"Politics is being upended. How can we make sense of this age of rebellion? This book is essential reading not just for those seeking to understand the contemporary far right but for modern politics and online culture more generally."

Jon Cruddas, *MP for Dagenham and Rainham, UK*

"Anyone who wants to be well-informed on rising levels of far-right extremism, populism and fascism in the Western world and beyond should read *The International Alt-Right*. This is a critical contribution by renowned experts on the face of fascism in the 21st century. And it is far more comprehensive than many other works about this movement, exploring areas that often receive little attention such as the manosphere or the role of this movement in Japan. I would highly advise those interested in rising extremism across the world to read this book."

Heidi Beirich, *Intelligence Project Director for Southern Poverty Law Center, USA*

"With impressive patience, the authors guide the reader through the murky and complex world of the alt-right. In this timely and necessary analysis, they show that the alt-right, despite the new terminology of 'incels', 'cucks' or metapolitics, is firmly rooted in the ideas of fascism and the radical right, and they thus sound a warning which needs to be heard very broadly."

Dan Stone, *Royal Holloway, University of London, UK*

"Anyone who wants to understand the truly global nature of the new far right should start right here. *The International Alt-Right* includes sharp observation of the movement's current figureheads, groups and the connections between them, and at the same time digs deep into the conspiracy theories, pseudoscience and reactionary ideas that underpin their thought. The authors provide some of the clearest explorations of the identitarian and neoreactionary movements, and sections on the manosphere and links to Russia and India are both comprehensive and fascinating. This book is a hard-headed and timely look at a growing and often frightening international phenomenon."

Mike Wendling, *author of* Alt-Right: From 4chan to the White House

"In the often loosely connected and sprawling world of extreme online politics, the new work, The *International Alt-Right: Fascism for the 21st Century?* provides a clear and detailed roadmap for understanding the many facets and manifestations of the contemporary alt-right movement. This book powerfully combines detailed research with an insightful theoretical analysis to create an inter-disciplinary and intersectional discussion of these pressing political activities and voices. The attention to gender, race, and global issues is particularly impressive and thorough. While theoretical in nature, this work is highly accessible for many types of readers, and can serve as an invaluable resource for classroom and academic use, as well as a guide for anyone committed to understanding and resisting present-day fascism."

Christa Hodapp, *University of Massachusetts Lowell, USA*

THE INTERNATIONAL ALT-RIGHT

The alt-right has been the most important new far-right grouping to appear in decades. Written by researchers from the anti-racist advocacy group HOPE not hate, this book provides a thorough, ground-breaking, and accessible overview of this dangerous new phenomenon. It explains where the alt-right came from, its history so far, what it believes, how it organises and operates, and its future trajectory.

The alt-right is a genuinely transnational movement and this book is unique in offering a truly international perspective, outlining the influence of European ideas and movements as well as the alt-right's development in, and attitude towards, countries as diverse as Japan, India, and Russia. It examines the ideological tributaries that coagulated to form the alt-right, such as white supremacy, the neo-reactionary blogosphere, the European New Right, the anti-feminist manosphere, the libertarian movement, and digital hate culture exemplified by offensive memes and trolling. The authors explore the alt-right's views on gender, sexuality and masculinity, antisemitism and the Holocaust, race and IQ, globalisation and culture as well as its use of violence. The alt-right is a thoroughly modern far-right movement that uses cutting edge technology and this book reveals how they use cryptocurrencies, encryption, hacking, "meme warfare", social media, and the dark web.

This will be essential reading for scholars and activists alike with an interest in race relations, fascism, extremism, and social movements.

Patrik Hermansson is a researcher at HOPE not hate and was responsible for the documentary, *Undercover in the Alt-Right* (2018).

David Lawrence is a researcher at HOPE not hate.

Joe Mulhall is a historian of fascism and senior researcher at HOPE not hate.

Simon Murdoch is a researcher at HOPE not hate.

ROUTLEDGE STUDIES IN FASCISM AND THE FAR RIGHT

Series Editors: **Nigel Copsey**, *Teesside University,* and **Graham Macklin**, *Center for Research on Extremism (C-REX), University of Oslo.*

This new book series focuses upon fascist, far right and right-wing politics primarily within a historical context but also drawing on insights from other disciplinary perspectives. Its scope also includes radical-right populism, cultural manifestations of the far right and points of convergence and exchange with the mainstream and traditional right.

Titles include:

A.K. Chesterton and the Evolution of Britain's Extreme Right, 1933–1973
Luke LeCras

Cumulative Extremism
A Comparative Historical Analysis
Alexander J. Carter

CasaPound Italia
Contemporary extreme-right politics
Caterina Froio, Pietro Castelli Gattinara, Giorgia Bulli and Matteo Albanese

The International Alt-Right
Fascism for the 21st Century?
Patrik Hermansson, David Lawrence, Joe Mulhall and Simon Murdoch

Failed Führers
A History of Britain's Extreme Right
Graham Macklin

The Rise of the Dutch New Right
An Intellectual History of the Rightward Shift in Dutch Politics
Merijn Oudenampsen

For more information about this series, please visit: https://www.routledge.com/Routledge-Studies-in-Fascism-and-the-Far-Right/book-series/FFR

THE INTERNATIONAL ALT-RIGHT

Fascism for the 21st Century?

Patrik Hermansson, David Lawrence, Joe Mulhall and Simon Murdoch

Routledge
Taylor & Francis Group

LONDON AND NEW YORK

First published 2020
by Routledge
2 Park Square, Milton Park, Abingdon, Oxon OX14 4RN

and by Routledge
52 Vanderbilt Avenue, New York, NY 10017

Routledge is an imprint of the Taylor & Francis Group, an informa business

© 2020 Patrik Hermansson, David Lawrence, Joe Mulhall, and Simon Murdoch

British Library Cataloguing-in-Publication Data
A catalogue record for this book is available from the British Library

Library of Congress Cataloging-in-Publication Data
A catalog record has been requested for this book

ISBN: 978-1-138-36340-3 (hbk)
ISBN: 978-1-138-36386-1 (pbk)
ISBN: 978-0-429-03248-6 (ebk)

Typeset in Bembo
by Taylor & Francis Books

CONTENTS

Introduction   1

PART I
Ideas and beliefs   **9**

1 The European roots of alt-right ideology   11

2 A global anti-globalist movement: The Alternative Right,
   globalisation and "globalism"   24

3 For whom the bell curves: The alt-right and pseudoscientific
   racism   35

4 The Alternative Right, antisemitism and the Holocaust   45

5 Right-libertarianism and the Alternative Right   54

6 Identitarianism in North America   65

7 The Dark Enlightenment: Neoreaction and Silicon Valley   81

PART II
Culture and activism   **105**

8 Art-right: Weaponising culture   107

9 The role of the troll: Online antagonistic communities and the
   Alternative Right   123

10   Alt-tech: Co-opting and creating digital spaces   139

11   Gaming the algorithms: Exploitation of social media platforms
     by the Alternative Right   153

PART III
Gender and sexuality   **161**

12   From anger to ideology: A history of the manosphere   163

13   Masculinity and misogyny in the Alternative Right   181

14   Sexuality and the Alternative Right   194

PART IV
International   **205**

15   Japan and the Alternative Right   207

16   Russia and the Alternative Right   218

17   Myth, mysticism, India, and the alt-right   235

Conclusion   251

Index   *259*

INTRODUCTION

In the wake of Charlottesville, with the world watching, President Trump gave his now infamous press conference in which he spoke of "very fine people, on both sides."[1] Jabbing a finger at a reporter, he demanded they tell him what the so-called "alt-right" actually is; "You define it. Define it for me. Come on. Let's go."[2] Trump's confusion here is perhaps unsurprising. In the last few years the alt-right has been painted as a radically new phenomenon and simultaneously derided as nothing more than a rebranding of traditional fascism. In the press and broadcast media, the term "alt-right" has been used to describe everything from hardcore nazis and Holocaust deniers through to mainstream Republicans in the US and right-wing populists in Europe. Even within the movement there remains debate over who is and who is not deserving of the moniker. Some vociferously reject the title yet comfortably fit within most definitions of it, while others have desperately claimed it yet do not.

In the minds of many, the link between Trump's election and the alt-right has become indivisible, not least because of the fallacy that the latter was the driving force behind the former. Within the alt-right itself its members certainly believed they were making a profound difference; Jason Reza Jorjani, formerly a leading American alt-right figure, would describe the movement as "the North American vanguard [...] most responsible for the electoral victory of President Trump."[3] The truth is that the alt-right's explosion onto the international scene was as much a symptom of Trump's election victory as a cause of it. Part of the confusion around the true influence of the Alternative Right is derived from the amorphous, baggy nature or complete absence of a definition for it. At present, the "alt-right" can be anything and thus is nothing. This is the primary issue that this book sets out to rectify by explaining how to define it, where it came from, what it believes, and how it operates.

What is the International Alternative Right?

We define the International "Alternative Right" as an international set of groups and individuals, operating primarily online though with offline outlets, whose core belief is that "white identity" is under attack from pro-multicultural and liberal elites and so-called "social justice warriors" (SJWs) who allegedly use "political correctness" to undermine Western civilisation and the rights of white males. Put simply, the "Alternative Right" is a far right, anti-globalist grouping that offers a radical "alternative" to traditional/establishment conservatism. The eclectic and disparate nature of its constituent parts makes for large areas of disagreement yet, together, they are united around a core set of beliefs. All reject what they believe to be the left-wing, liberal democratic, cultural hegemony in Western society and the rights derived from it. They reject what leading alt-right figure Jared Taylor has called the "dangerous myth" of equality which, in practice, means opposition to, *inter alia*, the rights of women, LGBT+ persons and ethnic and religious minorities or, if not these rights, at the very least the movements themselves that seek to advance those rights, such as feminism. Tracing the birth of the International Alternative Right is no easy task. It is an amorphous and mainly online political movement composed of a vast array of blogs, vlogs, websites, and podcasts with only a few offline organisations of note. As such, the movement has no single leader or even a dominant organisation but, instead, resembles a many-headed hydra made up of a collection of figures and groups, none of which fully control the loose movement's direction.

Due to the broadness of this definition it is necessary to subdivide the Alternative Right into two distinct branches: the "alt-right" and the "alt-lite." While both reject left/ liberal democratic hegemony, and the rights, freedoms and/or affiliated movements associated with it and both are concerned with the same set of issues – the left, globalisation, gender, the West, equality, and so on – they view these issues through fundamentally different lenses. While both are deeply critical of the conception of equality derived from the liberal consensus, the core concern of the alt-right is the threat it supposedly poses to the existence of white people, and so they advocate for the protection of their "race," usually through the creation of white ethnostates. As such, race forms the basis of its worldview. As Richard Spencer, the alt-right figurehead, has claimed: "almost every issue, political issue, cultural issue, sports, everything, almost everything – is based in race."[4] In contrast, the alt-lite perceives the liberal consensus as a threat to traditional Western culture and so is in favour of a Western chauvinist nationalism. Doubtless, both strands express an interest in the topic that forms the basis of the other's worldview. The alt-lite bemoans notions such as "white guilt" and "white privilege," while the alt-right frequently talks of pan-European civilisation and venerates classical Western culture. The difference comes down to the significance each places on these concepts. Gavin McInnes, a prominent figure in the alt-lite, sums this up when he states:

> Both sides have in common Western Chauvinism, they're not embarrassed about Whiteness [...], they don't think diversity is the be all and end all, but [the alt-lite] cares about Western Chauvinism and ideas. [The alt-right] says

"whites have to be a part of this", [the alt-lite] is inclusive and wants everyone to be friends as long as you accept the Western world as the best and refuse to apologise for creating the modern world.[5]

A conglomerate movement

While the Alternative Right is a distinct far-right movement, it is not an aberration conjured into existence in the last decade, nor is it born of fundamentally novel far-right ideas. Rather its distinctiveness is derived from the fact that it is a conglomeration of existing political and social movements that when fused together, created something new and different. It is, at its core, a convergence of three broad groups: the European New Right and Identitarian movement, the American Alternative Right and Online Antagonistic Communities. Each of these movements has its own history, structures, groups, and ideas and can, and in some cases, does, continue to operate quite independently of the Alternative Right but when the three overlap and interact they produce what we call the Alternative Right. The European New Right (ENR) is, broadly speaking, a current of thought derived from the ideas of the French far-right philosopher Alain de Benoist and his GRECE movement (*Groupement de recherche et d'études pour la civilisation européenne*) [Research and Study Group for European Civilisation] that was founded in France in 1968, along with subsequent strains of thought/activism such Guillaume Faye's Archeofuturism, Alexander Dugin's Eurasianism and the European Identitarian movement. The ENR movement sits comfortably within the far right and its ideas are best understood as a quest for the recovery of a mythical European identity. They fundamentally reject the ideals of the Enlightenment and of Christianity and fight back against "materialist" and modern ideologies from liberalism to socialism and, instead, posit a pan-European nationalism and a world of ethnically homogeneous communities.[6] Despite the explicit anti-Americanism of much of the ENR, in essence, the ideological core of the Alternative Right emerged when elements of ENR thought were merged with and adopted by the American far right. In its broadest sense this includes a multitude of radical or non-conservative right-wing and far-right traditions that offer an "alternative" to mainstream contemporary conservative Republicanism. This has included nazi and white supremacist individuals and groups, anti-government militias, and elements of the Ku Klux Klan (KKK).

However, the blend of ENR ideas with the American far right can only be considered the Alternative Right when it is also merged with what we call Online Antagonistic Communities. These we define as reactionary online communities built around various interests, but who all engage in exclusionary, antagonistic behaviour (be it through trolling, creating offensive symbolism or just espousing and voicing hatred and contempt). These are found on all sides of the political spectrum or can be non-political. However, when this behaviour is adopted by those within the Alternative Right their antagonism is directed at what they perceive as the left/liberal political and social hegemony.

In addition to these three main constituents is a plethora of smaller movements, cultures, and communities, elements of which have contributed in varying degrees or have been partly subsumed into the Alternative Right. Though many of them exist beyond and separately from the Alternative Right as broader ideological movements, they maintain large areas of crossover in terms of ideas and cooperation. For this reason, these elements have also, for some, acted as gateways into the Alternative Right. The three most significant, the manosphere, the Neoreactionary, and the right-libertarian movements are all covered in detail in this book. In addition to these are numerous further movements whose ideas have been of interest to elements within the Alternative Right such as paleoconservatism, survivalism and even right-wing national anarchism.

International and distinct

The two years following Trump's election have unsurprisingly seen an avalanche of books and articles on the alt-right and Donald Trump. One of the first out of the blocks was Jon Ronson with a short Kindle book, *The Elephant in the Room: A Journey into the Trump Campaign and the "Alt-Right"*, published in 2016.[7] In it he defines the alt-right as "a loose collection of internet conspiracy theorists and nationalists and some racists" and explains how "Trump delighted them, or derived inspiration from them."[8] While an amusing read that sheds some light onto the influential conspiracy theorist Alex Jones, the short book does not offer much of an insight into the alt-right as a movement. Then in 2017 came *Ctrl-Alt-Delete*, a small collection of essays including the especially useful "An Anti-fascist Report on the Alternative Right" by Matthew N. Lyons and a handy Glossary and Research Guide, offering short entries for some of the main alt-right individuals, organisations, factions, and events.[9] The first major book to tackle the movement properly was Angela Nagle's interesting yet controversial *Kill All Normies: Online culture wars from 4chan and Tumblr to Trump and the alt-right* in June 2017.[10] The book deserves much credit for illuminating "the online culture wars that formed the political sensibilities of a generation," as Nagle herself puts it.[11] Yet, while the book offers an interesting critique of certain unhelpful developments within progressive movements, especially online, she over-emphasises the role that left-wing online behaviour has played as a driver of the rise of the alt-right and, despite the merits of her critique, offers sometimes insufficiently nuanced stances on identity politics and political correctness.[12] Perhaps the book that best grasps the alt-right, as we define it, is Mike Wendling's *Alt-Right: From 4chan to the White House*.[13] While falling into the historically decontextualised trap of describing the alt-right as "in some ways unlike any other political force of modern times" he offers an engaging and informative overview of the movement that correctly understands it as "an oppositional force with no real organizational structure," a "creature of the internet, where many of its members, even some of the most prominent, are anonymous" and a "movement with several factions which shrink or swell according to the political breeze and the task at hand."[14]

In addition to these are a whole host of books that, while marketed as about the "alt-right," are actually better understood as explorations of the contemporary American right wing rather than explicitly about the international far-right movement explored in this book; though of course there is extensive crossover. The best of these is David Neiwert's adroit and engaging *Alt-America: The Rise of the Radical Right in the Age of Trump* which shows how the phenomenon of Trump actually has deep roots in the history of the American far right, most notably the anti-government militia movement which he covers in depth.[15] George Hawley's *Making Sense of the Alt-Right* is also well worth a read, and despite failing to offer a distinct definition of the alt-right, he covers the development of the movement, as we understand it, in interesting and informed detail.[16] Yet the book is overly Americentric, only briefly touching on the international element, and under-explores the role of gender and sexuality within the Alternative Right. Another thoroughly illuminating read is *Everything You Love Will Burn: Inside the Rebirth of White Nationalism in America*.[17] Vegas Tenold's immersive journey through the American extreme far right explores the "rebirth of white nationalism." While not a core focus of the book, he sees the "alt-right" as a renaming rather than a distinct or new movement,[18] a position that is understandable as he spends time with the KKK, the National Socialist Movement, and the Traditionalist Workers Party.

In addition to the quickly growing canon of works directly exploring the alt-right is a much more expansive collection of related literature that deals with specific and connected phenomena, much of which is used throughout this book. Some, such as the thoroughly useful *Key Thinkers of the Radical Right*, edited by Mark Sedgwick, surface throughout this book as its collection of articles offers interesting and important biographical and ideological insights into a number of the leading alt-right figures explored here.[19] Similarly, the recent book *The Identitarians: The Movement against Globalism and Islam in Europe* by José Pedro Zúquete provided valuable insights into a concurrent and affiliated movement which we explore in some depth throughout the book.[20] We also draw heavily on the work of historians when tracing the philosophical roots of the contemporary alt-right, with the work of scholars such as Tamir Bar-on and Roger Eatwell proving invaluable for exploring the role of European New Right thought, which we argue is an important part of the alt-right's ideology.[21] As we place significant emphasis on the centrality of misogyny and anti-feminism to the alt-right, we also draw on a number of recent studies that specifically deal with these issues. These include Michael Kimmel's *Angry White Men*, which, while only focusing on America, offers a useful framework for understanding the anger and sense of loss at the core of much organised anti-women politics.[22] Christa Hodapp's book *Men's Rights, Gender, and Social Media*, offers an especially useful overview of the contemporary men's rights movement with a theoretical analysis informed by philosophy and rooted in a firm grasp of how the movement has been shaped by the online world.[23] In addition to these are a huge range of works that inform single, specific chapters, be that Anton Shekhovtsov's *Russia and the Western Far Right* for our chapter examining "Russia and the Alternative Right," the work of Naoto Higuchi in that looking at Japan and the movement, Nicholas

Goodrick-Clarke's *Black Sun* in our "Myth, mysticism, India and the alt-right" chapter or Whitney Phillips' *This is Why We Can't Have Nice Things* in our chapter examining "Online antagonistic communities."[24] While our book is first and foremost the result of primary research, our adoption of such a holistic and broad approach to our exploration of the alt-right necessitated a reliance upon a rich and diverse range of secondary literature.

There are a number of commonalities across much of the published work that deals specifically with the alt-right, chief among which is that they are, understandably so, overly Americentric. By contrast this book takes a more holistic and consciously international approach, arguing that while the role of America is central, the movement is better understood as an international phenomenon. For that reason, this book outlines the European roots of alt-right ideology, the increasing influence of European Identitarianism in America, explores the influence of Hindu mysticism, the commonalities with contemporary Japanese far-right movements and the Alternative Right's relationship with Russia. However, in addition to arguing that it is an international movement we also argue that, in its purest form, the Alternative Right's outlook is transnational in nature. By that we mean core activists conceptualise their struggle beyond the borders of their nation-state; with the alt-right concerned with a transnational white "nation" and the alt-lite a transnational mythical West or Occident. That said, like numerous other transnational far-right movements there remains a tension between this and more traditional nation-state nationalism. While Richard Spencer has said, he is "ambivalent about America,"[25] and alt-lite vlogger Paul Joseph Watson talks much more about "the West"[26] than Britain or the States, the mobilising factors for Alternative Right activists often remain national or even hyperlocal. This, of course, is not a signifier of novelty with numerous prior transnational far-right movements operating similarly, be that Colin Jordan's World Union of National Socialists in the 1960s or the post-9/11 anti-Muslim Counter-Jihad Movement to name just two.[27]

Another misconception this book sets out to correct is that the Alternative Right is either brand new and completely novel or nothing more than a cynical rebranding exercise for the traditional far right. As is often the case, the truth is somewhere in the middle. While this movement is indeed replete with individuals and organisations whose far-right activism long predates the adoption of the term alt-right, such as Jared Taylor and Greg Johnson, and while we accept that many have indeed adopted it in an attempt to launder their image, we argue that the Alternative Right, while an amorphous conglomerate of disparate and sometimes even contradictory beliefs, can, and should, be understood as a distinct, modern international far-right movement. This requires using the term "alt-right" in a narrower sense than many do at present and rejecting its use as a catch-all term for any modern far-right activist or individual. For if the term can include anyone then it has little taxonomic value and is reduced to little beyond an insult or a rebrand depending on one's perspective. There are a number of individuals in this book who either did, or still do, self-define as alt-right, such as Andrew Anglin, who many would argue are simply neo-nazis. However, our definition doesn't make the two categories mutually exclusive. While it is true that not everyone in the alt-right is a nazi, and not every nazi is part of the alt-right, it is also true that some are. Anglin for example is part of the alt-right, partly because he self-identifies as such, but more importantly because the nature of his nazi activism, the means by which he does politics, the method by which he propagates his ideology, are all alt-right in nature. Like the alt-right more generally, his ideas lack novelty, but his activism does not.

In addition, having attended academic symposiums on the topic, it became evident to us that there is a huge need for an interdisciplinary approach to the study of the Alternative Right. At present, there seems to be a gap between those approaching this from the perspective of far-right and fascism research and those approaching it from a communications or digital perspective. The former sometimes fail to grasp the importance of the online spaces that have shaped the nature of the alt-right while the latter have a tendency to de-historicise and over-accentuate the novelty of the movement. We have sought to overcome this by including a broad range of articles covering the movement's history, its ideological roots and tributary movements but also explicitly addressing its means of online operation with articles on the role of trolling culture and alternative online spaces specifically used by the Alternative Right. Truncated and simplified versions of some of these chapters have been published online by the UK anti-fascist organisation HOPE not hate and via its U.S. based newsletter Ctrl Alt-Right Delete or as part of its 2017 report *The International Alternative Right: From Charlottesville to the White House.* However, all of this work has been updated and expanded and numerous brand new chapters added, meaning the majority of this book is completely new. Finally, all four authors of this book work for the British anti-fascist research organisation HOPE not hate and thus have spent time undercover inside different elements of the Alternative Right. Be it the tragic events at Charlottesville, the announcement of the creation of the AltRight Corporation in Stockholm, major National Policy Institute conferences in Washington DC or international manosphere and alt-right conferences in the UK, we have witnessed them first-hand, giving us a unique insight into the internal mechanisms of this movement, not possible from open source research alone.

Notes

1 Rich Klein, "Trump said 'blame on both sides' in Charlottesville, now the anniversary puts him on the spot," *ABC News*, 12 August 2018. https://abcnews.go.com/Politics/trump-blame-sides-charlottesville-now-anniversary-puts-spot/story?id=57141612
2 Natasha Bertrand, "Trump challenged a reporter to 'define the alt-right' – and his supporters are ecstatic," *Business Insider UK*, 15 August 2017. http://uk.businessinsider.com/trump-define-the-alt-right-2017-8
3 Red Ice TV, 2017, *Jason Reza Jorjani – Failure of Democracy – Identitarian Ideas IX* [Online video]. Available at: https://www.youtube.com/watch?v=Lvp8NZOauYw [Accessed 02 March 2017].
4 Richard Spencer in "Transcript: Richard Spencer Interview with James Allsup: 'The Alt-Right's Future in Trump's America'," *Sons of Europa*, 19 April 2017. http://sonsofeuropa.com/2017/04/19/transcript-richard-spencer-interview-with-james-allsup-the-alt-rights-future-in-trumps-america/

5 Rebel Media, *Gavin McInnes: What is the Alt-Right?*, [Online Video]. Available at: http s://www.youtube.com/watch?v=UQCZ9izaCa4 [Accessed 8 November 2018].
6 Tamir Bar-On, *Where Have All the Fascists Gone?*, (Abingdon: Routledge, 2007).
7 Jon Ronson, *The Elephant in the Room: A Journey into the Trump Campaign and the "Alt-Right"* (Kindle, 2016).
8 Ronson, *The Elephant in the Room* (the Kindle viewer only offers locations and not page numbers).
9 Matthew N. Lyons, It's Going Down, K. Kersplebedeb, Bromma, *Ctrl-Alt-Delete* (Montreal: Kersplebedeb Publishing, 2017).
10 Angela Nagle, *Kill All Normies: Online Culture Wars from 4chan and Tumblr to Trump and the Alt-Right* (Winchester: Zero Books, 2017).
11 Nagle, *Kill All Normies*, 9.
12 This is best typified by Chapter Five: "From Tumblr to the Campus Wars: Creating Scarcity in an Online Economy of Virtue." Nagle, *Kill All Normies*, 68–85.
13 Mike Wendling, *Alt Right: From 4 Chan to the White House* (London: Pluto Press, 2018).
14 Wendling, *Alt Right*, 5.
15 David Neiwert, *Alt-America: The Rise of the Radical Right in the Age of Trump* (London: Verso, 2017).
16 George Hawley, *Making Sense of the Alt-Right* (New York: Columbia University Press, 2017).
17 Vegas Tenold, *Everything You Love Will Burn: Inside the Rebirth of White Nationalism in America* (New York: Nation Books, 2018).
18 Tenold, *Everything You Love Will Burn, 162.*
19 Mark Sedgwick, *Key Thinkers of the Radical Right: Behind the New Threat to Liberal Democracy* (Oxford: Oxford University Press, 2019).
20 José Pedro Zúquete, *The Identitarians: The Movement against Globalism and Islam in Europe* (Notre Dame: University of Notre Dame Press, 2018).
21 Tamir Bar-On, *Where Have All the Fascists Gone?*, (Abingdon: Routledge, 2007); Roger Eatwell, *Fascism: A History* (London: Pimlico, 2003).
22 Michael Kimmel, *Angry White Men: American Masculinity at the End of an Era* (New York: National Books, 2017).
23 Christa Hodapp, *Men's Rights, Gender, and Social Media* (London: Lexington Books, 2017).
24 Nicholas Goodrick-Clarke, *Black Sun: Aryan Cults, Esoteric Nazism and the Politics of Identity* (New York and London: New York University Press, 2002); Naoto Higuchi, "The Radical Right in Japan", *The Oxford Handbook of the Radical Right*, 685 in: Jens Rydgren, (ed.), *The Oxford Handbook of the Radical Right* (Oxford: Oxford University Press, 2018); Whitney Phillips, *This is Why We Can't Have Nice Things: Mapping the Relationship between Online Trolling and Mainstream Culture* (Cambridge: MIT Press, 2015); Anton Shekhovtsov, *Russia and the Western Far Right: Tango Noir* (New York: Routledge, 2018).
25 Attended by author. Also available at: Truth against the World, 2016, *The Alt-Right Press Conference | Richard Spencer, Peter Brimelow & Jared Taylor* [Online Video]. Available at: https://www.youtube.com/watch?v=aJWLjRK2SRo [Accessed 21 October 2018].
26 Paul Joseph Watson video. Republished as: 3ilm MI (2016), *the west is the best* [Online Video]. Available at: https://www.youtube.com/watch?v=AeVyL5pLfZY [Accessed 4 November 2018].
27 For more details on Colin Jordan's World Union of National Socialists see: Paul Jackson, *Colin Jordan and Britain's Neo-Nazi Movement* (London: Bloomsbury Academic, 2016). For more information on the counter-jihad movement see: Joe Mulhall and Nick Lowles, *The Counter-Jihad Movement: Anti-Muslim hatred from the margins to the mainstream* (London: HOPE not hate Publications, 2015).

PART I
Ideas and beliefs

1

THE EUROPEAN ROOTS OF ALT-RIGHT IDEOLOGY

A watershed moment in the evolution of the alt-right came in Stockholm, in February 2017, at the Identitarian Ideas IX conference, when a new organisation simply called the AltRight Corporation was announced. This new venture saw the amalgamation of three of the movement's leading organisations: publisher Arktos Media Ltd led by Daniel Friberg, the web media group Red Ice Creations founded by Henrik Palmgren and the National Policy Institute (NPI) think tank led by Richard Spencer. The new group had a single board and an office in central Washington DC. For a period this became the hub and face of the movement, but in the seismic fallout of the Charlottesville Unite the Right Rally it has become dormant.

However, at the event, uncovered at the time by HOPE not hate and EXPO magazine,[1] Jason Jorjani, a co-founder of the AltRight Corporation, argued that the new organisation:

> represents nothing less than the integration of all of the [...] European right-wing schools of thought [the New Right (*Nouvelle Droite*), Archeofuturism, Identitarianism, and Aleksandr Dugin's Fourth Political Theory] with the North American vanguard movement most responsible for the electoral victory of President Trump.[2]

Despite the grossly exaggerated claims of their impact on Trump's victory, Jorjani's comments illustrated the extent of the convergence between the American far right and the European New Right (as well as its noted philosophical tributaries). Indeed, in recent years numerous European New Right (ENR) groups began to adopt the term "alt-right." At the same time, notable figures in this world, for instance, John Morgan, formerly of Arktos Media and now of US alt-right publisher Counter-Currents Publishing, have argued that these strands are "different in

a number of fundamental ways" and that they are better understood as "two distinct, if interrelated, phenomena."[3] What is certain is that the international movement known as the alt-right – generally viewed by many as an American
movement – in fact owes a huge debt to European far-right thought.

The long view: from Evola to the New Right

As the alt-right is a conglomeration of a number of pre-existing movements, it is no
surprise that aspects of its ideology are rooted in longstanding far-right notions with
origins outside of the US. The broad Alternative Right's rejection of liberal values,
especially, can be traced back at least as far as the work of the Italian fascist philosopher
Julius Evola who advocated anti-democratic, anti-egalitarian, anti-liberal, and radical
Traditionalist ideas.[4] Traditionalism is a worldview that in essence believes equality and
progress are illusions, and it has long been popular with the post-war far right. To the
amazement of many, the now-sacked Trump aide and former Breitbart News Network
executive Steve Bannon mentioned Evola in his now famous speech to a Vatican
conference in 2014.[5] Speaking to *The New York Times*, Mark Sedgwick, a leading
scholar of Traditionalism, rightly stated that "The fact that Bannon even knows [of]
Evola is significant."[6] Another fan of Evola is the above-mentioned leading American
alt-right figure, Richard Spencer. Spencer has remarked that "it means a tremendous
amount" that Bannon knows of Evola and Traditionalist thinkers, adding: "He at least
recognizes that they are there. That is a stark difference to the American conservative
movement that either was ignorant of them or attempted to suppress them."[7]

Bannon's knowledge of Evola and Traditionalism is emblematic of the influence
similar ideas have gained in recent years on both sides of the Atlantic. They are, especially in terms of their critique of modern society, the philosophical underpinning of the
current offensive against liberal democracy. In addition to Evola and Traditionalism,
European pessimistic philosophers have also influenced sections of the alt-right. As an
article published on the site of the Russian think tank Katehon, later republished on
Altright.com, put it: "Of particular interest [is the] Spenglerian theory of civilizational
decline, Nietzschean emphasis on aesthetics and temporal cycles of eternal return, and
[the] Schmittian concept of the Political."[8] Oswald Spengler's 1918 magnum opus *Der
Untergang des Abendlandes* [*The Decline of the West*] has long influenced far-right and fascist
thought. Spengler rejected unilinear theories of historical development as ahistorical and
Eurocentric, favouring instead a cyclical understanding of history with the rise and fall of
civilisations.[9] The great cultures were to be seen as organic and progressing through
prescribed stages, accomplishing "majestic wave-cycles." They would "appear suddenly,
swell in splendid lines, flatten again and vanish, and the face of the waters [would be]
once more a sleeping waste."[10] In another metaphor, Spengler claimed each civilisation
"passes through the age-phases of the individual man. Each has its childhood, youth,
manhood and old age."[11] It was Spengler's analysis that Europe was well past its prime,
and like Evola's Traditionalism, his ideas found advocates in the alt-right. As far back as
2012, Richard Spencer produced a podcast with the late British fascist, Jonathan
Bowden, to discuss Spengler's relevance to the contemporary far right.[12]

As noted above, another important influence on alt-right ideology is the work of the German philosopher, political theorist and Nazi Party member Carl Schmitt. Schmitt's Friend-Enemy Thesis, as explained in his 1927 work *Der Begriff des Politischen* [*The Concept of the Political*], declared that, "The specific political distinction to which political actions and motives can be reduced is the distinction between Freund und Feind [friend and enemy]."[13] For Schmitt, even in the abstract, the political is not immutable, but rather is "the most intense and extreme antagonism." Hence, "every concrete antagonism becomes that much more political the closer it approaches the most extreme point, that of the friend-enemy grouping."[14] The state's role then is the defence of friends against enemies. Thus, the identification of the enemy is critical as it dictates the actions to be taken by the state. Tellingly, Richard Spencer's entrance essay for the prestigious private Duke University was on Carl Schmitt. An article on the alt-right website Dissident Right places great significance on the role of Schmitt's ideas for the movement, when it explains how they are "considerably instructive in understanding the weakness of the Conservative mindset, as well as in coming to important conclusions that should be used to ground the ethnonationalist Alt-Right." It concludes, "When we begin to see politics the way Schmitt saw it, we understand both who we are as members of the Alt-Right (specifically, why we exist as a political unity) and why conservatism will perish."[15] What becomes clear when exploring the philosophical roots of the alt-right is that its ideas are born from the same ideological seedbed as countless far-right and fascist movements before them. The thinkers venerated by the movement, be it Evola, Nietzsche, Schmitt, Spengler or Heidegger, have long been important for fascists, both pre- and post-World War II, adding credence to the notion that when it comes to its ideas, the alt-right is a rebranding rather than a fundamentally new phenomenon with views distinct from other fascistic movements.

The New Right

While the ideas of the alt-right can be traced back to Traditionalists and older fascists like Evola, it is the philosophies of the comparatively more recent European New Right (ENR) that have been most influential in the ideological formation of the alt-right.

The ENR is, broadly speaking, a current of thought derived from the ideas of the French far-right philosopher Alain de Benoist and his GRECE organisation (*Groupement de recherche et d'études pour la civilisation européenne*) [Research and Study Group for European Civilisation] founded in France in 1968, along with subsequent affiliated strains of thought/activism such as Guillaume Faye's Archeofuturism, Alexander Dugin's Eurasianism and the European Identitarian movement. Its leading figure is de Benoist who set out to create a right-wing movement that would be both modern and intellectual, operating via articulate publications and discussion groups.[16]

The ENR claims it is an alternative to social democracy and conservative liberalism, a "laboratory of ideas," a "school of thought," a "community of spirit," and a "space of resistance against the system," that has transcended the existing political left–right schema.[17] Such claims can be dismissed as scholars have shown clearly the movement's direct ideological parallels with classical fascism and the historical continuity from then, through post-war fascism, until the emergence of the *Nouvelle Droite* in 1968.[18] In reality, the ENR sits comfortably within the far right, and its ideas are best understood as a quest for the recovery of a mythical "European Identity." It fundamentally rejects the ideals of the 18th century Enlightenment and of Christianity and fights back against "materialist" ideologies from liberalism to socialism. In their place, the ENR advocates a pan-European nationalism and a wider world of ethnically homogeneous communities.

GRECE came to be known as the French New Right (*Nouvelle Droite*) and, in 1999, de Benoist and Charles Champetier published a synthesis of their first 30 years of thought as a *Manifesto for a European Renaissance*. In it the duo talk of the "Crisis of Modernity" and examine "the main enemy," liberalism. In essence, de Benoist and Champetier argue that globalisation, liberalism, and hypermodernism have led to the "eradication of collective identities and traditional cultures"[19] and bemoan the "unprecedented menace of homogenisation"[20] wrought by immigration, which – in blanket fashion – is held to be an "undeniably negative phenomenon."[21] In place of liberal multiculturalism, they call for ethnopluralism: the idea that different ethnic groups are equal but ought to live in separation from one another. This is coupled with the "right to difference": "The right of every people, ethnos, culture, nation, group, or community to live according to its own norms and traditions, irrespective of ideology or globalist homogenization."[22] Furthermore, this right carries the assumption of "cultural differentialism": the idea that there are "lasting differences among and between cultures."[23]

Metapolitics

Aside from some of the roots of its ideas, what marks the alt-right out from most of its contemporaries on the far right is its conscious commitment to "metapolitical" activism. While some on the alt-right point to the Italian Marxist philosopher Antonio Gramsci as the wellspring for this belief, the current enthusiasm amongst the international alt-right for the notion – specifically, that "politics is downstream of culture"[24] – is primarily the result of the influence of the European New Right (GRECE) within their movement.

De Benoist and Champetier, in *Manifesto of the French New Right in the Year 2000*, explain that metapolitics:

> is not politics by other means. It is neither a strategy to impose intellectual hegemony, nor an attempt to discredit other possible attitudes or agendas. It rests solely on the premise that ideas play a fundamental role in collective consciousness and, more generally, in human history. [...] History is a result of human will and action, but always within the framework of convictions, beliefs and representations which provide meaning and direction. The goal of the French New Right is to contribute to the renewal of these sociohistorical representations.[25]

As explained by Tamir Bar-On in his essential *Where Have All the Fascists Gone?*, de Benoist and GRECE adopted Gramsci's Marxism "for their own partisan ends" and argued that "the most important route to political power was not elections or violent street combat, but in thoroughly changing the dominant *zeitgeist* and people's acceptable ideas and worldviews."[26] This concept has become absolutely central to the political project of the contemporary alt-right. For example, in his book, *Rising from the Ruins: The Right of the 21st Century*, published by Arktos, Joakim Andersen, co-founder of the Scandinavian ENR think tank Motpol, reiterates to his alt-right readers the "importance of metapolitics," reminding them of the "great risk if we focus entirely on politics and ignore metapolitics and culture," of the need for "our own ideas, institutions, and personnel" and how "Gramsci and the New Right are indispensable teachers in this aspect."[27] Within the wider European Alternative Right it is no great surprise that the concept of metapolitics has been so widely adopted as many, such as Daniel Friberg of Arktos or even the Identitarian movement, are essentially descendants of the *Nouvelle Droite*. However, this idea also sits at the core of the American alt-right's belief that they are in the midst of a cultural war that will precede a political takeover.

Central to the adoption of metapolitics by the US alt-right has been Greg Johnson, whose website and publishing house Counter-Currents Publishing was consciously launched to spread ENR ideas across the Atlantic and to create "a space for a dialogue in which a new intellectual movement, a North American New Right, might emerge."[28] As a central figure within the alt-right, Johnson has argued for the creation of:

> our own metapolitical organizations – new media, new educational institutions, and new forms of community – that can combat and replace those in anti-white hands. We must fight bad ideas with better ideas – institutional subversion with institutional renewal. [...] Actual politics comes later, once we have laid the metapolitical groundwork.[29]

With this in mind, Johnson has launched the New York Forum and the North-West Forum in Seattle, copying European groups such as the London Forum in the UK.

However, perhaps most important for spreading the idea of metapolitics within the alt-right has been Richard Spencer. In 2016 at the peak of press interest in the movement, he appeared alongside Jared Taylor of the white supremacist website American Renaissance and Peter Brimelow of the anti-immigration website VDARE at the Willard Hotel in downtown Washington to explain to the press "What is the alt-right?" Spencer explained to the gathered journalists that: "I don't think the best way of understanding the alt-right is strictly in terms of policy. I think metapolitics is more important than politics. I think big ideas are more important than policies."[30] Later, on 11 August 2017 on the eve of the disastrous Unite the Right rally in Charlottesville, he published "What It Means to Be Alt-Right: A meta-political manifesto for the Alt-Right movement" in which he states

"Spirit is the wellspring of culture, and politics is downstream of that. The Alt-Right wages a situational and ideological war on those deconstructing European history and identity."[31] As the best-known figure in the alt-right Spencer's advocacy for a metapolitical approach has been central for the alt-right's adoption of it.

Spencer has also been key in arranging for central ENR thinkers to speak in America. The 2013 National Policy Institute (NPI) conference, organised by Spencer, had a keynote speech from de Benoist and was also attended by Tomislav Sunic, the Croatian far-right author whose book, *New Right – Against Democracy and Equality* (1990), has been very influential among alt-right figures. Furthermore, the very creation of the AltRight Corporation involved the amalgamation of NPI with the Budapest-based publisher Arktos, which has been essential to the publishing of ENR texts in English and, as such, for an American audience. Arktos co-founder Daniel Friberg has used this new platform to promote the notion of metapolitics in the US. Writing for a primarily US audience at AltRight.com he explained how: "Any parliamentary struggle must be preceded, legitimised, and supported by a metapolitical struggle. Metapolitics, at its best, reduces parliamentarism to a question of mere formalities" and explained why he believes "metapolitical analysis must precede political action."[32] Interestingly though, this movement of people and ideas across the Atlantic is symbiotic. As well as ENR ideas heading across the Atlantic we are now also seeing them repackaged as "alt-right" and returning to Europe. A perfect example of this was the launch of a Scandinavian branch of Richard Spencer's AltRight Corporation.

Divergence between the alt-right and New Right

While the role of European far-right thought has, no doubt, been ignored in much analysis of the ideas and ideology of the alt-right, it would be wrong to understand the alt-right as a linear continuation or outgrowth of the ENR. Though the influences as outlined above are clear and central to the development of the alt-right, there are significant differences that are worth briefly exploring. Writing for Counter-Currents, Morgan went as far as to argue that "the Alt Right is a uniquely American creation that can't be exported wholesale into other cultural contexts, just as the European New Right is something very particular to Western Europe" and that while there is no "inherent conflict" between the two they should be understood as fundamentally "distinct."[33]

One of the major dividing lines between the ENR and the alt-right is the centrality of anti-Americanism to the platform of the former. Bar-On explains how GRECE's "anti-Americanism" had existed since 1975 and how in the post-1989 era "the ENR increasingly turned its venom to the remaining world superpower, the United States, seen as the ultimate embodiment of the most homogenizing, demonic and profit-hungry machine in world history," with GRECE even calling their 1991 colloquium "Danger: United States."[34] In the 1980s it adopted "philo-communism and [an] affinity for the Soviet Union,"[35] and as Eatwell argues, de Benoist "picked on American individualism and materialism as a greater danger than communism," a position that would seem a total anathema to most within the contemporary alt-right milieu.[36] While Richard Spencer has said he is "ambivalent about America,"[37] Americans and American nationalist movements were central to the development of the alt-right and as such anti-Americanism isn't part of the make-up of the movement and, at times, quite the opposite is true. In attempting to create a North American New Right Greg Johnson seems to have dealt with the ENR's anti-Americanism by simply ignoring it.

However, perhaps the most notable point of departure between the ENR and most of the alt-right is the latter's pre-occupation with race. As Graham Macklin shows in his biographical chapter of Greg Johnson in *Key Thinkers of the Radical Right*, the "European New Right thinkers, [...], consciously rejected biological racism as 'an erroneous doctrine, one rooted in time'," while Johnson has a "preoccupation" with race, something he shares with much of the contemporary alt-right.[38] This difference was pointed out by de Benoist himself in a 2013 interview with Jared Taylor's American Renaissance when he said:

> If I compare you and me, the first difference is that I am aware of race and of the importance of race, but I do not give to it the excessive importance that you do. For me it is a factor, but only one among others.[39]

This attitude to race is markedly different from most of the big names of the alt-right and some distance from Richard Spencer's Alt-Right Manifesto which opens by saying, "Race is real. Race matters. Race is the foundation of identity."[40] As Bar-On explains in his biographical chapter on Spencer in *Key Thinkers of the Radical Right*, "It is significant that race is the first point of the manifesto, because for Spencer the US should be a race-based ethnic state devoid of non-Europeans, nonwhites, blacks, and Jews."[41]

Interestingly, the emphasis on the indivisibility of race and identity and the need for ethnically-based states is also a point of divergence between the ENR and its closest ideological heirs and simultaneous influence on the alt-right, the European Identitarian movement. As José Pedro Zúquete points out in *The Identitarians*, for the Nouvelle Droite, "Neither the assimilation of the melting pot [...] nor the exclusion of apartheid was the ideal"[42] leading to de Benoist excoriating the excesses of "Identitarian tribalism" and bemoaning how Identitarians assign "ethnic factors the role that Karl Marx assigned to economic factors."[43] Of course, none of this is to say that the ENR was not racist itself. As Eatwell highlights, "there was widespread agreement among all critics that it was racist: for all its talk of cultural diversity, the New Right clearly did not envisage a multicultural France or Europe."[44] Thus, the divergence is not that one is a racist movement and one is not, but rather the emphasis placed on the issue differs.

However, de Benoist's failure to place race front and centre is perhaps one of the reasons that many in the alt-right and Identitarian movement have found greater affinity with the work of his one-time GRECE ally, Guillaume Faye, who was, in the later years of his life, much more open to overt racism. Stéphane François' chapter on Faye in *Key Thinkers of the Radical Right* argues that Faye is "responsible for the doctrinal renewal of French nativism" and neatly summarises his thought as the forging of "postmodern philosophy, some elements of Western counterculture, and racism."[45] Due to intellectual and financial disagreements with de Benoist, Faye left GRECE in 1987 and distanced himself from the ENR before re-emerging as a notable figure on the scene in 1998 after producing *Archeofuturism*.[46] Faye described his ideas as three connected theses: "that current civilisation, a product of modernity and egalitarianism, has reached its final peak and is threatened by the short-term prospect of a global cataclysm resulting from a convergence of catastrophes," that "the individualist and egalitarian ideology of the modern world is no longer suitable," and that "it will be more and more necessary to adopt an archaic mind-set, which is to say a pre-modern, non-egalitarian and non-humanist outlook."[47] This third claim lies at the heart of Faye's "Archeofuturist" thought, the principles of which he believes should guide how we "envisage the aftermath of the chaos, the post-catastrophic world."[48]

While both Faye and de Benoist have significantly influenced the alt-right, there are important differences between their ideologies with both developing along quite distinct trajectories throughout their careers. According to François, Faye has become "an important ideologue of nativism with a vehemently anti-immigration and anti-Islamic discourse in the name of defending the ethnic interests of Europeans. Since the late 1990s, he has championed a racialism that is reminiscent of the 1900s to the 1930s."[49] It is these elements of his work that made him so popular and influential within the modern alt-right and why he was so mourned after his death in 2019. The divergence from de Benoist is best seen in Faye's adaptation of the *Nouvelle Droite* motto of "cause of peoples" to "cause of *our* people" and his criticism of de Benoist and his ENR colleagues for "howling with the wolves against racism."[50]

Part of this divergence on the issue of race between the ENR and the alt-right includes the issue of antisemitism. As discussed in Chapter 4 in this book, antisemitism is a central tenet of the alt-right's worldview. Whether it is the conspiratorial anti-semitism prevalent amongst elements of the alt-lite, the pseudoscientific work of Kevin MacDonald or the crude and base Holocaust denial of the alt-right's more extreme online elements, antisemitism plays an open role in the alt-right that makes it markedly different from the ENR. Again, this is not to absolve the ENR, as while true that the ENR have in general eschewed open antisemitism, some, notably Harvey Simmons, have argued that its attacks on "Judeo-Christian" values may be a tactical way of presenting antisemitic views in a respectable manner.[51] As such the difference here is a matter of openness and emphasis.

One thing that exploring the points of divergence between the ENR and the alt-right reveals is the stark difference in the quality of each movement's thinkers and the nuance of their respective ideologies. The alt-right absorbs elements of right-wing philosophy when convenient and simply jettisons or ignores those contradictory or problematic elements as with the ENR's anti-Americanism. It also reveals the dearth of originality in alt-right thought. When one compares Greg Johnson, Richard Spencer, and Daniel Friberg to the thinkers of the ENR they are sorely lacking in originality, depth, and sometimes even understanding of the ideas they co-opt. The alt-right no doubt owes a great debt to European far-right thought, the ENR first and foremost, but it is a pick-and-mix fascist movement that has absorbed key elements of ENR ideology, namely a metapolitical approach, rather than being an American incarnation of it.

Ideas on the rise

For many years the people and groups espousing these ideas "perceived themselves as the rear guard of a dying world"[52]; what Evola described as "men among the ruins."[53] Yet, over the last decade confidence seems to have grown within the movement and as Philippe Vardon, a founder of the Identitarian movement in France, wrote: "Far from being the last expression of a world in its death throes, they [Identitarians] are the first pangs of a new birth."[54]

In 2013, de Benoist was the keynote speaker at a conference titled "After the Fall: The Future of Identity," organised by Spencer's NPI. The website for the event stated that the "identity of 'the West' that was promoted over the past half-century – 'democratic', 'tolerant,' 'liberal' – has begun to crack and splinter."[55] Clearly, well before Trump's election, the rise of Bannon, and the widespread public consciousness of the alt-right, those within the movement had already begun to see a possibility of the tide turning in their favour. In Europe in recent years these ideas have been manifested in the pan-European Identitarian movement that started in France in 2003 as a youth movement descended from the *Nouvelle Droite*. The term "Identitarians" is, as explained by Faye, drawn from the belief that what characterises humanity "is the diversity and singularity of its many people and cultures." Identity is central to this movement, therefore, since, as Faye adds, it sees "Every form of [humanity's] homogenisation [as] synonymous with death, as well as sclerosis and entropy."[56]

The 2013 book, *Die identitäre Generation: Eine Kriegserklärung an die 68er* [Generation Identity: A Declaration of War Against the '68ers] by the Austrian Markus Willinger is understood as the manifesto of the Identitäre Bewegung Österreich, the Austrian branch of the Identitarian movement. In it Willinger declares:

> A new political current is sweeping through Europe. It has one goal, one symbol, and one thought: Identity. [...] This book is no simple manifesto. It is a declaration of war. A declaration of war against everything that makes Europe sick and drives it to ruin, against the false ideology of the '68ers. This is us declaring war on you.[57]

While it would be easy to dismiss Willinger's manifesto as nothing more than an angry young man stamping his feet, *Generation Identity* is a lively and accessible articulation of the often dense and arcane ideas espoused by the likes of de Benoist. It is a reaction against the '68ers and the left's perceived cultural hegemony. Willinger rails against political elites who "disgust us"; condemns the increasing acceptance of LGBT+ people in society – what he calls "the union of nothing-ness" – and instead calls for a return to traditional gender roles as "Women want to be conquered."[58]

He also rejects multiculturalism outright, stating "we don't want Mehmed and Mustafa to become Europeans" and, like de Benoist, argues instead for ethnoplural-ism.[59] This new confidence is evident in the 2015 book *The Real Right Returns: A handbook for the true opposition* by Daniel Friberg. It opens by defiantly stating: "After more than half a century of retreat, marginalisation, and constant concessions to an ever-more aggressive and demanding Left, the true European Right is returning with a vengeance."[60] Friberg continues: "The real Right is now making a comeback all across Europe. In region after region, country after country, we are forcing the Left's disillusioned, demoralized, and feminized minions to retreat back to the margins of society, where their quixotic ideas and destructive utopias belong."[61] He goes on to lay out his plan to "reconstitute those ideals and values which were taken for granted in Europe prior to the advent of liberalism"[62] and to "develop an alternative to liberal modernity in its entirety."[63] Friberg's confidence in the victory of the alt-right reaches the point of hubris in his foreword to Joakim Andersen's *Rising from the Ruins*, when he writes "remember that our liberal-leftist opponents have already lost. They have just not stopped breathing yet."[64] Andersen himself is less definitive than Friberg but his book does exude a confidence that victory is within grasp:

> Today we have a good opportunity for victory. Nothing is guaranteed, but the combination of Spengler, Strauss-Howe, and Sam Francis reminds us that the post-bourgeois proletariat and the conservative Generation Z have a good chance to take over Faustian civilisation, and to create a system based on ascetic, heroic, and solidaric values.[65]

To achieve this, Anderson argues for the merging of the ideas of de Benoist and the European New Right with "Sorel's thoughts on the myth, with Le Bon's mass psychology, with Sloterdijk and Foucault's theories of the politics of language and dis-courses, and Francis', Dugin's, and Moldbug's thoughts about the relationship between groups and ideas."[66] In some ways his desire for the merging of ENR ideas with American thinkers popular within the alt-right, such as the neoreactionary blogger Curtis Yarvin (AKA Mencius Moldbug), was achieved with the launch of AltRight Corporation. While the Corporation has faltered in the wake of Charlottesville and its future remains very uncertain, this union itself continues to hold some symbolic sig-nificance as the first major manifestation of the metapolitical call for institution-building and Anderson's call for the combining of Transatlantic new far-right thought.

Nevertheless, the point here is not to argue that the alt-right and the ENR have become identical. Rather, it is to place the modern alt-right's worldview in its proper context and show that, while they may have slightly differing and divergent views of what the world should look like, there is a striking commonality when it comes to their critique of modernity and modern progressive society in America and Europe. Both agree the enemy is progressive, liberal democracy with its advancement of minority rights and its push towards multicultural, pluralist societies. What is so worrying is that this critique, while decades old, has begun to gain increasing traction in recent years and has emerged as a real threat to its target.

What was once a marginalised far-right philosophical debate, discussed by ignored "think tanks" in the back rooms of pubs or in conference centres booked under fake names, has now become an increasingly mainstream position. Whether movements like the American alt-right, the European New Right or the Identitarian movement have been successful at attracting people towards their way of thinking, or whether people have simply increasingly reached similar conclusions by themselves, is difficult to say (though the latter is much more likely). Whatever the case, the advancement of these ideas is an increasing challenge to the pillars of Western liberal democracy and the hard-won rights many take for granted.

Notes

1 Joe Mulhall, "Exclusive: New International Alt-Right Movement Formed," *HOPE not hate*, 26 February 2017. https://www.hopenothate.org.uk/2017/02/26/exclusive-new-interna tional-alt-right-movement-formed/
2 Red Ice TV, 2017, *Jason Reza Jorjani - Failure of Democracy - Identitarian Ideas IX* [Online video]. Available at: https://www.youtube.com/watch?v=Lvp8NZOauYw [Accessed 02 March 2017].
3 John Morgan, "Alt Right versus New Right," *Counter-Currents Publishing*, 28 February 2017. https://www.counter-currents.com/2017/02/alt-right-versus-new-right/
4 Mark J. Sedgwick, *Against the Modern World: Traditionalism and the Secret Intellectual History of the Twentieth Century* (Oxford: Oxford University Press, 2004).
5 Jason Horowitz, "Steve Bannon Cited Italian Thinker Who Inspired Fascists," *The New York Times*, 10 February 2017. https://www.nytimes.com/2017/02/10/world/europe/ bannon-vatican-julius-evola-fascism.html
6 Ibid.
7 Ibid.
8 John Undonne, "What is the Alt Right," *Katehon*, 27 January 2017. http://katehon. com/article/what-alt-right
9 Oswald Spengler, *The Decline of the West: An Abridged Edition* (Oxford: Oxford University Press, 1991), 12, 15–16.
10 Ibid., 73.
11 Ibid., 74.
12 Richard Spencer interview of Jonathan Bowden for the Vanguard Podcast. Transcript published as: Jonathan Bowden, "Understanding Spengler," *Counter-Currents Publishing*, 4 May 2016. https://www.counter-currents.com/2016/05/understanding-spengler/
13 Carl Schmitt, *Der Begriff des Politischen* (1927), 26. Cited in Joseph J. Bendersky, *Carl Schmitt: Theorist for the Reich* (Princeton: Princeton University Press, 1983), 88.
14 Ibid.
15 The *Dissident Right* website is now marked private. This quote was taken from an article originally at this address: https://dissidentright.com/2016/08/31/refusal-to-na me-the-enemy-carl-schmitt-political-reality-conservatism-and-the-alt-right/
16 Roger Eatwell, *Fascism: A History* (London: Pimlico, 2003), 313.
17 Andrea Mammone, Emmanuel Godin, Brian Jenkins (Eds.), *Varieties of Right-Wing Extremism in Europe* (Abingdon: Routledge, 2013), 55.
18 Ibid., 53–68.

19 Alain de Benoist and Charles Champetier, *Manifesto for a European Renaissance* (United Kingdom: Arktos Media Ltd, 2012), 15.
20 Ibid., 32.
21 Ibid., 34.
22 Guilliame Faye, *Why We Fight: Manifesto of the European Resistance* (Budapest: Arktos Media, 2011), 334.
23 George Ritzer, *Globalization: A Basic Text* (Chichester: Wiley-Blackwell, 2011), 207. This also assumes cultures are clearly demarcated entities linked to specific geographic locations. As Akhil Gupta and James Ferguson describe, this is an "[...] assumed isomorphism of space, place, and culture [...]". Akhil Gupta and James Ferguson, "Beyond 'Culture': Space, Identity, and the Politics of Difference," *Cultural Anthropology*, 7:1 (1992), 7.
24 Lawrence Meyers, "Politics Really Is Downstream from Culture," *Breitbart News Network*, 22 August 2011. https://www.breitbart.com/entertainment/2011/08/22/politics-really-is-downstream-from-culture/
25 Alain de Benoist and Charles Champetier, *Manifesto of the French New Right in Year 2000*, Available at: https://pdfs.semanticscholar.org/5388/a0f125887a784acd36b2d2166705d42ae678.pdf
26 Tamir Bar-On, *Where Have All the Fascists Gone?*, (Abingdon: Routledge, 2007), 35.
27 Joakim Andersen, *Rising from the Ruins: The Right of the 21st Century* (United Kingdom: Arktos Media Ltd., 2018), 300.
28 Greg Johnson (ed.), *North American New Right, Vol. 1* (San Francisco: Counter-Currents Publishing, 2012), 1.
29 Greg Johnson, "Politics, Metapolitics, & Hegemony," *Counter-Currents Publishing*, 1 February 2018. https://www.counter-currents.com/2018/02/politics-metapolitics-and-hegemony/
30 Author attended and filmed the event. Quote also available at: Marin Cogan, "The Alt-Right Gives a Press Conference," *Intelligencer*, 11 September 2016. http://nymag.com/daily/intelligencer/2016/09/the-alt-right-gives-a-press-conference.html
31 Richard Spencer, "What It Means to be Alt-Right," *Altright.com*, 11 August 2017. https://altright.com/2017/08/11/what-it-means-to-be-alt-right/
32 Daniel Friberg, "Metapolitics from the Right," *Altright.com*, November 2017. https://altright.com/2017/09/23/metapolitics-from-the-right/
33 Morgan, "Alt Right versus New Right."
34 Bar-On, *Where Have All the Fascists Gone?*, 82.
35 Bar-On, *Where Have All the Fascists Gone?*, 48.
36 Eatwell, *Fascism*, 314.
37 Attended by author. Also available at: Truth against the World, 2016, *The Alt-Right Press Conference | Richard Spencer, Peter Brimelow & Jared Taylor* [Online Video]. Available at: https://www.youtube.com/watch?v=aJWLjRK2SRo [Accessed 21 October 2018].
38 Graham Macklin, "Greg Johnson and Counter-Currents," in Mark Sedgwick (ed.), *Key Thinkers of the Radical Right: Behind the New Threat to Liberal Democracy* (Oxford: Oxford University Press, 2019), 213.
39 American Renaissance, "We Are at the End of Something – A Conversation with Alain de Benoist," accessed December 14, 2017, https://www.amren.com/features/2013/11/we-are-at-the-end-of-something/. Quoted in Macklin, "Greg Johnson and Counter-Currents," 10.
40 Richard Spencer, "What It Means to Be Alt-Right," 2017. https://altright.com/2017/08/11/what-it-means-to-be-alt-right/
41 Tamir Bar-On, "Richard B. Spencer and the Alt-Right" in Mark Sedgwick (Ed.), *Key Thinkers of the Radical Right*, 232.
42 José Pedro Zúquete, *The Identitarians: The Movement against Globalism and Islam in Europe* (Notre Dame: University of Notre Dame Press, 2018), 10–11.
43 De Benoist quoted in: Zúquete, *The Identitarians*, 11 and 14.
44 Eatwell, *Fascism*, 315.

45 Stéphane François, "Guillaume Faye and Archeofuturism," in Mark Sedgwick (ed.), *Key Thinkers of the Radical Right: Behind the New Threat to Liberal Democracy* (Oxford: Oxford University Press, 2019), 91.
46 Ibid., 93–94.
47 Guillaume Faye, *Archeofuturism: European Visions of the Post-Catastrophic Age* (United Kingdom: Arktos Media Ltd, 2010), 13–14.
48 Ibid., 14.
49 Ibid., 96.
50 Guillaume Faye quoted in: Zúquete, *The Identitarians*, 14.
51 Harvey Simmons, *The French National Front: The Extremist Challenge to Democracy* (Boulder: Westview Press, 1996), 212–215.
52 Vardon, P. Foreword to: Markus Willinger, *Generation Identity: A Declaration of War against the '68ers* (United Kingdom: Arktos Media Ltd, 2013), 9.
53 Evola, J. quoted in Daniel Friberg, *The Real Right Returns: A Handbook for the True Opposition* (United Kingdom: Arktos Media Ltd, 2015), 15.
54 Vardon, P. Foreword to: Willinger, *Generation Identity*, 9.
55 After the Fall: The Future of Identity: The National Policy Institute's 2013 Leadership Conference. http://www.npiamerica.org/2013-conference/
56 Faye, *Why We Fight*, 171.
57 Willinger, *Generation Identity*, 14–15.
58 Ibid., 24–27.
59 Ibid., 71.
60 Friberg, *The Real Right Returns*, 1.
61 Ibid., 15.
62 Ibid., ix.
63 Ibid., 15.
64 Daniel Friberg, Foreword to Anderson, *Rising from the Ruins*, xi.
65 Anderson, *Rising from the Ruins*, 304. "Strauss-Howe" refers to the Fourth Turning theory created by William Strauss and Neil Howe; they theorise that the history of a people moves in 80 to 100 year cycles called "saecula" and that is followed by an "ekpyrosis," a cataclysmic event that destroys the old order and brings in a new one.
66 Anderson, *Rising from the Ruins*, 304.

2

A GLOBAL ANTI-GLOBALIST MOVEMENT

The Alternative Right, globalisation and "globalism"

For many, the Alternative Right was viewed as a distinctly American phenomenon; a coterie of young white men with a deluded sense of aggrievement and a belief that they were the vanguard halting the "American carnage" Donald Trump railed against in his inauguration speech.[1] They saw themselves as defenders of the First Amendment, of memorialised Confederate generals, and of a vision of America that vehemently eschewed the 1965 Immigration Act and its commitment to admit the wretched refuse of all teeming shores.

This perception of the origins and interests of the Alternative Right is not entirely mistaken, but it overlooks the movement's truly global presence and outlook. Whilst the USA would play a pivotal role in the development of the Alternative Right, its ideology was shaped by a transatlantic conversation. Moreover, the reactionary movement this conversation would spawn was propelled by changes across the globe. Outside of the support for and faith in the economic, social and cultural policies of globalisation that bloomed after the fall of the Berlin Wall, resentment grew amongst some who were not the core beneficiaries of these policies, towards the advocates of this deterministic, globalised vision of the world. This anger was used by the far right to nurture the economic, cultural and racial nationalist wave, which the Alternative Right would ride upon as it emerged into the public eye in the mid-2010s.

For every injury – real or perceived – that these policies of globalisation led to for groups in the West, many in the far right would interpret them to be not just the fault of migrants and minorities, but more fundamentally that of a "globalist elite" who promoted policies and institutions that supported the free flow of people and trade across borders. Support for this was interpreted by the far right as ranging from overconfident and misguided adherence to a liberal economic and social doctrine, all the way to a deliberate plan to destroy (a highly mythologised notion of) white Western civilisation.

Of course, rumblings of such a backlash on the right could be heard early on in this period of wider support for globalisation. In his December 1991 announcement to contest George Bush Snr.'s presidency, Pat Buchanan warned of "our Western heritage" being "dumped onto some landfill called multiculturalism" and declared that "We must not trade in our sovereignty for a cushioned seat at the head table of anyone's new world order".[2] But in the US (and beyond) the Alternative Right would marry this America First-style nationalism to the postwar European fascist ideology developed by the European New Right (ENR) (or *Nouvelle Droite*) to produce a paradoxically global ideological outlook, that tied the "struggles" of each Western nation to that of all people of (white) European descent. Their enemies were to be not just the religious and racial groups that they perceived to fall outside of this group, but also the aforementioned elites; the "Davos Man" which Buchanan would declare in January 2016 was now haunted by the "Spectre of Trump."[3] Drawn together at an unprecedented scale by the globalising technologies of the digital age and spurred on by events which exemplified this connected world – from the "Global War on Terror" and the 2008 Financial Crash, to the rise of ISIS and the Mediterranean Refugee Crisis – our modern era set the stage for a thoroughly internationalist far right that propounds a racist and illiberal alternative to the vision of globalisation a generation grew up with.

Globalisation, globalism and the far right

Whilst a deep belief in the unbridled, continued success of modern globalisation entirely blinded some political observers to the growing dissent that fuelled the Alternative Right, others simply did not recognise its political significance. In part, this is because globalisation has been a process that unfolded over decades and so lacked the immediacy of a military conflict, for example. However, it is also due to confusions around what exactly constitutes "globalisation" and, even more so, the ideology described as "globalism." Globalisation scholars have noted the complexities of defining the former but as Bryan Turner and Robert Holton claim there is a degree of consensus that it involves:

> the compression of time and space, the increased interconnectivity of human groups, the increased volume of the exchange of commodities, people and ideas, and finally the emergence of various forms of global consciousness which [...] we may simply call "cosmopolitanism".[4]

Expanding on "cosmopolitanism" in turn helps in defining globalism. Similarly debated, Pauline Kleingeld and Eric Brown state nonetheless that a "nebulous core shared by all cosmopolitan views is the idea that all human beings, regardless of their political affiliation, are (or can and should be) citizens in a single community."[5] As Turner and Holton highlight, however, this shared view of people as citizens of a global community is just one possible result of the global consciousness that has emerged as a result of modern globalisation. Globalism, therefore, refers, in theory at least, to just "the cultural conditions of globalisation," without defining how open or hostile the culture in question is to the processes of globalisation.[6]

Increasingly the terms "globalism" and "globalist" are used by the Alternative Right as an epithet to describe cultural and economic elites conspiratorially wielding power for nefarious ends, often with implicit or explicit reference to Jews. As major American alt-right figure Greg Johnson wrote on his Counter-Currents Publishing website in 2015, "globalisation is not a path to universal freedom. It is the creation of one neck to bear a Jewish yoke for eternity."[7] Such conspiracies stem from long standing far-right ideas of Jews controlling institutions and of being "rootless cosmopolitans" who only have allegiances to Jewish interests. Both terms have for some time also taken on a broader connotation, referring more generally to any who support global economic and political institutions and agreements which foster the increased interconnectivity and exchange of commodities and people. Critics of globalism (on the left and the right) see its ideology symbolised by the likes of the United Nations, the European Union and the North American Free Trade Agreement. In addition to this, globalism is usually taken to be tied to a political outlook which urges legal, military, and regulatory oversight and intervention by (many, though not all) liberal democratic governments and supranational bodies such as the United Nations International Court of Justice, the North Atlantic Treaty Organization and the International Monetary Fund. In part, these institutions are taken to preserve the political and economic conditions that allow for the interconnectivity and exchange globalism prefers.

Opposition to parts or the whole of this worldview has long existed, most notably manifesting in recent decades with the international Occupy movement of the early 2010s and the "Battle of Seattle" protest against the World Trade Organization in 1999. These recent manifestations have meant anti-globalism has been associated with left-wing opposition to neoliberal regimes and the global free market, though the right also has a long history of opposition. Many on the right saw global institutions from their birth as vassals of secret – again, often believed to be Jewish-led – groups, as the prominent postwar British fascist A.K. Chesterton interpreted the Bretton Woods agreement, for example. Moreover, as populism scholar Cas Mudde has noted at the electoral level, "the national populist parties are [...] the most successful opponents of globalization."[8] Writing in 2004, Mudde added that for these parties "(anti-)globalization is not (yet) a central issue in their ideology and propaganda," in part because they reject the very historical, economically-focused determinacy that others – especially globalism's advocates – see globalisation as exemplifying.[9]

A reactionary movement for reluctant globalists

The Alternative Right placed the topic of globalisation front and centre, partly because of their perception that among those in positions of power globalism was becoming more widely accepted. For example, take the February 2008 article entitled *The Archaeology of Globalism* for the website Taki's Magazine (which, due to alt-right figurehead Richard Spencer's 2008–2010 stint as editor, was formative in the development of the Alternative Right). Contributor Matthew Roberts writes: "Almost all elitists seem to buy into [globalism] – whether one is a neoconservative supporting war, a Wall Street investor backing free trade or a Hollywood liberal adopting God knows how many children from around the world".[10] Roberts' observation articulated the sense among many who rejected the establishment right that they had to look elsewhere if they were to find a movement (and eventually representation) that rejected this pro-globalisation outlook. He concluded his article declaring:

> there is still hope. Despite all the propaganda in the media and academia, national polls show that the majority of Americans oppose the war in Iraq, free trade and mass immigration. If a charismatic politician were to rally round these three issues alone, he could foment a broad base of support.[11]

Rally around these issues candidates would. Yet, whilst the Alternative Right does oppose interventionist foreign policy[12] and the free flow of trade and people, this does not entirely capture what their brand of anti-globalism demanded. After all, centre-right, libertarian and left-wing arguments exist against these positions too. Instead, the Alternative Right's outlook was further informed by a different set of ideas, in particular the European New Right (ENR) movement that emerged in France in response to the political uprisings of May 1968, and which posited a pan-European nationalism and a world of ethnically homogeneous communities. The ENR articulated this as "ethnopluralism": the idea that different groups are equal but ought to live in separation from one another. This was argued to be out of a respect for the "right to difference" of such groups; their right to self-determination and ability to ensure that they do not lose their internal ethnic and cultural homogeneity.[13] The ENR argues that these communities share an "ethnocultural" identity, which posits an irreducible and unbreakable tie between ethnicity and culture. These ideas would descend from the ENR as a political ideology termed "Identitarianism," which manifested in Europe first as the French *Bloc Identitaire* party and later through the youth movement, *Génération Identitaire* (Generation Identity), which emerged in 2012. Though divergent with the wider Alternative Right in its origins, the European Identitarian movement frequently overlaps and finds supporters in the US Alternative Right and elsewhere.[14]

It was the translation of a text, *Manifesto for a European Renaissance*, co-authored by ENR thinkers Alain de Benoist and Charles Champetier, into English in 1999 which introduced notions such as ethnopluralism to the Anglophone far right more widely. Ostensibly, the adoption of ENR ideas by a movement with a large US contingent might seem jarring, since many anti-globalist arguments (from the left and right) have levelled criticism at the Americanisation of cultures and the ceding of control to this superpower that has come with much of modern globalisation. Moreover, parts of the ENR's output is distinctly anti-American; indeed, elements of even the US Alternative Right share this attitude.[15] At the same time, however, the utility of this position is also questioned. As ENR thinker Guillaume Faye declared in another text that would prove influential on the Alternative Right, *Why We Fight: Manifesto for a European Resistance*:

> The danger of anti-Americanism is in the virulence of its jeremiads, which are irresponsible and turn its proponents into hapless victims. Europeans are the leading actors in their Americanisation, in their submission to the United States —for the latter is strong only to the degree we are weak.[16]

In place of this attitude, Faye encouraged a multipolar anti-globalism, where America is Europe's "principal adversary, not [its] *principal enemy*."[17] Faye's aim here was to build on a distinction made by the German political theorist Carl Schmitt, which argued that politics begins with the designation of "friends" and "enemies," and the activity of politics is the competition that ensues between enemies.[18] For Faye, Europe's principal enemy was "the alien, the colonising immigrant masses, and Islam," whereas Europe's principal adversary was "America, which allies with Islam to weaken and dominate Europe."[19] Of course, there is nothing to prevent one's adversaries from becoming one's friends. Elaborating on Schmitt's notion of a political "friend," Faye explained:

> The political also entails designating the friend, that is, designating allies, but even more, designating one's co-religionists, comrades, and ethnic brothers, those who possess the same interests, the same origins, and the same values. Decadent civilisations designate their friends as enemies and their enemies as friends. Thus it is that Europe's governing elites demonise and ostracise as "fascists" whoever opposes the alien ethnic colonisers, even though these alleged "fascists" defend their people's identity and survival. By the same turn, the elites designate as friends and protect the alien masses colonising her.[20]

The Alternative Right has taken this to heart. After the "immigrant masses and Islam" appeared to them to be closing in across Europe and the US over the past two decades, the European and American far right forged a transatlantic partnership with their "co-religionists, comrades and ethnic brothers" across the Atlantic. As Mudde had noted, the far right had foreseen that the actions of globalists could help their own populist, nationalist causes. Yet, in a sense, the Alternative Right took its "enemies'" own increasing internationalisation – from the actions of parliamentarians in Brussels, to internationalised Islamist terror networks, and the efforts of European NGOs in the Mediterranean Refugee Crisis – as a sign that it can no longer assume that a populist, nationalist anti-globalism will simply win out. As a report of the speech of Alex Kurtagic, an early co-editor at Spencer's AlternativeRight.com, to a conference hosted by US alt-right organisation, American Renaissance, in 2012 stated, "[the movement] need[s] a positive enterprise of our own that is beyond politics and that simply ignores current orthodoxies."[21] It would have to stake out its own stance on the global political stage if only to destroy, or at least thoroughly refashion, the platform itself.

In an attempt to mobilise its global anti-globalism, the Alternative Right drew further still from the ENR by engaging in "identitarian metapolitics." Metapolitics, itself an adaptation of the ideas of Italian Marxist Antonio Gramsci, focuses on shifting the accepted positions in public discussion so as to create a political environment more open and potentially accepting of an ideology, prior to engaging in politics at an electoral and policy level. Faye's description of this approach to activism also brings out the grand, often global dimension of the political narratives promoted:

> [Metapolitics is the] social diffusion of ideas and cultural values for the sake of provoking a profound, long-term, political transformation. Metapolitics is an effort of propaganda – not necessarily that of a specific party – that diffuses an ideological body of ideas representing a global political project.[22]

As explained above, identitarianism is a political ideology that seeks to preserve ethnically and culturally rigid groups. Taking these two ideas together, this meant that the global cultural cause of the Alternative Right was to "protect" its (mythologised) white, Christian, European heritage from the inherent "threats" of migration from and influence of those that fell outside of this category. This is true even though American and European (and Australasian, Canadian, South African, and Latin American) identitarians simultaneously have their sights set on the comparatively local political project of affecting their national political landscape. At either level, Alternative Right identitarians on both sides of the pond view their enemies as the ethnic and cultural "aliens" Faye referred to and the pro-globalisation actors and policies that they see as allowing and encouraging these outsiders to "threaten" their identity.

Exiting together: Globalism viewed from the Alternative Right

How, then, should we understand this ostensibly paradoxical embrace of globalisation by the far right? One route is to consider the vision that emerges from what it *does* like about contemporary globalisation, chiefly its technological benefits. Not only have the web, social media, and various encrypted and anonymous communication platforms allowed the Alternative Right to network and propagandise at a tremendous scale for the far right, but crowdfunding (and, increasingly, cryptocurrencies) have allowed those belonging to the movement to support one another financially much more easily.

Yet, given the largely online origins and continued presence of the Alternative Right, 21st century global communications have also importantly provided the movement with a vision of what an alternative (anti-)globalist position could be. From the aesthetic, language and culture of its online forums, to the organised media manipulation strategies of its online activists, the movement has seen its growth and dominance of certain virtual spaces as a precursor for conventional, offline political actions. Indeed, it is as if they took a further statement of Faye's to heart: "Metapolitics is the occupation of culture, politics is the occupation of a territory."[23] A further useful perspective here is Lior Gelernter and Motti Regev's analysis of the relationship between ethnicity, diaspora, and the internet. Drawing on the work of Arjun Appadurai,[24] Gelernter and Regev note how the "Old homelands, new homelands and the mediated networks" between locales of a diaspora create new "ethnoscape[s]," which the internet "plays a central role in shaping [...] as it supports ubiquitous diasporic networks, offers a space in which identities and hierarchies are negotiated and allows for their political mobilization."[25] Viewed through this lens, the Alternative Right, especially the white nationalist element of the movement, has nurtured a white supremacist ethnoscape online by framing white Westerners of European descent across the world as a diaspora, who have gained greater racial and ethnic consciousness through the web and who must mobilise through it to face the "threats" of those outside of this diaspora.

That the Alternative Right considers its often radical global anti-globalist visions as options which would enjoy great swathes of support highlights the extent perhaps that the movement has been influenced by the illusory virtual "territories" it has created for itself online. This is perhaps best exemplified by an idea preferred by an obscure extreme of the contemporary far right: the "No Voice-Free Exit" strategy put forward by the "Neoreactionary" or "NRx" school of thought. The NRx developed largely online in the late 2000s and early 2010s and has acted as a tributary into the Alternative Right. In brief, NRx is a far right, anti-democratic movement that rejects enlightenment principles and advocates for a "patchwork" of "neo-cameralist" states, wherein a state is governed as if it were a business and its residents its customers.[26] Rather than a number of traditional geopolitical blocs, this instead emphasises the idea of competition between, often racially homogenous, states, which are governed in a manner closer to a corporation. In this scenario there is little democracy ("No Voice") save for allowing individuals the liberty to pick from the "market" of competing states ("Free Exit"). As the "Dark Enlightenment" Reddit.com subforum for the NRx community describes in its "Common Ideas" section, they wish for "A system of No Voice-Free Exit in large hyper-federalist states or small independent city states."[27]

Despite this extreme response to globalisation, it does speak to a broader undercurrent within the Alternative Right and the European identitarian movement, insofar as they generally opt not for working within the liberal democratic political arena that they take their globalist competitors to have created, but rather for various forms of secession from this. Closer to the reality of the successive national exit from the EU campaigns that have emerged in recent times, is the European identitarians' call for an alternative confederation of nations with little centralised control compared to the EU, as described by Austrian Generation Identity activist Markus Willinger in his *A Europe of Nations*.[28] Where Willinger's European confederation is conceived as one bloc in a multipolar competition against the US, China, the Islamic world and elsewhere, others in the American, Australasian, and European Alternative Right rally closer to the transnational and transcontinental idea of a bloc of white nationalist Western states, coming closer to traditional far-right ideas of the "Clash of Civilisations" between the white, Christian West and the rest. Writing for the alt-right *Radix Journal* in December 2016, for example, Charles Lyons, Chief

Administrative Officer of alt-right publisher Arktos Media, declared that the alt-right is both "The American Resistance" and part of "a global effort in alliance with European identitarians of all stripes."[29]

At the same time, for some in the Alternative Right, their secessionist response is more focused in the direction of localism. For example, US alt-right associate and advocate of tribalism Jack Donovan wrote in 2011 that the movement must "Hate Globally, Like Locally," and he is amongst others in the movement living in the US Pacific Northwest who have called for a state of "Cascadia" in the region to secede.[30] Similarly, Brad Griffin (AKA Hunter Wallace) of the Southern Confederalist alt-right blog Occidental Dissent, proposed a reimagined Southern Confederalism called the "Alt-South" in a speech to the alt-right Atlanta Forum gathering on 28 January 2017. Griffin claimed the term referred to "a space for everyone in Dixie who isn't some kind of leftist or mainstream conservative (i.e., nationalists, populists, reactionaries) to come together to discuss [the South's] past, present, and common future," and stated it "will blend the Alt-Right and Southern Nationalism."[31] In either case, however, there is a clear alliance with the political goals of those within the Alternative Right whose scale of interest is the national, transnational, and transcontinental.

The divergences between the European identitarian movement, the alt-right and its more regionally-focused elements brings out a tension which was noted by the ENR. As Alain de Benoist notes in *Confronting Globalisation*, "To resist globalisation does not necessarily imply a reassertion of the territoriality typical of the nation-state" since "identitarian, religious, ethnic, linguistic or cultural solidarities" can be transnational and so "opposed to territoriality."[32] Given this, faced by global out-looks or processes (such as multiculturalism or a global caliphate) which are seen as challenging these solidarities, "the nation-state appears more or less as an obsolete identitarian horizon."[33] Importantly, however, de Benoist is highlighting that, for these particularistic solidarities, the nation-state's obsolescence is a function of a (perceived) external threat, rather than as a result of something (at least as they see it) inherently contradictory about the pairing of nationalism and transnationalism. The alt-right is a white nationalist movement, the whiteness of which is defined by a mythologised concept of European identity, and in this regard they view their cause as transnational in nature. Yet, as the European identitarian movement, which influences the alt-right, will argue, this concept of European identity is a combination of both the supranational (European) and national (German, French, etc.) levels and, at a lower level, also the regional (for the French be it Brittany, Alsace, etc.).[34] In this respect, the US alt-right follows the same path in defining its identity but with an altered supra-national component: it is made up of Americans (perhaps with a particular regional identity) who also identify as being of European descent as opposed to European, which they usually tie to their white identity. In contrast, identitarians within Europe rarely refer to their supranational identity in racial terms, and treat "European" as a stand-in for "white" with little explicit reference to race when discussing identity.

In contrast to this is the more culturally-fixated, Western chauvinist alt-lite's response to globalisation. The alt-lite eschews white nationalism, though rallies against many of the same targets as the alt-right, namely non-Western immigrants and

Muslims. The alt-lite would agree with de Benoist that globalisation poses threats to a particular solidarity – in its case the West rather than white people – and would build its identity in much the same way as the alt-right, replacing "white" with "Western" (or European). However, their project is largely negative – keeping non-Western migrants and Islam out of the West – and as such has less in the way of an additional, radical, alternative political programme in the sense that the alt-right does (i.e. in the establishment of white ethnostates). Hence, whilst the likes of British alt-lite vlogger Paul Joseph Watson have declared "[...] we shouldn't be ashamed to defend Western civilisation"[35] and British alt-lite media personality Milo Yiannopoulos has asserted "I'm a Western supremacist,"[36] these are meant to buttress a loose coalition of Western chauvinist commentators and activists whose transnationalism functions as a means to "protecting" their respective Western nations, rather than as a means to establishing something substantial over and above this.

Whilst it is the practical global cooperation of the Alternative Right – its online networking, propagandising, organising, and financing – that is a more pressing concern than its hope of white nationalist geopolitical blocs and city-states run as corporations, its alternative visions of how a globalised and inegalitarian world could function should not be just dismissed as the deluded fantasies of the hateful. The anti-globalisation anger that the Alternative Right and the aforementioned nationalist and secessionist surge across Europe and America tapped into is real. It cannot be responded to with a reiteration of the previous prevailing pro-globalisation attitudes' lack of care for the real and perceived economic and cultural disadvantages it engendered. In the absence of novel and inspiring progressive alternatives, divisive outlooks may slowly begin to hold sway.

Notes

1 Donald J. Trump, "Inaugural Address," *Whitehouse.gov*, 20 January 2017. https://www.white house.gov/briefings-statements/the-inaugural-address/.
2 "Buchanan 1992 Announcement," 4 President. http://www.4president.org/speeches/buchanan1992announcement.htm [Accessed 15 September 2018].
3 Patrick J. Buchanan, "Is the Spectre of Trump Haunting Davos?" *Buchanan.org*, 21 January 2016. http://buchanan.org/blog/is-the-spectre-of-trump-haunting-davos-124642.
4 Bryan S. Turner and Robert J. Holton, "Theories of Globalization," in: Bryan S. Turner and Robert J. Holton, (Eds.), *The Routledge International Handbook of Globalization Studies Second Edition* (Abingdon: Routledge, 2015), 5.
5 Pauline Kleingeld and Eric Brown, "Cosmopolitanism," *The Stanford Encyclopedia of Philosophy*, 1 July 2013. https://plato.stanford.edu/entries/cosmopolitanism/.
6 Bryan S. Turner and Robert J. Holton, "Theories of Globalization," 10.
7 Greg Johnson, "The End of Globalization," *Counter-Currents Publishing*, 28 December 2011. https://www.counter-currents.com/2011/12/the-end-of-globalization/
8 Cas Mudde, "Globalisation: The Multi-Faceted Enemy?," *The Contemporary European Research Centre Working Papers Series*, 3 (2004), 16.
9 Ibid., 17.
10 Matthew Roberts, 'The Archaeology of Globalism', *Taki's Magazine*, 4 February 2008. http://takimag.com/article/the_archaeology_of_globalism/#axzz5WGvVtadk
11 Ibid.

12 For example, following the April 2018 US missile strikes in Syria, which led to wide-spread condemnation within the Alternative Right. Jason Wilson, "Why is the Far Right so Against US Intervention in Syria?" *The Guardian*, 13 April 2018. https://www.theguardian.com/us-news/2018/apr/13/syria-intervention-conservative-rightwing-opposition-trump

13 This line of thought has been employed in the rhetoric of some in both the Alternative Right and its contemporary, the European "identitarian" movement, when communicating their anti-migrant and anti-refugee positions. In addition to making claims that European ethnocultural identity is under threat from being "replaced" by these groups, they are also often presented as pawns controlled by globalist elites who actively desire or simply do not care about this "replacement." The German-based identitarian organisation, Alternative Help Association (AHA), launched in 2017, takes this a step further, and engages actively in efforts to prevent their movements into Europe through running local aid programmes in the countries of origin of migrants and refugees coming to Europe. Similar to this is the Italy-based *Solidarité Identités*, which claims to support groups "[...] struggling for their own survival, the safeguarding of their culture and the defense of their identity." "Home," Solidarité Identités. http://www.solid-onlus.org/. [Accessed 15 September 2018.]

14 For further discussion, see Chapter 1 "The European Roots of Alt-Right Ideology" in this book.

15 For example, as Jamie Weinstein reported in *The Guardian* in 2016, Richard Spencer is "indifferent or opposed to the US constitution." Jamie Weinstein, "The 'Alt-Right' Don't Belong in the American Conservative Tradition," *The Guardian*, 22 November 2016. https://www.theguardian.com/commentisfree/2016/nov/22/alt-right-dont-belong-american-conservatism-jamie-weinstein

16 Guillaume Faye, *Why We Fight: Manifesto of the European Resistance* (Budapest: Arktos Media, 2011), 91.

17 Faye, *Why We Fight*, 92.

18 Carl Schmitt, *The Concept of the Political* (Expanded Edition) (Chicago: University of Chicago Press, 2007), 26.

19 Faye, *Why We Fight*, 153.

20 Ibid.

21 Henry Wolff, "AmRen Conference Held in Tennessee," *American Renaissance*, 19 March 2012. https://www.amren.com/features/2012/03/amren-conference-held-in-tennessee/

22 Faye, *Why We Fight*, 272.

23 Ibid.

24 Arjun Appadurai, *Modernity at Large: Cultural Dimensions of Globalization* (Minneapolis: University of Minnesota Press, 1996).

25 Lior Gelernter and Motti Regev, "Internet and globalization," in: Bryan S. Turner and Robert J. Holton, (Eds.), *The Routledge International Handbook of Globalization Studies Second Edition* (Abingdon: Routledge, 2015), 83.

26 See: Mencius Moldbug, "Against Political Freedom," *Unqualified Reservations*, 16 August 2007. https://www.unqualified-reservations.org/2007/08/against-political-freedom/

27 "r/DarkEnlightenment," Reddit. https://www.reddit.com/r/DarkEnlightenment/. For further discussion of the NRx movement, see Chapter 7 "The Dark Enlightenment: Neoreaction and Silicon Valley" in this book.

28 See: Markus Willinger, *A Europe of Nations* (Budapest: Arktos Media, 2014).

29 Charles Lyons, "The Alt Right: The American Resistance," *Radix Journal*, 31 December 2016. https://radixjournal.com/2016/12/2016-12-31-the-alt-right-the-american-resistance/

30 Nathan Leonard, "Action is Key: An Interview with Jack Donovan," *Heathen Harvest*, 10 August 2014. https://heathenharvest.org/2014/08/10/action-is-key-an-interview-with-jack-donovan/

31 Hunter Wallace, "The Alternative South," *Counter-Currents Publishing*, 24 February 2017. https://www.counter-currents.com/2017/02/the-alternative-south/

32 Alain de Benoist, "Confronting Globalization," *Telos* 108 (1996), fn.37.

33 Ibid.

34 Brittany Pettibone, 2017, "What is Generation Identity" [Online video]. Available at: https://www.youtube.com/watch?v=DIZ3DVozFv8 [Accessed 17 September 2018].
35 Paul Joseph Watson, 2016, "Some Cultures Are Better Than Others" [Online video]. Available at: https://www.youtube.com/watch?v=2JXrDwtiqQs&feature=youtu.be&t=409
36 Sean Bruce, "'I'm A Western Supremacist' – Milo Yiannopoulos on Why He Thinks West Is Best," *Penthouse*, 10 October 2017. http://www.penthouse.com.au/videos/im-a-western-supremacist-milo-yiannopoulos-on-why-he-thinks-west-is-best

3

FOR WHOM THE BELL CURVES

The alt-right and pseudoscientific racism[1]

On 22 November 2015, then-Presidential Candidate Donald Trump took to Twitter to post a graphic with an array of crime statistics, including the claim that 81 per cent of white murder victims are killed by black people, while 97 per cent of black murder victims are killed by people of their own race. The following day the *Washington Post* described the figures as "wildly inaccurate" and explained that the "Crime Statistics Bureau – San Francisco" cited as the source on the graphic does not even exist.[2] As it turned out, the graphic itself actually originated from a neo-nazi Twitter account. A later report by the Southern Poverty Law Center (SPLC) explained that "The idea that black people are wantonly attacking white people in some sort of quiet race war is an untruthful and damaging narrative with a very long history in America."[3]

In many ways, this event encapsulates numerous facets of the alt-right's relationship with race, in that a long-standing racist trope about black violence was repackaged as a shareable meme, disseminated on social media, and made its way into political discourse, in this extraordinary case being picked up by the future President of the United States. In short, while there is very little that is new or unique about the alt-right's racism it has, as with its antisemitism, found modern means to repackage and disseminate it effectively in the digital age.

While many within the alt-right spend a lot of time and energy vocally trying to differentiate themselves from their far-right predecessors – bemoaning what they call "White nationalism 1.0"[4] – the majority of their ideas on race are drawn from individuals and organisations that long predate the emergence of the alt-right. This is no great surprise, considering the alt-right is a conglomerate movement that subsumed a whole plethora of existing racist movements under its umbrella, many of which have merely adopted the moniker as a rebranding exercise. As such, while it has done little in the way of innovation, the alt-right has helped facilitate something of a revival of pseudoscientific race science.

Repackaging old ideas

One beneficiary of this remarketing of long discredited ideas is Charles Murray and his infamous 1994 book, *The Bell Curve: Intelligence and Class Structure in American Life*, co-authored with Richard Herrnstein, in which the authors seek to explain racial difference in IQ scores.[5] According to Martin Lee in *The Beast Reawakens*, the book argued:

> that intelligence is a genetically linked characteristic of race, and precious resources should not be squandered on futile efforts to improve the lot of the permanently poor – and mainly black and brown – underclass consisting of genetically inferior people.[6]

While the book received large press interest and numerous positive reviews and editorials, experts were quick to weigh in with criticism. The evolutionary biologist Stephen Jay Gould, for example, wrote in *The New Yorker* that the book "contains no new arguments and presents no compelling data to support its anachronistic social Darwinism" and declared that "We must fight the doctrine of *The Bell Curve* both because it is wrong and because it will, if activated, cut off all possibility of proper nurturance for everyone's intelligence."[7] Writing in the *New York Times*, Bob Herbert was even more blunt, stating "Most serious scholars know that the conclusions drawn by Murray and Herrnstein from the data in 'The Bell Curve' are bogus" and wrote the book off as "an ugly stunt," declaring that Mr. Murray "can protest all he wants, his book is just a genteel way of calling somebody a nigger."[8] With time the furore died down and the book, thoroughly discredited, faded from discussion except amongst the racists of the far right.

However, a 2017 article in *Scientific American* opened simply by saying of Murray, "He's back" and talked about his "unfortunate resurgence" and his "resurging book sales."[9] Similarly, in the wake of protests against his appearance at Middlebury College in March 2017, the right-wing website PJ Media claimed that the *Bell Curve* had shot to number one on Amazon in the demographics category, number three in social sciences and number five in US history textbooks.[10] Nicole Hemmer, an Assistant Professor at the University of Virginia, has explained how *The Bell Curve* "has many new fans on the alt-right" and that its ideas have evolved into the language of "human biodiversity," the racist pseudoscience popular with the alt-right and discussed at length below.[11] Writing back in 1994 Gould said:

> I can only conclude that its success in winning attention must reflect the depressing temper of our time – a historical moment of unprecedented ungenerosity, when a mood for slashing social programs can be powerfully abetted by an argument that beneficiaries cannot be helped, owing to inborn cognitive limits expressed as low IQ scores.[12]

Sadly, it seems that 1994 was not "unprecedented," as *The Bell Curve* undergoes a contemporary revival.

Chief among the longstanding racists who have relaunched themselves as part of the alt-right is Jared Taylor of American Renaissance. In September 2016, Taylor joined fellow alt-right figureheads Richard Spencer and Peter Brimelow of the racist anti-immigration site VDARE at the Willard Hotel in downtown Washington DC for a press conference, designed to both explain what the alt-right is and to cement their positions as its leaders in the eyes of the gathered journalists.[13] During his speech, Taylor was unequivocal about the role of race in the alt-right's worldview. "Race is not just real: it is central to group and individual identity," he said.[14] He called for white people to:

> speak in these terms in self defense. Since orthodoxy has decreed that all groups are precisely equal, it permits only one explanation for non-white failure: white oppression. An entire industry has risen up to stoke white guilt and purge whites of "unearned privilege." We are not responsible for the shortcomings of others and we despise those who claim we are.[15]

For Taylor and his acolytes, the cause of racial inequality in America, and global inequality more generally, is to be understood as the result of innate racial difference born of divergent intelligence levels, rather than institutional and structural racism. As he puts it, "One of the most destructive myths of modern times is that people of all races have the same average intelligence."[16] Taylor believes "that genes account for much of the difference in intelligence between individuals"[17] and that the proof of this difference is born out in disparities in IQ scores between different racial groups. Here is not the place to debunk Taylor's pseudoscience, but needless to say, many of the ideas he promulgates are long discredited and disproved, not least because, as Dr Gavin Evans of Birkbeck University explains, "intelligence – even the rather specific version measured by IQ – involves a network of potentially thousands of genes, which probably takes at least 100 millennia to evolve appreciably."[18]

Despite now spreading such notions under the banner of the alt-right, Taylor has been espousing these ideas for decades. In 1990, he founded the white supremacist American Renaissance (AmRen), "in order to awaken whites to the crisis they face and to encourage them to unite in defending their legitimate interests as a race."[19] AmRen started as a monthly printed magazine promulgating "scientific" explanations for white "superiority" over black people. In 1994, AmRen launched a website and began organising conferences that have become key meeting points for far-right activists across the globe, bringing European far right and, importantly for the development of the alt-right, European New Right (ENR) ideas across the Atlantic, for example hosting a speech from the prominent ENR figure and Archeofuturism theorist Guillaume Faye in 2012. In January 2012, Taylor suspended publication of AmRen magazine, refocusing his efforts on the organisation's website, which it considers to be "the Internet's premier race-realist site."[20] The site posts daily news articles as well as longer opinion pieces, with contributions from figures influential on the Alternative Right, including Gavin McInnes, Tomislav Sunić, Francis Roger Devlin, Richard Spencer, Pat Buchanan, Jack Donovan, and Alex

Kurtagic. AmRen also publishes a regular podcast hosted by Taylor, runs an active YouTube channel and has published interviews with ENR philosopher Alain de Benoist.

AmRen came to be associated with the alt-right early in its development and Taylor is respected by many in the movement for his longevity and genial style. He generally strives to avoid much of the more extreme iconography and the crude racial epithets that are so common on other racist alt-right websites, and instead opts for a more "serious" approach and, unusually for the alt-right, generally avoids outright antisemitism. While Taylor has regularly provided platforms for extreme antisemites, he himself has stated that "AR [AmRen] has taken an implicit position on Jews by publishing Jewish authors and inviting Jewish speakers to AR conferences."[21]

The centrality of Taylor and AmRen to the alt-right project is in large part the result of his relationship with Richard Spencer, who is a longtime ally and admirer, once stating, "I can say that Jared Taylor red-pilled me, he was the person I looked to talk about race in a rational manner but also in an inspiring manner."[22] In a 2017 Q&A with the North Central Florida-based public broadcaster WUFT, Spencer's explanation of his position on race makes clear the lasting influence of Taylor, especially in regards to race and identity:

> [A]t the foundation of anyone's identity is race. That is something that one can't choose, something that one is born into. And race, as a foundation, informs everything. So, identity should not be equated with race. Identity is a lot more than race, but race is at the very foundation of everything. It's a sine qua non of who we are and who any individual is. So that, something, of how I would describe my starting point to thinking about politics.[23]

More succinctly he stated "I've recognized that race is real and race matters and race is the foundation of identity, [...]."[24] The relationship between Spencer and Taylor is an important one within the alt-right and in many ways archetypal of the movement, with Spencer adopting Taylor's old pseudoscientific ideas and seeking to disseminate them in new and modern ways to younger audiences.

Human biodiversity

While the works of Taylor and AmRen are popular within the alt-right, they are not alone in bringing pre-existing racist ideas into this modern movement. Alongside the traditional "race-realism" (a synonym for pseudoscientific racism) of Taylor is the similarly euphemistic race theory known as "human biodiversity" (HBD). Outside of racist and alt-right circles very little is written about HBD, but Ari Feldman, writing for the Jewish news outlet *Forward*, explains how:

> "Human biodiversity" appropriates scientific authority by posing as an empirical, rational discourse on the genetically proven physical and mental variation between humans. [...] The refrain of HBD bloggers and forum

commenters is that the (gene-driven, according to them) dissimilarities they outline are "non-negligible" or "non-trivial" and have, accordingly, social policy implications.[25]

One of the best-known figures within the "HBD-o-sphere" is "hbd chick," a popular figure among those within the alt-right interested in the issue of race. During an interview with the alt-right hub Counter-Currents Publishing, run by the white supremacist Greg Johnson, she argues that there is:

something about how these [racial] differences are the result of evolutionary processes. Also, that "groups" refers to all sorts of populations: men and women, different races, different ethnic groups – even subgroups within these larger groups, which a lot of people tend to overlook, I think.[26]

In *Rising from the Ruins*, Joakim Andersen, founder of the Swedish proto-alt-right think tank Motpol, explains how HBD bloggers:

have presented studies indicating that Europeans are on average more empathic than people from other continents, that White America is really several historical nations (such as New France, Yankeedom, and the Greater Appalachia), and that there are connections between alcoholism and how long a history of agriculture a society has. Within the HBD-sphere we also encounter fascinating studies of the so-called Hajnal line[27] showing significant connections between family patterns and things like high intelligence as well as economic and political success.[28]

However, the individual who has done more than any to advance the idea of HBD is Steve Sailer, who coined the phrase himself in the mid-1990s. Sailer is a prolific writer whose work on race has, while dismissed by critics "as pseudoscience at best and eugenics at worst," become extremely popular among sections of the alt-right.[29] Sailer graduated from Rice University in 1980 and began writing for *National Review* in the 1990s, a stint that ended when he was pushed out in 1997.[30] He now writes for several sites associated with the alt-right, such as VDARE, Taki's Magazine, and the Unz Review. However, while HBD is popular within the alt-right, Sailer has not wholeheartedly embraced the term himself, though he has written favourably of the movement in Taki's Magazine.[31] While Sailer, like other HBD advocates, would likely reject that he is racist and regularly lampoons the progressive movement for bemoaning the supposedly pervasive presence of racism in society, his pseudoscientific veneer barely covers a base and explicit racism. In his 2011 review of Jared Taylor's book *White Identity: Racial Consciousness in the 21ˢᵗ Century*, he wrote that, "Blacks tend to be colorful but not too competent; East Asians competent but colorless; Latinos culturally lethargic and unenterprising." He went on to explain how the most serious roadblock to the emergence of white identity politics is that "more Jews don't want it to happen than do want it to happen."[32] This sort of language has done nothing to dampen his influence within the alt-right and, in some cases, has no doubt aided it.

One common trait amongst HBD acolytes within the alt-right is a sometimes genuine, though often feigned, reluctance to accept the "truth" of racial intelligence difference based on genes. Many couch their advocacy for HBD in a faux-sadness and argue that, though they wish it were not true, the evidence was just too overwhelming. The genuineness of this varies between individuals but often their wider politics and previous statements indicate a predisposition to agreeing with racist pseudoscience. Perhaps the best example of this is the influential Canadian pseudo-philosopher Stefan Molyneux whose podcast, the Freedomain Radio show, has, according to him, had over 250 million downloads.[33] In a video entitled "Human Biodiversity and Criminality," Molyneux lamented:

> I mean, human biodiversity is one of [those] perspectives that I wished with all my heart was not the case. As far as it stands particularly, of course the increasing evidence for the genetic underpinnings for a lot of this sort of human group race or ethnic diversity differences. It is one of these things that you, for me at least I really had to grit my teeth and just say, man, if this was false, this would be the best thing ever but as the evidence tends to accumulate, you know we have to put away our childish [sic] and deal with what is if we wish to do the very best that we can in the world.[34]

This supposed reluctance, feigned or otherwise, is undermined by the near universal failure to explain *why* it is they explore the question of racial difference in the first place. In essence, their prejudicial drivers towards useful pseudoscientific explanations for their pre-existing prejudices are revealed by what they *do not* say. Writing in *Scientific American* about *The Bell Curve*, Eric Siegel rightly argues that:

> By never spelling out a reason for reporting on these differences in the first place, the authors transmit an unspoken yet unequivocal conclusion: Race is a helpful indicator as to whether a person is likely to hold certain capabilities. [...] The net effect is to tacitly condone the prejudgment of individuals based on race.[35]

This is certainly borne out when one looks at the political objectives of those within the alt-right who discuss HBD.

Most within the HBD-o-sphere claim that it is not an explicitly political project, but rather an objective apolitical scientific pursuit. HBD chick herself stated that: "I, personally, would prefer it – and I think it would be better for everybody concerned [...] – if the study of human biodiversity, sociobiology, was completely divorced from politics."[36] However, she herself admits in the very same interview that:

> HBD matters in all sorts of ways, from designing medical treatments for different populations (BiDil, for example) to thinking about immigration policies

(if different populations really are innately different in various ways, what are the potential implications of mass immigration?) [...].[37]

Similarly, in *Rising from the Ruins*, Andersen states that HBD "reminds us of the practical and ethical complications of subjecting multiple, differing groups of people to the same political and economic systems";[38] a coded way of explaining the need for separation of groups. Sailer, the father of HBD, is less guarded about its explicitly political ramifications, once stating in an interview with the H.L. Mencken Club that HBD is "both a field of study and a political movement."[39] As is so often the case when looking at racial theories within the far right, while framed as a merely academic exercise in pursuit of the truth, the reality is that they are used as an attempted justification for racist policies. As Feldman puts it, "Though it has a rational, policy-wonk zing to it, that's just Internet forum-ese for 'you're genetically distinct from us and should be treated differently.'"[40]

Ethnocultural identity and ethnopluralism

Within the broad Alternative Right there is the racial nationalist alt-right and the cultural nationalist or Western chauvinist alt-lite. The former draws on the ideas discussed above. However, this particular binary racial/cultural conception of identity is not universally held by the contemporary far right, and when seeking to understand the alt-right one has to consider the increasingly influential European Identitarian movement, whose ideas have, in recent years, become increasingly popular among alt-right circles in North America. The most significant network within the international Identitarian movement started in France with the launch of Génération Identitaire (GI), the youth wing of the far-right Bloc Identitaire.[41] It has since spread across the continent with affiliated groups, the most prominent of which, in addition to France, are based in Germany, Italy, and Austria.

According to GI, one's identity has an ethnic *and* a cultural side, as well as three levels: the regional, national, and civilisational (the latter being European civilisation, in the case of GI). The ethnic and cultural sides are reflected at all three levels. GI wants to preserve both sides of ethnocultural identity and argues that the mistake of traditional right-wing movements has been to reduce ethnocultural identity to just one side (racial nationalists) or the other (cultural nationalists). In the view of Martin Sellner, co-leader of the Austrian branch of GI and the movement's de facto spokesperson, it is because of the combination of both ethnicity and culture that assimilation and integration are possible but "only in certain amounts." This is because: "whilst culture is something you can assimilate into [...] the ethnic side is something you inherit that you cannot change," and "culture and people are linked together." So to believe that changes to ethnic populations "will not change our culture [...] [and] identity" is "sheer madness."[42]

Despite GI's claim that it rejects traditional racial nationalism, the concept of "ethnocultural" identity rigidly ties culture to ethnicity and so, as Dr. Raphael Schlembach of the University of Brighton argues, it "'biologises' and 'essentialises' cultures to such an extent that they are turned into the functional equivalents of race."[43] Despite the non-racist and non-prejudiced pretensions of GI, therefore, by employing the concept of ethnocultural identity it implicitly defines European identity by majority features of European ethnic (white) and cultural (in particular, non-Muslim) heritage.

As with the pseudoscience of the "race-realists" such as Jared Taylor or the HBD theorists, GI's understanding of race is not merely academic but rather makes up the foundation of its political objectives. For GI this means advocating for "ethnopluralism," the idea that different ethnocultural groups are ostensibly equal but ought to live in separation from one another out of respect for their "right to difference," their right to self-determination and ability to ensure that they do not lose their internal homogeneity. For GI this constitutes a rejection of the European status quo attitude of multiculturalism, seeing true "diversity" and "antiracism" to instead consist in a situation wherein, according to Sellner, "all peoples have a right to preserve and promote their group identity in their homelands."[44] Ethnopluralism is advocated as a response to a belief that ethnic Europeans are being replaced by non-European people, broadly understood as non-white and Muslim and is based on a belief that different ethnic groups living together is not desirable or workable. The introduction of such a policy involves the forced separation of ethnic groups via repatriation in the case of "illegal" migrants or by reducing living standards for legal migrants from these groups.

Whether it is the ethnopluralists of the Identitarian movement, the HBD advocates or traditional far-right pseudoscientific racists, all have a common belief that race is real, that different races have different inherent characteristics and that race and ethnicity are central to, and fundamentally defining of, one's identity. As political movements, they seek to use consciously contrived or shaky science to justify their pre-existing racial prejudices and to provide a justification for their advocacy of racist policies. The alt-right itself has done little to add to the canon of racist pseudoscience, with most of the ideas it propagates predating the birth of the movement. Yet, while it criticises "white nationalism 1.0," the movement is happy to regurgitate its racism and to take these pre-existing ideas and package them anew for a fresh and younger far-right audience, the result being a resurgence in long debunked and ostracised racist theories and thinkers.

Notes

1 There is also an American Renaissance article of this title: Jared Taylor, "For Whom the Bell Curves," *American Renaissance*, February 1995. https://www.amren.com/news/2017/09/charles-murray-bell-curve-race-and-iq-richard-herrnstein-jared-taylor/

2 Jon Greenberg, "Trump's Pants on Fire tweet that blacks killed 81% of white homicide victims," *PolitiFact*, 23 November 2015. https://www.politifact.com/truth-o-meter/statements/2015/nov/23/donald-trump/trump-tweet-blacks-white-homicide-victims/

3 Hatewatch Staff, "The Biggest Lie in the White Supremacist Propaganda Playbook: Unraveling the Truth about 'Black-on-White Crime'," *Southern Poverty Law Center*, 14 June 2018. https://www.splcenter.org/20180614/biggest-lie-white-supremacist-propaganda-playbook-unraveling-truth-about-%E2%80%98black-white-crime

4 Hunter Wallace, "Why White Nationalism 1.0 Failed," *Occidental Dissent*, 18 July 2017. http://www.occidentaldissent.com/2017/07/18/why-white-nationalism-1-0-failed/

5 Richard J. Herrnstein and Charles Murray, *The Bell Curve: Intelligence and Class Structure in American Life* (New York: Simon & Schuster, 1996).

6 Martin Lee, *The Beast Reawakens: The Chilling Story of the Rise of the Neo-Nazi Movement* (London: Little, Brown, 1997), 362.

7 Stephen Jay Gould, "Curveball," *The New Yorker*, 28 November 1994. http://www.da rtmouth.edu/~chance/course/topics/curveball.html

8 Bob Herbert, "In America; Throwing a Curve," *The New York Times*, 26 October 1994. https://www.nytimes.com/1994/10/26/opinion/in-america-throwing-a-curve.html

9 Eric Siegel, "The Real Problem with Charles Murray and 'The Bell Curve'," *Scientific American*, 12 April 2017. https://blogs.scientificamerican.com/voices/the-real-problem -with-charles-murray-and-the-bell-curve/

10 Tom Knighton, "Middlebury Riot Boosts Charles Murray's Book Sales," *PJ Media*, 30 March 2017. https://pjmedia.com/trending/2017/03/30/middlebury-riot-boosts-cha rles-murrays-book-sales/

11 Nicole Hemmer, "'Scientific Racism' is on the Rise on the Right. But it's Been Lurking there for Years," *Vox*, 28 March 2017. https://www.vox.com/the-big-idea/2017/3/28/ 15078400/scientific-racism-murray-alt-right-black-muslim-culture-trump

12 Gould, "Curveball."

13 Event attended by author.

14 Jared Taylor, "What is the Alt Right?," *American Renaissance*, 11 October 2016. https:// www.amren.com/news/2016/10/what-is-the-alt-right-jared-taylor/

15 Ibid.

16 "Our Issues," *American Renaissance*. https://www.amren.com/about/issues

17 Ibid.

18 Gavin Evans, "The unwelcome revival of 'race science'," *The Guardian*, 2 March 2018. https:// www.theguardian.com/news/2018/mar/02/the-unwelcome-revival-of-race-science

19 Jared Taylor, "Jews and American Renaissance," *American Renaissance*, May 2006. https:// www.amren.com/news/2006/04/jews_and_americ/

20 "About Us," *American Renaissance*. https://www.amren.com/about/

21 Taylor, "Jews and American Renaissance."

22 Richard Spencer in: "Truth against the World," 2016, *The Alt-Right Press Conference | Richard Spencer, Peter Brimelow & Jared Taylor* [Online Video]. Available at: https://www.youtube.com/watch?v=aJWLjRK2SRo [Accessed 21 October 2018].

23 Richard Spencer in: Mercedes Leguizamon, "Q & A with Richard Spencer," *WUFT*, 9 October 2017. https://www.wuft.org/news/2017/10/09/q-a-with-richard-spencer/

24 Ibid.

25 Ari Feldman, "'Human Biodiversity': The Pseudoscientific Racism of the Alt-Right," *Forward*, 5 August 2016. https://forward.com/opinion/national/346533/human-biodi versity-the-pseudoscientific-racism-of-the-alt-right/

26 Chip Smith, "Rebel Girl: An Interview with HBD Chick," *Counter-Currents*. https:// www.counter-currents.com/2013/09/rebel-girlan-interview-with-hbd-chick/

27 The Hajnal line is a border that runs from St Petersburg in Russia to Trieste in Italy and is said to dissect the continent into two distinct areas based on differing levels and times of marriage. See: https://hbdchick.wordpress.com/2014/03/10/big-summary-post-on- the-hajnal-line/

28 Joakim Andersen, *Rising from the Ruins: The Right of the 21st Century* (United Kingdom: Arktos Media Ltd, 2018), 188–189.

29 Park MacDougald and Jason Willick, "The Man Who Invented Identity Politics for the New Right," *Intelligencer*, 30 April 2017. http://nymag.com/intelligencer/2017/04/ste ve-sailer-invented-identity-politics-for-the-alt-right.html

30 Ibid.

31 Steve Sailer, "Political Punk Rock," *Taki's Magazine*, 07 September 2016. http://takima g.com/article/political_punk_rock_steve_sailer/#axzz4JkWqY4Sm

32 Steve Sailer, "White Identitarianism vs. Citizenism," *The Unz Review*, 23 November 2016. http://www.unz.com/isteve/white-identitarianism-vs-citizenism/
33 Stefan Molyneux, "About," YouTube. https://www.youtube.com/user/stefbot/about
34 Stefan Molyneux, 2017, "Human Biodiversity and Criminality: Brian Boutwell and Stefan Molyneux" [Online Video]. Available at: https://www.youtube.com/watch?v= uQBKn_GNHa4
35 Siegel, "The Real Problem with Charles Murray and 'The Bell Curve'."
36 Smith, "Rebel Girl: An Interview with HBD Chick."
37 Ibid.
38 Andersen, *Rising from the Ruins*, 189.
39 Feldman, "Human Biodiversity."
40 Ibid.
41 "A New Threat?: Generation Identity United Kingdom and Ireland," *HOPE not hate*, April 2018. https://www.hopenothate.org.uk/wp-content/uploads/2018/04/HNH% E2%80%93A-New-Threat.pdf
42 Martin Sellner in: Brittany Pettibone, 2017, What Is Generation Identity? [Online Video], Available at: https://www.youtube.com/watch?v=DIZ3DVozFv8 [Accessed 21 July 2018].
43 Raphael Schlembach, "Alain de Benoist's anti-political philosophy beyond Left and Right: Non-emancipatory responses to globalisation and crisis," Working Paper, Published Online, 10. https://www.nottingham.ac.uk/cssgj/documents/working-papers/wp 022-alain-de-benoists-anti-political-philosophy-beyond-left-and-right-non-emancipator y-responses-to-globalisation-and-crisis.pdf
44 Martin Sellner in: Brittany Pettibone, 2017, "What Is Generation Identity?" [Online Video]. Available at: https://www.youtube.com/watch?v=DIZ3DVozFv8 [Accessed 21 July 2018].

4

THE ALTERNATIVE RIGHT, ANTISEMITISM AND THE HOLOCAUST

In 1946, French philosopher Jean-Paul Sartre published *Anti-Semite & Jew*, in which he explored the causes of antisemitism. Sartre discusses the way in which antisemitism, like all forms of hate, is a matter of placing one's faith in a hateful passion, borne from insecurity and which necessitates the rejection of reason. In this lastingly insightful text Sartre gives a warning to those who fall for the knowing irrationality of some antisemites:

> Never believe that [they] are completely unaware of the absurdity of their replies. They know that their remarks are frivolous, open to challenge. But they are amusing themselves, for it is their adversary who is obliged to use words responsibly, since he believes in words. The anti-Semites have the right to play.
>
> They even like to play with discourse for, by giving ridiculous reasons, they discredit the seriousness of their interlocutors. They delight in acting in bad faith, since they seek not to persuade by sound argument but to intimidate and disconcert. If you press them too closely, they will abruptly fall silent, loftily indicating by some phrase that the time for argument is past.[1]

Though written over seven decades ago, Sartre's emphasis on the frivolous and consciously absurd nature of some antisemites rings presciently true in the age of the Jew-hating alt-right internet troll. Many in the alt-right have grown up within, and become politicised through, an internet culture that promotes an extreme, contrarian attitude towards liberal conventions. This penchant for the smashing of accepted social taboos, especially those deemed "politically correct," is merged with the prevalent conspiratorial antisemitism within many far-right movements, meaning that antisemitism sits *primus inter pares* alongside misogyny and other forms of racism within Alternative Right ideology. Of course the type of antisemitism

and the means of delivery differ significantly, be that the preoccupation with conspiratorial antisemitism amongst sections of the alt-lite, the pseudoscientific work of
Kevin MacDonald, Holocaust denial or the crude and ironised antisemitism
advanced by alt-right trolls.

The alt-lite and cultural Marxism

The Alternative Right's two wings – the especially culturally concerned, Western
chauvinist "alt-lite" and the especially racially concerned, explicitly white nationalist "alt-right" – each engage in antisemitism. The former is by no means universally antisemitic and many within the movement are genuinely appalled by the
anti-Jewish race politics of the more extreme alt-right, so much so that it can be
viewed as something of a dividing line between the two sides of the broad movement. That said, antisemitism remains present within the alt-lite's makeup, especially with respect to the widespread use of coded terms that perpetuate the notion
of disproportionate Jewish influence in various areas of society, whether consciously
or not. The most important manifestation of this is the widespread belief in the idea
of "cultural Marxism," a theory that asserts that the left wing has been engaged in a
decades-long plot to undermine and overthrow traditional Western values by infil-
trating cultural institutions and brainwashing populations, or otherwise enforcing its
ideas, so as to promote progressive counterculture and social movements.

Of course, the idea that Jews secretly brainwash society through the control of
cultural institutions is nothing new; be it the *Protocols of Zion* or the Nazis themselves, it is a longstanding antisemitic trope. However, in a 1998 speech, the US
paleoconservative William Lind claimed, "[cultural Marxism] is an effort that goes
back not to the 1960s and the hippies and the peace movement, but back to
World War I." This was a nod to the term's antisemitic roots in "cultural Bol-
shevism," which alleged that "Jews and Soviets were [...] working together to lay
low central European civilization." The cultural Marxism conspiracy theory went
on to pervade the online far-right following a 1999 documentary produced by
Lind, titled "Political Correctness: The Frankfurt School," which explored a group
of mainly Jewish academics who escaped Nazi Germany to come to the US and
whom many on the far right believe to be central to the plan to advance the
"cultural Marxist" agenda to destroy the West.

Though also used by other strands of the far right, the term is now widely
employed by the alt-lite, with the likes of vlogger Stefan Molyneux producing
videos with such titles as "Why Cultural Marxism is Destroying America" or Paul
Joseph Watson of InfoWars, who declared "From the 20th century onwards post-
modernist, moral relativist, critical theory-espousing cultural Marxist nihilists began
to seize control of society" in a video called "The Truth about Popular Culture."[2]
The overlap with Lind's propaganda is clear, given that in his aforementioned
speech he used this conspiracy theory to attack feminism, gay rights, and sexual
liberation, challenges to Christianity, the emergence of affirmative action, and the
growth of environmentalism. The alt-lite similarly believes a vast number of

cultural changes threaten the West; a variety that has allowed myriad reactionary voices to coalesce. That said, while conspiratorial antisemitism is always just below the surface of the cultural Marxist theory, there are many who have a belief in or promulgate the conspiracy theory who would reject its antisemitic inflection.

Kevin MacDonald and the alt-right

Meanwhile, antisemitism, known as the "JQ" (Jewish question), makes up a core tenet of the ideology of the race-obsessed alt-right. Many combine the conspiratorial belief that there is a "genocide" of white people with the idea that it is Jews who are secretly orchestrating it; an idea influenced heavily by the work of Kevin MacDonald and discussed at length below.

While much of the alt-right's antisemitism and Holocaust denial is disseminated via "humorous" and "unserious" means, it would of course be wrong to say that the alt-right themselves do not take antisemitism seriously. Amongst the more hardline elements of the alt-right, antisemitism is central to their worldview and their understanding of the causes of world events. The high priest of alt-right antisemitism is the academic and editor of webzine *The Occidental Observer* (TOO) and journal *The Occidental Quarterly* (TOQ), Kevin MacDonald. MacDonald's efforts to distil antisemitism into pseudo-scientific theory have been highly influential on the contemporary antisemitic far right, and though much of his work predates the emergence of the alt-right, he serves as something of an "elder statesman" to the movement.

MacDonald has long been controversial, making headlines back in 2000 when he freely testified as an "expert witness" for British Holocaust-denier David Irving when he unsuccessfully and disastrously bought a libel trial against US academic Deborah Lipstadt. With time, MacDonald's limited academic reputation became tarnished beyond repair and he became more openly aligned with far-right organisations. In 2001, he began working with the Charles Martel Society (CMS), a white nationalist group funded by William H. Regnery II. He quickly established himself as a leading voice in its TOQ journal, eventually taking over as editor. In 2007 MacDonald started the online webzine TOO which has since become his primary platform and helped to introduce his theories to a wider, younger audience.[3] MacDonald also writes intermittently for VDare and his research is featured on the website of Richard Spencer's National Policy Institute (NPI). He has also been active on the alt-right speaking circuit addressing events such as the London Forum in 2015, the US Northwest Forum in 2016 and at the NPI conferences in 2015 and 2016. However, he shot to international attention in August 2016 after he was retweeted by Donald Trump Jr.

Throughout the 1990s MacDonald developed his theories in a trilogy of books, *A People that Shall Dwell Alone* (1994), *Separation and Its Discontents* (1998) and most infamously *Culture of Critique* (1998), positing that Judaism should be understand as a "group evolutionary strategy" that manipulates larger populations in order to gain disproportionate access to resources and "that there is a fundamental and irresolvable friction between Judaism and prototypical Western political and social structure."[4] For MacDonald, Jews have consciously set out to undermine white European power in the West. In his essay "What Makes Western Culture Unique?" he argues that the:

> best strategy to destroy Europeans, therefore, is to convince the Europeans of their own moral bankruptcy. A major theme of my book, The Culture of Critique [...] is that this is exactly what Jewish intellectual movements have done. They have presented Judaism as morally superior to European civilization and European civilization as morally bankrupt and the proper target of altruistic punishment. The consequence is that once Europeans are convinced of their own moral depravity, they will destroy their own people in a fit of altruistic punishment.[5]

To achieve this "Activist Jews and the organized Jewish community" have supposedly sought to alter the nature of race relations in the United States, which has in turn "compromised legitimate White interests in a [sic] creating a culture of grievance and White guilt in which the genetically based tendencies of Blacks are ignored."[6] As with many conspiratorial antisemites, MacDonald does not stop there, also blaming Jews for "the cultural transformations in the areas of promoting a public culture of homosexuality, premarital sex, pornography, and adultery."[7]

The idea that powerful Jews are behind the alleged decline of society, and are to blame for declining white hegemony, is by no means a novel idea created by MacDonald. Yet, it is his work that has most effectively spread these ideas among the alt-right. He has consciously set out to explain to the so-called "race realists" within the movement that the real cause of "White dispossession" is actually undue Jewish power. He himself has laid out this process of radicalisation from anti-black racism towards antisemitism, explaining how many on the alt-right "begin with an awareness of White decline, race differences in traits like IQ, and minority hostility, and then progress toward an understanding of Jewish influence as they read more widely."[8] MacDonald has perhaps led more people along this road towards conspiratorial antisemitism than any other active within the contemporary alt-right.

The nature of alt-right antisemitism

Despite the pseudo-intellectual trappings of the likes of MacDonald, antisemitism in the alt-right has largely been typified by a more base, visceral, and heavily ironised tone. The Alternative Right developed largely online, on social media and in modern forums, such as Reddit.com and, especially, 4chan.org/pol/, the latter of which is particularly akin to a social network in its frenetic stream of content and ephemerality (4chan only archives posts for a short period of time and so much rapidly disappears from its homepage). Within these online spaces, an existing online behaviour, "trolling" – the act of being deliberately offensive or provocative with the aim of provoking a hostile, negative or outraged reaction, often with the stated aim of "merely" engaging in humorous ridicule – developed a distinctly extreme, antagonistic, and taboo-breaking style. Whilst not entirely new – the similar notion of "flaming" others online predates trolling and USENET groups (early forums) dedicated to "flaming" Jews and many other groups existed well before the likes of 4chan – the particular style of trolling found in these modern online spaces has aided the normalisation of extreme antisemitism, including with regard to the Holocaust, and is now documented to have catalysed many towards accepting extreme far-right beliefs. Mike Peinovich (AKA Mike Enoch), host of "The Daily Shoah" podcast and founder of the alt-right website TheRightStuff.biz highlights this when describing his site's origins:

> we started trolling, that's how we started The Right Stuff, that's where it came from. Literally, we wanted to bother liberals [...] We loved to trigger them. We loved to go in and just hit them on all their points and through this sort of opposition to that we actually developed some kind of coherent worldview, and that worldview centred around race politics.[9]

Most notably, Andrew Anglin, founder of the alt-right nazi site The Daily Stormer, who has stated that he is "at heart a troll," has claimed that it was through 4chan in 2010 that he "got into Hitler."[10] A style guide for contributors to the Daily Stormer, leaked in December 2017, reveals how radicalising individuals to antisemitism through humour has become a conscious tactic for the alt-right. The "prime directive" of the site, the guide details, is to "Always Blame the Jews for Everything," not for the purposes of building a movement but with a view to insidiously spreading "the message of nationalism and anti-Semitism to the masses."[11] Citing a propaganda doctrine from Mein Kampf as inspiration, Anglin explains that:

> The goal is to continually repeat the same points, over and over and over and over again. The reader is at first drawn in by curiosity or the naughty humor, and is slowly awakened to reality by repeatedly reading the same points. [...] The unindoctrinated should not be able to tell if we are joking or not.[12]

Anglin openly states that such "naughty humor" is a means to normalise extreme antisemitism and "the acceptance of violence" by readers, whilst avoiding the legal repercussions of actually promoting violence. Anglin admits that this tone "is obviously a ploy" as he does "actually want to gas kikes."[13] This tone is likewise employed in the site's regular Holocaust denial and revision, much of which covers the recent actions of traditional deniers and links to videos expressing their views (as well as in their occasional interviews with deniers, including Nicholas Kollerstrom in 2013). Users have shared links to traditional Holocaust denial literature on the forum's "Online Library" and expressed their support for traditional deniers. Following the death of Ernst Zündel in 2017, a user called "7x13_28 Stereotypical Badger" stated in a forum thread that "I am heartened by what he did for all of us, and the correspondence he and I shared 2008–2009."[14] Recognising the changing dynamics of communicating Holocaust denial in the social media age, a thread entitled "How would you debunk the Holocaust in 140 characters or less?" was started by a user named "Hadding" in July 2017.[15] The same user stated in the thread in December 2017 that they had "just finished an article for CODOH (Committee for Open Debate on the Holocaust)," and that "The article has been reviewed by [established denier] Germar Rudolf; so, it's good. Maybe somebody would like to use this as material for memes."[16]

However, while some alt-right activists clearly venerate the more traditional Holocaust deniers that preceded them, the contemporary movement has taken on a distinctly different form. An article on the Daily Stormer, in February 2018, epitomises the clashing of the old and new visions of Holocaust deniers. The article was addressing the criminal investigation of notorious denier Michèle Renouf after claims she allegedly made at a neo-nazi rally in Dresden, Germany that same month. The article ends with an embedded YouTube video of denier Fred Leuchter speaking at a Holocaust "revisionist" conference in the early 1990s. Leuchter, who claimed to be an engineer though had no relevant qualifications, declared in the speech that:

> I am an engineer and a scientist, not a revisionist [...] but because of what I have seen [...] I have a responsibility to the truth [...] because of this responsibility I am calling for [...] an international commission of scientists, historians and scholars.[17]

Despite promulgating content from pseudo-academic, traditional deniers, the Stormer's style guide extols the value of their writing being focused on "lulz" (i.e. on being humorous) and eschews grandiosity, encouraging writers to avoid "college words," for example. The article on Renouf itself is entitled "Germany: British Woman Investigated for Denying Kooky Fake Shower Room Hoax," typifying the casual way in which the alt-right engages with the Holocaust and antisemitism. Many in the alt-right who simultaneously deny or celebrate the Holocaust have little interest in attempting to feign "seriousness" as many traditional deniers did. Rather, this generation truly "delight[s] in acting in bad faith," as Sartre put it.[18]

Another fundamental difference between the nature of the alt-right's denial and the denial of more traditional far-right movements is the lack of importance placed on the Holocaust. For many traditional far-right antisemites, the Holocaust represented the primary obstacle to the resurrection of their fascist creed. However, as a result of the increasing distance from World War II and the young age of many alt-right activists, some perceive the Holocaust as ancient history. For many young far-right activists the Holocaust is shorn of historical significance, diminished by time and relatively absent from their collective consciousness, unlike the previous generations of postwar activists. This view is typified by a number of tweets by Peinovich (published on the UK's Holocaust Memorial Day in 2018):

Even if you think it happened despite lack of any real evidence, you should disregard the holocaust. It is used as a propaganda tool and moral blackmail against whites that want to stand up for their own interests. No more. #HolocaustMemorialDay[19]

On the same day he also tweeted:

Here's the thing Jews. Real or fake, I don't give a fuck about the holocaust, mmmkay. #HolocaustMemorialDay[20]

On 12 April 2018, Peinovich also tweeted:

No one gives a shit about "the holocaust" anymore. Lurid propaganda and obvious guilt tripping just pisses people off now. #HolocaustRemembranceDay[21]

Alt-right antisemitic iconography

As with much of the alt-right's ideology, its conspiratorial antisemitism is by no means unique or new, but it does become manifest and spread in new ways, often heavily inflected by the trolling culture from which many activists emerged. Memes play an important role in the dissemination of the ideas of the broad Alternative Right. The best known is the cartoon Pepe the Frog, a pre-existing meme adopted by the loose movement. Countless variations imbued with far-right imagery have been produced by the alt-right, including many antisemitic incarnations, for example of Pepe displayed with caricatured antisemitic features, or as a concentration camp guard.

Another widely-used antisemitic meme is the so-called "Happy Merchant," depicting a caricature of a Jewish man rubbing his hands together and smiling. Reminiscent of 1930s Nazi propaganda, it is intended as a nod to long-standing antisemitic tropes. The image itself predates the Alternative Right, with a 2015 Buzzfeed investigation putting its earliest use online to at least February 2001, though it has gained greater usage online due to the alt-right in recent years. The image was drawn by the pseudonymous artist "A. Wyatt Mann" (a pun on "a white man"), who has previously had illustrations published on the site of the US white supremacist organisation, Tom Metzger's White Aryan Resistance (WAR), Resist.com. The real identity of A. Wyatt Mann is disputed, with some suggesting it is Nick Bougas, a one-time Satanist film director and artist, who contributed to the anti-political correctness magazine *Answer Me!* in the early 1990s, while others suggest it is Wyatt Kaldenberg, an Odinist and former supporter of WAR. Buzzfeed's investigation stated Kaldenberg denied creating the image whilst a former colleague of Bougas from *Answer Me!* told the site he is A. Wyatt Mann.[22]

However, while antisemitic versions of Pepe and the Happy Merchant highlight the alt-right's penchant for causing offense, it is the "Echoes" meme that illuminates most about its ideology. The "Echoes" refer to the set of triple parentheses – "(((0)))" – placed around a name to allege that an individual or group is either of

Jewish heritage or controlled by Jews. The symbol originates from the podcast The Daily Shoah, which was launched in 2014 on the alt-right hub, The Right Stuff (TRS). In the show, Jewish surnames would be given an echo effect, which according to the TRS lexicon page refers to how "All Jewish surnames echo throughout history."[23] In an email to the online magazine *Mic*, the site's editors explained: "The inner parenthesis represent the Jews' subversion of the home [and] destruction of the family through mass-media degeneracy. The next [parenthesis] represents the destruction of the nation through mass immigration, and the outer [parenthesis] represents international Jewry and world Zionism."[24] The practice, which has become popular with the wider far right, gained mainstream attention following Google's removal in June 2016 of a browser extension that highlighted Jewish surnames via such parentheses. Some social media users have since co-opted the practice in an attempt to subvert it.

Antisemitic memes such as certain versions of Pepe, the Happy Merchant, and the Echoes are archetypal of the way in which the alt-right has adopted centuries old antisemitic tropes and sought to reinvent them for a new generation. Heavily inflected by the internet culture in which many within the alt-right emerged – a culture that venerates and encourages offense – the alt-right's antisemitism is not unique in form but it is new in style. However, whether it is "humorous" anti-semitic memes, the shocking casualness of their approach to the Holocaust or the consciously extreme language of sites like the Daily Stormer, the alt-right's anti-semitism is merely old wine in new bottles.

Notes

1 Jean-Paul Sartre, *Anti-Semite and Jew: An Exploration of the Etiology of Hate* (New York: Schocken Books, 1995), 13.
2 Paul Joseph Watson, 2017, *The Truth about Popular Culture* [Online Video]. Available at: https://www.youtube.com/watch?v=lyLUIXWnrC0 [Accessed 01 October 2018].
3 For biographical information about Kevin MacDonald see: "Kevin MacDonald," *Southern Poverty Law Center*: https://www.splcenter.org/fighting-hate/extremist-files/individual/kevin-macdonald
4 Kevin MacDonald, *The Culture of Critique: An Evolutionary Analysis of Jewish Involvement in Twentieth-Century Intellectual and Political Movements* (Bloomington: 1st Book Library, 2002), 317.
5 Kevin MacDonald, "What Makes Western Culture Unique?" *The Occidental Quarterly*, Summer (2002), 31.
6 Kevin MacDonald, "The Alt Right and the Jews," *Counter-Currents*, https://www.counter-currents.com/2016/09/the-alt-right-and-the-jews/
7 Ibid.
8 Ibid.
9 Mike Enoch, "Mike Enoch at the New York Forum 5–20–2017", The Daily Shoah [Podcast Audio], Available at: https://therightstuffbiz.libsyn.com/mike-enoch-at-the-new-york-forum-5-20-2017 [Accessed 4 November 2018].
10 "Andrew Anglin Profile," *Southern Poverty Law Center*. https://www.splcenter.org/fighting-hate/extremist-files/individual/andrew-anglin
11 "Daily Stormer Style Guide," Leaked Document, 10. Available at https://www.documentcloud.org/documents/4325810-Writers.html#document/p1

12 Ibid., 10–11.
13 Ibid., 11.
14 "Online Library," *Daily Stormer*, HOPE not hate Online Archive.
15 Username Hadding comment, on: Carolyn Yeager, "Greg Johnson echos [sic] Kevin MacDonald in opposing 'Holocaust' revisionism – One must ask why," *carolyneager.net*, https://carolynyeager.net/greg-johnson-echos-kevin-macdonald-opposing-holocaust-revisionism-one-must-ask-why
16 "Online Library," *Daily Stormer*, HOPE not hate Online Archive.
17 Video of Fred Leuchter speaking at a Holocaust "revisionist" conference in the early 1990s embedded in article: Andrew Anglin, "Germany: British Woman Investigated for Denying Kooky Fake Shower Room Hoax," *Daily Stormer*, 19 February 2018. https://dailystormer.name/germany-british-woman-investigated-for-denying-kooky-fake-shower-room-hoax/
18 Sartre, *Anti-Semite and Jew*, 13.
19 Tweet by Mike Peinovich (aka Mike Enoch), quoted in: Patrik Hermansson, David Lawrence, Joe Mulhall, Simon Murdoch, David Williams, *Rewriting History: Lying, Denying and Revising the Holocaust* (London: HOPE not hate, 2018), 18.
20 Ibid.
21 Tweet by Mike Peinovich (aka Mike Enoch), 12 April 2018, *HOPE not hate* Online Archive.
22 Joseph Bernstein, "The Surprisingly Mainstream History of the Internet's Favorite Anti-Semitic Image," *Buzzfeed News*, 5 February 2015. https://www.buzzfeednews.com/article/josephbernstein/the-surprisingly-mainstream-history-of-the-internets-favorit
23 Matthew Yglesias, "The (((echo))), explained," *Vox*, 6 June 2016. https://www.vox.com/2016/6/6/11860796/echo-explained-parentheses-twitter
24 Cooper Fleishman and Anthony Smith, "((((Echoes))), Exposed: The Secret Symbol Neo-Nazis Use to Target Jews Online," *Mic*, 1 June 2016. https://mic.com/articles/144228/echoes-exposed-the-secret-symbol-neo-nazis-use-to-target-jews-online#.1HATn9WVr

5

RIGHT-LIBERTARIANISM AND THE ALTERNATIVE RIGHT

The broad Alternative Right is a conglomerate movement, and so any deeper dive into its ideas, or study of its activists, will soon reveal overlaps and connections with other ideologies and political movements. The Alternative Right's overlap with right-libertarianism (henceforth referred to as simply libertarianism) as a movement and ideology is readily apparent.

This might seem like a contradiction. Libertarianism is individualistic, while the Alternative Right, with its focus on race and identity, is largely collectivist. Objectivist philosopher Ayn Rand, whose influence on, especially, American libertarianism was significant, wrote that "Racism is the lowest, most crudely primitive form of collectivism,"[1] while racism, as well as collectivist ideas around identity, are absolutely central to the Alternative Right, even celebrated. Libertarianism is anti-authoritarian and advocates for a minimal state, while some in the alt-right go as far as to glorify Nazism, representing one of the most authoritarian regimes in history. Despite these inherent contradictions, there is a convergence between the two movements, with libertarianism being both a route into the Alternative Right for some, and a distinct ideological strain within it. The two cross paths time and time again.

The convergence can be seen in the Alternative Right's appropriation of libertarian rhetoric and symbols. The Gadsden flag, depicting a rattlesnake above the words "DONT TREAD ON ME," has become a common sight at Alternative Right-linked rallies in the United States. Although the flag has traditionally been used by the libertarian movement as a reflection of anti-statist values, it is now also flown at rallies alongside swastikas and a myriad of extremist symbols belonging to various far-right groups, the main cause of whom is certainly not the protection of individual freedom, and who do not hold the non-aggression principle in high regard.[2]

Several key figures in the Alternative Right have previously described themselves as libertarians and some have credited the ideology as having played a role in their political development, or even credited experiences in libertarian circles and libertarian authors as having directly radicalised them into far-right worldviews. Some also continue to call themselves libertarian while being active in the Alternative Right. This pattern is readily observable in both the Western chauvinist faction of the Alternative Right, the alt-lite, and in the white nationalist alt-right. In the alt-lite there are several examples of figures who have called themselves libertarian, including Stefan Molyneux, Gavin McInnes and Milo Yiannopoulos, the last of whom is one of the key figures of a movement he calls "Cultural Libertarian[ism]."[3] This is no less common in the alt-right however, where we find the likes of Tim Gionet (AKA Baked Alaska), one of the planned speakers of the Unite the Right rally in Charlottesville in August 2017 who has since distanced himself from the movement, who used to call himself "a carefree, easygoing libertarian."[4] Alt-right figurehead Richard Spencer has also associated himself with libertarians and libertarianism. Spencer has credited libertarian senator Ron Paul for playing a role in his political awakening; he also introduced Paul at a conservative conference in 2007 and described himself as a supporter.[5] Spencer has also been the editor of Taki's Magazine, a news and opinion webzine that describes itself as libertarian but has consistently made overtures to the far right and played a meaningful role in the early Alternative Right by publishing many important figures, including Gavin McInnes, Colin Liddell, Steve Sailer, Jim Goad, Jared Taylor, Paul Gottfried, Paul Ramsey (AKA RamZPaul), and Matt Forney. Similarly, in 2017, Christopher Cantwell, who took part in the Unite the Right rally, explained the role of libertarianism in his political development:

> I instantly became fascinated with the history, and economics that libertarianism taught. I later became a big fan of Murray Rothbard, and Ayn Rand. You might be aware, these people are Jewish. Shocking to some then, that I am today a rather vocal antisemite.[6]

Ultimately few within the alt-right continue to call themselves libertarians, and most have at some point renounced the label. Often they find themselves disagreeing with the socially liberal elements of the movement, and see it as incompatible with the alt-right when it comes to notions of race, anti-immigration, and a return to traditional social values (or rejection, at least, of socially "deviant" behaviour, as Cantwell wrote when he complained that the libertarians he got in touch with "were more interested in promoting drugs"[7]). Others do not denounce the libertarian movement outright but argue, perhaps in contradiction, that it is not possible to achieve libertarian goals without the means of a strong state, and therefore come to embrace the state as a necessary means. Richard Spencer wrote in a tweet in February 2018, "We must get over libertarianism. We must embrace state power as a means of achieving dominance."[8]

A common cause

There are several core issues which factions of the Alternative Right and libertarians will agree on, although the motivation for doing so may fundamentally differ. A common libertarian position is to oppose affirmative action and other policies which introduce guidelines for (positive) discrimination beyond merit, on the basis that these disrupt free competition and the freedom of a business owner to run their business as they see fit. The Alternative Right also commonly opposes such policies, but not because of a breach of the ideal of freedom of the individual, businesses, and competition, but because these policies represent what they *perceive* to be unjust and harmful discrimination against white people. Given their divergent interests – protecting a collective versus protecting individuals – this represents a superficial, but important, ideological convergence.

Similarly, libertarians support a minimal state, or, in its anarchist factions, none at all, which while not in perfect alignment with far-right authoritarian ideas, does strike a common chord where there is a belief in conspiratorial ideas about the state being controlled by hidden powers and interests. This is particularly true of the conspiratorial antisemitic idea that the state is either run by a Jewish cabal, or that those in office are being influenced by a so-called "Deep State": rogue bureaucrats secretly controlling democratically elected administrations. Although it is broadly not against an extensive state, the Alternative Right is against most current liberal democratic governments, which are perceived to be corrupt. This is in line with what writer Joakim Andersen, of European New Right think-tank Motpol, sees as one of the historical achievements of classical liberalism. In his book *Rising from the Ruins* he praises the reactionary elements of libertarian ideas, saying that while they were unable to "take the state over [... they] could mitigate its growth and preserve spheres of freedom."[9]

Other overlaps include views on gun control, anti-interventionist foreign policy, anti-communism and anti-socialism, and of course, advocacy for (as well as weaponisation of) "freedom of speech." Importantly, anti-socialism and anti-communism are something that unites the Alternative Right with the libertarian and traditionalist right. The rhetoric of "free speech" has been exploited by the alt-right. Few ideologies emphasise the importance of freedom of speech as heavily as libertarianism, and the wider far right has long known the power of framing aspirations as a struggle for freedom. Far-right groups and figures often argue that breaking the bonds of the oppressive elite, whether it be the left's supposed war on freedom of speech or antisemitic ideas of undue Jewish control. It is an effective strategy because it manages to simultaneously exploit distrust in elites while mobilising around an idea that for most people has positive connotations. The Alternative Right has consciously made use of this freedom of speech discourse, especially when it comes to opposing political correctness. Presenting criticism as a threat to the value of freedom of speech is an effective way to mobilise sympathy for one's cause and gain legitimacy. The struggle between protecting freedom of speech and not giving support to the far right continues to confound liberals, conservatives, and libertarians alike, often to the benefit of the far right. An example is when the American Civil Liberties Union's (ACLU) commitment to defend absolute freedom of speech results in the organisation defending far-right groups. The ACLU controversially defended the right of nazis to march in Skokie, Illinois in court in 1978[10] and more recently defended the organisers of the Unite the Right rally in Charlottesville in August 2017. Its Legal Director David

Cole argued that "criticism comes with the territory, and does not dissuade us from defending the Bill of Rights, no matter how unpopular our clients may be."[11] However, a possible sign of change is that even within the ACLU, the position on the far right has been the subject of debate.[12]

What is apparent is that despite generally having different motives behind their policies, these superficial overlaps help explain how people sympathetic to Alternative Right ideas can fit quite comfortably in libertarian circles and, likewise, how the latter can be drawn into the former.

The libertarian to alt-right pipeline

The connection between libertarianism and the alt-right became the topic of debate after Matt Lewis of *The Daily Beast* published an article describing what he calls "The Insidious Libertarian-to-Alt-Right Pipeline."[13] Using the term "alt-right" to refer to the broader Alternative Right, Lewis points out that the role of libertarianism in bringing people further rightwards does not necessarily have to imply a broad ideological convergence between libertarians and supporters of the Alternative Right. Explaining the overlaps in a different manner, he argues that it is the similarity in the type of personality the two movements attract that is one of the most important factors tying them together, although he also acknowledges that there are certain issues that the two groups generally agree on. Lewis builds his argument on a quote from Kevin Vallier, an associate professor of philosophy at Bowling Green State University, Ohio and a writer at the left-leaning libertarian blog, Bleeding Heart Libertarians, who argues that personality traits might be the primary factor tying the two movements together:

> Libertarianism is an unpopular view. And it takes particular personality types to be open to taking unpopular views [...] some of these personality types simply enjoy holding outrageous and provocative views, who like to argue and fight with others, who like insult and and [sic] shock.[14]

Vallier touches on an interesting overlapping feature of libertarianism and the Alternative Right, beyond that of ideology. Vallier dubs this the "contrarian trap," arguing that "if you think you've rationally decided that millions and millions of people are completely wrong about something, it is natural to think they might be wrong about lots of other things as well," and that this by extension makes a contrarian open to ideas that deserve to be unpopular, such as racist and even directly violent ideas.

Vallier provides an explanation for why people with prior racist views might turn to the libertarian movement and later transition over to the alt-right (or adopt other far-right ideas). The former, while still somewhat fringe, remains less stigmatised than the alt-right and can offer a first step, as well as a framework for beginning to express underlying far-right positions. A different, but complementary explanation is made by Paulina Borsook, who has described how libertarianism is attractive to people entrenched in what she calls "tech culture," which she describes as prevailing among people working in (or aspiring to work in) high-tech industries.[15] Similar ideas are common in several of the online contexts in which the Alternative Right finds its supporters. Joshua Tait also identified this process in the intellectual trajectory of Curtis Yarvin (AKA Mencius Moldbug), a figurehead for the online "Neoreactionary" community, another tributary to the Alternative Right.[16] In this worldview, Borsook argues, computer programs and the rule-bound predictability of the laws of physics are seen as not much different from politics and society in general. This view can lead to a mechanistic understanding of society and political life, which turns these into problems that can be "solved" rather than processes involving a variety of always developing interests. The same veneration of science and technology can also lead to this view being extended to human biology, treating it as determinative, an idea that we see reflected in the discourse around race and intelligence. Libertarianism chimes well with this view because of its focus on efficiency and reliance on the market to provide solutions, largely ignoring social issues.

The appeal of this deterministic, "objective" claim to knowing the simple solutions to political problems has become an important rhetorical tool used by Alternative Right figures on social media, especially among figures in the alt-lite that also identify with the libertarian label. Stefan Molyneux (who has, himself, moved further down the pipeline) is one example. On his YouTube channel and website Freedomain Radio, Molyneux built a following by making use of crudely interpreted statistical data to make absolutist statements to discredit egalitarian ideas around race, gender, and other social issues.

Lewis' article in *The Daily Beast* also became a topic of discussion within the alt-right itself. In the 2019 book, *A Fair Hearing: The Alt-Right*, several members of the movement give their own accounts of the alt-right and of their motivations for engaging in it. In the book, Jared Howe, an alt-right podcaster with a history in the libertarian movement, wrote a chapter in direct response to Lewis' article. Framed as a direct denial of Lewis' account, the chapter in practice contains distinct traits of his and, maybe even more so, Borsook's argument:

> The young white men who were drawn to these ideas during Ron Paul's presidential runs were interested, above all, in knowing what is true. The Insidious Pipeline is actually a progression in one's understanding of certain fundamental aspects of our world. The process begins with intensive examinations of economics and state power, and then, if one is intellectually honest, advances to a study of what underlies and defines these things – human biology. And from there, unless one is actively working to remain ignorant, what must be confronted is who is determined to conceal the truth about these fundamentals from the general public, and why.[17]

Howe's description of his political journey as a search for absolute truths plays well with the description that Borsook gives. However, conspiratorial thinking also seems to play a significant role in Howe's thinking. This search leads to conspiratorial ideas of Jewish control, something that Cantwell also describes. Howe also describes the opposition towards the libertarian movement (and the presidential campaign of Senator Ron Paul in particular) from established media as something that pushed him to adopt these more extreme ideas, saying that, "One cannot return to naiveté about the extent of the rot in our system after observing the entire media and political establishment colluding to keep an honest man from being heard."[18]

One foot in each camp

Clearly, the relationship between libertarianism and the Alternative Right is more complicated than simply providing a less stigmatised alternative and a stepping stone into the far right. Speaking to there being room for far-right ideas within libertarianism are those who have one foot in each camp, and do not consider this contradictory. "Augustus Invictus" (born Austin Mitchell Gillespie), who was billed as one of the headline speakers at the Unite the Right rally in Charlottesville, has spoken at alt-right-associated rallies across the US. Yet, he also stood as a candidate for the Libertarian party in Florida in the 2016 Senate election. In his book, *The Structure of Liberty*, legal theorist Randy Barnett argues that "libertarian principles themselves are highly abstract – often too abstract to handle anything but the most basic social conflicts."[19] The effect is that concepts such as property rights and individual liberty can be used to defend ideas that are traditionally understood as incompatible with libertarianism. John Ganz, in an article for *The Washington Post*, argues that abstract notions of self-determination mean that "each person is free to concoct what is in their best interest, and because 'aggression' can be and has been defined in a variety of spurious ways."[20] Therefore, libertarian principles can be used to make conceptual space for racism. Ganz argues that this is what Cantwell is doing when he writes on his blog that:

> People should be free to exercise complete control over their own person and property. If blacks are committing crimes, or Jews are spreading communism, discriminating against them is the right of any property owner.[21]

Moreover, racist and far-right ideas such as ethno-nationalism can be made to fit in a libertarian framework, alleged to be a necessary precondition to a libertarian society. This idea is commonly expressed on libertarian subsections of far-right forums and image boards, such as 8chan's /liberty/ board, by users who differ from the mainstream alt-right in that they do not desire an ethnically homogenous state for its own sake, but believe that racial or ethnic homogeneity is a means to achieving their political end of a libertarian society. In an article on the foundational blog alternative-right.blogspot.com (renamed to affirmativeright.blogspot.com in 2018) titled "Can't have libertarianism without nationalism," libertarian Rik Storey argues:

> Without a high trust society, you won't have a significant capitalist class developing and, without that, you can kiss the manifestation of libertarian institutions good-bye. In short, if you love freedom, you've got to love homogeneity.[22]

For Storey and the alt-right more generally, a "high trust society" is one of the end-goals of the movement, envisioned as a society low on crime because of shared ethical values and contrasted with an ethnically diverse society whose internal differences supposedly lower trust. Again, while this is thinly-veiled racism, Storey is also attempting to argue that ethnic homogeneity is a precondition to the end goal of a functional libertarian society because it depends on respect for private property.

In a 2019 article, Cantwell expresses the same idea in more blunt terms, writing that "There will be no libertarianism in the absence of White people, which is why people who hate liberty keep on telling libertarians to purge 'racists' from their movement."[23] The idea of incompatibility between multicultural societies and libertarianism is expressed by some in the Alternative Right in a somewhat less racially charged manner. Youtuber Tarl Warwick (AKA Styxhexenhammer666), who has for periods identified as alt-lite as well as alt-right, while arguing that he is sympathetic to libertarianism, has stressed the need for borders for preserving culture. "I'm not an open borders libertarian because I'm intelligent, I'm intelligent enough to understand that a culture can't survive such a thing," he says and continues to stress the possibility of other nations to "deliberately organize the movement of people in massive numbers into your state."[24]

Paleolibertarianism

It is not possible to discuss the connection between the Alternative Right and libertarianism without covering "paleolibertarianism." Paleolibertarianism, and the figures connected to it, are examples of how the pathway from libertarianism into the far right has existed for some time and how this pipeline is being actively maintained. It combines libertarianism's core premise of a limited government with traditionalist social values, and commonly argues for nativist policies. The label paleolibertarianism began to be used in the early 1990s by libertarian writer and at one time congressional chief of staff of Ron Paul, Llewellyn Rockwell Jr.[25] and soon after by Murray Rothbard, the same scholar that Cantwell credited with his early fascination with libertarianism.[26] Rothbard has argued for the "voluntary" separation of races, as his paleolibertarianism builds on a Darwinian worldview where elite positions are naturally given. The title of Rothbard's 1992 publication *Egalitarianism as a Revolt against Nature* epitomises Rothbard's view that statism meddles in this natural hierarchy and should therefore be minimised.[27] The title is a good example of how paleolibertarians paved a way for mobilising libertarians towards ideas and rhetoric now common in the Alternative Right.

Ron Paul is arguably the most prominent face of this stream of thought and has been credited as an important link between the libertarian movement and the far right.[28] As a senator for the 22nd Texan congressional district and a three-time presidential candidate, his public persona garnered paleolibertarian ideas much attention. Paul unsurprisingly was against welfare spending and foreign intervention, but he also took a clear anti-abortion stance, expressed neo-Confederate views and during his 2008 campaign a set of newsletters sent out in his name in the 1990s sparked controversy for containing racist statements such as: "95 percent of the black males in that city [Washington DC] are semi-criminal or entirely criminal."[29] Paul denied writing the newsletters or having any knowledge of them but multiple sources alleged that they were written by Llewellyn Rockwell Jr, who was at one time employed as Paul's ghostwriter and was a close friend.[30]

Llewellyn Rockwell Jr, together with Murray Rothbard and Burton Blumert, founded the Ludwig von Mises Institute in 1982, which is now the premier paleolibertarian think tank. The institute is named in honour of Austrian-American libertarian scholar Ludwig von Mises, who was born in Austria in 1881 and emigrated to the USA in 1940, where he became influential in libertarian circles. He was frequently in touch with Ayn Rand and his students include well known libertarian Friedrich Hayek. In Mises' 1927 book *Liberalism*, published five years after Mussolini had come to power in Italy, he wrote:

> It cannot be denied that Fascism and similar movements aimed at the establishment of dictatorships are full of the best intentions and that their intervention has for the moment saved European civilization.[31]

Although Mises' conclusion was that fascism was not tenable as anything more than a "makeshift"[32] solution, the failure to distance himself from fascism is continued by the institute named after him. The Mises Institute is not as recognised as, for example, the libertarian Cato Institute, but it and its scholars are frequently cited by the Alternative Right and the Mises Institute's open flirtation with the far right continues to this day. Paul Gottfried, a man named as a mentor by Richard Spencer and often credited with introducing the term "alt-right" itself, is another commentator connected to the Mises Institute. Furthermore, in 2017 the current director of the institute Jeff Deist went so far as to make use of distinctly white supremacist rhetoric when he described his issue with mainstream libertarianism:

> In other words, blood and soil and God and nation still matter to people. Libertarians ignore this at the risk of irrelevance.[33]

Within the Mises Institute we also find a man that is particularly liked by some within the Alternative Right: Hans-Hermann Hoppe. Despite his criticism of the Alternative Right – arguing that Spencer "has gone so far as to even put up with socialism as long as it is socialism of and for only white people"[34] – Hoppe is still frequently quoted in Alternative Right circles. Spencer even says that Hoppe led him out of libertarianism and congratulated him on his birthday in November 2017.[35] Howe likewise has turned his back on paleolibertarianism, arguing that it, and the wider libertarian movement, are plagued by entryism from the progressive left and even undue influence from Jewish people.[36]

Hoppe is a libertarian scholar who incorporates decidedly far-right ideas into a libertarian framework, including those common in the Alternative Right. He said in 2017 that "restrictive, highly selective and discriminating immigration [policy] [...] is entirely compatible with libertarianism and its goal of freedom of association and opposition to forced integration."[37] According to Hoppe, "forced integration" is the effect of open immigration policies, providing another way to frame anti-immigration ideas inside the libertarian discourse of individual liberty, highlighting the ambiguity of the concept. He also underpins his anti-statism, similarly to Rothbard, with rhetoric that would feel at home in the alt-right, saying that "the state [...] promotes social degeneracy and pathology, thus [it] [...] promote[s] egalitarianism, affirmative action [...], multiculturalism and free mass immigration."[38] He also argues for a racial difference in what he calls "time preference," where a low time preference (alleged to be common among whites) means an ability to wait for future payoffs, harking back to far-right pseudoscientist works such as *The Bell Curve* by Charles A. Murray and Richard Herrnstein.[39] Hoppe also founded the Property and Freedom Society in 2006, an annual conference held in Turkey. It has not just included hints at far-right ideas by libertarians but also welcomed far-right speakers, including those connected to the alt-right, with open arms. Speakers have included prominent American white nationalist Jared Taylor, Paul Gottfried, Croatian far-right author Tomislav Sunić and again, Richard Spencer.[40]

Evidently, the ideals and institutions of libertarianism have become a fertile ground for the Alternative Right. One can of course find racists within adherents to most ideologies, but, perhaps more than anything, the distinctly abstracted nature of the libertarian conception of social relations has made those now drifting to the alt-right fit more comfortably here than in some other movements. The primary concern of libertarianism with negative rights and minimal state interference in the life of the individual, makes it often more accommodating to far-right positions and allows policies rooted in libertarian ideas to be supported by the Alternative Right. While the likes of Jared Howe deride what he perceives as progressive entryism into the libertarian movement, the real problem seems to be the reverse.

Notes

1 Ayn Rand, "Racism," *The Objectivist Newsletter* 2, no. 9 (New York, NY: Ayn Rand and Nathaniel Branden, September 1963), 33.
2 An ethical stance popular within libertarian circles that argues it is illegitimate to initiate physical force towards a person or their property.
3 AynRandHero, 2016, *Milo Yiannopoulos Nails It about Cultural Libertarianism and the Rise of Trump* [Online video]. Available at: https://www.youtube.com/watch?v=SnA4bDE qi5Q [Accessed 1 November 2017].

4 Oliver Darcy, "The untold story of Baked Alaska, a rapper turned BuzzFeed personality turned alt-right troll," *Business Insider UK*, 1 May 2017. http://uk.businessinsider.com/who-is-baked-alaska-milo-mike-cernovich-alt-right-trump-2017-4

5 kyle2796, 2017, *Ron Paul - Conservatism and Foreign Policy (Introduction by Richard Spencer)* [Online video]. Available at: https://www.youtube.com/watch?v=gAozR_FDFb8 [Accessed 21 October 2018].

6 Christopher Cantwell, "Why I Consider Myself Alt Right," *Radical Agenda*, 17 August 2017. https://christophercantwell.com/2017/08/17/consider-alt-right/

7 Ibid.

8 Richard Spencer (@RichardBSpencer). 12 February 2018, 10:37 pm, http://web.archive.org/web/20180325202051/https://twitter.com/richardbspencer/status/963301198458707970

9 Joakim Andersen, *Rising from the Ruins: The Right of the 21st Century* (United Kingdom: Arktos Media Ltd., 2018), 137.

10 "ACLU History: Taking a Stand for Free Speech in Skokie," *ACLU*. https://www.aclu.org/other/aclu-history-taking-stand-free-speech-skokie [accessed 4 April 2018].

11 David Cole, "The ACLU's Longstanding Commitment to Defending Speech We Hate," *ACLU*, 23 June 2018. https://www.aclu.org/blog/free-speech/aclus-longstanding-commitment-defending-speech-we-hate

12 Alex Blasdel, "How the resurgence of white supremacy in the US sparked a war over free speech," *The Guardian*, 31 May 2018. https://www.theguardian.com/news/2018/may/31/how-the-resurgence-of-white-supremacy-in-the-us-sparked-a-war-over-free-speech-aclu-charlottesville

13 Matt Lewis, "The Insidious Libertarian-to-Alt-Right Pipeline," *The Daily Beast*, 23 August 2017. https://www.thedailybeast.com/the-insidious-libertarian-to-alt-right-pipeline

14 "The Contrarian Trap: The Source of the Liberty Movement's Dark Side," *Bleeding Heart Libertarians*, 4 October 2014. http://bleedingheartlibertarians.com/2014/10/the-contrarian-trap-the-source-of-the-liberty-movements-dark-side/

15 Paulina Borsook, *Cyberselfish: a critical romp through the terribly libertarian culture of high tech* (New York: PublicAffairs, 2000).

16 Joshua Tait, "Mencius Moldbug and Neoreaction," in Mark Sedgwick (ed.), *Key Thinkers of the Radical Right: Behind the New Threat to Liberal Democracy* (Oxford: Oxford University Press, 2019), 190.

17 Jared Howe, "Regarding the Insidious Libertarian-to-Alt-right Pipeline," in George T. Shaw (ed.), *A Fair Hearing: The Alt-Right in the Words of Its Members and Leaders* (United Kingdom: Arktos Media Ltd., 2018), 74.

18 Ibid., 65.

19 Randy E. Barnett, *The Structure of Liberty: Justice and the Rule of Law* (2nd ed.) (Oxford: Oxford University Press, 2014), 353.

20 John Ganz, "Libertarians Have More in Common with the Alt-right than They Want You to Think," *The Washington Post*, 19 September 2017. https://www.washingtonpost.com/news/posteverything/wp/2017/09/19/libertarians-have-more-in-common-with-the-alt-right-than-they-want-you-to-think/

21 Cantwell, "Why I Consider Myself Alt Right."

22 Rik Storey, "Can't Have Libertarianism without Nationalism," *Affirmative Right*, 18 October 2016. https://affirmativeright.blogspot.com/2016/10/cant-have-libertarianism-without.html

23 Christopher Cantwell, "Radical Agenda S05E024 – Libertarian White Supremacy," *Radical Agenda*, 22 March 2019. https://www.theguardian.com/news/2018/may/31/how-the-resurgence-of-white-supremacy-in-the-us-sparked-a-war-over-free-speech-aclu-charlottesville

24 Styxhenhammer666, "True Libertarianism Cannot Support Open Borders or Forced Diversity," [Online video]. Available at: https://www.youtube.com/watch?v=0WDRR3QYTrs [Accessed 10 November 2018].

25 Mises Wiki, Lew Rockwell. https://wiki.mises.org/wiki/Lew_Rockwell [Accessed 8 November 2018].
26 Llewellyn H. Rockwell, Jr., "The Case for Paleo-libertarianism" in *Liberty magazine*, January 1990, 34–38. Available at: http://www.pericles.press/wp-content/uploads/2016/11/Liberty_Magazine.pdf
27 Murray Rothbard, *Egalitarianism as a Revolt against Nature, and Other Essays* (Auburn, AL: Ludwig von Mises Institute, 2000).
28 Matthew Sheffield, "A History of Hate: Long before Trump, white nationalists flocked to Ron Paul," *The Atlantic*, 9 December 2016. https://www.salon.com/2016/12/09/how-the-alt-right-became-racist-part-2-long-before-trump-white-nationalists-flocked-to-ron-paul/
29 Michael Brendan Dougherty, "The Story Behind Ron Paul's Racist Newsletters," *The Atlantic*, 21 December 2011. https://www.theatlantic.com/politics/archive/2011/12/the-story-behind-ron-pauls-racist-newsletters/250338/
30 Julian Sanchez and David Weigel, "Who Wrote Ron Paul's Newsletters?" *Reason*, 16 January 2008. https://reason.com/2008/01/16/who-wrote-ron-pauls-newsletter
31 Ludwig von Mises, *Liberalism: In the Classical Tradition* (3rd ed.) (Indianapolis: Cobden Press, 1985), 51.
32 Ibid.
33 Jeff Deist, "For a New Libertarian," *Mises Institute*, 28 July 2017. https://mises.org/wire/new-libertarian
34 Property and Freedom Society, *Hans-Hermann Hoppe, Libertarianism and the "Alt-Right"* *(PFS 2017)* [Online Video]. Available at: https://www.youtube.com/watch?v=TICdCM4j7x8 [Accessed on 1 November 2018].
35 Richard Spencer (@RichardBSpencer). 19 May 2016, 7:05 am, https://twitter.com/RichardBSpencer/status/733161511057821696. And: Richard Spencer (@RichardBSpencer). 2 September 2015, 6:07 pm, https://twitter.com/RichardBSpencer/status/927006139409227777
36 Howe, "Regarding the Insidious Libertarian-to-Alt-right Pipeline," 68–69.
37 Property and Freedom Society, *Hans-Hermann Hoppe, Libertarianism and the "Alt-Right"* *(PFS 2017)*.
38 Ibid.
39 Richard Herrnstein and Charles Murray, *The Bell Curve: Intelligence and Class Structure in American Life* (New York: Free Press, 1994).
40 Stephan Kinsella, "Past Speakers," *The Property and Freedom Society*, 7 November 2013. http://propertyandfreedom.org/past-speakers/

6

IDENTITARIANISM IN NORTH AMERICA

Often framed as an essentially American phenomenon, from its inception the alt-right has drawn heavily from various schools of European far-right thought, such as the *Nouvelle Droite* (New Right) that began in France in the late 1960s and the "identitarian" ideology and movement that descended from it. Yet, just as the latter recognised the need to get supporters onto the streets, and so created the activist organisation "Generation Identity" in 2012, so too did the alt-right, which realised the limitations of its largely online presence and the need for more real-world activism.

From alt-right figurehead Richard Spencer – who has described himself as an identitarian[1] – attempting to start an explicitly identitarian activist organisation in December 2017, to the now defunct American alt-right group Identity Evropa embracing Generation Identity's tactics, it is clear that the US contingent of this movement has looked across the Atlantic to draw on both European identitarian ideas and street activism. However, as shall be discussed, this transfer has not been not straightforward.

What is identitarianism?

One of the clearest self-descriptions of identitarianism comes from an American proponent, Joshua Bates (AKA Jossur Surtrson), a contributor to the site of Spencer's AltRight Corporation, and the founder of the defunct American identitarian groups Identity Vanguard and Southern Nationalists of Identity Dixie. In 2017 Bates described an identitarian as one who works to "influence political and socio-economic activity in an effort to protect and preserve racial, ethnic, and cultural identity."[2] Central to identitarianism is the rejection of liberal multiculturalism and the promotion instead of "ethnopluralism": the idea that different ethnic groups are equal but ought to live in separation from one another. This is coupled with the "right to difference": "The right of every people, ethnos, culture, nation, group, or community to live according to its own norms and traditions, irrespective of ideology or globalist homogenisation."[3] Furthermore, this right carries the assumption of "cultural differentialism": the idea that there are "lasting differences among and between cultures."[4] European identitarians' desire for ethnopluralism, and attachment to such a strict notion of ethnic and cultural identity, draws especially from a conspiratorial fear that the continent will succumb to "Islamification" from mass migration, which would eventually lead to a "Great Replacement" of "indigenous" Europeans.

Organised identitarian activism found its earliest incarnation in 2003 with the creation of the *Bloc Identitaire* party. This party (now an association, *"Les Identitaires"*), in turn, gave rise to a now independent youth-wing, *Génération Identitaire* (Generation Identity, or "GI"), launched in 2012 and which now has branches in 11 European countries, all of whom share a uniform brand and a core set of beliefs and political tactics. In the US the identitarian narrative has caught the attention of members of the far right who believe that similar demographic "threats" are posed by migrants, with Muslim migrants again being a particular focus. As the Anti-Defamation League reported in June 2017, the aforementioned Identity Evropa were at the helm of popularising a slogan drawing on the same theme – "You will not replace us" (at times interchanged for "Jews will not replace us") – amongst the alt-right that year.[5]

The American alt-right and identitarianism

Though not an exact copy, the importation of European New Right (ENR) thought to America was integral to the development of the American alt-right. In a December 2017 *Buzzfeed* profile of leading ENR philosopher, Alain de Benoist, the thinker recognised that some within the alt-right consider him "their spiritual father" though he did not consider them his "spiritual sons."[6] Nonetheless, de Benoist spoke at the 2013 conference of Richard Spencer's National Policy Institute (NPI), which became part of the AltRight Corporation, and it was *Manifesto for a European Renaissance*, co-authored by de Benoist and Charles Champetier and translated into English in 1999, which introduced notions such as ethnopluralism to the Anglophone-world more widely. This importing of far-right ideology has continued, with key contemporary European identitarian thinkers like Martin Semlitsch (AKA Martin Lichtmesz) speaking at a 2017 conference of the US organisation, American Renaissance, and Fabrice Robert, a founder of *Bloc Identitaire*, speaking there in 2013. Key US alt-right publishers Counter-Currents have also made a concerted effort to promote identitarianism. As its editor-in-chief, Greg Johnson, has stated, "Counter-Currents, particularly in our webzine, has given a great deal of coverage to Identitarianism in Europe because we wish to encourage an Identitarian movement adapted to North American conditions."[7]

Moreover, the ideological exchange exists in both directions, with Semlitsch, who is also a close associate of GI, for example translating *The Way of Men* by Jack Donovan, an early influence on the alt-right, from English to German in 2016, whilst US writer Michael O'Meara has translated texts from leading French identitarian thinker

Guillaume Faye for alt-right publishers Arktos Media. In the broader European identitarian milieu, early instances of interaction include the sharing of the NPI's first
promotional video by Zentropa, a long-running identitarian blog.

Nonetheless, the identitarian element of the alt-right went largely underreported
when it first entered the public's eye.[8] What would later emerge, however, was
indications that many in the American alt-right were increasingly looking not just
to mirror these European beliefs, but rather to embrace the terminology, identity,
and tactics of the European identitarian movement.

Defend Europe and the American alt-right

While prominent alt-right figures had long been looking across the Atlantic at the
European Identitarian movement, it was the headline grabbing "Defend Europe"
campaign in the summer of 2017 that really catalysed American far-right interest in
the activism of GI. This involved GI activists from across Europe disrupting the
work of NGOs working to save the lives of migrants and refugees crossing the
Mediterranean, initially by blocking an NGO ship in May 2017 in Sicily, and later
in the summer of that year by chartering a ship and sailing into the Mediterranean
to further disrupt their work.[9]

The action, which was largely a failure, nonetheless galvanised the international
far right and demonstrated their increased capability to work cooperatively on a
global scale. Defend Europe initially received wider attention via North American
vloggers Lauren Southern and Brittany Pettibone (the latter of whom became
engaged to key Defend Europe activist Martin Sellner, co-leader of the Austrian
branch of GI and *de facto* spokesperson for the movement) and had crowdfunding
coming in from across the world on US alt-lite troll Charles C. Johnson's
WeSearchr site. It also had international support from figures including Frauke
Petry (previously of Alternative for Germany), former UK Independence Party
donor Arron Banks' Brexit campaign Leave.EU, then-*Mail Online* columnist Katie
Hopkins, far-right news outlet Breitbart News Network, former Grand Wizard of
the Ku Klux Klan David Duke, alt-right figures Richard Spencer and Jared Taylor
and leading alt-right neo-nazi website, the Daily Stormer.

The campaign also served as a basis for growing the identitarian movement
in Europe, including with the initial launch of the UK and Ireland branch of
GI in October 2017. Furthermore, given that Defend Europe began, and was
predominantly carried out, in Catania, Sicily, the Italian branch of GI, *Generazione Identitaria*, attempted to recruit new activists across Italy during the
campaign.

In addition to visiting potential new GI activists following Defend Europe,
Sellner visited the US to meet with members of the alt-right during alt-lite
media personality Milo Yiannopoulos' failed "Free Speech Week" in Berkeley,
California in September 2017.[10] During his time there Sellner spoke with
Southern and Pettibone, and the three agreed that the issues are the same for
America and Europe (and Australia and New Zealand), with Sellner adding that

the exchange between Europe and America was at this point really one of "tactics."[11] Reaffirming that it is indeed an exchange, Pettibone noted that, "We've mastered the online activism and you've mastered the in-real-life activism."[12]

Identity Evropa and Generation Identity

The adoption of GI's tactics by North American far-right groups is most explicit for Identity Evropa (IE), a US identitarian and alt-right youth movement founded in 2016 which was "retired" with the emergence of the American Identity Movement (AIM) in March 2019.[13] In an interview with Greg Johnson in the same year, IE's founder Nathan Damigo told Johnson that European groups including Generation Identity: "got me really excited and motivated because I could see [their] models and say 'hey we can do this here in America [...] that seems to be working over there so why not build a model over here?'"[14] IE imitated common actions carried out by GI, such as banner drops, street theatre actions (including "die-ins" where activists pretend to be victims of Islamist terrorism or anti-white attacks in public places), distributing food to white homeless people and leafleting and engaging in "open dialogue" events on university campuses.[15] Moreover, at a deeper level IE's activism (so too for AIM) consciously follows GI's "metapolitical" strategy. As leading ENR thinker Guillaume Faye describes the approach in his 2001 book *Why We Fight* (a core recommended text by both GI and IE for their supporters): "Metapolitics is an effort of propaganda – not necessarily that of a specific party – that diffuses an ideological body of ideas representing a global political project [...] Metapolitics is the occupation of culture, politics is the occupation of a territory."[16]

The common cultural cause of identitarians across the international far right – namely, the "protection" of a shared, mythologised, white, Christian, European heritage from the inherent "threats" of immigration from those that fall out of this category – is precisely the kind of "global political project" Faye refers to and Defend Europe exemplified.[17] This is true even though American and European identitarians simultaneously have their sights set on the (comparatively) local political project of affecting their national political landscape. At either level, identitarians on both sides of the pond view their enemy as the "globalist" threat of left-liberal democratic politics and multicultural policy that is engendering the "threats" they face.[18]

This metapolitical outlook has resulted in an explicit adoption of progressive activist strategies. Core recommended texts for GI members include Srdja Popovic's *Blueprint for Revolution*, a guide to nonviolent action which draws from the author's involvement with progressive movements, and similarly the American alt-right community has explicitly adopted the strategies of central left-wing community organising text *Rules for Radicals*, by Saul Alinsky. This approach was replicated too by IE, as Damigo has explained that he had followed left-wing internet threads and saved comments that people made, in order to rework them to promote identitarianism.[19] A clear attention to marketing identitarian ideas to a wider audience is also reflected in the intentions behind the visual brands of GI and IE. Both have frequently employed romantic imagery of classical European art and architecture in their propaganda, and rely on logos (the black and yellow symbol of GI showing the Greek "lambda" letter, and the blue and white "Dragon's Eye" triangle of IE, an ancient Germanic symbol[20]) which eschew association with now widely-recognisable far-right movements.

The alt-right "doubles down" on identitarianism

The American alt-right as a whole reconsidered its public image following the events of 2017 – not least due to the murder of anti-fascist protestor, Heather Heyer, at the Unite the Right rally in Charlottesville, Virginia in August. As the Southern Poverty Law Center (SPLC) noted, the response of IE was to "[double] down on their identitarian label."[21] In January 2018, Pettibone spoke with Patrick Casey, the leader of IE (following the departure of Elliot Kline (AKA Eli Mosley) in November 2017, who had in turn taken over leadership following Damigo's departure in August 2017), who stated that they "want to have a very identitarian aesthetic [and] approach and we want our rhetoric to be identitarian."[22] Indication that there was European support for this came, for example, in IE revealing in September 2017 that they had partnered with the alt-right's central publishing organisation, Arktos Media, to "promote Identitarian literature with [US] students."[23] This partnership could have come about through William Clark, Former Registrar and North Atlantic Regional Coordinator for IE[24] who became head of Arktos' US operation in February 2018.[25]

More widely, as both GI and the alt-right were increasingly pushed away from mainstream platforms online in 2017 and 2018, both laid the foundations for means of organising online that could encourage transatlantic cooperation. For GI in Europe, this comes in the form of "Patriot Peer": a location-based social networking app which encourages users to visit cultural landmarks, meet other activists by attending events and meetings, and engage in activism. Interestingly, screenshots of the app, which was due to be rolled out worldwide though, at the time of writing, continues to have its launch postponed, advertises the Conservative Political Action Conference (CPAC), the key annual US conservative activism conference.[26]

For the alt-right, beyond IE, the most explicit indication of identitarian organising following the events of Charlottesville came from Richard Spencer, when he announced in December 2017 that he was launching "Operation Homeland" (OH), "a new organization dedicated to building a professional identitarian activist movement." The organisation was billed in a way that mimicked the structure of GI by relying on a "core of part- and full-time activists who provide leadership to the movement as a whole." Overseas cooperation is suggested too, as OH aimed to "foster collaboration among identitarians in America and around the world."[27] However, at the time of writing OH has not materialised beyond posters appearing bearing the organisation's name in February 2018 at the American University in Washington DC, and these were not confirmed as tied to Spencer's announced organisation.[28]

A discussion of the prospects for American identitarianism between Sellner, Pettibone, and US alt-right vlogger (and later IE member) James Allsup in January 2018, highlighted some of the issues for any American identitarian movement. The core stumbling block they located was that identitarianism's focal point – demographic change leading to the (supposed) erosion of identity – would not as easily be brought centre stage given that American identity is intimately tied now to civic nationalism, highlighting its prioritisation within American culture given the notion of America as an ethnic and cultural "melting pot." However, Sellner expressed his hopes when he argued that "American identitarianism exists already [...] in the voting group who voted for Trump," who are "becoming aware that they are a minority."[29] The three agreed that mainstreaming this discussion of demographics through an identitarian frame would allow more people to feel confident about being open about it. For Allsup, the people who voted for Trump are "right up to the edge with most of what we're saying, they just need to be pushed, then the floodgates will open."[30] Echoing the alt-right's rejection of the establishment right wing, Sellner added that the labels in US political debate muddy things and that a fresh new start is needed for the American right that avoids "fighting the lost battles of their grandfathers" when demographics should be the focus.[31]

IE leader Patrick Casey pushed forward with this approach, again explicitly drawing on the GI influences that Damigo had cited. In a post on his Maker Support funding page in January 2018 Casey responded to Brad Griffin (AKA Hunter Wallace) of the Occidental Dissent blog, explaining how IE "[...] want to depathologize ethnic/racial identity," something he believed Generation Identity "has proven [...] can be done."[32] As the SPLC noted, "Casey drew a distinction between '1.0' white nationalists like Griffin and identitarians like himself who, through the creation of their own culture, memes, and unique content, have created a space that appeals to a younger generation".[33] This, again, highlights how metapolitics is, as in Europe, front-and-centre for American identitarian activists.[34] As the SPLC described it, followers of identitarianism attempt "to discursively reconstruct whiteness: by talking about whites as just another ethnic group in our multiethnic society (or 'racializing' whiteness)," an effort which "gloss[es] over the impact of both historical and contemporary forms of white supremacy."[35] For European identitarians, this endeavour involves promoting coded terms for white, European identity – namely European "ethnocultural" identity – in an attempt to subtly alter people's conceptions of whiteness. Given the more explicit racial discourse in American politics, however, identitarians there have focused more intently on promoting the narrative that American society is fraught with "anti-white" racism, not just glossing over the impact of white supremacy in the US but actively perverting it.[36]

Canadian identitarianism

It is interesting to compare at this point the situation faced by the Canadian identitarian movement. Canada is home to what appears to be the first North American branch of Generation Identity, though its affiliation is ambiguous with only the

Slovenian GI branch acknowledging it on their website at the time of writing.[37] Its website states:

> ID Canada started off as Generation Identity–Canada back in December of 2014. As of August 2017, the organization came under new leadership. The new leadership team came to the quick realization that while the vast majority of our core Canadian tenets come from Europe, this organization needed its own unique Canadian brand. On January 1st, 2018, we officially re-branded as ID Canada.[38]

As of October 2018, ID Canada was believed to have chapters in Ottawa, Toronto, Montreal, Sudbury, Vancouver, Alberta, Manitoba, London, and Prince Edward Island, and claimed to have "hundreds of members and affiliates, spanning every major city across Canada" with expansion "into other cities and regions" occurring "rapidly."[39] In addition to ID Canada, other Canadian far-right groups have increasingly relied on identitarian themes – such as the Toronto-based Students for Western Civilisation, and the Quebec groups Fédération des Québécois de souche (FQS) and Atalante Québec.[40]

The prevailing conception of Canada is that it is a successful example of multiculturalism and this is borne out by the country's efforts to develop a particularly integrationist multiculturalism policy, often referred to as Canada's "Cultural Mosaic" in contrast to the United States' outlook of being an assimilationist "Melting Pot." For this reason, the concept of "ethnocultural" identity which identitarianism propounds is more familiar to Canadian society, albeit without the racism of the far-right's conception.[41] Indeed, as immigration lawyer Andy J. Semotiuk described in *Forbes* in October 2017, the Canadian government's influential 1971 multiculturalism policy:

> recognized Canada as a multicultural country, but did not talk about "multicultural groups" […] That was because there are no multicultural groups in Canada, only ethno-cultural communities. An ethno-cultural community is an open community based on a predominant ethnic origin, but made up of people of various races and backgrounds. It is distinguished not so much by a geographic base, as by a sense of belonging, an identification with it on the part of its members. For example, in the Ukrainian community there are Catholics, Orthodox, Baptists, Anglicans, Muslims and Jews. There are white, black and brown individuals. There are men, women and LGBTs. There are the disabled and there are seniors. All of them live and thrive in the Ukrainian community in Canada. Other ethno-cultural communities are exactly the same. Multiculturalism recognizes and celebrates this reality seeking to integrate but not assimilate immigrants as well as native born members of ethno-cultural communities into Canada's cultural mosaic.[42]

This recognises that there can be "predominant ethnic origin[s]" to an ethnocultural identity without suggesting that people of this origin are threatened by the inclusion in an ethnocultural community of others from outside this ethnic group.

As such, Canadian multiculturalism undermines the racism imbued in the identitarian conception of ethnocultural identity, which implicitly or explicitly suggests whiteness is essential to being European or American (and is threatened by non-white persons). Whilst this is not to suggest Canada does not face issues with racism, or that this "mosaic" image of Canada is not without issue itself (or indeed accepted by all), the context could hamper the spread of identitarian ideas in Canada.

Barriers to North American identitarianism

Activist infrastructure

North American identitarians may have successfully adopted some of the tactics of GI and diffused them further online and in their actions, but in terms of bringing supporters away from the web and out onto the streets they are still behind their European counterparts. One reason for this is that they lack the level of infrastructure that GI inherited from the preexisting identitarian movement in Europe. Not only does this movement have efficient activist organisations, but it is supported by a network of identitarian-run or identitarian-sympathising institutions, from bars, restaurants, and gyms, to social centers, publishers, think-tanks, and media bodies.[43] Both Canada and the US, of course, have pre-existing far-right networks and organisations, but given that North American identitarians wish to dissociate themselves from the traditional far right, they are ill-equipped to receive alternative support. Moreover, the alt-right movement was hardly able to recreate such a long-lasting infrastructure, leaving little inheritance to North American identitarians beyond having somewhat seeded identitarian ideas in North America.

The place of race

At the level of ideas, whilst the alt-right has drawn much from the European identitarian tradition, some of these remain difficult to translate to the US and Canada, especially the racially-coded "ethnocultural" concept of identity espoused by identitarianism. For many European identitarians American racial categories, especially, will fall short of the notion of identity they are concerned with. As John Morgan, a co-founder of Arktos Media who later joined Counter-Currents, told José Pedro Zúquete, the American conception of "white" will not translate to European identitarians, who view it as "rootless and cosmopolitan" compared to their more granular ethnic appeals (i.e. of being Celtic, Gallic, etc.).[44] Doubtless, in a US context, race is likely too central to mainstream politics to allow US identitarian activists to avoid being associated with traditional white supremacism when promoting such ideas as ethnocultural identity and ethnopluralism.

Importantly too, this understanding of race is something that would hamper European identitarian cooperation with North American identitarians. Sellner, for example, has stated that for US activists to be truly identitarian they have to "find a clear position against racism/racial supremacy and anti-semitism."[45] More bluntly, Regional Director for GI Berlin, Robert Timm, says that:

> we have a lot in common with the Alt-Right: we are patriots, we are against mass immigration, and we embrace the memetic culture. But they are much more radical. If you listen to their leader Richard Spencer, who says that America must remain a country of White people, I as an Identitarian cannot accept this. For a long time indeed, North America was a continent that remained White, but now it's not. Comparing the US and Europe in this regard is not entirely correct. Certainly, people in Europe and in the United States are against certain tendencies in the development of their countries, but the logic of the Alt-Right, and their idea of white supremacy ("white domination") does not suit us at all.[46]

Timm's perceptions are not quite accurate – the movement had no official leader and many in the alt-right believe they are indeed identitarians rather than traditional white supremacists, even if identitarianism belies supremacism. Nonetheless, such perceptions exist and whilst US and Canadian identitarian activists could potentially carry on regardless, it would undermine the supposedly transnational identity and cause they share with Europeans if their efforts were not recognised, or worse, were rejected, by European identitarians. As has been demonstrated above, there is an appetite for an identitarian turn in the North American alt-right and, indeed, it may be something they rely on as a lifeline for their continuation despite their internecine disputes and the declining attachment to the "alt-right" brand. As Zúquete has argued based on his interviews with many of the movement's leading figures, a uniting belief within the alt-right is the inevitable emergence of "a strong transatlantic identitarian alliance between the 'brother-peoples' of Europe and white America."[47]

Anti-Americanism

Whilst divergent conceptions of race and identity between European and North American identitarians could undermine support by the former towards the latter, it is unlikely to fuel active hostility. More troubling is the place of anti-Americanism in identitarian thought. Though the immediate targets of European identitarians are the processes of "Islamisation" and demographic "replacement" of white, ethnocultural Europeans, their latent target is the "globalist" elites whose immigration and multiculturalism policies and cultural hegemony they interpret as the catalysts for these processes. For many in the identitarian movement, this globalist outlook is synonymous with an idea of the West, or indeed the very notion of "the West," which is Americentric, has led to the Americanisation of cultures including those of Europe, and the ceding of control to this superpower – either directly or through relationships with supranational bodies such as the EU – at the expense of Europe.

For identitarians, this opposition stems largely from a critique of the Western worldview and the Christian and Enlightenment universalist and egalitarian ideas it inherited which they now see embodied in the left-liberal globalist hegemony.[48] The critique originates from the ENR movement from which the identitarian movement emerged and is explained in detail elsewhere in this book, so here the focus will instead be on how this anti-Americanism factors into the priorities of identitarian activists today.[49] Firstly, the alt-right itself undercuts the need for European identitarians to oppose the US so strongly. Both movements oppose this globalist elite, after all, and in that respect it ties them, and by extension North American identitarians, more closely together.[50] Secondly, opposition to the US as a world power chiefly plays out in the arena of geopolitics, a battleground which, albeit still of deep interest to some European identitarians, is for others less important. As Sellner has stated, geopolitical discussions "will become completely irrelevant if the Islamization of Europe continues in the way it does."[51] This should come as no surprise, of course, as the activist element of the European identitarian movement feels most viscerally that it is on the frontline of the impending "threat" of demographic "replacement" of white Europeans. As such, when the movement directs its actions towards those in positions of power, it does so closer to home. Moreover, even when it targets "globalist" elites in the European Parliament, for example, it does not appear to do so as a proxy for rallying against Americans it believes to be ultimately in control.[52]

A duty to "European blood and American soil": A possible trajectory for North American identitarianism?

The foregoing discussion of the primacy of identitarian fears about the impending "threat" of demographic change highlights a possible trajectory for North American identitarians and, indeed, for identitarian groups elsewhere in Australia, New Zealand, South Africa, and Latin America. Zúquete, characterising the ideological commitments of European identitarians, notes how:

> These self-proclaimed defenders of Europe do not proclaim allegiance to "tired" and "outdated" ideological categories but gather instead under the banner of Identity. This identity is ethnocultural and multilayered, with a nonexclusive attachment to its regional, national, and European dimensions, even if on the wide identitarian spectrum some individuals and groups may favour one side over the other, while always retaining Europeism as crucial. "Civilizationism," indeed is the key identitarian word.[53]

The civilisation invoked in European identitarian discourse is tied directly to the continent itself, rather than that of the Western world, and its interests – stopping "Islamisation" and ethnocultural "replacement" – are fixated on how these processes are supposedly playing out within Europe rather than across the world. Yet, the Europe it invokes is also deeply mythologised, meaning much of the civilisation it is trying to "preserve" exists ultimately as an idea (and, of course, always has done) and is, as a result, also in the minds of sympathisers elsewhere. Given European identitarians' perceptions that time is of the essence when it comes to stopping the "threats" Europe faces from Islam and immigration, this could lead identitarians around the globe to judge that efforts to preserve this mythologised European civilisation must rely more than ever on them. In this regard, the global support for the "Defend Europe" campaign should come as no surprise. In addition to helping European identitarians where they are, however, identitarians in North America and elsewhere may increasingly see this effort to "save" the European civilisation as one that encompasses their local efforts too, as it is solely they, in their eyes, who can carry on this myth in the event of white Europeans being "replaced" and the continent being "Islamised."

This sense of "duty" to European civilisation amongst North American identitarians again raises geopolitical considerations. One popular European identitarian geopolitical concept is a European confederation of nations with little centralised control compared to the EU, as described by Austrian Generation Identity activist Markus Willinger in his book *A Europe of Nations*.[54] Willinger's European confederation is conceived as one bloc in a multipolar competition against the US, China, the Islamic world, and elsewhere. In contrast, many in the American, Australasian, and European alt-right have typically rallied closer to the transcontinental idea of a bloc of global, white nationalist Western states, coming closer to traditional far-right ideas of the "Clash of Civilisations" between the white, Christian West and the rest. The Clash of Civilisations narrative has had a mixed reception by European identitarians,[55] but as members of the North American alt-right further embrace identitarianism, they may attempt to strike a balance between this and the multipolar picture invoked by Willinger.[56]

In a sense, North American identitarians have been conscious of this balance for some time, with IE, for example, using the slogan "European Roots, American Greatness." However, a more detailed approximation of what this may look like comes from, as Zúquete has highlighted, the relationship to Europe found amongst Latin American identitarian groups. Zúquete draws out how the Chilean identitarian group, Fuerza Nacional-Identitaria (FNI), is committed to race (as it argues, "an identitarianism that does not take into account the racial factor is doomed"[57]) but the group nevertheless "do not see themselves as identical to Europeans," because its members' identities have been "nurtured in a different territory."[58] Specifically, FNI claims: "We are no longer Europeans, we are Creoles, sons of European blood and American soil."[59] The centrality of maintaining a mythologised idea of European civilisation to this identity, and a sense that it is its duty to do so – both in Chile but also as part of a global cause – comes through in FNI's response to the "threat" of Europeans being replaced:

> If Europeans encourage and achieve the destruction of Europe thanks to their pusillanimous attitude, it's up to them, we will not let our Blood be lost in these lands and we will fight to preserve it. [But] if Europe decides to fight for its existence, there it will have us fighting at its side.[60]

The barriers to identitarianism's growth in North America remain and pose considerable challenges to the movement. Yet, the fragmentation of the US alt-right was not the result of a decline in support for its goals, and a growing association with the identitarian brand has emerged for some of its most active members and organisations. If they follow Latin American identitarians' territorially "creolised" model of European identity – in essence, accepting they occupy a pole apart from that of continental Europeans – but nonetheless believe it is an increasing duty to preserve this as part of a global effort to resist the "threats" posed to a mythologised Europe, we may see the continuation of North American identitarianism.[61]

Notes

1 Liam Stack, "Attack on Alt-Right Leader Has Internet Asking: Is It O.K. to Punch a Nazi?," *The New York Times*, 21 January 2017. https://www.nytimes.com/2017/01/21/us/politics/richard-spencer-punched-attack.html

2 Jossur Surtrson, "Identitarianism and the Great Replacement," *AltRight.com*, 12 May 2017. https://altright.com/2017/05/12/identitarianism-and-the-great-replacement/

3 Guillaume Faye, *Why We Fight: Manifesto of the European Resistance* (Budapest: Arktos Media, 2011), 334.

4 George Ritzer and Paul Dean, *Globalization: A Basic Text Second Edition* (Hoboken: Wiley-Blackwell, 2015), 207. This also assumes cultures are clearly demarcated entities specifically linked to specific geographic locations. As Akhil Gupta and James Ferguson describe, this is an "[…] assumed isomorphism of space, place, and culture […]." Akhil Gupta and James Ferguson, "Beyond 'Culture': Space, Identity, and the Politics of Difference," *Cultural Anthropology*, 7:1 (1992), 7.

5 ADL Blog, "White Supremacists Adopt New Slogan: 'You Will Not Replace Us'," *The Anti-Defamation League*, 9 June 2017. https://www.adl.org/blog/white-supremacists-adopt-new-slogan-you-will-not-replace-us

6 J. Lester Feder and Pierre Buet, "They Wanted to Be a Better Class of White Nationalists. They Claimed This Man as Their Father," *Buzzfeed*, 26 December 2017. https://www.buzzfeednews.com/article/lesterfeder/the-man-who-gave-white-nationalism-a-new-life

7 Greg Johnson, "Three Questions on Identitarianism," *Counter-Currents Publishing*, 10 March 2015. https://www.counter-currents.com/2015/03/three-questions-on-identitarianism/

8 An indication of the disconnect between the alt-right's embrace of identitarianism and the US media becoming aware of its central relationship to the alt-right, is evident from an statement to the press by Richard Spencer in 2015, in which he appears keen to show their connection early on as the alt-right began to receive more attention. Speaking to *The Washington Post* about the term "cuckservative" which became popular among the alt-right, he stated that the term "is a full-scale revolt, by Identitarians and what I've called the 'alt Right,' against the Republican Party and conservative movement." David Weigel, "'Cuckservative' – the conservative insult of the month, explained," *The Washington Post*, 29 July 2015. https://www.washingtonpost.com/news/the-fix/wp/2015/07/29/cuckservative-the-conservative-insult-of-the-month-explained/

9 See: "Crisis in the Mediterranean," *HOPE not hate*. https://www.hopenothate.org.uk/campaigns/crisis-in-the-mediterranean/

10 Specifically, activists in Malta and Scandinavia. Squatting Slav TV, 2017, *Squatting Slav TV: The Death of Europe? (ft. Martin Sellner)* [Online video]. Available at: https://www.youtube.com/watch?v=ZExTvmMJ7vM [Accessed 10 August 2018]

11 Martin Sellner, 2017, *The American and European Right – Lauren Southern, Brittany Pettibone & Martin Sellner* [Online video]. Available at: https://www.youtube.com/watch?v=cgwerO355t0 [Accessed 11 August 2018].

12 Ibid.

13 Patrick Casey (@PatrickCaseyUSA). 8 March 2019, https://twitter.com/PatrickCa seyUSA/status/1104243067278843904. There is ambiguity over the extent to which AIM is not simply a rebranding of IE though its leader has claimed it is not a rebrand.

14 CounterCurrentsTV, 2016, *Counter-Currents Radio Interview with Nathan Damigo* [Online video]. Available at: https://www.youtube.com/watch?v=qV_k0dNQdt4 [Accessed 11 August 2018]. Damigo also mentions in passing having been inspired by the British neo-Nazi organisation, National Action, who would be proscribed by the UK government in December 2016.

15 This mirrors the "I.B. Zones" – temporary stalls in public places – which GI activists in Austria and Germany have put up to discuss their politics with members of the public.

16 Guillaume Faye, *Why We Fight: Manifesto of the European Resistance* (Budapest: Arktos Media, 2011), 272. The book was translated into English by a founding partner of the AltRight Corporation, the publisher Arktos Media, in 2011.

17 Faye, *Why We Fight*, 272.

18 Amongst American identitarians, IE also followed European identitarians, particularly GI, at a policy level, for example by imitating the GI term "re-migration" to describe a programme which, in the US context, supports the movement of non-white, non-Western people living in the US to their "native homelands." Brittany Pettibone, 2018, *Identity Evropa: An American Identitarian Movement* [Online video]. Available at: https:// gloria.tv/video/HRt6f2hMcQcX3DTC94VdgddyT [Accessed 30 September 2018].

19 "Nathan Benjamin Damigo," *Southern Poverty Law Center*. https://www.splcenter.org/ fighting-hate/extremist-files/individual/nathan-benjamin-damigo [Accessed 12 August 2018].

20 As IE described it, its logo "is that of an ancient European design, the Dragon's Eye [...] The triangle represents the threat that we as a people are facing. The 'y' inside represents the choice that we have to make between good and evil. It is a symbol of protection that will grant us succor against the ongoing evil that seeks to destroy truth." Matt Pearce, "A Guide to Some of the Far-right Symbols Seen in Charlottesville," *Los Angeles Times*, 14 August 2017. https://www.latimes.com/nation/la-na-far-right-symbols-20170814-story.html

21 "Identity Evropa," *Southern Poverty Law Center*. https://www.splcenter.org/fighting-ha te/extremist-files/group/identity-evropa [Accessed 12 August 2018].

22 Brittany Pettibone, 2018, *Identity Evropa: An American Identitarian Movement* [Online video]. Available at: https://gloria.tv/video/HRt6f2hMcQcX3DTC94VdgddyT [Accessed 30 September 2018].

23 Identity Evropa (@IdentityEvropa), 7 September 2017, https://twitter.com/Identi tyEvropa/status/905756666217369601. GI have not publicly attempted to launch a US branch, though HOPE not hate revealed in March 2018 that a branch claimed to have been "officialized" in February 2018. See: Simon Murdoch, "Generation Identity: European Far-Right Group Launches in America," *HOPE not hate*, 12 March 2018. https:// www.hopenothate.org.uk/2018/03/12/generation-identity-european-far-right-group-la unches-america/. Separate evidence acquired by HOPE not hate in 2018 confirmed that GI had been thinking about ways to set up in the US but had failed to get anything off the ground.

24 "William Clark," *Arktos Media*. https://arktos.com/people/william-clark/ [Accessed 12 August 2018].

25 Arktos Media Ltd., "Arktos Moves Ever Forward," *Arktos Media*, 15 February 2018. http s://arktos.com/2018/02/15/arktos-moves-ever-forward/

26 "PatriotPeer, app identitaria per identitari," *Generazione Identitaria*, 18 February 2017. https://generazione-identitaria.com/2017/02/patriotpeer-app-identitaria-identitari/

27 Richard Spencer, "Introducing: Operation Homeland," *AltRight.com*, 2 December 2017. https://altright.com/2017/12/02/introducing-operation-homeland/

28 The Eagle Staff, "'No More Wars for Israel' Flyers Posted on School of International Service Building," *The Eagle Online*, 27 February 2018. http://www.theeagleonline. com/article/2018/02/no-more-wars-for-israel-flyers-posted-on-school-of-internationa l-service-building. According to the SPLC, following Kline's resignation from IE he

"began to work more closely with Spencer on [...] Operation Homeland." "Identity Evropa," *Southern Poverty Law Center*. https://www.splcenter.org/fighting-hate/extrem ist-files/group/identity-evropa [Accessed 13 August 2018]. A likely barrier to the development of OH has been the lawsuits facing Spencer and Identity Evropa after the Unite the Right rally. Brad Kutner, "Civil Lawsuit against Charlottesville Rally Organizers Can Move Forward," *Courthouse News Service*, 10 July 2018. https://www.courthousenews. com/civil-lawsuit-against-charlottesville-rally-organizers-can-move-forward/

29 *American Identitarianism (Martin Sellner, Brittany Pettibone, & James Allsup) Part 2* [Online video]. Available at: https://gloria.tv/video/i3bZYr6huFQk2WSZdoJrbZarY [Accessed 30 September 2018].

30 Ibid.

31 Ibid.

32 Patrick Casey, "Response to Hunter Wallace," *Maker Support*, 23 January 2018. https://web. archive.org/web/20180927121005/https://www.makersupport.com/post/5a6763577ef56 0253787bc76

33 "Identity Evropa," *Southern Poverty Law Center*.

34 In a divergence from GI, however, IE increasingly promoted its members' involvement in electoral politics and establishment Republican organisations. This includes the aforementioned Allsup, who was elected as a Precinct Committee Officer for Whitman County, in the Washington Republican party. Kelly Weill, "Charlottesville Hate Marcher Elected by Republican Party," *The Daily Beast*, 5 June 2018. https://www. thedailybeast.com/charlottesville-hate-marcher-elected-by-republican-party. Casey told NBC news in October 2018 that he is on a mission "To take over the GOP as much as possible." Anna Schecter, "White Nationalist Leader is Plotting to 'Take Over the GOP'," *NBC News*, 17 October 2018. https://www.nbcnews.com/politics/immigra tion/white-nationalist-leader-plotting-take-over-gop-n920826

35 "Identity Evropa," *Southern Poverty Law Center*.

36 European identitarians have tended, instead, to focus on altering conceptions about colonial guilt, by referring to "ethnomasochism," a term derived from the European New Right which suggests Europeans engage in needless and unjustified self-loathing directed at their ethnicity. Equally, where GI have rejected accusations of antisemitism, IE are public in their rejection of Jewish people, with their site's application form previously asking applicants whether they are of "European, non-Semitic heritage." "Apply," Identity Evropa. https://archive.is/yPo6S [Accessed 13 August 2018].

37 "IDENTITARNO GIBANJE V TUJINI," *Generacija Identite*. https://generacija-identi tete.si/identitarno-gibanje-v-tujini/. Indeed, the Canadian branch exemplifies the way in which identitarianism has become an "open-source ideology," as Zúquete describes it. Remarking on the various identitarian activist groups within Europe, he notes how they "share many grammars and repertoires of contestation" in part because the web "has enabled the copying and pasting everywhere of many of the identitarians' ideas, practices, even logos and graphics, sometimes giving rise to copycat movements." It has led, he argues, to a "source of international franchise of social political activism – show[ing] the primary role of the internet in the diffusion of consolidation of the identitarian movement." José Pedro Zúquete, *The Identitarians: The Movement against Globalism and Islam in Europe* (Indiana: University of Notre Dame Press, 2018), 367–368.

38 "Home," *ID Canada*. https://www.id-canada.ca/ [Accessed 13 August 2018]. Despite this statement, its Facebook page was founded in September 2012, which suggests Canadian identitarians may have set up their own branch of GI at this point but were not recognised by the European branches until 2014. This process of autonomous branch forming has occurred in Europe too.

39 "Home," ID Canada. https://www.id-canada.ca/ [Accessed 13 August 2018]. In May 2018 they declared that the "national leadership team of ID Canada traveled over 3,000 km across Canada's Atlantic provinces to meet with [...] affiliate chapters on the east coast" and stated these "Affiliate Chapters" had become "Official Chapters of ID Canada." ID Canada, Facebook Status Update, 29 May 2018, available at: https://www.

facebook.com/OfficialIDCanada/posts/2065297333757732?__tn__=-R [Accessed 13 August 2018]. During 2018, ID Canada have also come out in support of Canadian white nationalist and former Rebel Media presenter Faith Goldy, who at the time was running as a mayoral candidate in Toronto. ID Canada (@ID_Canada). 31 July 2018, https://twitter.com/ID__Canada/status/1024348823555059713

40 Notably, the magazine of FQS, *Le Harfang*, has featured both North American and European alt-right and identitarian figures. As they state, "Québec being favorably located at the crossroads of Europe and the United States, we are the only publication to have published collaborators as varied as Jared Taylor, Oscar Freyzinger, Pierre Vial, Herve Ryssen, Kevin MacDonald, Peter Brimelow, Tom Sunic Alain Escada, Ricardo Duchesne, Jean-Claude Martinez, Fabrice Robert and many others." "Le Harfang," Fédération des Québécois de souche. http://quebecoisdesouche.info/le-harfang/ [Accessed 3 March 2019].

41 The Canadian anti-racist organisation, The Canadian Ethnocultural Council, for example, was created in 1980. "About," The Canadian Ethnocultural Council. https://www.ethnocultural.ca/ [Accessed 13 August 2018].

42 Andy J. Semotiuk, "Multiculturalism – The Distinguishing Factor that Makes Canada Great," *Forbes*, 18 October 2017.

43 For example, in France, the Traboule restaurant in Lyon, the Citadelle bar in Lille, and the Agoge gym in Lyon, in Germany the Kontrakultur centre in Halle, and Verlag Antaios publisher and Institut für Staatspolitik think-tank in Steigra, and in Austria the AK Nautilus media organisation in Lieboch.

44 Zúquete, *The Identitarians*, 297. Interestingly, Identity Evropa had tended to focus less on regional, ethnic or national identities within Europe, something that GI have long emphasised alongside their national and pan-European identity. However, in October 2018 IE announced a new project along these lines called the "American Identity Showcase," which would "demonstrate the true cultural diversity of White Americans." *Identitarian Action | EP 21: American Identity Showcase* [Online video]. Available at: http s://www.youtube.com/watch?v=aHnw7cZcxpc [Accessed 1 October 2018]. This approach may also develop further if additional, regionally-focused American identitarian movements emerge to compete with AIM, as exemplified by "Identity Acadia" (IA), a "Franco-Louisiana Identitarian organization with a focus on Cajun identity." Abdul Aziz, "The Secret, All-White Committee Advising New Orleans' Black Woman Mayor on the Fate of Confederate Statues," *Splinter*, 22 May 2018. The IA website was registered in January 2018. See: https://www.whois.com/whois/identityacadia.com

45 Zúquete, *The Identitarians*, 314.

46 3ndscape, "Identitarians – Who Are They?," 3ndscape.com. https://web.archive.org/web/20170629213246/http://3ndscape.com/blog/2017/06/17/identitarians-not-radica ls-europe-lost-common-sense/ [Accessed 25 March 2019].

47 Zúquete, *The Identitarians*, 307.

48 N.B. Though many identitarians oppose Christian universalist, egalitarian ethics, much of European Christian heritage is also frequently celebrated within the identitarian movement. Ibid., 219–220.

49 For further discussion of this, see Chapter 1 "The European Roots of Alt-Right Ideology" in this book.

50 Moreover, some European identitarians view certain American nationalist movements which preceded the alt-right, including Southern secessionist nationalists, as outside the America synonymous with the West and globalism. Zúquete, *The Identitarians*, 166–167.

51 Ibid., 253.

52 For further discussion of this, see Chapter 2 "A Global Anti-Globalist Movement: The Alternative Right, Globalisation and 'Globalism'" in this book.

53 Zúquete, *The Identitarians*, 365. Cf. Roger Brubakers, "Between Nationalism and Civilizationism: the European Populist Moment in Comparative Perspective," *Ethnic and Racial Studies*, 40:8 (2017), 1191–1226.

54 See: Markus Willinger, *A Europe of Nations* (Budapest: Arktos Media, 2014).

55 Zúquete, *The Identitarians*, 163.
56 Of course, there are further geopolitical possibilities in which European identitarianism moves further away from North America. As Zúquete has highlighted, there are European identitarian sympathisers with the Russia-partnered "Eurasianist" or "Eurosiberian" movements. Ibid., 241–248 (as well as a Russian branch of GI that has been active since at least November 2017. See: https://vk.com/identarist [Accessed 25 March 2019]). There is also, as Zúquete has noted, the "Mare Nostrum" ("Our Sea") concept of a geopolitical pole of Mediterranean civilisation, propounded particularly by the identitarian-sympathising, Italian neo-fascist organisation, CasaPound. Zúquete, *The Identitarians*, 218. Likewise, it is worth remembering that many in the US and Canadian alt-right have not doubled-down on an identitarian brand in place of the fragmentation of the alt-right, and instead appear to have sought alternative partnerships with the European far right which are less closely tied to the identitarian movement. Most notably, Greg Johnson of the US publishers Counter-Currents, which was long associated with the alt-right, has increasingly interacted with the Ukrainian, neo-nazi-linked Azov group, who have advocated the concept of "Intermarium," a bloc of central and eastern European countries, a move which has been well-received. Cf. Oleksiy Kuzmenko, "'Defend the White Race': American Extremists Being Co-Opted by Ukraine's Far-Right," *Bellingcat*, 15 February 2019.
57 Zúquete, *The Identitarians*, 318.
58 Ibid.
59 Patricio Villena, "¿Qué es ser criollo?," *Círculo de Investigaciones PanCriollistas*, 1 March 2014. Available at: https://pancriollismo.com/2014/03/01/que-es-ser-criollo/ [Accessed 25 March 2019].
60 Ibid.
61 For further discussion of this, see Chapter 2 "A Global Anti-Globalist Movement: The Alternative Right, Globalisation and 'Globalism'" in this book.

7

THE DARK ENLIGHTENMENT
Neoreaction and Silicon Valley

In the early hours of 9 November 2016, whilst much of the world watched in disbelief at the dawning election of Donald Trump, an obscure Silicon Valley computer programmer came to learn that the billionaire tech magnate, with whom he was watching the events unfold, was "fully enlightened."[1] The programmer was Curtis Yarvin (AKA "Mencius Moldbug"), an erstwhile blogger whose grandiose online musings in the late 2000s about the need to destroy progressive liberal democracy (or, as he liked to refer to it, the "Cathedral") would play a role in the development of the white nationalist alt-right. The billionaire was Peter Thiel, a serial tech entrepreneur who declared in 2009 that he "no longer believe[d] free-dom and democracy [were] compatible,"[2] who has expressed his interest in "para-biosis"[3] – a supposed means of forestalling aging by injecting the blood of the young – and who has invested in 477 acres of New Zealand land, seemingly to jet off to in the case of an apocalyptic collapse of American society.[4] Here was a key ideologue of the modern American far right having an election night party with a highly influential Trump ally – a story in and of itself. Yet when one explores the ideas of Yarvin and the movement of which he is part, and considers the influence it has amongst elements of the tech community, the story takes on an even darker hue.

The term "Neoreactionary" (NRx) describes a largely online, far-right political subculture that took shape in the first two decades of the 21st century. From the broader blogging "reactosphere" this movement took shape as various bloggers saw that their various core interests – from gender, to race, religion, governance, and much else – all shared a rejection of the liberal democratic attitudes towards these that have grown in the West following the Enlightenment.

As yet, no concise or consensual definition has emerged for the movement. Benjamin Noys, Professor of Critical Theory at the University of Chichester described this so-called Dark Enlightenment as "an acceleration of capitalism to a fascist point."[5] Park MacDougald, staff editor at *Foreign Affairs* argues that it is "less a single ideology than a loose constellation of far-right thought, clustered around three pillars: religious traditionalism, white nationalism, and techno-commercialism."[6] However, we define neoreaction as a far right, anti-democratic movement that rejects Enlightenment principles and seeks to meld a regressive return to a monarchical past with a fetishised post-human future, all structured within a neo-cameralist state.

Given this, the ideological inspirations for NRx are varied and extend far back to pre-Enlightenment (and early anti-Enlightenment) thought. It also shares parallels with a postwar far-right European school of thought, Archeofuturism, developed by French philosopher Guillaume Faye, one theme of the postwar European New Right movement that began as a reaction to the political uprisings of 1968.[7] A more recent influence is accelerationism, a political philosophy that grew out of the work of, amongst others, Nick Land, previously of the Department of Philosophy at the University of Warwick in the United Kingdom in the 1990s and who would become a core NRx figure. Nonetheless, as a meaningful community, the origins of NRx can be traced back to the early 2010s.

Best thought of as a disparate blogosphere rather than a cohesive movement, it has acted as both a tributary into and a constituent part of the alt-right. However, where the alt-right grew to gain a large public profile, the NRx community has remained essentially online and within small, obscure forums and blogs. Yet, despite this, this fringe online world found adherents and supporters in a major emerging political arena of the 21st century, Big Tech and Silicon Valley.

NRx ideology

Outlining the ideology of NRx is no easy task. The rambling, often purposefully impenetrable blogs and essays that make up the movement's ideological wellspring are often rife with laughable a-historical reference points, dogged by semi-comprehensible and sprawling tangents, manufactured words and phrases, sometimes heavy irony and a sense of unwarranted philosophical importance. Philip Sandifer in *Neoreaction as Basilisk* correctly identifies the "triptych of core works of the movement"[8] as Land's *The Dark Enlightenment* and Yarvin's *Open Letter* and *Gentle Introduction* (to Unqualified Reservations [UR]), the latter of which he opens by saying "unfortunately, I'm lying. There is no such thing as a gentle introduction to UR. It's like talking about a 'mild DMT trip.' If it was mild, it wasn't DMT."[9]

Tracing the birth of the NRx movement is not straightforward either. NRx adherents venerate a plethora of thinkers both past and present. One key influence is the 19th century Scottish philosopher Thomas Carlyle, best known for his "Great Man" theory of history, although it is his rejection of democracy that most appeals to his contemporary NRx admirers, famously stating: "I do not believe in the collective wisdom of individual ignorance."[10] Other touchstones for the movement include the Italian esotericist and philosopher Julius Evola and the Austrian economists Ludwig von Mises and Hans-Herman Hoppe. Also well read by NRx supporters is the collaborative work of the French philosopher Gilles

Deleuze and the French psychoanalyst Félix Guattari, especially their work on deterritorialisation and its influence on the idea of "accelerationism," a right-wing form of which is a key tenet of NRx thinking.

What NRx rejects

Central to the NRx critique of contemporary society is a visceral, vocal, and outright rejection of democracy. In Land's primary contribution to the NRx canon, *The Dark Enlightenment*, he offers a cutting and caustic appraisal of it:

> For the hardcore neo-reactionaries, democracy is not merely doomed, it is doom itself. Fleeing it approaches an ultimate imperative. The subterranean current that propels such anti-politics is recognizably Hobbesian, a coherent dark enlightenment, devoid from its beginning of any Rousseauistic enthusiasm for popular expression. Predisposed, in any case, to perceive the politically awakened masses as a howling irrational mob, it conceives the dynamics of democratization as fundamentally degenerative: systematically consolidating and exacerbating private vices, resentments, and deficiencies until they reach the level of collective criminality and comprehensive social corruption. The democratic politician and the electorate are bound together by a circuit of reciprocal incitement, in which each side drives the other to ever more shameless extremities of hooting, prancing cannibalism, until the only alternative to shouting is being eaten.[11]

Yarvin concurs, calling democracy the "castle of *evil*" in his 2010 essay *Divine-Right Monarchy for the Modern Secular Intellectual*, explaining that "we have no trouble in diagnosing the fundamental disease of democracy. The condition (which is incurable) is *imperial decay* – that is, the broadening of the decision process, from a single executive decision to a universal-suffrage election."[12]

Importantly, in *Key Thinkers of the Radical Right*, Joshua Tait makes salient how the NRx rejection of democracy does not begin straightforwardly from a desire for authoritarianism. Reflecting Yarvin's own intellectual journey,[13] it is an ideology with deeply libertarian roots, and recognising what he and others in the NRx community (and, indeed, for some who later became part of the wider Alternative Right) perceived as a failure of traditional libertarianism is essential to understanding its thinking. Tait argues that a core NRx assumption is that "humans desire power," and since democracy offers people a degree of power, NRx adherents contend that "society trends toward greater division of power" (both through suffrage and the expansion of the state) and "a concomitant erosion of order."[14] In contrast, "Strong government with clear hierarchies [...] remain small and narrowly focused," and on this basis Yarvin "justifies authoritarianism on libertarian grounds. The minimal state is achieved by making government strong, not by weakening it."[15] Of course, one could argue that the justification is not made on libertarian grounds, since the imposition of an authority undermines, necessarily, personal liberty to some extent. However, Tait argues "[Yarvin] remains committed to radical libertarianism, but he believes libertarianism has failed because it presupposes order. Without order, agitating for liberty creates chaos and violence, which inhibits freedom far more than the state does."[16] Doubtless, as Tait adds, "By prioritizing order above all, [Yarvin] left behind Mises and Rothbard – even Hoppe and Burnham" – his libertarian and (in the latter case) conservative influences – and "embraced reaction."[17] Yarvin would likely argue that what he offers in place of democracy, as will be discussed below, is the greatest possible liberty at the smallest price.

Coupled with NRx's rejection of democracy is its attack on the media and academic structure it believes props up the current system, the so-called "Cathedral." Yarvin defines it as the left's "party of the educated organs, at whose head is the press and universities. This is our 20th-century version of the established church [...] although it is essential to note that, unlike an ordinary organization, it has no central administrator."[18] More succinctly, Michael Anissimov's "Neoreactionary Glossary" describes the Cathedral as "the self-organizing consensus of Progressives and Progressive ideology represented by the universities, the media, and the civil service."[19] While regressive, the NRx movement is by no means conservative but rather radical and revolutionary in that it wants the destruction and replacement of the contemporary system, the destruction of the Cathedral. Yet their radicalism is not always matched with a cogent plan for revolution. Jason Lee Steorts, writing in the conservative *National Review* magazine, describes reading Yarvin's work as akin to "listening to somebody who informs you of his plan to take care of the termites by burning his mansion down and then starts romanticizing life in a log cabin despite never having lived in one."[20]

In the place of liberal democratic, multicultural globalism Yarvin invokes a mythical past born of his historical ignorance; an imagined time of great, all-powerful leaders overseeing stable kingdoms. As he puts it:

> And at the top? Versailles. Louis XIV. Elizabeth I. The greatness of Britain. The greatness of Europe. The fire of yesterday, untarnished by time! The glory of princes! Cardinals, in their red hats! Black-robed Jesuits, terrible, intense! Against them, the burning martyrs of the Reformation! What a world! A gleaming, cloud-borne Olympia in the blue, far above our wet gray reality. Gentlemen, we have only our butts to turn around. Why not climb, and fast? Two steps in a jump? Three?[21]

His belief that the warring monarchical dynasties of yesteryear offered superior societal stability to contemporary liberal democratic states is, of course, historically untenable, but this mythical pre-democratic past is an important element of the NRx belief system.

In place of democratic nation states, NRx thinkers propose what they call "neocameralism." According to Land, "Neocameralism could be understood as 'corporatist' and 'dictatorial'. It treats the state as a corporation, founded upon freely alienable primary or sovereign property. It is 'dictatorial' in the manner of all corporate control (i.e. run by stock-holders, not enfranchised customers, or by employees)."[22] He offers Hong Kong and Singapore as "approximate templates." However, these states are not uniform in nature but rather a "patchwork" of competing states with differing ideological models. Land claims to reject "regime homogeneity" stating "If leftists have nowhere to go, the outcome will be suboptimal."[23]

In this model of competing states where individuals choose their state like they do their utilities supplier or bank, elections are deemed superfluous as productive and effective governments would self-legitimise or fall based on the merit of their actions, just as a company does. Should leaders fail to relinquish power when stripped of their legitimacy Yarvin offers a techno-utopian means of holding authority to account in his 2008 text *Patchwork: A Political System for the 21st Century*:

> The standard Patchwork remedy for this problem is the *cryptographic chain of command*. Ultimately, power over the realm truly rests with the shareholders, because they use a secret sharing or similar cryptographic algorithm to maintain control over its root keys. Authority is then delegated to the board (if any), the CEO and other officers, and thence down into the military or other security forces. At the leaves of the tree are computerized weapons, which will not fire without cryptographic authorization.[24]

The idea is that cryptographic locks could be activated by shareholders, thereby rendering the existing leader's ability to enact violence upon the people null and void.

While there will supposedly be place for leftist states in this future patchwork of competing neocameral states, NRx supporters often envisage their utopian option as being a racist ethnostate or believe Yarvin's neocameralism to offer the chance for a competition driven ethnopluralist future.[25] When asked about ethnopluralism Land explained that he took it as "meaning resilient geopolitically-distributed cultural diversity, as opposed to a homogenized 'world culture', rather than anything that necessitates a predominance of 'ethnostates' in the narrow sense."[26] Tait notes that Yarvin attempts to distinguish NRx from such associations, by arguing historical proponents of nationalism and fascism were mistaken in embracing democracy in their pursuit of order and authority, and it is this which required another "motivating force like anti-Semitism or nationalism," which are dangerous "precisely because [they are] democratic." Underlining how core the rejection of democracy is for the NRx, Tait notes how such historical revisionism attempts to "place the blame for the horrors of the twentieth century squarely at the feet of democracy."[27]

Yarvin and Land seem to suggest that social conflict is merely the product of people not having (or not having enough) alternatives. Not only does this rely on a deeply simplistic analysis of why conflict emerges, but the very notion of patchwork government – and its supposed superiority over liberal democracy – is based, it is important to remember, essentially on conjecture. Moreover, as is clear, both

Yarvin and Land's broader anti-progressivism implies a deep distaste for the possibility of (and an assumption that people would avoid) a patchwork world containing an abundance of multicultural societies. Indeed, the dichotomy between ethnopluralism and the homogenised "world culture" Land invokes is not only false, but would only come to mind for someone who considered liberal multiculturalism to be something problematic (and, moreover, could see no progressive alternatives to liberal multiculturalism). Given this predilection, it should come as no surprise that beyond these ideologues, in practice NRx forums are replete with open racism and as MacDougald correctly states, "even the non-white-supremacists tend towards a hereditarian determinism that bleeds easily into outright racism."[28]

Importantly, and likewise revealingly, for much of the NRx community this journey from liberal democratic, multicultural globalism (in its present form) to corporatist, dictatorial ethnopluralism is considered inevitable. In essence, neoreactionaries adopt a Hegelian or Marxist, namely materialist, conception of history that sees the shift as unavoidable and often desirable. Hence why the concept of accelerationism is so popular within the NRx movement, as it argues that capitalism will and should accelerate towards its collapse. For true NRx believers a neocameralist future of competing ethnopluralist states is not just desirable but inevitable, and they are determined to accelerate towards it.

From the "reactosphere" to the NRx

> There is a second conservatism haunting the internet [...] my suspicion is, in the long term, little by little, the Anti-Enlightenment is winning on the right.
>
> *Midwestballadreview.tumblr.com, 10 April 2012*[29]

As a community and distinct political ideology, NRx emerged from the "reactosphere,"[30] a loose constellation of reactionary political bloggers that had existed online since the early 2000s. According to the *Reaction Times* site run by NRx blogger "Free Northerner" (and tied to the NRx group, "The Hestia Society"), many in the reactosphere:

> began to coalesce around the writings of the blogger Mencius Moldbug, who brought forth a strong critique of modernism during a period of prolific writing in 2007–2009. Following that period, Moldbug's rate of writing began to decline, but others, such as Foseti, kept producing neoreactionary critique. Neoreaction experienced strong growth in 2012–2014.[31]

It is important to emphasise that whilst Yarvin's writing was essential to the development of NRx, his ideas emerged from the existing reactosphere discussions. Nonetheless, given Yarvin's undoubtedly unparalleled influence in the creation of NRx, his initial blogging provides an ideal point at which to construct a timeline of this movement's development.

Yarvin's blog, Unqualified Reservations, began with his "Formalist Manifesto" posted on 23 April 2007, a day after it had first appeared on the reactosphere "2blowhards" blog, founded in 2002. Yarvin had commented at 2blowhards since at least late 2006 (one of the site's administrators, "Michael" posted on 25 April 2007 praising the development: "We did it: [Yarvin] is now blogging. Bookmark that sucka"[32]). Yarvin used the term "neoreactionary" in 2008,[33] though others in the community refer to a more conscious coining of the term "neo-reactionaries" by a user called "Martin B" on 14 January 2009 on the "Mangans" blog (where Yarvin also comments). To understand how the term became one that individuals identified with, however, requires understanding what developments outside of Yarvin's writing catalysed the NRx community's emergence in the first place.

Yarvin had already been a contributor to another preexisting and occasionally overlapping blogging community, sometimes referred to as the "Rationalist Sphere," which is concerned with various topics but which centres on a deep interest in rationality, cognitive science, and technology and has been associated with blogs such as Overcoming Bias, Slate Star Codex and LessWrong. Key figures in this latter community, including Eliezer Yudkowsky (founder of LessWrong) and Alexander Scott (founder of Slate Star Codex) would reject the emerging NRx ideology,[34] though interaction with Yarvin (and vice versa) and approval of his blog from commenters on Rationalist Sphere sites would continue, albeit as a minority.

Yarvin's output dwindled somewhat towards the early to mid-2010s but the broader NRx community had already coalesced by this point. A summary of the community's activities in 2013 – referred to as an "Anti-Progress Report" – published on the "Radish Magazine" site (inactive since 2014, inactive on Twitter since 2017) by the "Thomas Carlyle Club for Young Reactionaries (Students Against a Democratic Society)," details this coalescence.[35] Importantly, the year appeared to mark the point at which the NRx community was encouraged to present a united front to others for two reasons. First, the community was beginning to see some mainstream media interest, which was increasingly encouraging those who subscribed to its ideas to discuss how they ought to present themselves to the outside world. Writing on 29 September 2013 on his Outside In blog (a popular spot for the NRx community launched in February 2013), Land said that the journalist Matt Sigl was in touch with him and he encouraged readers to contribute in the comments to help shape the article. Secondly, the wider Rationalist Sphere had stepped up its disavowal of NRx, with Yudkowsky questioning it in the comments of a LessWrong post in November 2012[36] and Alexander Scott summarising his understanding of the movement in March 2013[37] and publishing an "Anti-Neoreactionary FAQ" on Slate Star Codex in October.[38] In this sense, individuals sharing writing by Yarvin and other early NRx bloggers were being isolated from a portion of the wider blogging community they partially grew out of. In response to this, blogs were set up to more explicitly offer an alternative, including "MoreRight" which its creator, key early NRx figure Michael Anissimov, declared was:

A group blog [...] to discuss the many things that are touched by politics that we prefer wouldn't be, as well as right wing ideas in general. It grew out of the correspondences among like minded people in late 2012, who first began their journey studying the findings of modern cognitive science on the failings of human reasoning and ended it reading serious 19th century gentlemen denouncing democracy.[39]

On 9 May 2013 Land had posted on Outside In noting, under the title "Cambrian Explosion," that there had been a quick growth in NRx blogs within the previous month. In the comments section of this post, many of the blog's most active members appeared to notice this change as well, with the top comment stating "I think early-to-mid-2013 will be known as 'the' time the nascent neo-reactionary blogosphere coalesced into an identifiable movement."[40] It is worth noting that Land likely played a role in catalysing this too. Writing for *Viewpoint Magazine* in 2017, Shuja Haider noted that "In 2012, [Land] took it upon himself to systematize the Moldbug ideology, and [...] christened it 'The Dark Enlightenment.' His sequence of essays setting out its principles have become the foundation of the NRx canon."[41] In addition to the term "Dark Enlightenment" catching on, Haider highlights that Land's essays were useful precisely because, quoting Anissimov from his MoreRight blog in September 2013, "Very few of Moldbug's fans have read anywhere near his entire corpus."[42]

The NRx blogger, "Scharlach," posted on their blog "Habitable Worlds" on 21 April 2013 that "the neoreactionary movement has begun to go 'meta' on itself. Scholars of the Dark Enlightenment are beginning to ask self-reflexive questions about who they are, where divisions lie, and what it all means." Scharlach created a visual representation of the "Neoreactionary Space" online at the time, which showed its constitutive blogs, their overlapping subgroups and the ties between these subgroups.[43] On 2 May 2013 another visualisation of the movement, created by "Nick B. Steves" editor of the "Social Matter" NRx website, appeared on Land's Outside In blog attempting to pin down the divisions and overlaps within the NRx community.[44]

The community was beginning to increasingly see itself as a distinct – if still often internally divided[45] – political movement, rather than just an inert constellation of blogs. Some bloggers considered steps forward, offering "Advice for the Student Reactionary"[46] and engaging in some of the first meetups,[47] though Land was amongst those who were sceptical that ideological differences would not force the NRx "movement" to come apart.[48] Whilst it would not come apart, the movement would not witness a straightforward growth following its initial "Cambrian Explosion."

The first organised NRx group to emerge was the "Hestia Society for Social Studies," which appears to be solely a web entity and not a formal organisation of any kind. Registered online on 2 February 2014, its site stated that: "It's become clear over the past year (mid 2014 to mid 2015) that 'Neoreaction' is suffering a tragedy of the commons and lack of formal structure." As a result, the Society expressed its desire to take on "formalizing [...] stewardship of Neoreaction."[49] It also added that the "Hestia leadership team [...] consists of Henry Dampier, Hadley Bennett, Anton Silensky and Warg Franklin."[50] The aforementioned "Free Northerner" NRx blogger stated after the launch of Hestia that "The first two are names most reactionaries will know from their work at their own blogs [...] [but] The latter two are new names."[51]

Since its origins the NRx community had consciously prioritised theorising over activism, and Hestia's team made clear that they would uphold this. On its site the society declared early on that though it was "building a new system of government [...] a synthesis of modern business practice and historically successful political wisdom," it would "try not to rock the boat." Instead, it held that if the NRx community was to offer "a better deal to stakeholders" (i.e. members of the public), it must first "Test and prove" its ideas "on smaller projects."[52] As such, Hestia focused on building infrastructure to nurture theorising within the NRx community. As it described it, its "job [was] to ensure that the spirit of free inquiry that makes Neoreaction so exciting will be nourished and protected."[53]

Nonetheless, by virtue of the NRx community otherwise remaining largely unorganised, the infrastructure the Hestia Society created became the *de facto* channel where much NRx activity occurred. The NRx community more broadly also appeared to have maintained a focus on theorising, with Hestia stating as of August 2017 that it was engaged in a "systematic research program" carried out by "full-time researchers and [the] wider [NRx] intellectual community," the creations of which were to be published on the (inactive since mid-2019) "Social Matter" website.[54] Two further blogs, "The Future Primaeval" (inactive since January 2017) and "Post-Anathema" (inactive since October 2018), published writing and images intended to display the aesthetic of NRx, respectively.[55] The Hestia Society, which had billed itself as a "fraternal network," also stated on its site as late as August 2017 that it had chapters in Vancouver, San Francisco, Los Angeles, New York City, Baltimore, Washington DC and Raleigh.[56]

NRx and the Alternative Right

As noted, NRx grew out of the existing, amorphous "reactosphere" of reactionary online political blogs.[57] In this sense, NRx discussions could quite naturally flow into online spaces where the Alternative Right was taking shape, though it had enough divergent interests and positions to mean it did not simply get subsumed into this other nascent ideology. This ambiguity is evident in a set of playing cards designed by the NRx *Radish Magazine* site in May 2013, well-shared amongst the reactosphere blogs at the time, that displayed the "Heroes of the Dark Enlightenment."[58] In addition to the likes of Yarvin and Land are figures very much associated with the alt-right, including John Derbyshire, Steve Sailer, Jared Taylor, Richard Spencer, Alex Kurtagic, and Jack Donovan. Moreover, core figures in the alt-right have stated that the NRx played a role in the development of the movement. Notably, Scottish alt-right vlogger Colin Robertson (AKA "Millennial Woes") stated in September 2017 that:

before the alt-right became as big as it is say 2013–2014 back then there was the neoreactionary movement, which still exists today of course, but back then it was more at the forefront of things if you are involved in this in this field.[59]

Moreover, this overlap extended to interactions offline. A September 2014 post on the Hestia Society's Social Matter site encouraged readers, in lieu of an NRx conference, to attend the annual conference of the H.L. Mencken Club, an annual event which would prove important to the alt-right's growth.[60] The recognition appears to have been mutual as well, with one user commenting that, "I happen to know that many in the Mencken Club are quite interested in the thing that has come to be known as 'Neoreaction'."[61]

Where the NRx and Rationalist communities shared an interest in technical debates, experimental political structures and technological utopianism, the former and the Alternative Right share an interest in rejection of the establishment right and a desire for a return to traditional social values.[62] Yet, for many in the alt-right, NRx thought does not go far enough. Writing on the site of the alt-right publishers Counter-Currents Publishing in December 2013, Matt Parrott of the US Traditionalist Workers Party, which sought to align itself with the alt-right, argued that many in the NRx community were simply earlier on in their process of moving to the far right, by virtue of not embracing outright antisemitism and racial nationalism. However, he saw them as useful in this respect, since:

> By limiting the scope of their work to avoid naming specific enemies or getting too specific about solutions, they're capable of reaching a much large [sic] audience than otherwise possible, given the internalized taboos and external disincentives attached to either "racism" or "antisemitism."[63]

Greg Johnson, founder of Counter-Currents, and a leading figure in the alt-right, concurred with Parrott's assessment in a comment on his article, adding that "We are the true Dark Enlightenment, in that we are more Enlightened than the other guys, and further from the mainstream and therefore 'darker' from their point of view."[64] Yet, these divisions are not clear cut; many in the NRx world agree with the antisemitic and racial nationalist views espoused by the alt-right. The differences, perhaps, lie more in the NRx community's greater emphasis on rejecting democracy over discussing Jews and race; as the NRx blogger, Donovan Greene, wrote in response to Parrott, "It isn't that we're necessarily against discussing either of those things, our minds are just elsewhere."[65]

The influence of NRx

The ambitious aims of the NRx mission – the creation of "Statecraft for the American Restoration," as the Social Matter website described it[66] – and its focus on conducting much of this theorising in secluded blogs, would suggest that it is unlikely that the movement has had or is continuing to have any influence outside of its portion of the fringe far right, let alone closer to the mainstream of politics.

Despite this, the NRx movement has been touted as having close ties to, or at least considerable influence on, one of the major emerging political arenas of the 21st century: Big Tech and Silicon Valley. Some of this is simply misplaced and borne from conflation of NRx with the broader Alternative Right of which it has been a tributary (though this is not to say that adherents to the latter do not exist within Silicon Valley).[67] Given that coverage of the Alternative Right has frequently inflated its level of support, it is unsurprising that this would spill over into suspicions about NRx influence upon Silicon Valley.[68] Nonetheless, the links between these two communities are worth exploring in detail.

The relationship is best understood as one predominantly of partial ideological convergence, resulting from a pre-existing libertarianism prevalent within this tech community that means interests and occasionally positions are shared with the NRx world. As Klint Finley wrote for *Techcrunch* in 2013:

> You may have seen [neoreactionaries] crop-up on tech hangouts like Hacker News and Less Wrong [...] though neoreactionaries aren't exactly rampant in the tech industry, PayPal founder Peter Thiel has voiced similar ideas, and Pax Dickinson, the former CTO of Business Insider, says he's been influenced by neoreactionary thought. It may be a small, minority world view, but it's one that I think shines some light on the psyche of contemporary tech culture.[69]

The clearest connection to this psyche – and indeed the NRx community – is Peter Thiel, co-founder of PayPal, an early Facebook investor and a co-founder of, amongst numerous other organisations, Palantir, a data analytics company used for US government surveillance.[70] Thiel has been the focal point of speculation about NRx/Silicon Valley links for two reasons. Firstly, his views have appeared to align closely at times with those of the NRx community, in particular, when it comes to his criticisms of progressive politics and the subject of democracy especially. He famously wrote in a 2009 essay that he "no longer believe[d] that freedom and democracy are compatible" on the basis that the latter endangers the former.[71] He has also expressed the view that companies should be run in a manner that stops short of outright dictatorship. In 2012 Thiel gave a series of lectures to students at Stanford University and Blake Masters, who attended the lectures and who went on to work for Thiel, published his notes online, paraphrasing Thiel as follows:

> A startup is basically structured as a monarchy. We don't call it that, of course. That would seem weirdly outdated, and anything that's not democracy makes people uncomfortable. [...] [But] Importantly, it isn't an absolute dictatorship. No founder or CEO has absolute power. It's more like the archaic feudal structure. People vest the top person with all sorts of power and ability, and then blame them if and when things go wrong.

We are biased toward the democratic/republican side of the spectrum. That's what we're used to from civics classes. But the truth is that startups and founders lean toward the dictatorial side because that structure works better for startups. It is more tyrant than mob because it should be. In some sense, startups can't be democracies because none are. None are because it doesn't work. If you try to submit everything to voting processes when you're trying to do something new, you end up with bad, lowest common denominator type results.[72]

Thiel's preference here for a "strongman" style of organisational control is tempered by a recognition that:

pure dictatorship is unideal because you can't attract anyone to come work for you. Other people want some power and control too. So the best arrangement is a quasi-mythological structure where you have a king-like founder who can do more than in a democratic ruler but who remains far from all-powerful.[73]

Thiel is talking specifically about startups here, but the parallels with the NRx community's preferred form of neocameralist governance discussed above are substantial.[74] Interestingly, in 2011 Stanford Law School's Mark Lemley interviewed Thiel after the entrepreneur taught a class at the university on the theme of "sovereignty, globalisation and technological change" (a class he reprised in 2018). Lemley notes that one of the questions discussed in the class was "Is there something analogous to starting a company and starting a country?"[75]

The second reason Thiel has attracted so much attention is because he has been a serious investor in experiments in this simultaneously pro/anti-libertarian ideal of governance, and with organisations with direct ties to the NRx community. Most significant is his venture capital firm's investment in Tlon, a company founded by Yarvin in 2013. Tlon focuses on an internet decentralising project which Yarvin has been developing since 2002 called Urbit, the aim of which is to remove control of web services from major tech companies. Another direct link comes through Thiel's investment in the Seasteading Institute, an organisation which aims to build floating cities in the sea and which was founded by Patri Friedman, grandson of influential libertarian Milton Friedman ("seasteading" is seen by some in the NRx community as a means of escaping liberal democratic states and implementing neocameralism, though it has enjoyed support otherwise within Silicon Valley).[76] In a January 2014 Facebook post Patri Friedman stated that he was happy to discover "that [Yarvin] is no longer an obscure single voice, but has somehow managed to inspire an entire school of red pill political philosophy." He added, however, that he was hoping to create "a more politically correct dark enlightenment [sic] [...] adding anti-racism and anti-sexism."[77] Beyond these ties to NRx-inflected experiments, Thiel was linked to the NRx figure Michael Anissimov, by way of the Machine Intelligence Research Institute (MIRI), where Anissimov worked from 2004 until 2013. (Anissimov would go on to leave MIRI and self-publish a book in 2015 that argued multiculturalism had "made it difficult for intelligent Europeans to thrive in the United States.") An artificial intelligence organisation, MIRI was co-founded by Yudkowsky, Brian Atkins, and Sabine Stoekel in 2000 and Thiel has been one of its largest donors.[78]

The extent of Thiel's ideological overlaps with NRx thinking more broadly is evident from his wider criticisms of progressive politics. Most notably, he co-wrote *The Diversity Myth: Multiculturalism and Political Intolerance on Campus* in 1996, which criticised multicultural policies in universities and called date rape "belated regret."[79] In October 2016 he apologised for the book's "insensitive, crudely argued statements" in a statement to *Forbes*, adding that "Rape in all forms is a crime."[80] Yet, as *Forbes* notes, Thiel did not say which specific statements were "crudely argued," nor did he explicitly denounce his criticism of multicultural policies in education.[81] Thiel also founded the student paper *The Stanford Review* whilst a student at the same university in 1987, which argued that Stanford "should focus on 'institutionalized liberalism' rather than [its] supposed 'institutionalized racism'."[82] *Stanford Politics'* Andrew Granato reported that, during the after-party of the 30th anniversary for the *Review*, held at Thiel's home, a former editor of the student paper had been told by Thiel that "his apology was just for the media, and that 'sometimes you have to tell them what they want to hear.'"[83] Granato also reported that Thiel had told a former editor at the event that Yarvin was "interesting" but "crazy," and he would "lecture you for an hour."[84] He adds that "the editor remembered that Thiel did offer to set up a meeting between Yarvin and [a current] Review staff member who asked about him."[85]

Thiel's ideological roots are libertarian,[86] and it appears that it is from this direction that his critique of multiculturalism in education – specifically the claim that it undermines intellectual rigour – arises. As he told vlogger Dave Rubin on his *Rubin Report* YouTube show in September 2018: "Diversity of ideas is to be valued, but you don't have real diversity when you have people who look different and think alike [...] The diversity myth is that it's not about diversity at all. It's about conformity."[87]

Of course, under the guise of protecting a "diversity of ideas" it is possible for extreme positions to be given an equal platform. Thiel veered into this territory in 2016, after it was revealed that he was due to speak at the annual meeting of the Property and Freedom Society (PFS) in Turkey. The PFS was founded in 2006 by Hans-Hermann Hoppe, an influential libertarian scholar who, in a speech to the PFS in 2017 on "Libertarianism and the Alt-Right," declared that "restrictive, highly selective and discriminating immigration [...] is entirely compatible with libertarianism and its *desideratum* of freedom of association and opposition to forced integration."[88] Thiel's name was removed from the list of speakers after it was announced that he was due to speak and a spokesperson stated that he would not be attending the event.[89] Nonetheless, that Thiel was due to speak at meeting of a society which had previously hosted far-right thinkers including Peter Brimelow, John Derbyshire, Tomislav Sunic, Jared Taylor, Richard Spencer, and Paul Gottfried is concerning.

Fertile ground

That mainstream figures could come into contact personally with these ideas in Silicon Valley is less bizarre when one takes into account the history of the San Francisco Bay Area, where Silicon Valley is situated, as a home for fringe and experimental subcultures. As Julia Galef, a co-founder of the Center for Applied Rationality (CFAR), which has ties to Yudkowsky's Machine Intelligence Research Institute (MIRI), explained in a post on LessWrong in September 2013, "The Bay Area is unusually dense with idea-driven subcultures that mix and cross-pollinate in fascinating ways, many of which are already enriching rationalist culture."[90] Galef accompanies the post with a flowchart of what she sees as the area's ideological subcultures from the previous 50 years, describing it as its "memespace."[91] The diagram does not mention NRx but does place "Seasteaders" in a box labelled "Libertarians."[92]

Despite this, NRx seems to remain largely at arm's length from most in Silicon Valley; it appears to be known of by elements of the latter and sometimes an ideology of interest to them, and so is tolerated if not accepted. Yarvin, for example, was disinvited from the 2009 Seasteading Institute annual conference after complaints from a fellow invited speaker about the content of Yarvin's blog, though in a statement the Institute cited the "gratuitous personal attacks" made by Yarvin towards a speaker as the basis of the disinvitation rather than his extreme writing.[93] Indeed, they write with regret, there "are so few political theorists on competitive government that we must admit to some sadness at such a conflict manifesting."[94] Aside from open support for Urbit, Yarvin's acceptance by Silicon Valley remains somewhat ambiguous. Tweeting in January 2018, Thiel associate Eric Weinstein – who coined the phrase "Intellectual Dark Web" in 2018 to describe a network of high-profile, contrarian right-wing and libertarian figures in the public eye – said that he and Yarvin "ran into each other at a dinner" and joked about their respective movement's names.[95]

A greater insight into this ambiguous relationship is revealed by the annual surveys the LessWrong blog has carried out of its visitors, given the role this community played in fostering the NRx community. In 2009, the survey did not provide much insight into how many held right-wing views though "conservatives" were a minority (4.3%) out of 166 respondents and even more so in 2011 (2.8%) when there were 1090 respondents, though by the latter survey some commentators were curious about whether any of those identifying with the right were influenced by Yarvin.[96] In 2012 there was much greater clarity, with 30 respondents out of 1195 claiming to be "Reactionary" (2.5%) and 19 more specifically identifying as "Moldbuggian" (1.6%).[97] In 2013, out of 1636 respondents, "Reactionary" made up 40 (2.4%) of respondents, in 2014, out of 1503 respondents, 29 (1.9%) identified as "Neoreactionary." From what appears to be the most recent published survey at the time of writing in 2016 (no 2015 survey appears to have been undertaken), 28 (0.92%) respondents out of 3060 identified as "Neoreactionary."[98] Interestingly, 112 respondents (3.66%) claimed in this survey that the site was "Too tolerant of Neoreaction," when it came to consideration of the site's community issues.

What is evident from these surveys is that the NRx community, insofar as it overlaps with the tech world found in Silicon Valley and beyond who frequent sites like LessWrong (almost a third of 2016 respondents worked in academic or practical computing occupations), has been and remains a somewhat tolerated fringe contingent. What may have allowed it to remain so is precisely that enough NRx adherents – at least in its early stages – were part of the tech community already. Moreover, away from the hardline libertarianism of NRx that might attract the likes of Thiel, many of Silicon Valley's moderate libertarians and liberal-left share with much of the NRx community a deep conviction about technology's capacity to act as a panacea for society's ills, a belief in radical alternatives to the current political system (another overlap here is the shared interest for many in each camp in accelerationist economic ideas), and a commitment to an acutely rationalist worldview.[99] As a description of NRx in relation to LessWrong on the key alt-lite outlet Breitbart News Network highlighted in 2016:

> LessWrong urged its community members to think like machines rather than humans. Contributors were encouraged to strip away self-censorship, concern for one's social standing, concern for other people's feelings, and any other inhibitors to rational thought. It's not hard to see how a group of heretical, piety-destroying thinkers emerged from this environment.[100]

Where they differ, of course, is with regard to what they want society to become. In contrast to the reactionary, "Dark" enlightenment encouraged by the likes of Yarvin, the liberal tech-utopians of Silicon Valley see themselves – however sometimes inaccurately – as continuing many Enlightenment ideals. As Yudkowsky told *Harpers* magazine in 2015: "We're part of the continuation of the Enlightenment, the Old Enlightenment. This is the New Enlightenment," he said. "Old project's finished. We actually have science now, now we have the next part of the Enlightenment project."[101]

The prospects for NRx

NRx has been the subject of conspiracy, with shady connections to tech elites and political figures, yet the connections remain cryptic. The key example of this is its relationship to Steve Bannon, former Breitbart executive chairman and former chief strategist to President Trump. *Politico* reported in February 2017 that Yarvin had "opened up a line to the White House, communicating with Bannon and his aides through an intermediary," according to an unnamed source.[102] Yarvin denied this in an interview with *Vox* but speculation remained for a number of reasons.[103] The first is his links to Thiel, who served on Trump's transition team, the second is Breitbart's coverage of Yarvin in a March 2016 article,[104] suggesting Yarvin may be on Bannon's radar, and the third comes from an October 2017 *Buzzfeed* revelation that former Breitbart contributor, Milo Yiannopoulos, had sought advice from Yarvin for an article about the Alternative Right.[105] *Buzzfeed* also reported that

Yarvin had told Yiannopoulos that he had been "coaching [Peter] Thiel" and that he had watched the 2016 US election at Thiel's house.[106] Less of a tangible connection, but still an indication of the reach of NRx thinking, is the praise for Yarvin given by Sam Bowman, former senior fellow and executive director of the British think-tank, the Adam Smith Institute. In a 2014 post entitled "Where my beliefs come from" from his now deleted blog, Bowman listed Yarvin's work and stated "I am not a neo-reactionary, but sometimes I think Mencius Moldbug is the greatest living political thinker."[107]

The NRx community takes a long view when it comes to affecting political change and so whilst developing connections with those in positions of power may be desirable for some within the movement, many will argue that their focus should remain on developing their ideas.[108] In this respect, the Hestia Society's Social Matter site was the hub for the movement, working as an aggregator of sorts as well as producing its content (including, notably, an interview on the *Myth of the 20th Century* podcast with the former president of the British National Party, Nick Griffin, in September 2018).[109] Outside of Hestia, parts of the broader reactionary right may provide potentially fertile areas for NRx activity. The first of these is the right-wing of the accelerationist movement, of which Land has been an advocate. Accelerationism is a school of economic thought which argues, as Brian Willems describes it, that "the best way to carve out alternatives to a dominant system is by speeding up the system's own mechanisms."[110] The movement has left- and right-wing adherents, who share a belief that "technology, particularly computer technology, and capitalism, particularly the most aggressive, global variety, should be massively sped up and intensified" as Andy Beckett describes, either "because this is the best way forward for humanity, or because there is no alternative."[111] This has overlaps, of course, with the Silicon Valley techno-utopian ethos described earlier, and so developing links to the NRx community here is plausible.

Another area of development could come from alliances with standard reactionary, or traditionalist, groups, such as the Sydney Traditionalist Forum. This Australian organisation describes itself as "an association of 'old school' conservative, traditionalist and paleoconservative individuals who live, work and study in Sydney, New South Wales"[112] and hosts conferences which have featured prominent alt-right figures. Though not explicitly an NRx organisation, it describes itself as "in fellowship" with Hestia, distinguishing this from "support[ing]" the work of other organisations including the Traditional Britain Group, the Mencken Club and the American Society for the Defense of Tradition, Family and Property.[113]

These possible avenues for the NRx community highlight that it is, as Land predicted, fragmenting somewhat along its fault lines. Indeed, the earlier cited diagram from Nick B. Steves could indicate that the "Theonomist" (religious) branch of NRx may move towards working with the wider religious right, the "Ethnicists" branch of NRx towards the alt-right and wider nationalist and racialist right and the "Techno-Commercialists" towards the libertarian, accelerationist (and perhaps Silicon Valley-located) right.[114]

Notes

1 Joseph Bernstein, "Alt-White: How the Breitbart Machine Laundered Racist Hate," *Buzzfeed News*, 5 October 2017. https://www.buzzfeednews.com/article/josephbern stein/heres-how-breitbart-and-milo-smuggled-white-nationalism#.rmomGXmLr
2 Peter Thiel, "The Education of a Libertarian," *Cato Unbound*, 13 April 2009. https://www.cato-unbound.org/2009/04/13/peter-thiel/education-libertarian
3 Jeff Bercovici, "Peter Thiel is Very, Very Interested in Young People's Blood," *Inc.*. https://www.inc.com/jeff-bercovici/peter-thiel-young-blood.html
4 Mark O'Connell, "Why Silicon Valley Billionaires Are Prepping for the Apocalypse in New Zealand," *The Guardian*, 15 February 2018. https://www.theguardian.com/news/2018/feb/15/why-silicon-valley-billionaires-are-prepping-for-the-apocalypse-in-new-zealand
5 Benjamin Noys, quoted in: Olivia Goldhill, "The Neo-fascist Philosophy that Underpins Both the Alt-right and Silicon Valley Technophiles," *Quartz*, 18 June 2017. https://qz.com/1007144/the-neo-fascist-philosophy-that-underpins-both-the-alt-right-and-silicon-valley-technophiles/
6 Park MacDougald, "The Darkness Before the Right," *The Awl*, 28 September 2015. https://www.theawl.com/2015/09/the-darkness-before-the-right/
7 For further discussion of this movement, see Chapter 1 "The European Roots of Alt-Right Ideology" in this book.
8 Elisabeth Sandifer, *Neoreaction as Basilisk: Essays on and around the Alt-Right* (Charleston: CreateSpace, 2018), 26.
9 Curtis Yarvin (Mencius Moldbug), "A Gentle Introduction to Unqualified Reserva-tions," *Unqualified Reservations*, 8 January 2009. https://www.unqualified-reservations.org/2009/01/gentle-introduction-to-unqualified/
10 Thomas Carlyle quoted in: Sam Chaltain, "The Wisdom of Crowds, Untapped," *Huffington Post*, 3 July 2013. https://www.huffingtonpost.com/sam-chaltain/the-wisdom-of-crowds_b_3162296.html?guccounter=1
11 Nick Land, "The Dark Enlightenment," *The Dark Enlightenment*.http://www.theda rkenlightenment.com/the-dark-enlightenment-by-nick-land/
12 Curtis Yarvin (Mencius Moldbug), "Divine-Right Monarchy for the Modern Secular Intellectual," *Unqualified Reservations*, 18 March 2010. https://www.unqualifie d-reservations.org/2010/03/divine-right-monarchy-for-modern/
13 "Moldbug's intellectual trajectory was a rightward march. He shifted from the liber-alism of his family, through the cultural libertarianism of Silicon Valley, in and out of mainstream American conservatism and radical libertarianism, and ultimately arrived at neoreaction." Joshua Tait, "Mencius Moldbug and Neoreaction," in: Mark Sedgwick (Ed.), *Key Thinkers of the Radical Right: Behind the New Threat to Liberal Democracy* (Oxford Scholarship Online, February 2019), 190.
14 Ibid., 195.
15 Ibid., 192.
16 Ibid., 193.
17 Ibid.
18 Curtis Yarvin (Mencius Moldbug), "A Gentle Introduction to Unqualified Reserva-tions," *Unqualified Reservations*, January 2009, 15–16. http://atavisionary.com/wp-con tent/uploads/2015/08/A-gentle-introduction-to-unqualified-reservations.pdf
19 Michael Anissimov, "Neoreactionary Glossary," *More Right*, 19 September 2013. http://www.moreright.net/neoreactionary-glossary/
20 Jason Lee Steorts, "Against Mencius Moldbug's 'Neoreaction'," *National Review*, 5 June 2017. https://www.nationalreview.com/2017/06/problems-mencius-moldbug-neorea ction/
21 Curtis Yarvin (Mencius Moldbug), "Divine-Right Monarchy for the Modern Secular Intellectual."
22 Email to the author.

23 Ibid.
24 Curtis Yarvin (Mencius Moldbug), "Patchwork: A Political System for the 21st Century," *Unqualified Reservations*, 13 November 2008. https://www.unqualified-reserva
    tions.org/2008/11/patchwork-positive-vision-part-1
25 Through his blog, Yarvin's addressal of race also came from the direction of attacking
    the supposed restraints and control of the Cathedral. As Joshua Tait highlights, Yarvin
    considers assumptions of "'human neurological uniformity' and antiracism" as "central
    pillars" of the universalist, egalitarian ethic the Cathedral promotes. Joshua Tait,
    "Mencius Moldbug and Neoreaction," 194.
26 Email to the author.
27 Joshua Tait, "Mencius Moldbug and Neoreaction," 196.
28 MacDougald, "The Darkness Before the Right." Strangely, due to a contingent
    within the movement being keen believers in transhumanism, there can be a tension
    between those who believe in the preservation of their race via a neocameral ethnos-
    tate and those who want to move beyond the human race all together.
29 "Derbyshire's firing is an ideological matter," *Midwest Ballad Review*, 10 April 2012.
    http://midwestballadreview.tumblr.com/post/20860366027/derbyshires-firing-is-a
    n-ideological-matter
30 Bryce Laliberte, "A Taxonomy of the Reactosphere," *Anarcho Papist*, 9 August 2013.
    https://web.archive.org/web/20150404162616/https://anarchopapist.wordpress.com/
    2013/08/09/a-taxonomy-of-the-reactosphere/
31 "Introduction," *Reaction Times*. https://neorxn.com/introduction/
32 Michael, "Elsewhere," *2Blowhards*, 25 April 2007. http://www.2blowhards.com/a
    rchives/2007/04/elsewhere_236.html
33 Curtis Yarvin (Mencius Moldbug), "An Open Letter to Open-Minded Pro-
    gressives: Chapter 3 The Jacobite History of the World," *Unqualified Reservations*, 1
    May 2008. https://www.unqualified-reservations.org/2008/05/ol3-jacobite-histor
    y-of-world/; Curtis Yarvin (Mencius Moldbug), "An Open Letter to Open-
    Minded Progressives: Chapter X: A Simple Sovereign Bankruptcy Procedure,"
    Unqualified Reservations, 19 June 2008. https://www.unqualified-reservations.org/
    2008/06/olx-simple-sovereign-bankruptcy/
34 Eliezer Yidkowsky Comment on, arborealhominid, "Why is Mencius Moldbug so
    popular on Less Wrong? [Answer: He's not.]," *LessWrong*, 16 November 2012. http
    s://www.lesswrong.com/posts/6qPextf9KyWLFJ53j/why-is-mencius-moldbug-so-p
    opular-on-less-wrong-answer-he-s#TcLhiMk8BTp4vN3Zs; see also: Eliezer Yid-
    kowsky, "no title," *Optimize Literally Everything*, 8 April 2016. http://yudkowsky.tum
    blr.com/post/142497361345/this-isnt-going-to-work-but-for-the-record-and; Alex-
    ander Scott, "The Anti-Reactionary FAQ," *Slate Star Codex*, 20 October 2013.
    http://slatestarcodex.com/2013/10/20/the-anti-reactionary-faq/
35 "The 2013 Anti-Progress Report," *Radish*, 31 December 2013. https://radishmag.
    wordpress.com/2013/12/31/the-2013-anti-progress-report/
36 Eliezer Yudkowsky comment on, arborealhominid, "Why is Mencius Moldbug so
    popular on Less Wrong? [Answer: He's not.]." https://www.lesswrong.com/posts/
    6qPextf9KyWLFJ53j/why-is-mencius-moldbug-so-popular-on-less-wrong-a
    nswer-he-s#TcLhiMk8BTp4vN3Zs
37 Scott Alexander, "Reactionary Philosophy in an Enormous, Planet-Sized Nutshell," *Slate
    Star Codex*, 3 March 2013. http://slatestarcodex.com/2013/03/03/reactionary-philosop
    hy-in-an-enormous-planet-sized-nutshell/
38 Scott, "The Anti-Reactionary FAQ."
39 Michael Anissimov quoted in: mstevens, "[Link] More Right Launched," *Less-
    Wrong*, 5 May 2013. https://www.lesswrong.com/posts/2X6zJwWTrMbf73q5R/
    link-more-right-launched
40 Nick Land, "Cambrian Explosion," *Outside in*, 09 May 2013. http://www.xenosystem
    s.net/cambrian-explosion/

41 Haider, "The Darkness at the End of the Tunnel." Also, in personal correspondence, Land himself reckoned that he "probably [came across Moldbug and the reactosphere] via right libertarian online discussion."

42 Michael Anissimov, "Neoreactionary Glossary," *More Right*, 19 September 2013. http://archive.is/QXmhG

43 "Visualizing Neoreaction," *Habitable Worlds*, 21 April 2013. http://habitableworlds. wordpress.com:80/2013/04/21/visualizing-neoreaction/. The diagram groups the blogs into "Techno-Commercialists/Futurists," "Economists," "Neoreactionary Political Philosophy," "Secular Traditionalists," "Masculine Reaction," "Feminine Reaction," "Ethno-Nationalists," "HBD" (an abbreviation of "Human Biodiversity") and "Christian Traditionalists."

44 Graphic Image, "Visual Trichotomy," *Outside in*, 02 May 2013. http://www.xenosystem s.net/visual-trichotomy/. The visualisation is a Venn diagram with three intersecting circles, described as "Techno-Commercialists," "Theonomists," and "Ethnicists Nationalists." The intersection describes the "Neoreactionary fusion" as consisting in "natural hierarchy," "deep heritage," "race-realism," "sex realism," "microeconomics," "federalism," "subsidiarity," "freedom," and "exit."

45 Though many attempted to codify its positions e.g. "Reactionary Consensus," *The Reactivity Place*, 9 November 2013. https://web.archive.org/web/20131109222301/http:// nickbsteves.wordpress.com:80/reactionary-consensus/; Michael Anissimov, "Twelve Points of Neoreaction," *More Right*, 27 June 2013. https://archive.is/DI7fe

46 Bryce Laliberte, "Advice for the Student Reactionary," *Anarcho Papist*, 31 August 2013.   https://web.archive.org/web/20150404173453/https://anarchopapist.wordp ress.com/2013/08/31/advice-for-the-student-reactionary/

47 "Minutes of the DC Area Reactionary Meetup Thingy (2013/06/01)," *The Reactivity Place*, 03 June 2013. https://web.archive.org/web/20131027100229/http://nickb steves.wordpress.com/2013/06/03/minutes-of-the-dc-area-reactionary-meetup -thingy-20130601/

48 Nick Land, "2014: A Prophecy," *Outside in*, 5 January 2014. http://www.xenosystem s.net/2014-a-prophecy/

49 The Hestia Team, "Official Statement on the Leadership of NRx," *The Hestia Society*. https://archive.is/1YNIY

50 Ibid.

51 "Authority," *Free Northerner*, 24 May 2015. https://freenortherner.com/2015/05/ 24/authority/

52 The Hestia Team, "Our Plan for Civilization," *The Hestia Society*. https://image2. owler.com/7862288-1450072750383.png

53 The Hestia Team, "Official Statement on the Leadership of NRx."

54 The Hestia Team, "About Us," *The Hestia Society*. https://image2.owler.com/ 7862288-1502599206126.png

55 Specifically, a mixture of science fiction, cityscapes, nature, and classical European art. Post-Anathema also archived a series of posters found on the *Radish Magazine* site: http://post-anathema.tumblr.com/tagged/infographics. These included quotes from Julius Evola, Joseph de Maistre, and Thomas Carlyle below statements intended to highlight the NRx communities' departure from assumptions of mainstream political opinion, for example: "Liberals want a big government, conservatives want a small government. Reactionaries want a functioning government whether not every fool has a vote."

56 The Hestia Team, "About Us."

57 A good demonstration of this amorphousness can be seen here: J. Arthur Bloom, "The 41 best alt-right websites of 2013," *missionary ground*, 27 December 2013. http://ja rthurbloom.tumblr.com/post/71329484893/the-41-best-alt-right-websites-of-2013

58 "17. Heroes of the Dark Enlightenment," *Radish*, 24 May 2013. https://archive.fo/ EoNzl

59 Millennial Woes, 2017, *The Cathedral Stands Up* [Online video]. Available at: https://www.youtube.com/watch?v=Gzwf4oIAvU0 [Accessed 20 October 2018]. Robertson has also attributed his "red-pilling" (a term popular within the Alternative Right which refers to coming to see the "truth" of the Alternative Right's claims) to the NRx vlogger Davis Aurini: Millennial Woes, 2014, *Introduction: About Me (v3)* [Online video]. Available at: https://www.youtube.com/watch?v=1y-1vU2hXDc&t=1067s [Accessed 20 October 2018].

60 Hubert Collins, "Looking to the Mencken Club and What Lies Beyond," *Social Matter*, 13 September 2014. https://archive.is/RUbrC.

61 Ibid.

62 Some in the alt-right have expressed an interest in technological utopianism. Greg Johnson of Counter-Currents Publishing wrote in September 2018 that "technological utopianism is not only compatible with ethnic nationalism but also that liberalism and globalization undermine technological progress, and that the ethnostate is actually the ideal incubator for mankind's technological apotheosis." See: Greg Johnson, "Technological Utopianism and Ethnic Nationalism," *Counter-Currents Publishing*, 17 September 2018. https://www.counter-currents.com/2018/09/technological-utopianism-and-ethnic-nationalism/

63 Matt Parrott, "The 'Dark Enlightenment' is New Right Lite," *Counter-Currents Publishing*, 9 December 2013. https://www.counter-currents.com/2013/12/the-dark-enlightenment-is-new-right-lite/

64 Ibid.

65 Donovan Greene, "A Schema for Understanding the Reaction," *The Legionnaire*, 15 December 2013. https://iamlegionnaire.wordpress.com/2013/12/15/a-schema-for-understanding-the-reaction/

66 Homepage, *Social Matter*. https://www.socialmatter.net/

67 Josh Harkinson, "Meet Silicon Valley's Secretive Alt-Right Followers," *Mother Jones*, 10 March 2017. https://www.motherjones.com/politics/2017/03/silicon-valley-tech-alt-right-racism-misogyny/

68 An early example occurred in some media coverage of Google software engineer Justine Tunney, a prominent Occupy activist turned Yarvin enthusiast. Arthur Chu, "Occupying the Throne: Justine Tunney, Neoreactionaries, and the New 1%," *Daily Beast*, 1 August 2014. https://www.thedailybeast.com/occupying-the-throne-justine-tunney-neoreactionaries-and-the-new-1

69 Klint Finley, "Geeks for Monarchy: The Rise of the Neoreactionaries," *Tech Crunch*. https://techcrunch.com/2013/11/22/geeks-for-monarchy/

70 Peter Waldman, Lizette Chapman and Jordan Robertson, "Palantir Knows Everything About You," *Bloomberg*, 19 April 2018. https://www.bloomberg.com/features/2018-palantir-peter-thiel/

71 Thiel, "The Education of a Libertarian"; Peter Thiel, "Your Suffrage Isn't in Danger. Your Other Rights Are," *Cato Unbound*, 1 May 2009. https://www.cato-unbound.org/2009/05/01/peter-thiel/suffrage-isnt-danger-other-rights-are

72 Blake Master, "Peter Thiel's CS183: Startup – Class 18 Notes Essay," *Blake Masters*, 6 June 2012. http://blakemasters.com/post/24578683805/peter-thiels-cs183-startup-class-18-notes

73 Ibid. In 2016, *The Verge* also reported that Thiel appeared to be due to give a seminar at the private education institute, The Berkeley Institute, on "Heterodox Science" which would discuss "fields of study that dissent from mainstream science," including "biology and human nature; evolution and sexual differences; and economics and urban social policy." After it was reported the seminar was removed from the site's course listings. See: Melissa Batchelor Warnke, "Peter Thiel is almost definitely behind this mysterious 'Heterodox Science' course," *The Verge*, 21 December 2016. https://www.theverge.com/2016/12/21/14025760/peter-thiel-heterodox-science-class-berkeley-institute

74 Specifically, it aligns very close to the "No Voice, Free Exit" concept at the heart of the NRx ideology. This is the idea of competition between (for many neor-eactionaries, racially segregated) dictatorial poles of power, which reduces democracy ("No Voice") whilst allowing individuals the liberty to pick from the "market" of competing states ("Free Exit"). As the "Dark Enlightenment" Reddit.com subforum for the NRx community describes in its "Common Ideas" section, they wish for "A system of No Voice-Free Exit in large hyper-federalist states or small independent city states." See: https://www.reddit.com/r/DarkEnlightenment/

75 "On Innovation, Entrepreneuralism, and Law: A Conversation with Peter Thiel and Mark A. Lemley," *Stanford Lawyer*, 31 May 2011. https://law.stanford.edu/stanford-la wyer/articles/q-a-legal-matters-with-peter-thiel-92-ba-89-bs-89-and-mark-a-lem ley-ba-88/

76 Corey Pein, "The Moldbug Variations," *The Baffler*, 9 October 2017. https://theba ffler.com/latest/the-moldbug-variations-pein. Kyle Denuccio, "Silicon Valley Is Let-ting Go of Its Techie Island Fantasies," *Wired*, 16 May 2015. https://www.wired. com/2015/05/silicon-valley-letting-go-techie-island-fantasies/

77 Patri Friedman, Facebook Status Update, 26 January 2014, available at: https://www.fa cebook.com/patri.friedman/posts/10152224034719766 [Accessed 7 November 2018].

78 "Top Contributors," *Machine Intelligence Research Institute*. https://intelligence.org/top contributors/

79 David O. Sacks and Peter A. Thiel, *The Diversity Myth: Multiculturalism and Political Intolerance on Campus* (Oakland: The Independence Institute, 1998), 113.

80 Ryan Mac and Matt Drange, "Donald Trump Supporter Peter Thiel Apologizes for Past Book Comments on Rape," *Forbes*, 25 October 2016. https://www.forbes.com/sites/rya nmac/2016/10/25/peter-thiel-apologizes-for-past-book-comments-on-rape-and-race/

81 Ibid.

82 Andrew Granato, "How Peter Thiel and the Stanford Review Built a Silicon Valley Empire," *Stanford Politics*, 27 November 2017. https://stanfordpolitics.org/2017/11/ 27/peter-thiel-cover-story/

83 Ibid.

84 Ibid.

85 Ibid.

86 Thiel, "The Education of a Libertarian."

87 The Rubin Report, 2018, *Peter Thiel on Trump, Gawker, and Leaving Silicon Valley (Full Interview)* [Online video]. Available at: https://www.youtube.com/watch?v= h10kXgTdhNU [Accessed 5 October 2018].

88 Hans-Hermann Hoppe Speech delivered at the 12th annual meeting of the Property and Freedom Society in Bodrum, Turkey, on September 17, 2017. Available at: http s://www.youtube.com/watch?v=TICdCM4j7x8

89 Ben Walsh, "Trump's Top Tech Backer Won't Attend 'White-Nationalist Friendly' Event," *Huffington Post*, 26 July 2016. https://www.huffingtonpost.co.uk/ entry/peter-thiel-donald-trump_us_5796598ee4b0d3568f840ee3

90 Julia Galef, "A Map of Bay Area memespace," *LessWrong*, 21 September 2013. https:// www.lesswrong.com/posts/WzPJRNYWhMXQTEj69/a-map-of-bay-area-memespace

91 Ibid.

92 Ibid.

93 "Conference Schedule, Ground Rules, The Market for Ideas, and Reality," *The Seasteading Institute*, 21 September 2009. https://www.seasteading.org/2009/09/con ference-schedule-ground-rules-the-market-for-ideas-and-reality/

94 Ibid.

95 Eric Weinstein (@EricRWeinstein), 31 January 2018. https://twitter.com/ericrwein stein/status/958873451229360133?lang=en

96 Scott Alexander, "Survey Results," *LessWrong*, 12 May 2009. https://www.lesswrong. com/posts/ZWC3n9c6v4s35rrZ3/survey-results And: Scott Alexander, "2011 Survey

Results," *LessWrong*, 5 December 2011. https://www.lesswrong.com/posts/HAEPbGa MygJq8L59k/2011-survey-results

97 Scott Alexander, "2012 Survey Results," *LessWrong*, 7 December 2012. https://www. lesswrong.com/posts/x9FNKTEt68Rz6wQ6P/2012-survey-results. The survey also notes that "These are the only ones that had more than ten people. Other responses notable for their unusualness were Monarchist (5 people), fascist (3 people, plus one who was up for fascism but only if he could be the leader)." For some qualification on how much support Yarvin had at the time, though, see: arborealhominid, "Why is Mencius Moldbug so popular on Less Wrong? [Answer: He's not.]."

98 In addition, 5 (0.16%) identify as "Fascist", 5 (0.16%) as "Monarchist": "Quick statistics Survey 554193 'LessWrong Diaspora 2016 Survey'," jdpressman.com.

99 A view somewhat shared by key figures in the movement, including Land, who in personal correspondence with the author suspected that the perception that NRx ideas had been an influence on Silicon Valley could be accounted for by "deeper cultural currents."

100 Allum Bokhari and Milo Yiannopoulos, "An Establishment Conservative's Guide to the Alt-Right," *Breitbart News Network*, 29 March 2016. https://www.breitbart.com/tech/2016/03/29/an-establishment-conservatives-guide-to-the-alt-right/. Tait draws attention to Paulina Borsook's analysis of how libertarianism enters quite naturally into tech culture. It is a "rational, rule-bound, and solvable" world, wherein "software and hardware are the dominant metaphors for society" (thinking that "dovetails with the ironclad assumptions about human and market behavior of the Austrian School of Economics"); its common work ethic "accords with libertarianism's concentration on efficiency and 'solving' government"; it venerates science, allowing for the treatment of "human biology as determinative," confirming to "mechanistic assumptions about humanity." Nonetheless, Tait notes that these tech libertarians "are not nostalgic for a mythical past." This would jar more with NRx if it weren't for the fact that it is also a culture in which, precisely because a futuristic-orientation is central, interest in science fiction abounds. Given this is a genre which, as Tate notes, has been used "to explore libertarian concepts and imagine possible alternative regimes," an interest in historical forms of governance could enter, as they did for Yarvin. Moreover, as the web itself offered some technoutopians in the 1990s a vision of a future, stateless society, the stage was set even more perhaps for a movement like NRx to emerge. On closer inspection, it should be no surprise that quite aside from his own reading of libertarian theory, a technolibertarian worldview "saturates" his writing. Joshua Tait, "Mencius Moldbug and Neoreaction," 190.

101 Sam Frank, "Come With Us If You Want to Live Among the Apocalyptic Libertarians of Silicon Valley," *Harper's Magazine*, 30 January 2015. https://www.hedweb.com/social-media/apocalyptic-libertarians.pdf

102 Eliana Johnson and Eli Stokols, "What Steve Bannon Wants You to Read," *Politico Magazine*, 7 February 2017. https://www.politico.com/magazine/story/2017/02/steve-bannon-books-reading-list-214745

103 Dylan Matthews, "Neo-monarchist Blogger Denies He's Chatting with Steve Bannon," *Vox*, 7 February 2017. https://www.vox.com/policy-and-politics/2017/2/7/14533876/mencius-moldbug-steve-bannon-neoreactionary-curtis-yarvin

104 Allum Bokhari, "Programming Conference Rejects SJW Demands to Ban Speaker over Political Views," *Breitbart News Network*, 29 March 2016. https://www.breitbart.com/tech/2016/03/29/sjws-urge-programming-conference-to-ban-speaker-over-political-views/

105 Bernstein, *Alt-White*.

106 Ibid.

107 Sam Bowman, "Where my beliefs come from," *Sam Bowman's blog*. https://archive.is/zc2S2#selection-969.39-979.74

108 As Tait describes, Yarvin discourages activism, "'violent or harmless, legal or illegal, fashionable or despicable.' Even voting is borderline. Instead, [he] advocates 'the Steel

Rule of Passivism.' He counsels readers that 'since you believe others should be willing to accept the rule of the New Structure, over which they wield no power, you must be the first to make the great refusal.' [Yarvin's] rationale is that progressivism feeds on right-wing opposition. By remaining passive, neoreaction 'starves' progressivism of a necessary enemy. Without a 'loyal opposition,' 'progressivism collapses into sclerosis.' Eschewing politics also safeguards neoreaction from cooption by those attracted to power, 'vaccinat[ing] itself against Hitler.'" Joshua Tait, "Mencius Moldbug and Neoreaction," 190.

109 Adam Smith, "Nationalism in the Shadow of Empire – Nick Griffin," *Myth of the 20ᵗʰ Century*, 12 September 2018. https://myth20c.wordpress.com/2018/09/12/nationa lism-in-the-shadow-of-empire-nick-griffin/

110 Brian Willems, "Every Which Way but Loose," *Los Angeles Review of Books*, 21 November 2014. https://lareviewofbooks.org/article/every-way-loose/#!

111 Andy Beckett, "Accelerationism: how a fringe philosophy predicted the future we live in," *The Guardian*, 11 May 2017. https://www.theguardian.com/world/2017/may/ 11/accelerationism-how-a-fringe-philosophy-predicted-the-future-we-live-in

112 "Home Page," Sydney Traditionalist Forum. https://sydneytrads.com/

113 Ibid.

114 In an email to the author, this is the wing Land identified with and, of the alt-right, he claimed "They know I am not in their camp."

PART II
Culture and activism

8

ART-RIGHT

Weaponising culture

Metapolitics – the technique of altering our culture, to prepare the way for political change – is the primary strategy of the White Nationalist movement […] But to change the culture, we must become part of it.–

Charlie Farnsbarns, Counter-Currents Publishing[1]

The white nationalist alt-right is a "metapolitical" movement, defined by Arktos Media CEO Daniel Friberg as "a war of social transformation, at the level of worldview, thought and culture."[2] The alt-right has adopted this perspective from the European New Right (ENR),[3] which regards metapolitics to be the "social diffusion of ideas and cultural values for the sake of provoking a profound, long-term, political transformation," in the words of the late ENR thinker Guillaume Faye.[4] Key figures have therefore sought to mould the alt-right into a "turbocharged, highly active *cultural vanguard* to break the dominant taboos," in the words of Brad Griffin (AKA "Hunter Wallace") of the alt-right Occidental Dissent website.[5]

Whilst all far-right movements have, to some degree, sought to propagandise through the arts, the metapolitical outlook of the alt-right elevates the arts to a crucial battleground in the war for society. Utilising the internet and digital technology, the movement has, with varying degrees of success, sought to disrupt, appropriate, and provide alternatives to the existing mainstream culture, which is considered to be "degenerate" and inherently anti-white due to the alleged infiltration of "cultural Marxists"/Jews into cultural institutions. In adopting this cultural focus, the alt-right hopes to distinguish itself from bygone generations of racist movements preoccupied with the political process or violent revolution, often pejoratively dubbed "White Nationalism 1.0."[6]

This chapter provides an overview of the alt-right's engagement in the mediums of visual aesthetics, music, film, television, animated web series, gaming, and fashion, and explores the multitude of competing styles and tropes adopted by the loose, decentralised movement.

Meme aesthetics

The visual aesthetic perhaps most closely associated with the alt-right is a deliberately crude, low-resolution cartoon style displayed in many of the movement's most recognisable memes. The style has roots in 4chan, the popular image board that, since its launch in 2003, has become a key influence on the development of online meme culture as a whole. The aesthetic is designed for easy reproduction and modification, resulting in endless variations,[7] and so is ideal for the 4chan tradition of "shitposting" (derailing an online conversation through irrelevant or offensive posting), a key modus operandi in the alt-right's cultural war. Such seemingly random images are used to provoke and bewilder "normies," who are forced to take childish cartoons seriously (and be exposed to the far-right ideas they espouse). As Vicky Osterweil writes in *Real Life Magazine*, "The fundamental mundanity of the alt-right aesthetic is a crucial part of its power," in part because it is intended to "produce conditions of sufficient confusion, apathy, irony, or symbolic distance about what they are trying to do."[8]

The most pertinent example is Pepe, an anthropomorphised cartoon frog originating from Matt Furie's comic *Boy's Club* in 2005, which was adopted by 4chan around 2008 and became widely used online. The broad Alternative Right subsequently appropriated the meme and has produced endless variations imbued with far-right imagery, and developed an entire lore asserting that Pepe is the modern-day equivalent of the frog-headed Egyptian deity, Kek. As Andrew Anglin of the neo-nazi Daily Stormer site wrote in August 2016, "Our aesthetic has been largely formed by keky memes, which wholly represent the spirit of our movement. This happened organically."[9] The broad Alternative Right's use of the meme has been prolific to the point that it has come to symbolise the loose movement in popular consciousness.

Whilst the original Pepe meme had no explicit far-right connotations, and so was inherently ambiguous and adaptable, the cartoon aesthetic has also helped to provide a sheen of irony and humour to images that are forthrightly racist. Examples include the "Sheeeit" meme, and the "Amerimutt/Le 56% Face" meme, crude racial stereotypes rendered on Microsoft Paint. Particularly notorious is the Happy Merchant meme, which depicts a caricature of a Jewish man greedily rubbing his hands together. This image encapsulates the movement's antisemitism, so crude in its racism and presentation that it appears satirical, but this faux-irony masks a real prejudice.[10]

A degree of tension exists between the gleeful use of the cartoon aesthetic by the alt-right's shitposters and the more sombre, high-culture pretensions of institutions such as American Renaissance, which have aligned themselves with the movement. However, whilst some may be somewhat bemused that the movement they regard as having the deadly serious mission of protecting the white race has come to be represented by a cartoon frog, they recognise the propaganda power of such images. For example, Joakim Andersen of the Swedish proto-alt-right think-tank Motpol, writes:

The postmodern era is sometimes described as borderline illiterate; people are losing their reading ability while sounds and pictures battle for their attention. Memes are an expression of this development, which in turn is at its core a step in the Great Worsening. At the same time this opens new possibilities to dodge the gatekeepers of the collective unconscious, bypass the official ideology and taboos of the *ersatz*-religions.[11]

Echoing these sentiments, Anglin is quoted in David Neiwert's book *Alt-America*:

A movement which meets all of the SPLC's [Southern Poverty Law Center's] definitions of Neo-Nazi White Supremacism using a cartoon frog to represent itself takes on a subversive power to bypass historical stereotypes of such movements, and thus present the ideas themselves in a fun way without the baggage of Schindler's List.[12]

The ironic ambiguity of memes such as Pepe has indeed provided the movement some of its most widely celebrated victories. For example, future president Donald Trump tweeted an image of himself characterised as Pepe in October 2015, and the image was decried on Hillary Clinton's campaign website as "sinister" in September 2016. Anglin has claimed, with apparent sincerity, that "Pepe the frog did a hundred times more for white people than all of the pro-white protest movements since WWII combined."[13] The alt-right as a whole has benefited enormously from its use of meme culture, aided in part by this cartoon aesthetic.

Classical motifs

In stark contrast to the deliberately lowbrow aesthetic outlined above, the alt-right also regularly incorporates artistic and architectural motifs from Greco-Roman antiquity into its propaganda, aiming to give the movement a more sophisticated and "high culture" sheen. For example, the now-notorious 2016 "Become Who We Are" conference of Richard Spencer's National Policy Institute (NPI) incorporated a photograph of Michelangelo's David into its promotional material, and the American group Identity Evropa (IE) (since replaced by American Identity Movement) adorned campuses around the US with posters bearing images of classical statues and slogans such as "Protect Your Heritage."

Plundering classical antiquity for motifs is not an original tactic; as Donna Zuckerberg writes in her book *Not All Dead White Men: Classics and Misogyny in the Digital Age*, "Political and social movements have long appropriated the history, literature, and myth of the ancient world to their advantage," including the far-right tradition, such as the Nazi Party in Germany.[14] As with previous far-right groups, in incorporating classical motifs the alt-right is, as Heidi Morse of the University of Michigan writes, drawing on "the iconicity and cultural capital of the sculptures as an overt appeal to a supposedly 'white' classical tradition linked to white European heritage."[15] The alt-right seeks to appeal to white men, and references to classical art are intended to invoke a sense of racial achievement, for which modern white men can claim vicarious credit. A critique of Zuckerberg's book on Counter-Currents Publishing affirms this view, stating:

> For those on the dissident Right, an appreciation of the classical world follows naturally from our respect for our Indo-European heritage and for the ideals of greatness, beauty, and heroism. We are not "misappropriating" the classical tradition: we are its rightful heirs.[16]

Incorporating motifs from classical art also invokes a sense of a lost past, to be contrasted with the supposed degeneracy and decay of modern architecture and art, which is sometimes regarded as the outcome of a Jewish conspiracy to undermine Western identity. For example, in a post called "Classical Art vs. Modern Nihilistic Jew Crap," Anglin states that "the death of beauty has played a key role in the death of Western civilization."[17] Unsurprisingly, no attempts are made by the likes of Anglin to reconcile their stated opposition to the erosion of European art with their heavy use of 4chan memes, as the alt-right is rife with inconsistencies. The classical motifs used the alt-right's propaganda function as a shorthand for white "superiority."

Fashwave

Classical motifs are also commonly incorporated into "fashwave," a visual and musical aesthetic heavily used by the alt-right, which essentially updates existing fascist tropes with heavy layers of 1980s kitsch and a digital, synthetic gloss, apt for a largely millennial movement operating primarily online.

Fashwave aesthetics were co-opted from "vaporwave," a scene that developed online in the early 2010s and which combines retro 1980s and 1990s visuals and sounds, sci-fi tropes, grainy digital effects, and glitches to create audio and visual works that have been interpreted by some as satirical of consumer-capitalism.[18] The alt-right widely adopted the style in August 2016, after Anglin recommended abandoning established but "pretty dated" far-right musical traditions in various rock subgenres to embrace synthwave, the "Whitest music ever," as the "Official Soundtrack of the Alt-Right."[19] Anglin shortly thereafter began the "Fashwave Fridays" series, posting retro sci-fi images and sounds onto his website. It should be noted that whilst Anglin's endorsement marks the alt-right's official adoption of the style, the aesthetic was already used by some online nazis. Daily Stormer contributors Andrew Auernheimer (AKA "weev") and Gabriel Sohier Chaput (AKA "Zeiger") accredit the now-defunct neo-nazi forum Iron March, and specifically forum user Benjamin Raymond, founder of the now-banned UK nazi terror group National Action (NA), as originating fashwave through his graphic designs.[20]

Since Anglin's endorsement, autonomous alt-right graphic artists and musicians have honed fashwave into a deeply formulaic genre of visual and audio propaganda. Visually, fashwave art simply overlays neon filters and digital visuals over some combination of classical motifs, sci-fi imagery, photographs of historical fascists, white supremacist symbols, and simple right-wing slogans.[21] War is a common focus, sometimes depicted as glorious and heroic, sometimes as tragic, or celebrated with a death-worshiping nihilism. The sonic counterpart is sometimes more tongue-in-cheek, for example the upbeat, bouncy synth anthem "Hail Victory" by British producer Xurious, and at other times more overtly fascistic, for example the dark soundscapes produced by CYBERNΔZI, which are heavily derivative of early video games and 1980s movie soundtracks.[22] As reported by *VICE*, CYBERNΔZI considers himself a "direct heir" to Futurism, an early 20th century artistic movement that blended new technological forms with a veneration of violence and war, and which became an artistic inspiration for Italian Fascism.[23] Fashwave's retro-futurist style is also often reminiscent of the themes prevalent in Faye's book *Archeofuturism* (popular with the alt-right), which envisions a future society that combines futuristic technology with archaic traditions.

Allie Conti in *VICE*, referencing the work of Leeds Beckett University Professor Karl Spracklen,[24] posits that white supremacists have traditionally been attracted to certain musical genres, such as English folk, because they are evocative of an idealised white past.[25] In its heavy aesthetic nods towards the 1980s, the alt-right seeks to tap into a similar appeal, with Richard Spencer claiming that the 1980s represented "halcyon days, as the last days of white America,"[26] and Anglin stating that synthwave is "the spirit of the childhoods of millenials [sic]."[27] As *VICE* notes, in the 2010s, 1980s nostalgia has experienced a boom in the mainstream, demonstrating that the aesthetic tropes of the decade have an intrinsic appeal for many millennials. To some degree, fashwave helps to deepen the allure of white supremacist propaganda to millennials by incorporating reassuringly familiar tropes from their childhoods.[28]

Whilst fashwave remains both a one trick novelty and highly derivative, the style has been celebrated by many in the alt-right, described by Spencer as "the music of the future,"[29] and the Daily Stormer as "The Vision and Sound of a New Modernity!"[30] Whilst such claims are obvious overstatement, this enthusiasm stems from the fact that fashwave does indeed constitute an identifiable aesthetic scene the movement can plausibly call its own, and is significant if solely for this reason.

Parody music

Whilst the synth sounds of fashwave may be the closest the alt-right has to an identifiable musical scene, the movement's ironic sensibilities and penchant for co-opting and distorting mainstream artistic forms have led to a natural embrace of the parody music form. The alt-right simply co-opts existing popular tunes and re-dubs them with racist lyrics, the audio equivalent of the Daily Stormer's meme campaign of overlaying Hitler quotes on images of American pop star Taylor Swift. The practice is deliberately infantile, relying on ever more extreme and novel juxtapositions between the racist lyrics and the backing track to produce a shock humour effect. Examples include Blink 1488's "All the Rapefugees" (a racist version of Blink 182's "All the Small Things") produced by Right Wing Death Squad (RWDS), and "Summer of 88" (an openly nazi version of Bryan Adams' "Summer of 69"), produced by the Daily Shoah podcast co-host Jesse Dunstan (AKA "Seventh Son" or "Sven"). The pursuit of the most offensive parodies has even resulted in white nationalist Disney songs, as produced by now-deleted YouTube channel Uncuck the Right.

The parody musical form typifies the alt-right's puerile sense of fun, a key facet of much of its cultural output. Michael Billig has highlighted the links between humour and hatred, and in his study of the racist humour in Ku Klux Klan-affili-ated websites notes Sigmund Freud's observation that jokes enable a socially accepted means of breaking taboos and "saying the unsayable." Billig also notes that humour often entails an expression of aggression towards targets, often through unflattering stereotypes, whilst enabling recourse to the excuse "it was just a joke."[31] Jazzhands McFeels, host of the podcast Fash the Nation, recognised the taboo-breaking potential of the alt-right's comedic sensibility when he told George Hawley, author of *Making Sense of the Alt-Right*, that "Humor [...] can be utilized to disarm our opposition, unravel their narratives, and pierce their arguments with elements of taboo truths we use to tactically nuke their agenda."[32]

The inherent humour of the parody form typifies the alt-right's weaponisation of humour; as the content producer for the Uncuck The Right channel told Counter-Currents, his songs are intended to be "upbeat and funny" and "edgy enough to draw young people in, but smart enough to get them thinking."[33] Weaving extreme racist messages into catchy, recognisable songs also serves to lower the guard of the listener, potentially making them more susceptible to the message in the lyrics. An SPLC study makes reference to the Daily Shoah's parody songs as a gateway into antisemitism. "You get them hooked in with Sven's songs" one forum user wrote, "then when they're all relaxed, Mike [Peinovich, AKA Mike Enoch] comes in and cracks them over the head with some real shit."[34] Whilst the parody form is, of course, inherently unoriginal and cannot be con-sidered the hallmark of a fresh far-right artistic scene, it remains a weapon in the alt-right's recruitment arsenal, and indicative of the satirical sensibility woven through the alt-right's cultural output as a whole.

Film, television and web series

The mediums of film and television are at the forefront of modern popular culture, and are recognised by some in the alt-right as carrying enormous propaganda potential. Greg Johnson writes under the pseudonym Trevor Lynch that by "integrating so many art forms, film [and television] can communicate more, and more deeply, to more people, than any single art form," going on to claim that film is "the greatest tool ever invented for shaping people's ideas and imagina-tions."[35] However, as the alt-right lacks the resources for feature-length film pro-duction and has proved too toxic for television, the movement has focussed on creating its own animated web series, on providing reviews and interpretations of television shows and film from white nationalist perspectives, and on incorporating references from film and TV culture into its propaganda.

One exception to the alt-right's blanket exile from television came courtesy of Sam Hyde and his troupe Million Dollar Extreme (MDE), providing a highly significant case study of how the alt-right's partial obfuscation of its politics through humour and irony can provide it a degree of cover. MDE started as a comedy YouTube channel, coming into prominence in 2013 following Hyde's notorious TED conference talk, in which he ridiculed the TED style with ironic and absurdist pronouncements,[36] and for stand-up routines containing racist messages.[37] After building an online following, in 2016, six episodes of MDE's sketch show, *World Peace*, aired on Cartoon Network's evening programming slot, Adult Swim. The show featured off-kilter humour with racist, sexist, and homophobic themes, as well as direct references to the alt-right's Moon Man meme and former Ku Klux Klan leader and veteran white supremacist David Duke.[38] As *VICE* journalist Allie Conti noted, *World Peace* reached an average of almost 900,000 viewers a week, making it "one of the few alt-right cultural products to ever break through to the mainstream", enabled by the fact that Hyde's comedic style made it difficult to discern whether or not "he was just playing a caricature of an alt-right persona in order to enrage liberals and didn't actually believe the ideas he was pushing."[39] As per Billig's theory, the ability to fall back on the "it's just a joke" excuse enabled *World Peace* to broadcast alt-right content to national audiences for its short running time, despite blatant displays of bigotry and references to white nationalism.[40]

World Peace remains, however, an anomaly, and in lieu of shows on television, there have been some attempts among the alt-right to establish its own web series, using easily accessible animation software such as Flash and releasing the products on YouTube and alternative platforms, all of which are also heavily soaked in humour. One example is animator Emily Youcis' series of surrealist, *The Ren & Stimpy Show*-inspired shorts featuring a character named Alfred Alfer, a 4chan-using anthropomorphic dog with an "ultra fashy alter personality, Dictator Alfred."[41] The most popular of the alt-right's web series is *Murdoch Murdoch*, a lo-fi cartoon heavily incorporating pre-existing memes and stock images. The show, which is openly influenced by South Park and Adult Swim,[42] revolves around three characters (all represented by the Wojak/Feels Guy meme popular amongst the alt-right) who loosely represent different factions of the movement. The characters explore current debates within the alt-right with an abundance of gutter racism and extremely distasteful jokes; for example in one episode the trio execute the National Alliance leader William Luther Pierce by gassing, to demonstrate "the generational divide between the current alt-right and its predecessors."[43] Again, an SPLC study of alt-right radicalisation narratives notes the humour in *Murdoch Murdoch* as a gateway into radical antisemitism.[44] The show is unique, however, in the fact that it has been relatively consistent in its output and has been able to establish a dedicated fan base within the alt-right.

A form of engagement with film and television more commonly used by the alt-right is simply to analyse and strategically misinterpret mainstream films and shows, seeking to tap into and subvert the power of the mediums. Johnson, for example, believes that although the film industry is dominated by "an alien and hostile people, the Jews," the act of reviewing mainstream films from a white nationalist perspective can expose their supposed anti-white messages, thus nullifying the alleged propaganda power of the industry. Johnson considers this practice to be "cultural warfare at its best."[45] To this end, Johnson has published, under his alias, the essay collection *Trevor Lynch's White Nationalist Guide to the Movies*.[46] Beyond decoding "anti-white propaganda" in film, the alt-right also delights in identifying supposed right-wing themes in mainstream movies and TV shows, subsequently using familiar pop culture references in its propaganda and memes as shorthand for far-right concepts. For example, *The Lord of the Rings* trilogy has been interpreted as a battle between the noble races of the West (Europe) against orcs (immigrants), invading their homeland,[47] a theme that has then been used to produce racist memes depicting orcs as sexually aggressive immigrants. The alt-right also delights in deliberately distorting films and TV shows with liberal and left-wing messages, for example alleging that the black empowerment superhero film *Black Panther* holds a pro-ethnostate message,[48] or that John Carpenter's critique of 1980s capitalism, *They Live*, is about a Jewish conspiracy.[49] Others still have been co-opted for the sheer absurdity, for example reading extreme racist themes into the 1980s/90s children's show *Saved by the Bell*.[50] Overlaying right-wing themes on the cultural products of the 1980s/90s also further enables the alt-right to exploit millennial nostalgia, as explored in the section on fashwave above.

By cloaking propaganda in film and television references, the viewer is also provided with a new framework through which racist notions can be interpreted, and thus be made more easily understandable and appealing. The most widely used metaphor across the broad Alternative Right is the "red pill" scene from *The Matrix*, in which the character Morpheus offers the protagonist Neo a choice between blissful ignorance (the blue pill) and accepting a harsh reality (the red pill). To the alt-right, accepting the red pill means to become aware to issues supposedly kept hidden by ruling elites, such as "Jewish power" and "race realism." Ignoring the obviously jarring aspects of the scene in question – Morpheus is played by Lawrence Fishburne, a black actor – the alt-right uses a simple film reference to recast radicalisation into extreme racism and antisemitism as an act of heroism worthy of a well-known pop culture protagonist, contrasting with the mindless docility of a tolerant society. The alt-right may be unable to engage wholesale in film and TV production, but the mediums have still provided an important dimension to its propaganda, a resource that can be plundered for culturally resonant tropes.

Gaming

The alt-right has long regarded the gaming community as a potentially fecund recruiting pool, being a majority white and male pastime in the US,[51] with long-standing issues around casual hate speech on the live chat functions of consoles such as Xbox Live.[52] Whilst some within the alt-right have alleged that the hobby is an organ of Jewish control, channelling the energy of men into unproductive arenas,[53] the alt-right has broadly sought to appeal to gamers by presenting gaming culture as a "last bastion" of white male hegemony under threat from feminism and cultural Marxism. The alt-right has also produced a handful of original games and modifications (mods) of existing games, which contain heavy racism and alt-right themes.

A highly significant moment in the development of the Alternative Right was the Gamergate scandal of 2014, when elements of the gaming community, the manosphere,[54] 4chan and its offshoot 8chan rallied together to unleash a barrage of abuse against female game developers. The scandal, ostensibly a backlash against the perceived encroachment of feminism into gaming culture, has been described by Angela Nagle as "possibly the biggest flame war [heated online argument] in the history of the Internet so far."[55] Figures aligned with the burgeoning Alternative Right, such as Theadore Beale (AKA Vox Day) and Milo Yiannopoulos, sought to narratively tie the scandal into a broader cultural battle between white men and interfering "social justice warriors" (SJWs). Manosphere writer Matt Forney, for example, described Gamergate as "the first successful backlash against cultural Marxism in most of our lifetimes. The white men of gaming saw leftists trying to subvert their favourite hobby, one they retreated to after society rejected them, and they said 'No more. Enough. This line you shall not cross'."[56]

Gamergate emboldened the emerging Alternative Right as a whole, and the alt-right has continued to court gamers, one noteworthy example being the Daily Stormer encouraging the distribution of nazi fliers at the offline sites of "gyms" (battle areas) of the augmented reality mobile game *Pokémon Go*.[57] Marcus Follin (AKA "The Golden One") has written that the gaming community is "largely dominated by young Western men, and in our current predicament it is important to network and talk to other people in the same situation."[58] The alt-right's heavy use of popular gaming chat apps Discord and Steam is indicative of both the roots the movement has established in gaming culture, and of its hopes to continue recruiting in this sphere.[59]

In a bid to appeal to gamers – and again to imbue race hate with a sense of fun – the alt-right has also produced a small number of original games and modifications (mods) of existing games. In doing so, the alt-right is contributing to a tradition of explicitly racist games that enable the player to enact extreme violence against minorities, the most notorious example being the 2002 first person shooter *Ethnic Cleansing*.[60] The only original alt-right example of note is *Angry Goy*, a retro, basic 16-bit game made available for free download on the Daily Stormer.[61] The game, which features a CYBERNΔZI soundtrack and references to Sam Hyde, allows the main character (voiced by the nazi Natt Danelaw) to massacre refugees, left-wingers, police officers, and gay people in a struggle against a Jewish conspiracy, throwing a Jewish professor in an oven in the process. An alt-right 'Moon Man' mod for the influential 1993 first person shooter game *DOOM* simply transforms the monsters in the game to feminists, Jews, and African Americans, who make chimpanzee noises and throw watermelons as they are annihilated by the protagonist (a choice between "Moon Man," "Zyklon Ben," or Adolf Hitler). According to gaming blog *Kotaku*, alt-right mods also exist for historical games such as *Hearts of Iron IV*, allowing the player to elect Richard Spencer as president and rebuild America as an ethnostate.[62] Whilst such games are potentially potent recruitment tools, transporting the player to a world of racist violence,[63] the alt-right has failed to fully exploit the genre, something partially attributable to the technical expertise required to produce such games.

More pertinently, however, many on the alt-right perceive there to be little need for producing original games, as white males already dominate the medium's mainstream. Some within the alt-right have, as with film, sought to read right-wing themes into computer games, an often simple pursuit given that the protagonists are usually white,[64] they often contain violent themes, and non-white characters are often stereotyped.[65] In addition, as gaming journalist Alfie Brown has highlighted, games are "often biased – even when their designers intend them to be impartial – towards conservative, patriarchal and imperialist values such as empire, dominion and conquering by force."[66] For example, Counter-Currents writer Michael Bell has argued that fantasy game *The Elder Scrolls V: Skyrim* is "saturated with racially healthy themes, heroic values, and references to Indo-European culture", continuing that "With a game like Skyrim, much of our work is already cut out for us. Players are exposed to a world where racial differences not only exist, but impact the gaming experience."[67] Both the themes in computer games such as *The Elder Scrolls V: Skyrim*, and the demographic makeup of the gaming community, lead Follin to write:

> We noble philosophers of the Real Right must realise the importance of gaming as a part of the metapolitical war, and we must defend our hegemony here with vigour. Should the blasphemous forces of Cultural Marxism gain too strong a foothold in this industry, one of the last refuges of sane thought will be compromised![68]

Indeed, the notion that computer games can serve as a gateway into the right wing is taken seriously by some commentators. Brown, for example, has written that "Games attracted rightwing players because they carried rightwing messages and produced rightwing pleasures, and, even more worryingly, they prepared apolitical gamers for the later embrace of rightwing values."[69] Unlike with the mediums of music, film, and television, gaming occupies an unusual cultural space for the alt-right, as the emphasis lies on protecting mainstream culture, rather than taking it back.

Fashion

With greater media attention, personal appearance and fashion have become increasingly important for the alt-right, which is anxious to distinguish itself from the skinhead/hillbilly Klansmen styles of other racist subcultures and the basement-dwelling, unkempt nerd stereotype of the gamer/4chan user. However, rather than establishing one distinct subcultural style, the movement has largely focused on appearing clean cut, well-educated and "respectable," and in doing so, as the Anti-Defamation League

(ADL) highlights, follows in the footsteps of suit-wearing white supremacists such as David Duke and Jared Taylor of American Renaissance.[70] The importance of looking "normal" has even been recognised by Anglin, who represents the alt-right's most overtly fascistic and wilfully offensive tendencies, who rejects the militant look in favour of simple clothing which "can be bought at H&M or Zara very cheaply."[71]

The adoption of a more refined look has resulted in some flattering coverage in the press. Spencer has long recognised that many people are repelled by the caricature "redneck, tattooed, illiterate, no-teeth" racist,[72] whereas his own smart dress sense has seen him described as a "dapper white nationalist"[73] in a tweet from *Mother Jones* in 2016, and as "An articulate and well-dressed former football player with prom-king good looks" in an article by the same outlet.[74] Typifying the preppy aesthetic of the alt-right is Identity Evropa (IE), whose members wore full suits or white polo shirts and khakis to aid its attempts to recruit "high-quality individuals from doctors to lawyers to economists."[75] An image of one young IE member, wielding a tiki torch and wearing a white polo stamped with the group's logo, became one of the most widely used images of the Charlottesville events, in part because it defied expectations of how a white supremacist should appear. The white polo/khakis look has had less traction in Europe, where IE's forebears from the ENR-inspired identitarian movement have courted a more fashionable style that has unhelpfully led some in the press to describe them as "hipster fascists."[76] Spencer was criticised within the alt-right for the negative "optics" of appearing at a college tour with his black-clad, jackbooted, militant bodyguards of the now-defunct neo-nazi street movement, the Traditionalist Workers Party (TWP), who engaged in an ugly mass brawl with antifascists in March 2018 at Michigan State University. The debacle was seen by some as a setback for a movement that had, to an extent, successfully distinguished itself visually from its forebears in the eyes of the press until that point.[77]

In her study of German far-right youth culture *The Extreme Gone Mainstream*, Cynthia Miller-Idriss writes that "Since the early 2000s, far right youth have gravitated away from the singular, hard-edged skinhead style in favor of sophisticated, fashionable, and highly profitable commercial brands that deploy coded far right extremist symbols."[78] The alt-right has largely refrained from attempting to hijack existing commercial brands (although Gavin McInnes' alt-lite "Western Chauvinist" fraternity Proud Boys has adopted yellow and black Fred Perry polo tops, to the chagrin of the brand).[79] Anglin has declared footwear brand New Balance the "Official Shoes of White People" after the brand's vice president of public affairs endorsed Donald Trump,[80] and called clothing company H&M "the official clothing brand of the Alt-Right" after accusations of racism in its advertising.[81] However, such proclamations should be read primarily as press-baiting provocations, as he has even described fast-food chain Wendy's the "official burger of the Neo-Nazi Alt-Right movement."[82] The alt-right's most recognisable stylistic signal is not a brand but rather the "fashy haircut," a severe undercut sported by the likes of Spencer and former IE leader Nathan Damigo. The haircut has a far-right tradition but also a degree of chic, due to its adoption by some hipsters and celebrities in the mid-2010s. Therefore, in accordance with Miller-Idriss' thesis, the haircut contains a degree of ambiguity and deniability to "normies," whilst still recognisable to those in the scene.

The emphasis of alt-right leaders on presenting a refined, polished outer appearance reveals something of the movement's aspirations. The fact that Anglin has to advise his followers to dress "sexy" and like a "Chad" (slang for alpha male) reveals that he knows that many of them do not already meet this standard.[83] However, the focus on personal appearance in media appearances has provided the alt-right with some small victories. As Anna Silman perceptively wrote in *The Cut*, the alt-right's emphasis on fashion is designed to "disarm opponents," continuing that "We can't be shocked when someone like Richard Spencer looks 'normal', because presenting as a legitimate, familiar, 'dapper' man is the whole point."[84] The fact that the press has been late to understand this has unfortunately played into the alt-right's hands.

Metapolitics

Whilst the alt-right's metapolitical strategy necessarily requires engaging in artistic spheres, it is fair to say that the alt-right has broadly failed in its aspiration of creating "something new, something that is our own," in the words of Joakim Andersen.[85] The alt-right's engagement in visual art, music, film/television, gaming, and fashion has largely been to directly appropriate, if not heavily imitate, existing works, styles, and scenes. It may celebrate its derivative aesthetics, such as fashwave, with wild hyperbole, but the alt-right remains, for the most part, incapable of true originality. In claiming existing figures and forms as their own, be it *Lord of the Rings*, Taylor Swift or *Skyrim*, the alt-right can give the illusion that it has a rich culture. However, even an article on Counter-Currents ponders whether the alt-right's tendency to view existing culture from far-right perspectives is "just wishful thinking," admitting that "there is a tendency to claim things that aren't ours as ours to give the impression that White Nationalism is more relevant than it actually is."[86] The movement may present itself as a vibrant creative force, but at times, it is not even able to convince its own acolytes.

To focus solely on the alt-right's failure to realise its rhetoric around artistic innovation, however, is to miss the point. In confounding its opponents by donning a suit or cloaking its politics in "ironic" humour, the alt-right has touched the edges of the mainstream, be it through complimentary remarks in the press, a tweet from a future president, or a short-lived show on television. The irony and humour pervading much of the alt-right's cultural output, in its music, its visual aesthetic, and its web series remains its most potent weapon, providing a sense of "fun" and thinly masking its extreme dehumanisation of minorities and at times genocidal urges. Moreover, the wholesale appropriation and distortion of popular cultural icons has helped to provide easy points of reference for its propaganda, broadening both the appeal of the message and the attractiveness of the movement.

Although the alt-right's engagement in the arts may often simply boil down to stealing pop culture and repackaging it with old racist ideas, its cultural efforts have appealed to new audiences, and won tangible victories, thereby actualising the metapolitical doctrines of the ENR and distinguishing itself from other post-war white nationalists preoccupied with the ballot or the bullet.

Notes

1 Charlie Farnsbarns, "A Reminder that England Still Exists: Detectorists," *Counter-Currents Publishing*, 3 October 2018. https://www.counter-currents.com/2018/10/a-reminder-that-england-still-exists/
2 Daniel Friberg, *The Real Right Returns: A Handbook for the True Opposition* (United Kingdom: Arktos Media Ltd., 2015), 20.
3 For more on the European New Right, the alt-right and metapolitics see Chapter 1 "The European Roots of Alt-Right Ideology."
4 Guillaume Faye, *Why We Fight: Manifesto of the European Resistance* (United Kingdom: Arktos Media Ltd., 2011), 193.
5 Brad Griffin (AKA Hunter Wallace), "Why White Nationalism 1.0 Failed," *Occidental Dissent*, 18 July 2017. http://www.occidentaldissent.com/2017/07/18/why-white-nationalism-1-0-failed/
6 Ibid.
7 Vicky Osterweil, "Mass Appeal: How contemporary fascist aesthetics ask, excuse, and normalize violence," *Real Life Magazine*, 15 June, 2017. http://reallifemag.com/mass-appeal/
8 Ibid.
9 Andrew Anglin, "The Official Soundtrack of the Alt-Right," *Daily Stormer*, 13 August 2016. https://dailystormer.name/the-official-soundtrack-of-the-alt-right/
10 For more on antisemitism in the Alternative Right, see Chapter 4 "The Alternative Right, Antisemitism and the Holocaust."
11 Joakim Andersen, *Rising from the Ruins: The Right of the 21st Century* (United Kingdom: Arktos Media Ltd., 2018), 210.
12 Andrew Anglin quoted in David Neiwert, *Alt-America: The Rise of the Radical Right in the Age of Trump* (London: Verso, 2017), 256.
13 Andrew Anglin, "Decision Time for the Alt-Right: Which Way White Man?" *Daily Stormer*, 22 March 2018. https://dailystormer.name/decision-time-for-the-alt-right-which-way-white-man/
14 Donna Zuckerberg, *Not All Dead White Men: Classics and Misogyny in the Digital Age* (Cambridge, Massachusetts: Harvard University Press, 2018). Quote from Introduction [Online – Google Books].
15 Heidi Morse, "Classics and the Alt-Right: Historicizing Visual Rhetorics of White Supremacy," *Learn Speak Act: Liberal Arts in the Moment*, 15 February 2018. https://sites.lsa.umich.edu/learn-speak-act/2018/02/15/classics-and-the-alt-right/
16 Alex Graham, "Classics in an Age of Confusion," *Counter-Currents Publishing*, 22 October 2018. https://www.counter-currents.com/2018/10/classics-in-an-age-of-confusion/
17 Andrew Anglin, "Classical Art vs. Modern Nihilistic Jew Crap," *Daily Stormer*, 27 June 2014. https://dailystormer.name/classical-art-vs-modern-nihilistic-jew-crap/
18 For an informative article on vaporwave and the development of fashwave with a focus on the utilisation of classical artwork in the genre, see: Jip Lemmens, "Putting the 'Neon' in 'Neo-Nazi': The Aesthetic of Fashwave," *Eidolon Classics Journal*, 19 October 2017. https://eidolon.pub/putting-the-neon-in-neo-nazi-4cea7c471a66
19 Anglin, "Decision Time for the Alt-Right: Which Way White Man?"
20 薄熙来, *Race Ghost Roast to Roast 3 - Eulogy for Ironmarch | Weev podcast* [Online video]. Available at: https://www.youtube.com/watch?v=uFkpkWagpBE [Accessed 14 July 2018].
21 Lemmens, "Putting the 'Neon' in 'Neo-Nazi': The Aesthetic of Fashwave."

22 Penn Bullock and Eli Kerry, "Trumpwave and Fashwave Are Just the Latest Disturbing Examples of the Far-Right Appropriating Electronic Music," *Thump: VICE*, 30 January 2017. https://thump.vice.com/en_uk/article/mgwk7b/fashwave-trumpwave-far-right-appropriating-electronic-music

23 Bullock and Kerry, "Trumpwave and Fashwave Are Just the Latest Disturbing Examples of the Far-Right Appropriating Electronic Music."

24 Karl Spracklen, "Nazi punks folk off: leisure, nationalism, cultural identity and the consumption of metal and folk music," *Leisure Studies* 32:4 (2013), 415–428.

25 Alice Conti, "The Alt-Right Is a Subculture without a Culture," *VICE*, 4 April 2018. https://www.vice.com/en_uk/article/evm7wm/the-alt-right-is-a-subculture-without-a-culture

26 Bullock and Kerry, "Trumpwave and Fashwave Are Just the Latest Disturbing Examples of the Far-Right Appropriating Electronic Music."

27 Anglin, "Decision Time for the Alt-Right: Which Way White Man?"

28 Bullock and Kerry, "Trumpwave and Fashwave Are Just the Latest Disturbing Examples of the Far-Right Appropriating Electronic Music."

29 Richard Spencer (@RichardBSpencer), 29 May 2016, 6:02PM. https://twitter.com/RichardBSpencer/status/737092092300660737

30 Colonel Gunter Brumm, "Fashwave Friday: The Dawn of Fashwave Fridays," *Daily Stormer*, 19 August 2016. https://dailystormer.name/fashwave-friday-the-dawn-of-fashwave-fridays/

31 Michael Billig, "Humour and Hatred: The racist jokes of the Ku Klux Klan," *Discourse and Society*, 12:3 (2001), 267–289.

32 Jazzhands McFeels, quoted in: George Hawley, *Making Sense of the Alt-Right* (New York: Columbia University Press, 2017), 76.

33 Dorin Alexandru, "Making Memes Memorable: Interview with 'Uncuck The Right'," *Counter-Currents Publishing*, 29 January 2016. https://www.counter-currents.com/2016/01/interview-with-uncuck-the-right/

34 Hatewatch Staff, "McInnes, Molyneux, and 4chan: Investigating pathways to the alt-right," *Southern Poverty Law Center*, 19 April 2018. https://www.splcenter.org/20180419/mcinnes-molyneux-and-4chan-investigating-pathways-alt-right

35 Greg Johnson (AKA Trevor Lynch), "Why I Write," *Counter-Currents Publishing*, 1 August 2011. https://www.counter-currents.com/2011/08/why-i-write-11/

36 drewwerds, 2013, *Sam Hyde's 2070 Paradigm Shift* [Online video]. Available at: https://www.youtube.com/watch?v=KTJn_DBTnrY [Accessed 27 July 2018].

37 MDE Never Dies, 2015, *Sam Hyde Migrant Crisis stand up routine Sept 29th, 2015* [Online video]. Available at: https://www.youtube.com/watch?v=h5oWcqUwDAU [Accessed 27 July 2018].

38 Conti, "The Alt-Right Is a Subculture without a Culture."

39 Ibid.

40 Ibid.

41 Emily Youcis, *Emily Youcis – The Ascent of Art in the Alt-Right – Radio 3Fourteen* [Online video]. Available at: https://www.youtube.com/watch?v=H7oIRfzdaIo [Accessed 23 July 2018].

42 Murdoch Murdoch quoted in Hannibal Bateman, "A Conversation with Murdoch Murdoch," *Radix Journal*, 15 April 2016. https://radixjournal.com/2016/04/2016-4-15-murdoch-murdoch-speak/

43 Ibid.

44 Hatewatch Staff, "McInnes, Molyneux, and 4chan: Investigating pathways to the alt-right."

45 Johnson, "Why I Write."

46 Leah Nelson, "Hating On Hollywood," *Southern Poverty Law Center*, 16 May 2013. https://www.splcenter.org/fighting-hate/intelligence-report/2013/hating-hollywood

47 Greg Johnson (AKA Trevor Lynch), "The Fellowship of the Ring," *Counter-Currents Publishing*, 17 July 2010. https://www.counter-currents.com/2010/07/the-fellowship-of-the-ring/

48 James Dunphy, "Toward a White Wakanda," *Counter-Currents Publishing*, 23 February 2018. https://www.counter-currents.com/2018/02/toward-a-white-wakanda/

49 John Patterson, "They Live: John Carpenter's Action Flick Needs to be Saved from Neo-Nazis," *The Guardian*, 9 January 2017. https://www.theguardian.com/film/film blog/2017/jan/09/they-live-john-carpenter-neo-nazis

50 Andrew Anglin, "What the Fuck is a Neon-Nazi?" *Daily Stormer*, 27 June 2018. https://dailystormer.name/what-the-fuck-is-a-neon-nazi/

51 "Distribution of gamers in the United States as of April 2015, by ethnicity," Statista, https://www.statista.com/statistics/494870/distribution-of-gamers-by-ethnicity-usa/ and "Distribution of computer and video gamers in the United States from 2006 to 2018, by gender," Statista. https://www.statista.com/statistics/232383/gender-split-of-us-computer-and-video-gamers/

52 K.L. Gray, "Deviant Bodies, Stigmatized Identities, and Racist Acts: Examining the experiences of African-American gamers in Xbox Live," *New Review of Hypermedia and Multimedia*, 18:4 (2012), 261–276.

53 Charles Chapel, "Weaning Ourselves from Entertainment Media," *Daily Stormer*, 29 March 2014. https://dailystormer.name/weaning-ourselves-from-entertainment-media/

54 For more information on the manosphere and its relationship to the alt-right, see Chapter 12 "From Anger to Ideology: A History of the Manosphere."

55 Angela Nagle, *Kill All Normies: Online Culture Wars from 4chan and Tumblr to Trump and the Alt-Right* (Croydon: Zero Books, 2017), 21.

56 Red Ice TV, 2017, *Matthew Forney – White Men Say No More – Identitarian Ideas IX* [Online video]. Available at: https://www.youtube.com/watch?v=4MepvhcofBg [Accessed 22 June 2017].

57 Neiwert, *Alt-America*, 261.

58 Marcus Follin, "Gaming: Making it Glorious Instead of Degenerate," *AltRight.com*. http s://altright.com/2015/11/09/gaming-making-it-glorious-instead-of-degenerate/

59 Jacob Davey and Julia Ebner, "The Fringe Insurgency: Connectivity, Convergence and Mainstreaming of the Extreme Right," *Institute of Strategic Dialogue Report*, 2017. https://www.isdglobal.org/wp-content/uploads/2017/10/The-Fringe-Insurgency-221017.pdf

60 "Games Extremists Play," *Southern Poverty Law Center*, 5 March 2002. https://www.sp lcenter.org/fighting-hate/intelligence-report/2002/games-extremists-play

61 Andrew Anglin, "'Angry Goy' The Ethnic Cleansing Game Starring Natt Danelaw," *Daily Stormer*, 1 January 2017. https://dailystormer.name/angry-goy-the-ethnic-clea nsing-game-starring-natt-danelaw/

62 Luke Winkie, "The Struggle over Gamers Who Use Mods to Create Racist Alternate Histories," *Kotaku*, 6 June 2018. https://kotaku.com/the-struggle-over-gamers-who-use-mods-to-create-racist-1826606138

63 Andrew Selepak's essay provides useful background and analysis of the phenomenon of racist games: Andrew Selepak, "Skinhead Super Mario Brothers: An Examination of Racist and Violent Games on White Supremacist Web Sites," *Journal of Criminal Justice and Popular Culture*, 17:1 (2010), 1–47.

64 B. Mitchell Peck, Paul R. Ketchum and David G. Embrick, "Racism and Sexism in the Gaming World: Reinforcing or changing stereotypes in computer games?" *Journal of Media and Communication Studies*, 3:6, 2011, 212–220.

65 Gray, "Deviant Bodies, Stigmatized Identities, and Racist Acts: Examining the experiences of African-American gamers in Xbox Live," *New Review of Hypermedia and Multimedia*.

66 https://www.theguardian.com/games/2018/aug/13/video-games-are-political-here s-how-they-can-be-progressive

67 Michael Bell, "The Elder Scrolls V: Skyrim," *Counter-Currents Publishing*, 11 November 2011. https://www.counter-currents.com/2011/12/the-elder-scrolls-v-skyrim/

68 Follin, "Gaming: Making it Glorious Instead of Degenerate."

69 Alfie Brown, "How Video Games Are Fuelling the Rise of the Far Right," *The Guardian*, 12 March 2018. https://www.theguardian.com/commentisfree/2018/mar/12/video-games-fuel-rise-far-right-violent-misogynist

70 "Re-Branding White Supremacy," *Anti-Defamation League*, 16 December 2016. https://www.adl.org/blog/re-branding-white-supremacy

71 Andrew Anglin, "Self-Help Sunday: Fashion is Not a 'Sense,' It is a Science," *Daily Stormer*, 1 July 2018. https://dailystormer.name/self-help-sunday-fashion-is-not-a-sense-it-is-a-science/

72 Richard Spencer in: Lauren M. Fox, "The Hatemonger Next Door," 29 September 2013. https://www.salon.com/2013/09/29/the_hatemonger_next_door/

73 Mother Jones (@MotherJones). 3 November 2016, 12:15 AM. https://twitter.com/motherjones/status/794075448334491648?lang=en

74 Josh Harkinson, "Meet the White Nationalist Trying to Ride the Trump Train to Lasting Power," *Mother Jones*, 27 October 2016. https://www.motherjones.com/politics/2016/10/richard-spencer-trump-alt-right-white-nationalist/

75 M. L. Nestel, "Veteran Posts Signs at Colleges Telling White to Be "Great Again'," *The Daily Beast*, 10 October 2016. https://www.thedailybeast.com/veteran-posts-signs-at-colleges-telling-whites-to-be-great-again

76 Paul Bracchi, "The Hipster Fascists: Well-dressed, highly educated and from respectable families. Why this new British far-Right group is the most sinister and dangerous yet," *The Times*, 20 May 2018. https://www.thetimes.co.uk/article/the-hipster-fascists-breathing-new-life-into-the-british-far-right-6hvtmq63k

77 Greg Johnson, 'Interview on Unite the Right 1 & 2', *Counter-Currents Publishing*, 9 August 2018. https://www.counter-currents.com/2018/08/interview-on-unite-the-right-i-and-ii/ and Andrew Anglin, *Decision Time for Alt-Right: Which Way, White Man?* 22 March 2018. https://dailystormer.name/decision-time-for-the-alt-right-which-way-white-man/

78 Cynthia Miller-Idriss, *The Extreme Gone Mainstream: Commercialization and Far Right Youth Culture in Germany* (New Jersey: Princeton University Press, 2017), 1–2.

79 Kyle Swenson, "The Alt-right's Proud Boys Love Fred Perry Polo Shirts. The feeling is not mutual," *The Washington Post*, 10 July 2017. https://www.washingtonpost.com/news/morning-mix/wp/2017/07/10/the-alt-rights-proud-boys-love-fred-perry-polo-shirts-the-feeling-is-not-mutual/?utm_term=.d524db886003

80 Andrew Anglin, "Your Uniform: New Balance Just Became the Official Shoes of White People," *Daily Stormer*, 12 November 2016. https://dailystormer.name/your-uniform-new-balance-just-became-the-shoes-of-white-people/

81 Andrew Anglin, "Official Alt-Right Clothing Retailer H&M Doubles-Down on Nigger-Hate, Putting 'Allah' on Socks!," *Daily Stormer*, 29 January 2018. https://dailystormer.name/official-alt-right-clothing-retailer-hm-doubles-down-on-nigger-hate-putting-allah-on-socks/

82 Andrew Anglin, "After Pepe Post, Daily Stormer Endorses Wendy's as the Official Fast Food Chain of the Alt-Right," *Daily Stormer*, 4 January 2017. https://dailystormer.name/after-pepe-post-daily-stormer-endorses-wendys-as-the-official-fast-food-chain-of-the-alt-right/

83 Andrew Anglin, "PSA: When the Alt-Right Hits the Street, You Wanna be Ready," *Daily Stormer* 19 August 2017. https://dailystormer.name/psa-when-the-internet-becomes-real-life-and-the-alt-right-hits-the-street-you-wanna-be-ready/

84 Anna Silman, "For the Alt-Right, Dapper Suits Are a Propaganda Tool," *The Cut*, 23 November 2016. https://www.thecut.com/2016/11/how-the-alt-right-uses-style-as-a-propaganda-tool.html

85 Andersen, *Rising from the Ruins*, 301.

86 Farnsbarns, "A Reminder that England Still Exists: Detectorists."

9

THE ROLE OF THE TROLL

Online antagonistic communities and the Alternative Right

It is impossible to understand the broad Alternative Right – both the racial nationalist alt-right and the cultural nationalist alt-lite – without understanding how it operates online. Though the traditional far right has, of course, used the internet as a tool, the Alternative Right's use of a specific online trolling subculture has allowed it to advance its cultural war and attract a younger audience than most existing far-right movements. Moreover, while the Alternative Right is a movement that brings American groups and European far-right ideas together, it is also partly borne from online spaces, and one in particular which began as part of a non-political forum. Not only would this online world provide the Alternative Right with a style and means of engaging in harassment of those whom it deemed inferior, but its gradually politicised virtual spaces would act as a channel for many towards the movement.

The origins of Alternative Right trolling

Such harassment is emblematic of what HOPE not hate designates as "Online Antagonistic Communities": online communities built around a variety of interests but all of which engage in exclusionary, antagonistic behaviour.[1] Such communities are found on all sides of the political spectrum, and can also be non-political. Their point of convergence with the Alternative Right occurs when their antagonism is directed against what they perceive as the left-liberal political and social hegemony. Key to this antagonism is the use of trolling: the act of being deliberately offensive or provocative online with the aim of provoking a hostile, negative, outraged reaction.[2] Trolling as a behaviour dates as far back as the late 1980s but it is the subculture of anti-progressive individuals self-identifying as trolls, which emerged primarily from the 4chan.org forum in the 2000s and especially on the 4chan.org/pol/ subforum founded in 2011, that became so important in the formation of what is now known as the Alternative Right.[3]

Progenitors to this style of trolling were already prevalent in the 2000s across the web – including on mainstream social media platforms like Facebook and Twitter. Moreover, both "ironic" and entirely serious expressions of extreme bigotry (and sharing of extreme content more generally) have been part-and-parcel of 4chan since its inception, partly given the site's design which placed few restraints on users: there is no sign-up, they can post anonymously and threads are deleted if they become inactive.[4] Despite this, 4chan's politics were not so widely and self-consciously far right in nature earlier on. The targets of trolls' harassment – if political at all – were often groups and figures on the right as well as the left. As Whitney Phillips has noted, early on "historically dominant groups" were also frequent targets, with "White Christians and Republicans in particular" generating "a great deal of trollish taunting."[5] Figures in the far right were also targets of 4chan campaigns, including Hal Turner, a white nationalist who lost thousands of dollars after his site was taken down by hackers that he believed originated on sites including 4chan.[6] Moreover, the widely-adopted "Anonymous" label for activists and hackers originating on 4chan, included many supportive of the Wikileaks whistleblowing site[7] and the progressive "Occupy" movement, for example.[8]

Yet, once one considers what such a variation in targets reveals about the implicit cultural logic of this trolling subculture, 4chan's rightward turn begins to make more sense. As Phillips notes:

> there [was] a through line in the trolls' targeting practices: the concept of exploitability. Trolls believe that nothing should be taken seriously, and therefore regard public displays of sentimentality, political conviction, and/or ideological rigidity as a call to trolling arms[9]

No community can exist in a political vacuum, of course, and the prioritisation of exploitability by 4chan's trolls highlighted the burgeoning underlying political current of this subculture. As Phillips elaborates:

> Trolls [...] are champions of the idea that the practical ability to accomplish some goal ("I am able to troll this person") justifies, if not necessitates, its pursuit ("therefore it is my right to do so"). Nontrolls are quick to reject this line of reasoning on the grounds that it is callous, solipsistic, and exploitative. In other contexts, however, "I can, therefore, I should be able to" is taken for granted, and in some circles is explicitly fetishized.[10]

Within this subculture, then, a distinctly libertarian and often chauvinist perspective emerged which, through coupling a rejection of "political conviction" and "ideological rigidity" (at least when it came to others) with a playful, ironic detachment from engagement with taboos, created fertile ground for, and a predisposition towards, exposure to extreme ideas. Ostensibly, this could have allowed exposure to such ideas from the left just as much as the right, yet the desire to ridicule and harass all, including the oppressed, necessarily carries with it an equal platform for expressions of bigotry, prejudice, and inegalitarianism. Moreover, in maintaining that the freedom to exploit all views for the sake of trolling is the community's one inviolable principle, this means protecting such expressions from being silenced. (This also obviously puts the already oppressed at a further disadvantage in this realm, since these protected expressions are precisely aimed at silencing them.)

This presumption of unfettered freedom of expression and speech would be a thread running throughout the Alternative Right's developing self-conception. Reliance on this argument is not a new tactic for far-right movements, yet Phillips' analysis of its partial origins in this online subculture in this particular case goes some way towards explaining precisely why it would be so integral to the – especially American – Alternative Right. As she notes:

> trolls' more extreme actions call attention to the ugly side of free speech, which so often is cited by people whose speech has always been the most free [...] to justify hateful behavior towards marginalized groups. In these cases, claims to protected speech are often less about the legal parameters of the First Amendment and more about not wanting to be told what to do, particularly by individuals whose perspective one doesn't respect.[11]

Given the ephemerality of content on 4chan, establishing how quickly it took a far-right turn is difficult. Nonetheless, more recent research suggests that between 2015 and 2018 /pol/, at least, saw a steady rise in racist and fascist terms.[12] Prior to this, it appears the above-discussed logic of an implicit veering toward, and protection of, expressions of extreme right-leaning ideas began to play out fully with the increasingly rightward turn of its "/new/" subforum, added 7 April 2006 and removed on 17 January 2011 because of its racist focus (the basis also for an earlier removal).[13] The most extreme contingent frequenting /new/ migrated in part to a duplicate forum, "4chon," until the creation of the "politically incorrect" or "/pol/" subforum created on 4chan on 10 November 2011. Seen by many as a means of isolating far-right content to a single forum on the site, /pol/ nonetheless has proved to be a key hub for far-right activity on the web ever since, with much of its users' creations and campaigns spreading onto other sites, to social media and at times into the mainstream media. Of course, previous sites and forums existed for far-right discussion, most notably the white nationalist Stormfront forum which had been running since 1995. However, /pol/ is unprecedented as a point of origin for far-right online campaigns, likely due to the similar pre-existing practices of the trolling subculture from which it emerged.

Moreover, given that /pol/ was a replacement of the already right-leaning /new/ subforum on 4chan, it had already developed its political tendencies independently of the first explicitly Alternative Right-linked forums online, such as the "r/altright" subforum on Reddit.com (a hugely popular forum site dedicated to numerous topics other than just the far right) created on 3 March 2010 and Richard Spencer's AlternativeRight.com website, created 28 March 2009.[14] Other later alt-right communities online, such as TheRightStuff.biz created on 4 October

2012 and the Daily Stormer site created on 4 July 2013, exemplify the increasing convergence of these two online communities – /pol/'s far-right tendency and the explicit white nationalism of the Alternative Right – given their mixture of trolling and serious engagement with far-right ideas.

In addition to the rightward turn of 4chan's trolling subculture being explained by the logic of its internal norms playing out quite naturally, there is evidence of some external recruitment efforts by the far right early on. Most notable, on the aforementioned Stormfront, which has a subforum referred to as "Swarmfront" that has existed since 2011 and is dedicated to seeding interest in white nationalist politics on other sites. Posts on Swarmfront suggest there was an active discussion of recruiting on both 4chan[15] and Reddit[16] that began independently in January 2014. Sites that were part of the Alternative Right themselves also discussed recruitment, including the aforementioned Daily Stormer in an article posted in March 2015, declaring "We brought 4chan over to our side long ago. Now, we need to focus on Reddit."[17]

Gamergate and the Alternative Right's impact on the alternative media

A key moment in the development of this trolling subculture's underlying politics was the "Gamergate" phenomenon, which exemplified and catalysed both this subculture's radicalisation and what it would contribute to the Alternative Right. In 2014, the ex-boyfriend of a female US game developer alleged online that she had cheated on him with various men in the video game industry, including gaming journalists. Though refuted, this led to a discussion on ethics in video game journalism and culminated in sexist elements from within and without the gaming community seizing the opportunity to criticise an alleged overreach of feminism into the supposedly male spaces of gaming. While this centred on the gaming community, of whom only a part will have overlapped with the trolling subculture discussed above, it acted as a catalyst for this contingent to be radicalised further and established a firm link between this subculture and the wider Alternative Right. Whilst the uniting interest for many across the two camps was initially a general anti-political correctness stance, it is now well understood that Gamergate acted as a pathway to the Alternative Right for many.[18] Likewise, the events acted as a stepping stone in the careers of figures in the Alternative Right, most notably Milo Yiannopoulos, who was at that time technology editor at the far-right Breitbart News Network website during Gamergate and who used the unfolding events to further establish his reputation as a far-right media personality.[19]

Gamergate involved extensive internet harassment, including rape and death threats aimed at feminist critics of the gaming community.[20] Such tactics were implemented by several factions that were – or would become – constituent parts of the Alternative Right and, since then, the movement has continued to use trolling and harassment both to gain publicity and as a form of intimidation. This has included the aforementioned alt-lite figure Milo Yiannopoulos, who played both a crucial role in stoking up the harassment around Gamergate and a subsequent role in the online harassment of actor Leslie Jones (which resulted in his permanent ban from Twitter). Another notable case is that of alt-right figure Andrew Anglin from the aforementioned Daily Stormer website whose own "Troll Army" has engaged in multiple antisemitic harassment campaigns. Importantly, antagonistic trolling has deeply influenced the conduct of the Alternative Right beyond its use of online harassment. It has helped to shape its broader rhetorical strategies of offensively stereotyping and ridiculing minority groups and opponents on the left and right as well as its manipulation of the media through strategically amplifying fake news. This is often achieved through the use of bots – computer software which interacts with systems and users and so can be used on social media to spread information – and extensive social media networks of real users who can quickly organise online campaigns.[21]

While this more extreme online culture emerged on sites like 4chan, it has also informed the tone and style of much of the wider Alternative Right, including the alternative media which have grown alongside the activists themselves. This right-wing alternative media stretches from the edges of the mainstream – most notoriously Breitbart – to mid-level online media organisations like Rebel Media and InfoWars and down to social media communities and individuals engaged in citizen journalism and political and social commentary, such as vloggers Carl Benjamin (AKA "Sargon of Akkad"), who emerged from the Gamergate community, and Lauren Southern. While portraying themselves as "news" platforms, outlets in this alternative media world have adopted many of the rhetorical strategies and antagonistic attitudes of 4chan's trolling subculture, when engaging in their hostile journalism and commentary (consider the Breitbart headline, "Would you rather your child had Feminism or Cancer?"[22]).

Also drawing on this particular troll culture is the use of media manipulation strategies by figures in the Alternative Right-wing media community. For example, former Rebel Media correspondent Jack Posobiec was pivotal in amplifying the #MacronLeaks disinformation campaign. The attack was a deliberate attempt to misinform the French electorate prior to the final round of the 2017 French presidential election by mixing in fake documents with genuine hacked documents from Emmanuel Macron's campaign team. Nicolas Vanderbiest of UC Louvain demonstrated that Posobiec ran early with the hacked documents and was key in spreading awareness of them across Twitter.[23] Furthermore, an analysis by the Atlantic Council's Digital Forensics Research Lab of Posobiec's Twitter "reporting" of the leaked documents (which he told the BBC he had been alerted to by the 4chan user who first posted them online) also suggested the use of automated bots to amplify his tweet, as it received 87 retweets in the first 5 minutes. Their analysis concludes: "[…] the #MacronLeaks hashtag was initially launched in the US and was driven by a cluster of alt-right accounts and probable bots. It was then picked up by Le Pen supporters, and probable bots, and passed on to the French audience."[24]

It is also worth noting that a feature of online antagonistic communities' approach to manipulating the media converges with an influential idea within the Alternative Right that has its roots in the European postwar far-right *Nouvelle Droite* (European New Right) movement. Amongst other ideas, the Alternative Right took from the ENR the notion of "metapolitics."[25] This is the idea, itself adopted from the Italian Marxist Antonio Gramsci, that activism must focus on affecting culture before anything else, so as to shift the accepted topics, terms, and positions of public discussion to create a social and political environment more open and potentially accepting of an ideology. This approach to activism overlaps somewhat with what Phillips describes as trolls' use of *détournement* (or, "misappropriation"). As she explains:

> détournement is the process by which the existing meaning of a particular statement or artifact is turned against itself [...] détournement challenge[s] dominant ideals through creative and often absurdist appropriation [...] by détourning [...] trolls [...] [allow] a particular statement or artifact to indict itself through itself.[26]

To some extent, the Alternative Right's metapolitical goal has been to engage in a series of campaigns aimed at *détournement* of popular left-liberal ideas and terms. One example is their subversion of the phrase "cultural enrichment," initially denoting the benefits multiculturalism can bring in the form of exposure to other cultures, the Alternative Right recast the phrase sarcastically in reference to what they see as the harms brought by peoples of non-white and non-Western culture.

Who are the trolls?

Whilst there are numerous high-profile public figures within the Alternative Right, the majority of the movement's adherents are anonymous and confine their activism to the web. It is incredibly difficult to track these faceless activists engaging in online abuse as their contributions can quickly disappear under a deluge of further such content or, as is often the case on 4chan.org/pol/, go entirely unarchived. Despite this, the profile of public figures in the Alternative Right, along with the behaviour of its anonymous members online, allows us to reasonably infer a general picture of the average person within the movement. The public figures of the Alternative Right are overwhelmingly white middle- and lower-middle-class men from the USA, UK, and northern Europe. Interpretative studies of those identifying, or expressing aligning beliefs with the Alternative Right found across online trolling subcultures point to the same demographic.[27] Communicated by their comments and memes is support for white, Western, male, cisgendered, heterosexual identity politics and the ridicule and harassment of groups that they view as inferior or a threat to this identity acts as an exclusionary tool against members of these groups. The assumption among those belonging to these online communities, therefore, is that they are spaces populated by, and mainly for, such men.[28]

Of course, as Amelia Tait has highlighted in a profile of female alt-right 4chan users, this assumption can lead others to doubt the identity of someone claiming to be female even when they are in fact so.[29] Moreover, this is potentially true for users whose identity does not align with this assumed demographic in further ways. Coupled with this is the likely possibility that many other users will choose to hide facets of their identity which are precisely those being excluded and attacked. Given such possibilities, even 4chan's own claim that ~30% of its users are female, for example, may be conservative.[30] Nonetheless, the key takeaway here is not what the exact demographics of these trolling spaces are – something we can never precisely determine, given their nature – but what their social norms reveal about the supremacist assumptions they maintain. As Ryan Milner contends in *The World Made Meme: Public Conversations and Participatory Media*, whiteness and masculinity can frequently be "dominant in mediated collectives" like the trolling subculture on 4chan.[31] With the veer towards widespread support of far-right politics within these virtual spaces, however, the dominance that was previously largely presumed and maintained through exclusionary, offensive ridicule, gave way to increased explicit support (often, nonetheless, alongside such "humour").

It is also worth noting evidence from these online spaces that suggests the Alternative Right finds much more international support, or at least ideological overlap, than is often assumed. Though reliable demographic data from these online spaces is hard to come by, an in-depth study of the user base of 4chan.org/pol/ from Hine et al. suggests that "while Americans dominate the conversation in terms of absolute numbers, many other countries (both native English speaking and not) are well represented in terms of posts per capita."[32] An important caveat here is that users can use proxies to hide their true locations. However, when the researchers tried to control for this by tying frequent region-specific posts to users' country flags, "the majority of posts from countries seem[ed] to match geographically."[33]

Another area of insight concerns trolls' economic and social signifiers. With respect to their lifestyles, writer Dale Beran summed up the popular external stereotype of 4chan users, stating they were:

> a group of primarily young males who spent a lot of the time at the computer, so much so they had retreated into virtual worlds of games, T.V., and now the networks of the internet. This was where most or all of their interaction, social or otherwise took place. The real world, by contrast, above their mothers' basements, was a place they did not succeed, perhaps a place they did not fundamentally understand.[34]

Beran goes on to note that the activities of certain groups on 4chan suggested a more varied picture, from political hackers to "professionals and successful people [...] who used it only for amusement."[35] Nonetheless, the majority still maintain "a culture of hopelessness, of knowing 'the system is rigged'," a worldview reflected in the self-conception of many within these online communities.[36] This includes a deep sense of economic failure or despair, exemplified by a popular self-identity amongst these users of being a "NEET," taken from a 1999 UK government report classifying those aged 16–24 who were "Not in Education, Employment or Training."[37] Similarly, a popular self-conception on these online spaces concerns users' sense of sexual and romantic failure or disaffection, exemplified by the "incel" subculture of the anti-feminist and misogynist "manosphere" community that overlaps with the Alternative Right. This term is short for "involuntary celibate": someone who, as one manosphere forum describes, "tries to find romantic relationships without success and is very pessimistic about his chances."[38]

Finally, it is also worth considering how the development of the trolling element of the Alternative Right was an alternative reaction to the increasingly pessimistic political environment in which this subculture developed. Given the global social, economic and political upheavals throughout the 2000s and 2010s, it makes sense that a subculture that is focused on exploiting the topics of the day in an ugly and juvenile manner would be in its element given the number of sensitive and polarising topics that were emerging in news headlines. Philips draws attention to this when quoting an entry from the trolling mainstay, the "Encyclopaedia Dramatica" website, concerning "lulz" – a term referring to trolls' professed object of desire, namely the humour of their cruel ridicule:

> "Lulz is engaged by internet users who have witnessed one major economic/environmental/political disaster too many," the entry reads, "and who thus view a state of voluntary, gleeful sociopathy over the world's current apoplectic state, as being superior to being continually [emotional]."[39]

The role of economic, social/romantic and political pessimism undoubtedly played a role in the emotional detachment required for the nascent trolling Alternative Right to engage in extreme online harassment and politics. For some, this pessimistic outlook will have catalysed a retreat into nihilism, but it also served as the basis for both individual trolls' developing sense of identity[40] as well as the building blocks of their sense of community with one another.[41]

Trolling, irony, pseudo-intellectualism, and far-right sympathies

Racist, homophobic, and sexist "shitposting" (posts intended to derail an online conversation by being pointless and often offensive) on sites such as 4chan long predate the coalescence of the Alternative Right. As a 2011 study was already able to point out: "Communities like 4chan have immense impact on Internet culture [and its] anonymous, ephemeral community design is playing a strong role in that cultural influence."[42] The prevalence of this trolling behaviour online meant the Alternative Right was imbued from the start with a highly casual attitude towards symbols of hatred. The aforementioned Andrew Anglin of the Daily Stormer, which makes heavy use of extreme racist imagery and terms, has stated in a description of his radicalisation that he "had always been into 4chan, as I am at heart a troll" and referred to the moment at which he "got into Hitler" being when

4chan's "/new/" subforum was "going full Nazi."[43] Daily Stormer site administrator, Andrew Auernheimer (AKA weev), also gained notoriety as a troll long before he openly adopted white supremacy.[44]

In an insightful remark, Mike Peinovich (AKA Mike Enoch) of the The Right Stuff said the following when describing his site's origins:

> we started trolling, that's how we started The Right Stuff, that's where it came from. Literally, we wanted to bother liberals [...] We loved to trigger them. We loved to go in and just hit them on all their points and through this sort of opposition to that we actually developed some kind of coherent worldview, and that worldview centred around race politics.[45]

Peinovich's comment highlights the possibility that, for many in the Alternative Right, an initial impulse to troll liberal sensibilities with "ironic" extreme opinions eventually led them to a sincere belief in far-right politics. As Richard Spencer told *Vice* in a December 2016 interview:

> I have actually met some kids from 4chan who started reading some Identitarian ... or some of Kevin MacDonald's work, or anything critical of race relations, immigration, uhh, Jewish influence, so on, and they actually read this stuff so that they could troll people. [...] That was their entrance to it but after reading it they were actually convinced by it.[46]

Both Peinovich's and Spencer's anecdotes bring out the fact that trolling humour was not entirely reserved for the avowed far right. Rather, it was well in tune with the irony-heavy popular culture that arose in the 2000s. As Philips argues, trolls "digest" the culture of the time through their trolling output[47] and so what they trolled and the manner in which they did it already resonated far beyond the Alternative Right's most obscure, dark corners of the web. It should come as little surprise, then, that the more popular, alt-lite (the non-racial nationalist wing of the Alternative Right) vloggers will poke fun at the widely ridiculed stereotype of the "Social Justice Warrior," and receive interest from those with little prior familiarity with far-right politics. The wider resonance of trolling-influenced humour is so central to the Alternative Right that it has spilled over into the offline world in various ways. Given its hatred of the liberal establishment, the Alternative Right has trolled mainstream media organisations by tricking them into thinking otherwise innocuous symbols are being used with the intention of covertly expressing far right beliefs. These include the images of milk as a symbol of white supremacy, the use of the "OK" hand gesture as a symbol of white power, and the "peace" sign gesture as a denial of non-binary gender identity.[48] This impulse explains the popularity of Pepe the Frog, a cartoon frog that has been a perpetual representation of the Alternative Right's trolling subculture. After Hillary Clinton's campaign site published an article referring to Pepe as "sinister" and a "symbol associated with white supremacy," many in the Alternative Right celebrated the fact that Clinton had decried a cartoon frog as the pinnacle of their trolling achievement.[49] Even following Richard Spencer's now notorious National

Policy Institute 2016 conference speech that ended with the words "Hail Trump, hail our people, hail victory!" (leading several members of the audience to throw Nazi salutes), Spencer returned to the microphone to shout "Pepe!"[50]

Offline rallies by the Alternative Right have also made heavy use of the internet imagery associated with their trolling subculture. In addition to references to Pepe the Frog, another popular symbol for the Alternative Right at political demonstrations has been the fictional nation of "Kekistan" – invented on 4chan.org/pol/ as a "home" for shitposters – and its associated flag; a green, white and black banner that deliberately mimics a German Nazi war flag and has the 4chan logo in one corner. The relationship between the Alternative Right's trolling and real world behaviour runs in both directions too, with individuals at marches quickly being presented as memes themselves. These include the alt-lite figure Kyle Chapman (AKA Based Stick Man), who first appeared at a pro-Trump rally on 4 March 2017 attacking anti-fascist protestors with a stick while wearing a helmet and carrying a shield. The fact that Chapman, infamous for real political violence, later crowdfunded for a graphic novel based on his "character" demonstrates the depth of the unreality and ambiguous, trolling irony at the heart of the Alternative Right.

One major attraction to such trolling for the Alternative Right is that, as Data & Society's Dr Alice Marwick notes, "irony has a strategic function. It allows people to disclaim a real commitment to far right ideas while still espousing them."[51] The growing popularity for "ironic" support of far right politics in order to "trigger" liberals is highly useful for those who sincerely support fascism. With a culture imbued with such "irony," the Alternative Right has been well poised to attract those frustrated with the liberal-left consensus – as well as mainstream conservatism – but who might be reluctant to openly support the far-right politics they may prefer instead. As author Alexander Reid Ross told *The Guardian*:

> the anger, the sense of betrayal, the need for revenge, the resentment, the violence. They're putting forward the male fantasies, the desire for a national community and a sense of unity and a rejection of Muslims. They're doing all of that, but they're not stating it.[52]

The Alternative Right have also relied on an opposite response to this frustration, which likewise allows them to dress up far-right beliefs as something other than what they are. Within the Alternative Right there is a streak of pseudo-intellectualism that is employed to allow undeniably prejudiced and bigoted views an airing on the basis of encouraging free, rational, objective political debate. Be it the culture of autodidacticism within the YouTube "Sceptic" community that often overlaps with the Alternative Right, the vague, selective use of statistics within alt-lite vloggers' discussions of migration and Islam, or the alt-right National Policy Institute's *Radix Journal*. Just as "ironic" humour is used by the Alternative Right to allow far-right beliefs to become talking points, so too is the use of faux-objective pontificating on racial or sexual differences, or the threat of Islam, for example, used to lend once rightly rejected beliefs an air of acceptability.

Whilst a familiar tactic for the far right to employ, this, too, can be traced in part to the Alternative Right's trolling roots. Phillips recognised this feature of this community prior to its overlap with the Alternative Right and their pseudo-intellectualising of far right beliefs in the name of "objective" debate. It was already prevalent, she notes, in trolls' valorising of the "adversary method" of argument.[53] This refers to a tradition associated with Western philosophy and legal theory, wherein the two sides to a theory or case present their positions and engage in a formal discussion, or dialectic, aimed at establishing the truth of the matter at hand (or, in the case of law, this is done by a third, impartial party, namely a jury). Whilst a normal and acceptable means of inquiry, the adversarial method can be exploited if interlocutors employ rhetorical tricks with a view to merely give the impression of having "won" the argument, as opposed to actually establishing the truth of the matter at hand. Examples include *ad hominem* attacks, which aim to discredit one party to the discussion and, it is hoped therefore, give the impression that their argument is flawed also. Trolls, Phillips notes, "[...] take a similar approach, explicitly eschewing the pursuit of truth [...] in favor of victory, and more importantly, dominance."[54]

This trolling trait has continued within the Alternative Right, most evidently in the "bloodsports" genre of YouTube videos within the Alternative Right's alternative media milieu. As Jared Holt of Right Wing Watch describes, this sees "[...] prominent alt-right personalities on YouTube [...] [debate] against 'classical liberal,' libertarian and 'anti-social justice warrior' YouTube talkers."[55] Likewise, even when not brazenly engaged in for the sake of competition (or financing, or recruitment) rather than productive dialogue, the Alternative Right's pseudo-intellectualising comes through in a condescending, similarly androcentric tone which attempts to employ rhetorical tricks to "win" arguments with their critics in a manner not only redolent of but, likely in many cases, directly inherited from an earlier feature of the trolling subculture. As Phillips notes:

> Not only does "knowing how to rhetoric" [...] serve as a point of pride for trolls, it provides a built-in justification for their antagonistic behaviors. After all, if cool rationality is in fact superior to "softer" modes of thinking, then denigrating and attempting to silence the feminized other isn't just warranted, it is the trolls' cultural duty (in response to their target's distress "you're welcome" was an attitude frequently expressed by the trolls I worked with).[56]

This more explicitly brings out the androcentrism of the Alternative Right's pseudo-intellectualising. Phillips highlights that:

> in addition to establishing the ground rules for "proper" argumentation, the adversary method presupposes the superiority of certain male-gendered traits (rationality, assertiveness, dominance) over female-gendered traits (sentimentality, cooperation, conciliation). In the process, it privileges and in fact reifies an explicitly androcentric worldview while simultaneously delegitimizing less confrontational discursive modes.[57]

In this regard, two core influences of antagonistic trolling on the Alternative Right – extreme "ironic" humour and the valorisation of the adversary method – act as both means of cloaking hateful ideas, as well as means of excluding others through policing what kinds of behaviour are acceptable for its members.

The trolls are sincere

The online activities of the (mainly) frustrated young men attracted to the Alternative Right are often put down to the disinhibiting effects of the internet – its tendency to lead people to dissociate or distance themselves from the consequences of their actions online, trolling being a prime example. Yet, as Phillips and Milner emphasise in a review of the empirical evidence, this is not an inevitability, for while "anonymity in digitally mediated spaces can facilitate toxic expression, the disinhibiting effects of anonymity can also facilitate compassion and emotional openness as easily as aggression."[58] A better explanation comes from the observation that, online, "Participants actively choose to wear that particular mask, in that particular moment, because it's a mask they want to wear."[59] What this suggests is that, while the "mask" of far-right beliefs worn by the young trolls of the Alternative Right may involve some pressures – the norms of the shitposting communities they are a part of online, for example – it is, all the same, a mask they choose over others and so is a mask that reflects, at some level, what they sincerely feel and believe. This doesn't mean, of course, that far-right trolls themselves are able to always recognise this. In her interviews with trolls who engaged primarily on Facebook, and so, unlike those on 4chan who had near complete anonymity, had to create more stable personae online, Phillips notes how they would "mention some amusing thing [their] profile had done, as if the profile were somehow separable from the person whose profile it was," and she "eventually came to realize that, in the trolls' minds, their profiles were separable from their 'true' selves."[60]

This captures the bind which the Alternative Right ultimately faces when it comes to the role of the troll in the movement. Speaking at the alt-right "Scandza Forum" conference in Oslo in 2017, Greg Johnson of Counter-Currents Publishing recognised the tension when he explored the upside and downside of the ironic distance that trolling culture has created between their movement's ideas and the people who express putative support for them online. Johnson compares the irony-laced virtual spaces of the alt-right to the ideological equivalents of changing rooms and car test drives, in the sense that these spaces allow people to try something out before committing to them. He notes that as people are "not overly eager to commit to being part of something that radical and marginal," these spaces are all the more useful for the alt-right as, "if you don't have to fully commit upfront to something, [then] you're more likely to try it and if you try it then it's possible for you to commit."[61] At the same time, he adds that the movement must "never lose sight of the fact that if we're talking about defending something as central to us as our identity, that you can't be ironic about."[62] As such, whatever benefit an ironic distance has for allowing people to "try out" far-right ideas, he believes that if society maintains that detachment from political sincerity is the superior attitude, it can be "deadly" for the alt-right's interests.[63] As a result, Johnson argues that the movement must "figure out how to close the deal with these people who come and play around", because:

> in the end the people who are going to create a revolution and save our civilization are going to be the people who are a hundred percent committed to it and own up to that commitment because it's a matter of who they are, not something that they can just jump back from and pretend like it's all just a game.[64]

Notes

1 Patrik Hermansson, David Lawrence, Joe Mulhall, Simon Murdoch, *The International Alternative Right: From Charlottesville to the Whitehouse* (London: HOPE not hate, 2017), 10.
2 Ibid., 10.
3 There is scholarly consensus that a distinctive trolling subculture emerged during the mid-to-late 2000s, with a major catalyst being "the ascendancy of 4chan, originally conceived in 2003 as a content overflow site for a particularly NSFW ["Not Safe For Work" – i.e. inappropriate and often shocking] Something Awful subforum called 'Anime Death Tentacle Rape Whorehouse'," as Whitney Phillips describes in *This is Why We Can't Have Nice Things: Mapping the Relationship between Online Trolling and Mainstream Culture* (Cambridge: MIT Press, 2015), 18. Its founder, fifteen-year-old Christopher "moot" Poole, was a regular contributor. Ibid. Likewise, as Phillips notes, "a great deal of overlap existed between proto- and early trolling spaces, particularly on the so-called shock sites of the late 1990s and early 2000s, including Rotten (1996), Hard OCP (Hardware Overclockers Comparison Page) (1997), Totse (1997), Stile Project (1999), Something Awful (1999), Gen May (2002), and finally 4chan (2003)." Phillips, *This Is Why We Can't Have Nice Things*, 20.
4 4chan's key inspiration, the Japanese "2channel" site, experienced the same issues of extreme content. As Lisa Katamaya reported in 2008, "2channel is becoming increasingly controversial. There have been stalking incidents and suicide pacts supposedly planned through the site." Lisa Katamaya, "Meet Hiroyuki Nishimura, the Bad Boy of the Japanese Internet," *WIRED*, 19 May 2008. https://www.wired.com/2008/05/mf-hiroyuki/
5 Phillips, *This Is Why We Can't Have Nice Things*, 25. This continued after the development of the Alternative Right with establishment right figures being accused, for example, of being "cuckservatives." The term is meant to suggest establishment conservatives who agree with the liberal-left are the political equivalents of "cuckolds"; a term referring to a situation in which a married man accepts other men engaging in sexual relationships with their wife. The Alternative Right's usage of the term normally is intended to connote also a category of online pornography featuring the white wives of submissive husbands having sex with (usually) black men, hence the term has become filled with racial meaning.
6 Louis Doré, "Five of Anonymous's Most Infamous Trolling Operations," *The Independent*, 26 November 2015. https://www.indy100.com/article/five-of-anonymouss-most-infamous-trolling-operations–ZkJCpfhCte
7 Adbusters Blog, "Anonymous Joins #OCCUPYWALLSTREET," *Adbusters*, 23 August 2011. https://web.archive.org/web/20111009004643/http://www.adbusters.org/blogs/adbusters-blog/anonymous-joins-occupywallstreet.html
8 Anonymous and spin-off movements would also engage in repeated campaigns against far-right groups, including the "Operation Blitzkreig" campaign launched in 2012. See: Marilyn Elias, "Anonymous Hacking Collective Declares 'Operation Blitzkrieg' Against Neo-Nazi Websites," *Intelligence Report*, 25 May 2012. https://www.splcenter.org/fighting-hate/intelligence-report/2012/anonymous-hacking-collective-declares-operation-blitzkrieg-against-neo-nazi-websites

9 On 4chan, a long-running disagreement between trolls centred around those who engaged in principled online campaigns (referred to by their fellow troll critics as "moralfagz") and those who were not consciously driven by a political conviction but rather by a focus solely on cruel humour (referred to as "lulzfagz").

10 Phillips, *This Is Why We Can't Have Nice Things*, 132.

11 Ibid., 133.

12 Andrew Thompson, "The Measure of Hate on 4chan," *Rolling Stone*, 10 May 2018. http s://www.rollingstone.com/politics/politics-news/the-measure-of-hate-on-4cha n-627922/

13 Poole stated that it had become like the white nationalist forum, www.stormfront.org, "ages ago." The "/r9k/" subforum – added on 19 February 2008 – was also removed at this time, in part because it had become focused on "misogyny, and self-loathing." Christopher Poole, "Why were /r9k/ and /new/ removed?," *content.4chan.org*, 17 January 2011. https://www.webcitation.org/6159jR9pC?url=http://content.4chan.org/tmp/r9knew.txt. It was reinstated on 10 November 2011 and became a hub for the extreme misogynist "Incel" community. It has been described as "famous for its stories of social awkwardness and nostalgia [...] as well as discussion of abnormal social behaviour. It[s] [users] hold anger and disdain over males with active social and sexual lives." "r9k," *Know Your Meme*. https://knowyourmeme.com/memes/sites/r9k. [Accessed 21 August 2018].

14 Archives of the r/altright subforum also suggest it was created by the owners of AlternativeRight.com. "r/altright," Reddit. https://web.archive.org/web/20100307212807/http://www.reddit.com:80/r/altright [Accessed 21 August 2018].

15 Blue Wolf, post on "4chan /pol/–surprising allies," 23 January 2014. https://www.stormfront.org/forum/t1019254/ [Accessed 22 August 2018]. Some 4chan users speculated in 2013 that Stormfront's efforts had started earlier too, and that Stormfront users had possibly contributed to the /pol/ predecessor subforum "/new/" also. See: "/q/ 4chan Discussion" 4chan Data. http://4chandata.org/q/Stormfront–4chan-Specifically-p ol–a374189 [Accessed 22 August 2018].

16 WakeUpWhiteMan, post on "Swarming on Reddit," 18 January 2014. https://www.stormfront.org/forum/t1018437/ [Accessed 22 August 2018].

17 Michael Slay, "Reddit is Fertile Ground for Recruitment," 5 March 2015. https://a rchive.is/7lQiA. [Accessed 22 August 2018].

18 Hatewatch Staff, "McInnes, Molyneux, and 4chan: Investigating Pathways to the Alt-Right," *Southern Poverty Law Center*, 19 April 2018. https://www.splcenter.org/ 20180419/mcinnes-molyneux-and-4chan-investigating-pathways-alt-right

19 Zaid Jilani, "Gamergate's Fickle Hero: The Dark Opportunism of Breitbart's Milo Yiannopoulos," *Salon*, 28 October 2014. https://www.salon.com/2014/10/28/gamerga tes_fickle_hero_the_dark_opportunism_of_breitbarts_milo_yiannopoulos/. Gamergate had lasting knock-on effects on the trolling subculture from which it partially emerged too. After Poole stated that planning of Gamergate-related campaigns would be censored from 4chan, many users migrated to the openly extreme far-right 8chan forum, where a dedicated subforum for the topic was established. Christopher Poole, "Regarding Recent Events," *4chan*, 18 September 2014. https://archive.is/IlYMw [Accessed 22 August 2018].

20 Nick Wingfield, "Feminist Critics of Video Games Facing Threats in 'Gamergate' Campaign," *The New York Times*, 15 October 2014. https://www.nytimes.com/2014/ 10/16/technology/gamergate-women-video-game-threats-anita-sarkeesian.html

21 Alice Marwick and Rebecca Lewis, *Media Manipulation & Disinformation Online* (New York: Data & Society Research Institute, 2017), 38.

22 Breitbart Tech, "Would You Rather Your Child Had Feminism or Cancer?," *Breitbart*, 19 February 2018. https://www.breitbart.com/video/2016/02/19/would-you-rather-your-child-had-feminism-or-cancer/

23 Robert Mackey, "There Are No 'Macron Leaks' in France. Politically Motivated Hacking is Not Whistleblowing," *The Intercept*, 6 May 2017. https://theintercept.com/ 2017/05/06/no-macron-leaks-politically-motivated-hacking-not-whistleblowing/

24 Megha Mohan, "Macron Leaks: The Anatomy of a Hack," *BBC*, 9 May 2017. https://www.bbc.co.uk/news/blogs-trending-39845105
25 For further discussion see Chapter 1 "The European Roots of Alt-Right Ideology" in this book.
26 Phillips, *This Is Why We Can't Have Nice Things*, 67. Interestingly, like the ENR's adoption of a left-wing thinker's concept, Phillips notes that *détournement* is "most closely associated with the Situationist International and the Letterist International, radical Marxist collectives founded in the 1950s." Ibid., 68.
27 See, for example: Ryan M. Milner, "FCJ 156 Hacking the Social: Internet Memes, Identity Antagonism, and the Logic of Lulz," *The Fibreculture Journal: Trolls and the Negative Space of the Internet*, 22 (2013), 62–92.
28 As Phillips notes: "Our raced, classed, and gendered bodies are encoded in our online behaviour, even when we're pretending to be something above or beyond or below what we really are IRL (in real life)." Phillips, *This Is Why We Can't Have Nice Things*, 41.
29 Amelia Tait, "We Need to Talk About the Online Radicalisation of Young, White Women," *The New Statesman*, 18 August 2017. https://www.newstatesman.com/science-tech/internet/2017/08/we-need-talk-about-online-radicalisation-young-white-women.
30 "Advertise," 4chan. https://www.4chan.org/advertise [Accessed 23 September 2018].
31 Ryan M. Milner, *The World Made Meme: Public Conversations and Participatory Media* (Cambridge: MIT Press, 2016), 122.
32 Gabriel Emile Hine, Jeremiah Onaolapo, Emiliano De Cristofaro, Nicolas Kourtellis, Ilias Leontiadis, Riginos Samaras, Gianluca Stringhini, Jeremy Blackburn, "Kek, Cucks, and God Emperor Trump: A Measurement Study of 4chan's Politically Incorrect Forum and Its Effects on the Web" (2017). In: Sandra González-Bailón, Alice Marwick and Winter Mason (Eds.) *Proceedings of the 11th International AAAI Conference on Web and Social Media (ICWSM 2017)* (Montreal: Association for the Advancement of Artificial Intelligence, 2017), 100.
33 Ibid., 98. Unfortunately, the authors of the study do not specify the exact figure.
34 Dale Beran, "4chan: The Skeleton Key to the Rise of Trump," *Medium*, 14 February 2017. https://medium.com/@DaleBeran/4chan-the-skeleton-key-to-the-rise-of-trump-624e7cb798cb
35 Ibid.
36 Ibid.
37 The Social Exclusion Unit, *Bridging the Gap: New Opportunities for 16–18 Year Olds Not in Education, Employment or Training, Presented to Parliament by the Prime Minister by Command of Her Majesty* (London: Stationery Office, 1999).
38 "Incel Subreddit FAQ," Reddit. https://archive.is/YRJUw [Accessed 24 September 2018]. For further discussion of this see Chapter 12 "From Anger to Ideology: A History of the Manosphere" in this book.
39 "Lulz," Encyclopedia Dramatica. https://encyclopediadramatica.rs/Lulz. In: Phillips, *This Is Why We Can't Have Nice Things*, 121.
40 As Beran describes this identity, it is about "embracing your loserdom, owning it. […] it is what all the millions of forum-goers of 4chan met to commune about. It is, in other words, a value system, one reveling in deplorableness and being pridefully dispossessed." Beran, "4chan: The Skeleton Key to the Rise of Trump."
41 "Concurrently […] [trolling] provide[d] both entertainment and a basic feeling of connection between participants." Phillips, *This Is Why We Can't Have Nice Things*, 33. Furthermore, "The mask of trolling thus establishes a clear insider/outsider distinction. More important, it necessitates an affective reorientation to content." Ibid, 35.
42 Michael S. Bernstein, Andrés Monroy-Hernández, Drew Harry, Paul André, Katrina Panovich, Greg Vargas. "4chan and /b/: An Analysis of Anonymity and Ephemerality in a Large Online Community" (2011), *Proceedings of the Fifth International AAAI Conference on Weblogs and Social Media (ICWSM 2011)* (Montreal: Association for the Advancement of Artificial Intelligence, 2011), 56.

43 "Andrew Anglin," *Southern Poverty Law Center*.https://www.splcenter.org/fighting-hate/extremist-files/individual/andrew-anglin [Accessed 24 September 2018].
44 See: Mattathias Schwartz, "The Trolls Among Us," *The New York Times*, 3 August 2008. https://www.nytimes.com/2008/08/03/magazine/03trolls-t.html
45 Mike Enoch, "Mike Enoch at the New York Forum 5–20–2017," *The Daily Shoah* [Podcast audio]. Available at: https://therightstuffbiz.libsyn.com/mike-enoch-at-the-new-york-forum-5-20-2017 [Accessed 24 September 2018].
46 *Vice News*, 2016, *"We memed alt-right into existence": Richard Spencer Extended Interview* [Online video]. Available at: https://www.youtube.com/watch?v=aN8w7lUMc1o [Accessed 24 September 2018].
47 Phillips, *This Is Why We Can't Have Nice Things*, 10.
48 Some in the Alternative Right did, of course, intend to express these positions when employing these symbols, but importantly the *primary* intention was often to provoke media coverage of what were otherwise innocuous symbols so as to ridicule the media for supposedly whipping up a needless moral panic.
49 Similarly, after a man was heard shouting "Pepe!" after Clinton's first public mention of the alt-right in a speech on 25 August 2016, 4chan posts revealed he had been encouraged to do so by 4chan users during the speech. "Anon Heckles Hillary's Pepe Rally," Imgur. https://imgur.com/gallery/cC90P#AFaFAkl [Accessed 24 September 2018].
50 *Red Ice TV*, 2016, *"Richard Spencer – NPI 2016, Full Speech"* [Online video]. Available at: https://www.youtube.com/watch?v=Xq-LnO2DOGE [Accessed 24 September 2018].
51 Jason Wilson, "Hiding in Plain Sight: How the 'Alt-Right' is Weaponizing Irony to Spread Fascism," *The Guardian*, 23 May 2017. https://www.theguardian.com/technology/2017/may/23/alt-right-online-humor-as-a-weapon-facism
52 Wilson, "Hiding in Plain Sight: How the 'Alt-Right' is Weaponizing Irony to Spread Fascism."
53 Phillips, *This Is Why We Can't Have Nice Things*, 124.
54 Ibid., 125. Phillips notes that this feature of the trolling subculture is so ingrained that a text describing these rhetorical methods, *The Art of Controversy* (also translated as *The Art of Being Right*), by influential German philosopher Arthur Schopenhauer is regarded by some in this subculture "as a blueprint for modern trolling" and adds that it "was recommended to [her] by one of [her] troll [interviewees]." Ibid., 124.
55 The Alternative Right's trolling-inflected focus on treating discussions as a vehicle for entertainment – in this case debates in which one person "beats" the other akin to a competition – is emphasised by the fact that, as Holt highlights, these videos are effective revenue streams and recruitment platforms. Jared Holt, "Welcome To YouTube 'Bloodsports,' The Alt-Right's Newest Recruiting Tool," *Right Wing Watch*, 31 January 2018. http://www.rightwingwatch.org/post/welcome-to-youtube-bloodsports-the-alt-rights-newest-recruiting-tool/
56 Phillips, *This Is Why We Can't Have Nice Things*, 126.
57 Ibid., 124.
58 Whitney Phillips and Ryan M. Milner, *The Ambivalent Internet: Mischief, Oddity, and Antagonism Online* (Cambridge: Polity, 2017), 70–71.
59 Ibid., 70.
60 Phillips, *This Is Why We Can't Have Nice Things*, 79.
61 *Red Ice TV*, 2017, *Scandza Forum Oslo, 2017 – Greg Johnson* [Online video]. Available at: https://www.youtube.com/watch?v=YXQGwmmOL5Q [Accessed 25 September 2018].
62 Ibid.
63 Ibid.
64 Ibid.

10

ALT-TECH

Co-opting and creating digital spaces

The nazi website the Daily Stormer calls itself "The Most Censored Publication in History."[1] While such claims are hyperbolic, the site has indeed faced significant opposition. The website's domain name was seized by Google and its hosting provider, GoDaddy, kicked the site off its servers after the Unite the Right rally in Charlottesville, Virginia in August 2017. This was in part a response to the Daily Stormer calling Heather Heyer, the anti-racist activist murdered at the rally, a "fat, childless, 32 year-old slut"[2] and site administrator Andrew Auernheimer (AKA weev) claiming that he wanted to "get people on the ground" at her funeral.[3] The site has subsequently moved between hosting providers and, as of October 2018, has had 14 domain names seized, effectively limiting its access to one of the most basic infrastructure services that make up the internet.

The Daily Stormer is not the only example of the deplatforming of Alternative Right-affiliated figures and organisations. Online troll Charles Johnson was one of the first high profile Alternative Right figures to be permanently banned from Twitter after he made violent threats towards civil rights activist DeRay Mckesson in May 2015.[4] The following year Milo Yiannopoulos, then the star of Breitbart News Network and a central figure of the Western chauvinist "alt-lite" wing of the Alternative Right, was forced off the platform, as were the accounts of the *Radix Journal* and the National Policy Institute (NPI), organisations led by Richard Spencer, a figurehead of the "alt-right" racial nationalist wing of the movement, a few months later.

However, in the late summer in 2017, after the events in Charlottesville, the pressure on social media platforms, as well as internet platforms more generally, to take a stand against the far right's use of their services grew significantly. The rally had been organised and promoted on mainstream platforms and many of these companies reacted by deplatforming alt-right activists. These included Twitter, YouTube, Discord (a group chat platform) and Facebook. Payment providers and other internet service companies such as PayPal, GoDaddy, Uber and AirBnB also limited access to their platforms or deplatformed users connected to the rally.

The bans have limited the ability of sections of the Alternative Right to reach an audience as they had previously. While part of the origin of the Alternative Right has accurately been assigned to the blogosphere and to imageboards such as 4chan, mainstream social media platforms such as Twitter remain important for the movement.[5] These platforms allow for mainstream recognition and continue to be the primary way the Alternative Right disseminates information, attracts new supporters, and conducts its activism.

Considering that among the most important tactics of the Alternative Right is the practice of trolling and the use of coordinated hate campaigns as a way of attracting the attention of the mainstream media, thereby inflating its influence and helping to normalise its ideas, denial of this attention can be an effective way to combat the movement. However, the lack of a consistent approach between platforms has made the effect of deplatforming weaker than it could have been. After Charlottesville, social media companies in particular deplatformed a significant number of far-right users, but the platforms have different codes of conduct, resulting in inconsistencies. At the time of writing the influential alt-right vlogger Colin Robertson (AKA Millennial Woes) is banned from Twitter but not YouTube, and Facebook has banned Richard Spencer and the alt-right hub Counter-Currents Publishing, while Twitter has not. The Daily Stormer has once again managed to register its main domain name, dailystormer.com, with a different provider. Some influential activists have simply returned to Twitter under different user names, meaning that they still have outlets to communicate with their audiences. These inconsistencies have lead Bharath Ganesh from the Oxford Internet Institute to call the online far right and related groups "ungovernable." He points out that inconsistencies in legislation between territories and between platforms have been exploited by far-right activists.[6] Not only have they attempted to claim that the bans are evidence of their victimisation and unfair treatment, and thus render them more sympathetic to the mainstream, but they exploit it by moving between web hosts and social networks after getting suspended, relying on inconsistent applications of suspensions, in order to keep channels open to their audience, who are quick to follow.

Regardless, the Alternative Right has increasingly found that the internet is no longer the safe haven it once was. Groups and figures associated with the movement and the wider far right are regularly denied access to social media platforms, payment providers, direct communication platforms, basic internet infrastructure, and even dating platforms. Consequently, the movement has been forced to find solace on alternative, more marginal, platforms, find ways to circumvent their bans on the mainstream platforms or create their own.

Online separatism

"We need parallel everything. I do not want to ever have to spend a single dollar at a non-movement business," Pax Dickinson wrote on his now-suspended Twitter account in June 2017.[7] Dickinson is a former Chief Technology Officer at the financial publication *Business Insider* and one of the founders of WeSearchr (along with Charles Johnson). WeSearchr was launched in 2015 and was a crowdfunding platform dedicated to fundraising for, especially, media productions connected to the Alternative Right. It was created in response to the mainstream fundraising site GoFundMe's denial of access to a far-right cause.[8] The same month Dickinson launched Counter.Fund, another fundraising platform but this time with the ambition to fund political action against "Marxist political correctness and the globalist progressive Left."[9]

In an article published two months later on the official blog of Gab, an Alternative Right-associated social media platform, a new sub-movement within the Alternative Right dubbed "The Free Speech Tech Alliance," or "alt-tech," started to take shape. The article paints a picture of an increasingly hostile climate to far-right ideas online, at the time exemplified by the firing of Google employee James Damore for writing and circulating a manifesto that railed against the company's efforts to close the gender pay gap.[10] "The time is now for patriots and free thinkers inside and outside of Silicon Valley to organize, communicate in a safe way, and start building,"[11] the article declares. It continues to outline the need for alternative platforms and infrastructure outside of the control of the "liberal" Silicon Valley giants.

The alt-tech movement represented an intensification of an existing trend within the Alternative Right, attempting to solve the issue of being hugely dependent on internet platforms while not being in control over them. For several years, following cancellations of accounts and moderation of content on other platforms, alternative platforms had been sporadically created, such as an alternative to the popular forum site Reddit called Voat, launched in 2014. In addition, many sought to overcome their reliance on online payment processors like PayPal and standard bank transfers by using decentralised cryptocurrencies (digital currencies secured by cryptographic means instead of any central authority).

It is important to point out that the far right has long recognised the potential of the internet, and carved out its own spaces on it. Stormfront, a white supremacist forum, went online in 1995 after its 1990 launch in the form of a bulletin board (several months before the inception of what we today call the World Wide Web).[12] Even earlier, in 1984 Louis Beam, a leading member of the Ku Klux Klan and the man who popularised the terrorism tactic of "leaderless resistance,"[13] launched the first white supremacist bulletin board, Aryan Nation Liberty Net. In the "Inter-Klan Newsletter & Survival Alert" he wrote:

> Imagine, if you can, a single computer to which all leaders and strategists of the patriotic movement are connected. Imagine further that any patriot in the country is able to tap into this computer at will in order to reap the benefit of all accumulative knowledge and wisdom of the leaders. "Someday," you may say? How about today? Such a computer is already in existence and operational. We hereby announce Aryan Nation Liberty Net.[14]

While attempts to create alternative spaces online for the benefit of the far right are nothing new, a series of recent developments means that the intensity and focus of this trend has increased. Over the last few years figures associated with the Alternative Right have gone beyond making use of the internet as a dissemination platform and made it central to their activism. Online platforms allow not just the dissemination of information but a way to network within a movement and across ideological and national boundaries, allowing its supporters to share and reinforce a world view.[15]

Free speech platforms

The at least superficial dedication to an absolutist interpretation of free speech is something Gab shares with all platforms in the alt-tech world. The team behind the site market it in opposition to mainstream platforms, which they argue assert varying degrees of illegitimate censorship over their movement. Gab uses the motto "people and free speech first," while Reddit alternative Voat, for example, uses the more subtle tagline: "Have your say."

Evidently, bans by mainstream platforms have fed into this narrative of free speech being under threat and the Alternative Right as a suppressed movement. The bans implemented by these platforms continue to mobilise a common narrative within the Alternative Right, which portrays the movement as an underdog in a populist attempt to gain sympathy for its cause and to make it appear righteous and thereby more attractive to potential and current supporters. Framed in this way, moving over to new platforms becomes an act of resistance itself; one of the competitive advantages the alternative platforms have compared to the likes of Facebook and Twitter. The honesty of this rhetoric can of course be questioned; Richard Spencer has himself stated that the alt-right does not actually support freedom of speech.[16] Moreover, whilst there is little reason to question the ideological conviction of the founders of most of these platforms, similar to the mainstream platforms, while having strong political motives, the alt-tech platforms are not free of profit motive. Thus, statements such as those of Gab's founder of running a platform "for the people" should be taken with a grain of salt. Like any for-profit business portraying an ethical image, these platforms capitalise on the free speech narrative (in addition to others, such as the fears of data mining by mainstream social media corporations).

A far-right safe space

Probably the most successful example of a new alternative platform is Gab, an independently-developed platform that positions itself as a competitor to Twitter and Facebook, started in 2016 by Andrew Torba, a 25-year-old entrepreneur from Pennsylvania.[17] Gab has taken many features from Twitter with some additions from other social media networks, such as groups, and special features for paying members. The platform quickly gained traction in the alt-right as a Twitter alternative after a number of high-profile activists were banned from Twitter in the wake of Charlottesville and policy changes on the platform in December 2017. Gab made early nods towards the alt-right by making a green frog, similar to the Pepe meme, its logo. Although it did not admit direct support for the movement at first, instead positioning itself in opposition to "big tech" and for freedom of speech. The platform became the focus of media attention after it was revealed that the killer of eleven Jewish people at the Tree of Life Congregation Synagogue in Pittsburgh, on 28 October 2018, had posted white supremacist and antisemitic content and glorified violent far-right groups on the platform without being suspended.

It should not come as a surprise that Gab has attracted the alt-right, as Torba and Gab as an organisation have increasingly expressed support for several of the causes of the Alternative Right. Torba appeared on far-right conspiracy theorist Alex Jones' Infowars YouTube channel after Jones' ban from many of the mainstream social media platforms in August 2018. In the interview Torba argued that the far right need "to stop playing on the left's playgrounds," as opposed to its mainstream competitors.[18] Torba, as well as Gab's official channels on other social media, have also increasingly made use of memes associated with the Alternative Right. Even clearer indications of the ideological direction of Gab could be found on the platform's now-deleted blog, where readers published articles replete with alt-right rhetoric such as "EXPOSED: Anti-White 'Hate Speech' on Twitter By CNN, Buzzfeed, NYT, and LA Times Reporters" and "The Social Justice Sham of Silicon Valley." Gab has, however, continued to claim that the platform is "for everyone,"[19] sometimes using the highly anecdotal piece of evidence that there are "independent rap artists from socially liberal viewpoints in Canada" on the platform as proof of its dedication to diversity of opinion.[20]

Even if such a user actually exists, they are better described as the exception that proves the rule, rather than a reflection of the average user on the platform. While Gab, like many other alt-tech platforms, claims that "All are welcome,"[21] it has become dominated by figures associated with the far right. The free-for-all attitude to racism and other forms of hate found on the site unsurprisingly makes the atmosphere on the platform toxic. Many figures within the movement have expressed support for Gab and a brief look at the most followed accounts indicates that the Alternative Right is driving much of the growth of the platform. As of October 2018, among the top 20 most followed accounts we find that all but one express support for the Alternative Right and most are well-known figures associated with the movement, including Paul Joseph Watson (the most followed account on the platform), Alex Jones, Milo Yiannopoulos, Stefan Molyneux, Ricky Vaughn, and Mike Cernovich.

Alt-everything

Gab is just one of many alternative social media platforms, albeit possibly the most successful. Numerous others present themselves as alternatives to Facebook or provide their own models. The combined urgency of the need to replace the mainstream services after suspensions, the relative ease of publishing a new website and the tech savviness of some of the supporters of the Alternative Right has pushed the movement to iterate platforms quickly. However, most are comparatively small, and their lifespans have tended to be short.

There are, for example, dating platforms aimed at the alt-right and the wider far right. One of them is WASP Love (WASP meaning "White Anglo-Saxon Protestant"), which was launched in early 2016 and claims to cater for "Reformed Christian, Quiverfull, Confederate, Homeschooled, Christian Identity, white nationalism, altright, Sovereign Grace Singles."[22] For dating sites, censorship is not the main issue but rather the skewed gender balance within the Alternative Right. Stonewall, the founder of WASP Love, told *VICE* that the service needed to "beef up the female members."[23] A competitor to WASP Love is the descriptively named WhiteDate, which even had a section on its website titled "How to Invite Women to WhiteDate," complete with its own printable flier.[24]

However, among the most important types of platform for the Alternative Right are those aimed specifically at video as well as fundraising. Social media scholar Zeynep Tufekci has argued that YouTube "may be one of the most powerful radicalizing instruments of the 21st century."[25] Therefore, it is especially worrying that, compared to other mainstream platforms, YouTube has been relatively forgiving to Alternative Right users.[26] While there are cases of users being blocked from the platform, a more common practice on YouTube is to take down a single video rather than the whole account, or to "demonetise" (removing the ability to make profits on advertisement) videos or users. Alternatives to YouTube have therefore sprung up, which also position themselves as "free speech" advocates and vow not to moderate their users' content. However, video content presents specific difficulties as well, since compared to primarily text-based platforms video sites are more expensive to run, due to storage and data-transfer costs, requiring more funding or more creative approaches to the hosting of video content. It is therefore no coincidence that YouTube's alternatives represent some of the more technologically innovative approaches to alternative platforms.

BitChute is one of the main alternatives to YouTube that makes use of decentralisation technology, and it has been increasingly adopted by the alt-right, especially by those who believe themselves to be at risk of YouTube bans. It is used by several key organisations and figures, including Red Ice Creations and Colin Robertson (AKA Millennial Woes).

Funding platforms

YouTube should be seen as both a funding platform and a dissemination platform as it allows its creators to take a part of the advertisement revenue as well as allowing viewers to donate money during live streams in "super chats." The latter function is frequently used by Alternative Right YouTubers, some of whom make part, or all, of their livelihood by producing media content. Corporate sponsorships are naturally a rarity among the Alternative Right, but many make significant sums of money from advertisements on YouTube along with donations from their followers. The movement's supporters have proven willing to support its central figures with both spontaneous and recurring donations.

Figures and groups in the Alternative Right also make extensive use of online payment and donation platforms to fund their livelihood, raise funds for events, actions, travel costs, and to sell books and merchandise. However, this too has faced opposition from mainstream platforms since, in addition to YouTube's demonetisation practices, crowdfunding site GoFundMe has denied access to numerous Alternative Right figures, such as Tim Gionet (AKA Baked Alaska) and Kyle Chapman (AKA Based Stick Man). Similarly, Patreon, a service that provides a subscription-based model for donations, has banned a long list of far-right figures and organisations, including Richard Spencer, Brittany Pettibone, Lauren Southern, Defend Europa, and Faith Goldy. Attempts have therefore been made to replace these platforms with specifically Alternative Right replicas. In place of GoFundMe came GoyFundMe ("goy" being a Hebrew term for non-Jewish people and a common meme amongst the alt-right), and Patreon was replaced by Hatreon and MakerSupport. Several other similar platforms have also been set up, such as Charles Johnson's WeSearchr and Freestartr; platforms whose closest mainstream analogue would be Kickstarter. None of these remain active, mainly because payment processors have cut their ties with the platforms.[27]

The relatively small number of payment services available and the common conception that they carry more responsibility for the transactions on their network than, for example, a domain registrar for its customers' content, means that payment processors are less accessible for the alt-right. Moreover, the reliance on online payments has become one of the primary targets of activists and media aiming to disrupt the movement's ability to organise. The potential impact of disrupting funding streams has meant that campaigns have formed with the specific purpose of hurting far-right groups financially. Sleeping Giants, for example, is a social media activism group that describes itself as "A campaign to make bigotry and sexism less profitable,"[28] and regularly calls out payment processors and companies that advertise on far-right websites.

Limited successes

The limited successes that the alt-tech movement has achieved to date have often come after high-profile bans on mainstream platforms, which has led key far-right activists to publicise their move to alternatives, thereby bringing such alternative platforms renewed attention and attracting new supporters. Daily Stormer's Andrew Anglin, for example, has one of the most active and high-profile accounts on Gab, which remains his only public social media platform alongside BitChute. Torba himself has attributed the site's recent growth to bans of high-profile far-right activists on other platforms, the largest of which is that of Alex Jones and his conspiratorial site InfoWars in August 2018.[29]

However, overall the successes of alternative platforms have been few and far between. Out of the multiple projects detailed in this chapter, only a fraction are still online and even fewer can be considered successful. Those which remain active, such as Gab, Voat, and WrongThink, still suffer from issues relating to reliability, a relatively inactive user base and a lack of mainstream attention.

While Gab continues to grow, overall its users remain quite inactive. A study by Zannettou et al. showed that only 20 percent of the users on the social network change their profile description and 43 percent had never posted to the site.[30] Gab still suffers alt-right ghettoisation; despite being larger than other alt-tech platforms its user base remains homogeneous and few posts spark discussion. In other words, the platform is still *too* alternative. It provides a place for users kicked off Twitter, a safe-haven of sorts, but the possibility of unmoderated speech is in itself not enough of a reason for some to engage. Many high-profile Alternative Right figures turned to Gab but stayed only a short time before leaving the platform again, instead focusing their energy on their mainstream accounts or attempting to circumvent their suspensions. At the time of writing Mike Cernovich's last post was sixteen months ago, while he posted on average 238 times a day to Twitter for the month of October 2018. Even Milo Yiannopoulos, who is banned from Twitter, has not been active in seven months, instead using Facebook. Colin Robertson (AKA Millennial Woes), despite being banned from Twitter in September 2018, did not post more than a handful of Gab posts about his Twitter ban before going inactive. He has instead returned to Twitter under a pseudonym and is active on Instagram.

It is clear that even ardent supporters of the Alternative Right do not necessarily want to move to alternative platforms but do so only when forced. Thus, both Gab and BitChute in essence act as backups to mainstream platforms. Moreover, the alternative platforms do not have potential targets for harassment campaigns, nor do they have the same potential to reach new audiences and the attention of mainstream media. The primary importance of mainstream platforms remains, an indication of which is the legal cases brought against Twitter by both Jared Taylor's American Renaissance and Charles Johnson in the spring of 2018 following their bans. As Colin Robertson explained in a since deleted YouTube video, there is a "unique maelstrom of activity that takes place on Twitter."[31]

Other issues are more practical in nature, reflecting the quality of the platforms themselves. Voat regularly returns error messages and BitChute's decentralised video technology, while impressive in theory, remains slow compared to traditional video hosting sites. The polish of mainstream platforms like Facebook, Twitter, and YouTube has ultimately made the general user picky and impatient when it comes to competing platforms. Competing with the resources of these giants remains a challenge.

Taking control of the infrastructure

However, the Alternative Right faces a deeper issue than attracting users to its social media platforms. A well-constructed platform is of no use if the domain name is seized or its hosting is shut down. This was the fate suffered by the Daily

Stormer in 2017, alongside Richard Spencer's *Radix Journal* and the alt-right group Identity Evropa, after the hosting provider Squarespace cancelled their accounts.[32] Similarly, a funding platform cannot function without the capability to process payments which often rely on mainstream options such as PayPal.

Therefore, the question of control over the infrastructural services upon which the modern web relies has increasingly become a central issue for the alt-tech movement. A modern website commonly relies on several important services that are increasingly centralised. These include hosting, domain registration, distributed denial-of-service (DDOS) protection, payment processors, and access to mobile app stores.

For these reasons a contingent of the Alternative Right, including many of the founders of the platforms mentioned above and those amongst the "Free speech tech alliance," argue for a need to control every part of the infrastructure. This aim is supported by various actors, one of which is the alternative news outlet Defend Europa, which set out a plan in a May 2018 article for an alt-right domain registrar, web host, and payment processor, concluding that "No-one is going to build these platforms for us, and if we can build them, we can build anything. It's time to put our people to work."[33] However, many have little faith in the ability of the Alternative Right to match the services of the giants of Silicon Valley, who have had decades head start, vast resources, and who have inserted themselves as vital nodes in the internet today. The world's largest CDN provider (a service that protects against DDOS attacks against websites), Cloudflare, was used by at least 10% of the most visited sites on the internet as of April 2017.[34] Similarly, Apple and Google are the near absolute arbiters of what software we are able to run on our smartphones.

Neither alternative platforms nor infrastructure (for example, a domain registrar) under the control of Alternative Right sympathisers alleviates the fundamental issue of trusting a small number of individuals and organisations with the power as gatekeepers. The far right is fraught with ideological schisms and bitter infighting, and the Alternative Right is no different. Given this, many are uneasy about the centralisation of control, even within the disparate movement itself.

The movement's fear of a continued reliance on technologies that remain under the control of a few was heightened when Gab itself banned white nationalist Paul Nehlen for doxing (revealing the true identity of) alt-right activist Ricky Vaughn in April 2018. The suspension from the "free-speech" platform resulted in significant criticism from within the movement.[35] It highlights how, besides building a functional platform, maintaining trust from users is a challenge alt-tech also has to overcome. This is not an insignificant issue because of the paranoid nature of the far right, which fears anti-fascist and government infiltrations. A thread on the Daily Stormer's forum from October 2018 highlights these worries. In it, a user expressed concern about the newly launched Freezoxee social network which advertises itself as a free-speech platform, albeit one with a policy to block "authoritarian ideologies."[36] The user writes that they "have to conclude that the real reason [the site's creators are] starting a new site is so [they] can be the one making the ultimate decisions on who to ban."[37]

Decentralisation is therefore another prominent stream of thought discernible among Alternative Right figures concerned about their future on the internet. As opposed to building alternative platforms and services and thereby taking control into their own hands, but inevitably in a centralised manner no different from how most of their mainstream competitors work today, the decentralisation philosophy takes a different approach: doing away with any concentrated point of power (and single point of failure) online.

It is important to note that another movement for a more decentralised internet existed long before the Alternative Right and was, and remains, unaffiliated to it. Anarchist, techno-libertarian programmers and internet activists living under authoritarian rule have long built platforms that enable a decentralised internet outside of the control of either governments or big corporations.[38]

Some early decentralisation projects have become well-known, such as the Torrent protocol. This is most commonly understood as a way to pirate copyrighted material, but the technology underneath allows people to coordinate the sharing of large files between thousands of computers with unstable internet connections, without any central server. If any of the computers uploading a file goes offline, it has no impact on the availability of the file and only minimally on the download speed. It is comparatively a much more complex method than how we regularly download files directly from a server to our computers in a steady stream, one bit after the other. In the latter case, all it takes to make content unavailable is to take the server offline, or delete the file. It also makes it relatively easy to check which computer downloaded the file and from where.

The strive towards a decentralised internet has intensified in recent years, in part because of increased awareness of abuse of personal data by large mainstream platforms such as Facebook. Interest in alternatives relying on some form of decentralisation, as well as encryption, has subsequently increased the number of projects aiming to address these issues. The motives or origin of most of these projects are unrelated to the far right but elements of the far right have found a use in these technologies for their own purposes nonetheless. Unsurprisingly, this was taken up early on by violent far-right groups. National Action (NA), a British neo-nazi group now proscribed under terrorist legislation, warned its members about providing too much information to Google, which it described in a guide on tech as run by "sneaky little Jews" who "keep your records of everything to make more money and to appeal to their overlords."[39] The guide continued to inform the reader on how to use encrypted messaging and detailed how to obscure one's identity online.

In the Alternative Right the drive towards decentralisation has gone especially far when it comes to the issue of funding. As outlined above, being denied access to payment processors and demonetisation are some of the most common hurdles for the Alternative Right. Far-right actors have, therefore, long been interested in cryptocurrencies, due to the lack of regulation and level of anonymity afforded by them. Cryptocurrency transactions, since they do not rely on any form of identification except for a cryptographic key, make it relatively easy to obfuscate who is actually behind a transaction. Moreover, the decentralised blockchain technology underpinning cryptocurrencies, which keeps an immutable and cryptographically verified record of all transactions ever made through the currency, means that assets cannot be seized or transfers stopped as they can in the traditional banking system.

There is also an ideological component to the Alternative Right's interest in cryptocurrencies and decentralisation more generally. As David Golumbia of Virginia Commonwealth University argues in his book *The Politics of Bitcoin: Software as Right-Wing Extremism*, bitcoin's central purpose is to "satisfy needs that make sense only in the context of right-wing politics" and that the technology is reliant on the cyberlibertarian school of thought which has overlaps with far-right ideas.[40] Not least, decentralised finance evokes the traditional antisemitic trope of banks being controlled by Jews. The Daily Stormer, for example, has described cryptocurrency as a potential means to "free us from the Jew-dominated central banking institutions."[41] Alt-right figurehead Richard Spencer claimed in March 2017 that "Bitcoin is the currency of the alt-right."[42] NA recommended using Bitcoin in 2015, as "a great way to help protect your identity when making purchases."[43]

Other projects aim at decentralising the hosting of websites and media content, a few of which have been used by the Alternative Right. Regular web hosting remains centralised, meaning providers can choose to terminate the service or be pressured to do so. While there is an abundance of hosting providers available and these can be changed relatively quickly, it results in downtime and often increased costs. Furthermore, hosting can come with high costs, especially for video sharing websites. Therefore, projects like BitChute make use of the Torrent file sharing protocol to let the users themselves offset some of the data transfer costs, by uploading the video to other users from their personal computers while they are watching them. This dramatically lowers the costs of running a video platform.

While Torrent technology is not a viable alternative for completely offsetting the need for traditional hosting, other projects have sought to address this issue. The InterPlanetary File System (IPFS) aims to offset the need for any single, core servers at all by distributing content entirely across a network while preventing any node from altering the data.[44] The technology allows for the hosting of both websites and specific pieces of content, meaning in essence that a platform such as BitChute could be completely decentralised. While new, this technology has already caught the attention of the Alternative Right as a way to ensure that its material remains accessible. In a thread entitled "IPFS Volunteers Needed" on the Daily Stormer forum, Andrew Auernheimer (AKA weev) asks for volunteers to run IPFS nodes for the archiving of material he is afraid could be lost. "I've thought a lot about the content shoahs and have decided IPFS is going to be the transit of the future for podcasts, PDFs, and video content," he writes. The subsequent thread received over one hundred responses and several IPFS servers have been set up by other forum members.[45]

Bans and the victim narrative

The trend of the Alternative Right and the wider far right towards creating its own platforms is a consequence, and likely an unavoidable side effect, of banning associated accounts on various mainstream platforms. While the project of creating separate platforms has proven difficult, this should not be taken as an indication that this will continue to be the case. Alternative platforms will continue to be sought with increased intensity as mainstream social media continue to limit access to the far right. This is both a positive development, as it marginalises far-right groups, and a challenge, as more private forums can provide effective context for recruitment and radicalisation. It is a relatively tech-savvy movement and the innovations of separate movements striving for a more decentralised, as well as encrypted, internet will undoubtedly be taken advantage of by the Alternative Right. Therefore, the techno-libertarian movement as well as the wider Open Source community need to be conscious of entryism from the far right. Moreover, while Gab currently seems to be kept alive by the symbolism of an alternative space and the hope of what it can be rather than what it is, as the network grows the platform becomes more attractive for others to join. Judging from previous bursts of growth, more high-profile figures moving to the platform could likely accelerate this process.

To exclude far-right accounts from mainstream platforms does, however, remain an important tactic. It limits their ability to reach and radicalise potential supporters, their influence over societal debate, and the damage done to other users on those platforms and in the offline world. At the same time, the bans highlight an important issue of our time, that of the dependency on private companies as platforms for public debate. Putting the arenas for public debate at the whims of a relatively small number of private institutions is something that many are concerned about. The Alternative Right has tapped into this concern. This begs the question of how bans should be carried out in order not to amplify the narrative of suppression which has become an increasingly important source of in-group definition for the conglomerate movement, reaching across the divide between the racial nationalist alt-right and the cultural nationalist alt-lite. Furthermore, it has proven successful for reaching outside of the Alternative Right itself. While framed differently, the issue cuts across the Alternative Right, as well as nazi groups like National Action and other parts of the far right. The anti-Muslim activist Stephen Yaxley-Lennon (AKA Tommy Robinson), for example, has received an almost unprecedented level of support from sections of the alt-right as well as elected politicians and sections of the general public after having been sentenced to prison in 2018. It is therefore vital to strive to make bans as consistent as possible, but also to examine the effect of bans, not just for the individual platforms but for the wider network and movement. The inconsistent application of terms of use has undoubtedly created a feeling of arbitrariness to bans that can attract attention and help far-right figures present themselves as martyrs.

Notes

1 Daily Stormer, Homepage. https://dailystormer.name [Accessed 4 November 2018].
2 Andrew Anglin, "Heather Heyer: Woman Killed in Road Rage Incident was a Fat, Childless 32-Year-Old Slut," *The Daily Stormer*, 13 August 2017. https://dailystormer.name/heather-heyer-woman-killed-in-road-rage-incident-was-a-fat-childless-32-year-old-slut/

3   Andrew Auernheimer (AKA weev) in: Will Worley, "Neo-Nazi website asks readers to target funeral of Heather Heyer who died in Charlottesville violence," *Independent*, 16 August 2017. https://www.independent.co.uk/news/world/americas/america-top-neo-nazi-website-daily -stormer-orders-followers-harass-funeral-heather-heyer-victim-a7895496.html

4   Amanda Hess, "Why Did Twitter Ban Chuck C. Johnson?" *Slate*, 28 May 2015. http://www.slate.com/articles/technology/users/2015/05/chuck_c_johnson_suspended_from_twitter_why.html.

5   See Chapter 9 "The Role of the Troll: Online Antagonistic Communities and the Alternative Right" in this book. Also: Whitney Phillips, *This is Why We Can't Have Nice Things: Mapping the Relationship between Online Trolling and Mainstream Culture* (Cambridge: MIT Press, 2015).

6   Bharath Ganesh, "The Ungovernability of Digital Hate Culture," *Journal of International Affairs*, 71:2 (2018), 37.

7   Tweet by Pax Dickinson, 7 June 2017, HOPE not hate Online Archive.

8   Michelle Castillo, "The Far Right Uses this Site to Fund its Favorite Causes – and its Founder Hopes to Build a 'Very Profitable Business'," CNBC, 24 June 2017. https://www.cnbc.com/2017/06/24/wesearchr-charles-johnson-alt-right-causes.html

9   Counter.Fund, Homepage. https://web.archive.org/web/20170618191058/https://counter.fund/ [Accessed 4 November 2018].

10 James Damore, "Google's Ideological Echo Chamber," July 2017. https://assets.documentcloud.org/documents/3914586/Googles-Ideological-Echo-Chamber.pdf.

11 Gab, "Announcing the Free Speech Tech Alliance," *medium.com/@getongab*, 10 August 2017. https://web.archive.org/web/20180918112907/https://medium.com/@getongab/announcing-the-alt-tech-alliance-18bebe89c60a

12 Carol M. Swain and Russ Nieli, (eds.), *Contemporary Voices of White Nationalism in America* (Cambridge: Cambridge University Press, 2003), 154.

13 Southern Poverty Law Center, "Louis Beam." https://www.splcenter.org/fighting-hate/extremist-files/individual/louis-beam [Accessed 5 September 2018].

14 Louis Beam (ed.), *Inter-Klan Newsletter & Survival Alert* (Ud. 1984), 2.

15 Helen Margetts, Peter John, Scott Hale and Taha Yasseri, *Political Turbulence: How Social Media Shape Collective Action* (New Jersey: Princeton University Press, 2015).

16 RightWingWatchdotorg, 2018, *RWW News: Richard Spencer Says the Alt-Right Doesn't Support Free Speech* [Online video] Available at: https://www.youtube.com/watch?v=-X5si3DA63w [Accessed 3 October 2018].

17 Joshua Brustein, "How a Silicon Valley Striver Became the Alt-Right's Tech Hero," *Bloomberg*, 9 October 2017. https://www.bloomberg.com/news/articles/2017-10-09/how-a-silicon-valley-striver-became-the-alt-right-s-tech-hero

18 NewsBlip, 2018, *Andrew Torba of Gab.ai Visits Alex Jones* [Online video]. Available at: https://www.youtube.com/watch?v=anXYG7V8t0Q [Accessed 3 October 2018].

19 Gab, "Introducing gab.com: The Home of Free Speech Online," *medium.com/@getongab*, 16 December 2017. http://web.archive.org/web/20181016185100/https://medium.com/@getongab/introducing-gab-com-the-home-of-free-speech-online-588fd22906bb

20 Anisa Subedar and Will Yates, *Gab: Free Speech Haven Or "alt-right safe space"?*, BBC World Service, Broadcast 10 December 2016. https://www.bbc.co.uk/programmes/p04k0075

21 Gab, Homepage. https://gab.ai [Accessed 20 October 2018].

22 WASP Love, Homepage. https://wasp.love/ [Accessed 20 October 2018].

23 Mack Lamoureux, "Inside the Sad World of Racist Online Dating," *VICE*, 19 December 2016. https://www.vice.com/en_uk/article/wndk85/inside-the-sad-world-of-racist-online-dating

24 "Mini Flyer – How to Invite Women to WhiteDate," WhiteDate. https://www.whitedate.net/miniflyer/

25 Zeynep Tufekci, "YouTube, the Great Radicalizer," *New York Times*, 10 March 2018. https://www.nytimes.com/2018/03/10/opinion/sunday/youtube-politics-radical.html.

26 Rebecca Lewis, *Alternative Influence* (New York: Data & Society Research Institute, 2018).

27 Faith J. Goldy, 2018, *NATIONALISTS ARE NOT ALLOWED TO MAKE A LIVING!?* [Online video] Available at: https://www.pscp.tv/w/1vAxRERYqqVJl [Accessed 16 October 2018].

28 Sleeping Giants (@slpng_giants), profile description. https://twitter.com/slpng_giants [Accessed 20 October 2018].

29 Lucas Nolan, "Social Media Platform Gab to Silicon Valley: 'You Will Be Replaced'," *Breitbart*, 20 September 2018. https://www.breitbart.com/tech/2018/09/20/social-media-platform-gab-to-silicon-valley-you-will-be-replaced/

30 Savvas Zannettou, Barry Bradlyn, Emiliano De Cristofaro, Haewoon Kwak, Michael Sirivianos, Gianluca Stringhini and Jeremy Blackburn, "What is Gab? A Bastion of Free Speech or an Alt-Right Echo Chamber?" *WWW '18 Companion* (2018), 4.

31 Video by Count Dankula (AKA Mark Meechan), 3 October 2018, HOPE not hate Online Archive.

32 Colin Lecher, "Squarespace Says it's Removing 'a Group of Sites' as Internet Cracks Down on Hate Speech," *The Verge*, 16 August 2017. https://www.theverge.com/2017/8/16/16159106/squarespace-removing-websites-charlottesville

33 redsquirrel, "Alt-Tech: Making It Happen," *Defend Europa*, 5 May 2018. https://www.defendevropa.com/2018/culture/alt-tech-making-it-happen/

34 Tom Arnfeld, "How We Made our DNS Stack 3x Faster," *Cloudflare*, 11 April 2017. https://blog.cloudflare.com/how-we-made-our-dns-stack-3x-faster/

35 Hatewatch Staff, "In Another Major Stumble for the Alt-right, Pundit "Ricky Vaughn" Allegedly Doxed by Paul Nehlen," *Southern Poverty Law Center*, 3 April 2018. https://www.splcenter.org/hatewatch/2018/04/03/another-major-stumble-alt-right-pundit-ricky-vaughn-allegedly-doxed-paul-nehlen

36 Freezoxee, user homepage. https://friends.freezoxee.com [Accessed 25 November 2018].

37 Mathias, comment on "Matthew Bracken's social media platform banned me twice for my GAB posts," *The Goyim Know*, 9 October 2018, https://bbs.thegoyimknow.to/t/matthew-brackens-social-media-platform-banned-me-twice-for-my-gab-posts/301327/2 [Accessed 20 November 2018].

38 Ronald J. Deibert, "Black Code: Censorship, Surveillance, and the Militarisation of Cyberspace," *Millennium*, 32:3 (2003), 527.

39 National Action, "Security and Anonymity in the Digital Age – A Nationalist Perspective," 2015, 14.

40 David Golumbia, *The Politics of Bitcoin: Software as Right-Wing Extremism* (Minneapolis: University of Minnesota Press, 2016), 12.

41 Joe Jones, "An Explanation of Blockchain Technology, Cryptocurrency. and the PsyOps Being Pushed Regarding Them," *Daily Stormer*, 21 January 2018. https://dailystormer.name/an-explanation-of-blockchain-technology-cryptourrency-and-the-psyops-being-pushed-regarding-them/

42 Richard Spencer (@RichardBSpencer). 18 March 2017, 2:04 PM., https://twitter.com/RichardBSpencer/status/843206485794471937

43 National Action, "Security and Anonymity in the Digital Age – A Nationalist Perspective," 2015, 16.

44 IPFS, Homepage. https://ipfs.io/ [Accessed 18 October 2018].

45 weev, "IPFS Volunteers Needed," *The Goyim Know*, 23 March 2018, https://bbs.thegoyimknow.to/t/ipfs-volunteers-needed/279468

11

GAMING THE ALGORITHMS

Exploitation of social media platforms by the Alternative Right

The Alternative Right marks itself out from earlier far-right movements in the way it has made use of online platforms. While far-right movements have traditionally used the internet as one tool among many, much of the influence of the Alternative Right can be attributed to its online activism. A variety of platforms serve as recruitment and radicalisation pathways and organising forums, and are used for the dissemination of its ideas as well as the arenas for its activism, often in the form of harassment campaigns and trolling.

The Alternative Right has thrived online. Techno-libertarian notions of online freedom and accessible mass communication have been exploited by far-right movements and especially the Alternative Right.[1] It has run harassment campaigns against countless individuals and organisations, orchestrated disinformation campaigns, attempted to influence national elections and the agenda of mainstream media channels. Even more worryingly, it has spread its ideas to new and younger audiences. This chapter will look more closely at tactics used by primarily the racial nationalist "alt-right" and its activists to circumvent censorship and exploit features and weaknesses of mainstream social networks to advance their agenda.

The attempts by the alt-right to implement more traditional social movement tactics have been less successful. Its public rallies have generally attracted small crowds, far from the numbers that could be expected from a movement which regards itself as playing a significant role in the election of a US president.[2] Moreover, such rallies have often resulted in negative backlash, sometimes with damaging legal repercussions or doxings (exposure of someone's identity) of participants.[3] The Unite the Right rally in Charlottesville, Virginia in August 2017 was the largest public gathering of alt-right supporters. It attracted worrying numbers on the streets but it was not the *tour de force* that its supporters wanted it to be or bragged about beforehand.[4]

Clearly, there is a marked asymmetry in the movement's abilities online and offline, with its ability to organise and achieve successful outcomes online being vastly stronger. This is not to say that there is a clear boundary between online and offline activism. Online action does have offline impact, something which has been noticed and courted by more established far-right political parties. Marine Le Pen of the French far-right National Rally (previously National Front), for example, thanked the "online combatants" for their support during her French presidential election campaign in 2017.[5]

The alt-right is often characterised as "tech-savvy," something given credence by the many documented cases of the alt-right's detailed strategies to inflate its influence online.[6] However, tech savviness does not itself explain every aspect of its growth and impact. Giving too much explanatory power to its skill in using online platforms (primarily social media) risks looking at the alt-right's successes (and failures) in a decontextualised way. Instead, what must also be considered is how the context and design of online platforms might have been beneficial for this movement's cause.

The attention economy

Firstly, it is important to answer the basic question of what the general aims of the alt-right's actions are, what it counts as success, and what it does to achieve it. Its main method of causing change is "metapolitical" work, with much of its activism aiming to influence culture and shift the boundaries of acceptable debate in order to create the necessary preconditions for lasting political change.[7] Secondly, trolling is a central tactic to the alt-right. Trolling can be defined as the act of being deliberately offensive or provocative online with the aim of provoking an outraged reaction, something the movement has inherited from antagonistic communities online on sites such as 4chan.org.[8] Trolling dates as far back as the late 1980s and does not necessarily have to be politicised, but it has deeply influenced the conduct of the alt-right. It has helped to shape the loose movement's broader rhetorical strategy of offensively stereotyping and ridiculing that is so effective in evoking strong responses from people and organisations otherwise difficult for the alt-right to influence or be noticed by.

These two seemingly unrelated concepts are both, at their core, dependent on attention, aimed at reaching as many eyes and ears as possible in order to shift values and radicalise. As such the alt-right primarily measures the success of its actions in terms of attention.

There is no doubt that social media platforms and the internet more generally have proven useful for the far right, just like they have for many progressive social movements. Long before the rise of the alt-right, far-right groups realised the potential of the internet.[9] Online platforms afford such groups a degree of anonymity they could not have had offline, lowering the social cost of engagement and making it easier to express ideas that are socially stigmatised. Additionally, it has allowed activists to connect with each other globally and thereby grow supporter bases without concern for national borders or vast geographical distances.[10]

However, certain aspects of social media platforms are particularly well-suited to the alt-right's metapolitical objectives. As the free-to-use model has been established as the norm, advertising is the main source of income for all of the large social media networks. Advertising revenue in turn depends on the amount of time users spend on the platform, hence techno-sociologist Zeynep Tufekci has concluded that attention is "the crucial resource of the digital economy."[11] In other words, social media platforms and the alt-right measure success in similar terms.

Social media platforms have become unprecedented and accessible tools for political influence campaigns, because of their importance as arenas of public debate in combination with means to quantify and evaluate performance. In addition to quantifiable measures such as number of shares a social media post has received, modern social media platforms offer users increasingly advanced tools, primarily built for advertisers, which give deep insights into the efficacy of a post or campaign. This allows alt-right activists running campaigns online to quickly iterate and find the most efficient approach. A good example can be found in leaks from a Discord channel (a group chat service commonly used among far-right activists) belonging to alt-right inspired German "identitarians" (a European far-right movement), which include screenshots of spreadsheets where the performance of a hashtag campaign on Twitter had been painstakingly measured and recorded.[12]

The role and consequences of algorithmic decision-making have been given extensive attention in recent years and it is commonly argued that algorithms do not "exist in isolation [...] but are instead embedded in multi-faceted ecologies of social, cultural and political interactions, and therefore reflect particular ways of conceiving the world," in the words of Emiliano Treré.[13] Algorithms mediate our communication on social media platforms and will therefore skew the content we consume in one direction or another. For example, evidence strongly suggests YouTube's recommendation algorithm leads viewers to increasingly more extreme content in order to retain the viewer's attention, and thereby can become the beginning of a radicalisation pathway into the alt-right.[14]

Ico Malay from Tilburg University highlights how social media platforms in essence have turned popularity into a "coded and quantified concept and as such [...][made it] manipulable."[15] In other words, the knowledge and understanding of these algorithms provides a way to make use of them in order to increase the popularity of a message, or conversely decrease someone else's visibility. When this practice is used with political motives it has been dubbed "algorithmic activism" or "algorithmic resistance."[16] The shape of this practice necessarily varies from decisions as simple as the choice of keywords for a blog post or thumbnail picture for a video, to much more intricate tactics. A report by Data & Society analysed the Alternative Right's presence on YouTube and found that key far-right accounts use practices common among mainstream YouTubers to increase their reach on the platform, but with the difference that they "also explicitly [...] promote reactionary ideology."[17] These practices include search engine optimisation (techniques to make search engines favour a web page), linking to each other's accounts in order to gain followers, and manufacturing controversies and conflict to be favoured by recommendation algorithms. Examples of figures who have used such techniques include figures such as Stefan Molyneux, Colin Robertson (AKA Millennial Woes), Lauren Southern, and Andy Warski.

Sockpuppets and mass actions

However, other methods involve direct misuse of social media platforms in ways that were not intended or are directly aimed at causing offence or harm to other users. Often these are the types of actions that are penalised by the platforms, if discovered. Here manipulation tactics are combined with the trolling culture of the alt-right to silence and harass opponents, inflate its own size and disseminate its ideas to wide audiences.

The use of sockpuppet accounts is a simple and efficient, albeit somewhat cumbersome, tactic used by those seeking to manipulate social media conversations. Sockpuppets are accounts created to deceive other members on the platform that it is a genuine user while it in fact is just one of multiple accounts run by the same person in order to instigate conflict and debate. It is often done to start a comment thread or inject a conversation with conflict and attract authentic users' attention. Additionally, it is commonly used as a way to inflate the apparent size of a group or campaign to make it more likely that it starts trending and attracts media attention.[18]

The use of sockpuppets is well documented. The Gamergate harassment campaign, where mainly male gamers reacted to the perceived encroachment of feminism on the game industry which ostensibly was one of the first rallying points of the alt-right, was in part driven by the help of sockpuppets and other manipulation tactics. Chat logs and forum threads later revealed coordinated use of the tactic and several important accounts promoting the campaign showed clear signs of being imposters.[19] There is also the case of Joshua Goldberg, a participant in the campaign who was arrested by the FBI in 2015. In the ensuing investigation, several of Goldberg's personas were revealed, one of which pretended to be a Jewish lawyer and was used to inflame discussions.[20] Goldberg has continued to specialise in impersonation tactics. In 2018 he was found guilty of planning a bomb attack on the anniversary of 9/11, posing as an IS terrorist.[21]

Leaked documents from a German identitarian chatroom have provided detailed insight into how the tactic is employed in practice. One of the documents includes detailed step-by-step instructions on how to make them and deploy them efficiently. By making use of specific browser extensions the writer claimed to run up to 100 YouTube accounts and details the potential use of fake accounts on YouTube:

> How you use the burn accounts tactically is up to you. But keep in mind that it should be useful in the context of our cause, our goals. You can appear as an antifa troll to discredit them with nonsensical comments and conversely, to give the patriots a better reputation with clever commentary. Be creative.[22]

A similar document was published by an anonymous user in June 2016 on paste-bin.com (a service often used to create easily shareable but anonymous links to documents) and subsequently shared on 4chan's /pol/ board. It details how sockpuppet accounts should be used to spread anti-Clinton memes ahead of the Presidential elections, saying that "We need to create a feeling of disgust towards

Hillary."[23] As opposed to the document released in the German identitarian chat-room, this document focuses on Twitter and explains how to get a significant number of followers for fake accounts by "follow[ing] a hundred or so people every day per account, and unfollow the ones who don't follow back after a couple days. After a few weeks, you'll have #XXX - #XXXX followers per account" and details how "normies" (people who are not supporters of the Alternative Right) can best be reached. It includes advice such as: "Use hot girl usernames/pics (Bonus points for ethnic sounding usernames). – These are best for gaining massive amounts of followers."[24]

The tactics highlight how the simplistic, quantitative measurements of popularity (such as number of followers) can be exploited to inflate importance and thereby ability to reach wider audiences and how the difficulty of verifying who is behind an account on online platforms can be exploited by the alt-right.

Often sockpuppet accounts can be used to make other types of manipulative tactics more effective. Mass downvoting content on YouTube or mass reporting opponents for infringing platform rules is a relatively common practice and a technique that has several times been used by alt-right supporters. The tactic aims to get a victim's account suspended by making it seem like a large number of users find the account problematic or framing specific content produced by the account as offensive. *Buzzfeed News* editor Katie Notopoulos became a victim of mass-reporting after alt-right associated users found an old post on her Twitter account that they argued constituted racism against white people, resulting in her being locked out of Twitter.[25]

Strategic amplification and fake news

Disinformation in the form of complete fabrications, rumours or heavily-skewed news items based on actual events are another common tactic employed by the alt-right. Social media platforms are well suited for the spread of fabricated stories because of the difficulty of assessing the origin of information. Even if the source is found, verifying the intent and validity of the information itself can still prove difficult. The speed of the networks on these platforms further means that by the time it can be debunked it can very well have researched thousands if not hundreds of thousands of people.[26]

Efforts to spread conspiracy theories and fake news and to troll mainstream media often rely on strategic amplification. Using the power of their networks and possibly other amplification techniques, manipulators can strategically push a story to a specific mainstream media outlet or in a local area and hope that if it takes hold there, it can then travel "up the chain" of successively larger outlets that are willing to trust a somewhat smaller outlet. An item might be posted on an imageboard such as 4chan's /pol/ board, where barriers of entry are low or non-existent and from which other users can pick it up and share it on mainstream social media platforms. Fringe alternative news sites, such as *The Gateway Pundit*, regularly republish content produced by Alternative Right activists on their social media channels, and are large enough to regularly be referred to by Fox News, which would be less likely to republish content produced by such social media activists.[27] *The Gateway Pundit* has, for example, spread several conspiracy theories with support in the far-right, including the claim that students who survived the Stoneman Douglas High School shooting in Parkland, Florida, were actors.[28] A concrete example of how the site has played a role in amplifying unfounded stories originating from minor far-right activists is an article from April 2017 originally based on a tweet by Swedish anti-Muslim activist Jan Sjunnesson. He posted a picture of a McDonald's flier with Arabic writing on it along with the caption "McDonalds i Södertälje" (meaning "McDonalds in Södertälje," a town in Sweden). Sjunnesson tweets in Swedish and was not shared extensively, but conspiracy theorist Peter Imanuelsen (AKA Peter Sweden), who had 13 times more followers than Sjunnesson, copied the content of the tweet and translated it to English. Imanuelsen, who has also written for other far-right conspiracy sites, was picked up by *The Gateway Pundit*,[29] the nazi Daily Stormer[30] and a four days later also by the Russian state-funded Sputnik News.[31] While the two former sites published decisively conspiratorial articles, Sputnik's narrative was more restrained but had the potential to reach a much larger audience.

Since the Unite the Right rally in Charlottesville in 2017 the tech industry has stepped up their efforts to deplatform far-right activists. All major platforms have made changes and have somewhat more consistently refused access to the far right. However, their platforms remain useful for those who spread far-right ideologies and they continue to be exploited in ever evolving ways. That will likely continue to be the case as long as attention is the primary measurement of success and the technologies are developed in a context dependent on cyberlibertarian notions of complete online freedom, the result of which is sometimes unethical methods to keep users on the platform, such as recommendation algorithms that favour divisive content and thereby play into the hands of the alt-right. Furthermore, the lack of insight into the workings of the platforms and algorithms themselves impede users, researchers, and legislators abilities from pushing for changed in an informed way. Exemplified by the many ways that the alt-right have abused social media platforms to the benefit of their cause, there are clearly multiple aspects of their services that the current platforms can address to minimise the potential impact of influence campaigns and the spread of far-right propaganda.

Notes

1   Jessie Daniels, "The Algorithmic Rise of the 'Alt-Right'," *Contexts*, 17:1 (2018).
2   Red Ice TV, 2018, *Richard Spencer – NPI 2016, Full Speech* [Online video]. Available at: https://www.YouTube.com/watch?v=Xq-LnO2DOGE [Accessed 14 October 2018].
3   Right Response Team, "The Alt-Right since Charlottesville," *Southern Poverty Law Center*, 19 August 2018. https://hopenothate.com/2018/08/19/alt-right-since-charlottesville/
4   Bill Morlin, "Extremists' 'Unite the Right' Rally: A Possible Historic Alt-Right Showcase?" *Southern Poverty Law Center*, 7 August 2017. https://www.splcenter.org/hatewatch/2017/08/07/extremists-unite-right-rally-possible-historic-alt-right-showcase

5 Marine Le Pen (@MLP_officiel). 24 April 2017, 5:00 pm, https://twitter.com/mlp_officiel/status/856523138183577600

6 George Hawley, *Making Sense of the Alt-Right* (New York: Columbia University Press, 2017), 81–90.

7 Joakim Andersen, *Rising from the Ruins: The Right of the 21ˢᵗ Century* (United Kingdom: Arktos Media Ltd., 2018), 300. Also see Chapter 1 "The European Roots of Alt-Right Ideology" in this book.

8 See Chapter 9 "The Role of the Troll: Online Antagonistic Communities and the Alternative Right" in this book. Also: Whitney Phillips, *This is Why We Can't Have Nice Things: Mapping the Relationship between Online Trolling and Mainstream Culture* (Cambridge: MIT Press, 2015).

9 Jessie Daniels, *Cyber Racism: White Supremacy Online and the New Attack on Civil Rights* (Lanham, Md: Rowman & Littlefield Publishers, 2009). Also see Chapter 10 "Alt-Tech: Co-opting and Creating Digital Spaces" in this book.

10 Caiani, Manuela, Donatella Porta, and Claudius Wagemann, "Networking Online." In Manuela Caiani, Donatella della Porta, and Claudius Wagemann (ed.), *Mobilizing on the Extreme Right: Germany, Italy, and the United States* (Oxford: Oxford University Press, 2012), 54–55.

11 Zeynep Tufekci, "How Social Media Took Us from Tahrir Square to Donald Trump," *MIT Technology Review*, 14 August 2018. https://www.technologyreview.com/s/611806/how-social-media-took-us-from-tahrir-square-to-donald-trump/

12 Jacob Davey and Julia Ebner, "The Fringe Insurgency: Connectivity, Convergence and Mainstreaming of the Extreme Right," *Institute for Strategic Dialogue*, 2017, https://www.isdglobal.org/isd-publications/the-fringe-insurgency-connectivity-convergence-and-mainstreaming-of-the-extreme-right/

13 Emiliano Treré, "Digital Activism to Algorithmic Resistance." In Meikle Graham (ed.), *The Routledge Companion to Media and Activism* (New York: Routledge, 2018), 368.

14 Rebecca Lewis, *Alternative Influence* (New York: Data & Society Research Institute, 2018).

15 Ico Maly, "Populism as a Mediatized Communicative Relation: The birth of algorithmic populism," *Tilburg Papers in Culture Studies*, paper 213 (2018), 10.

16 Emiliano Treré, "Digital Activism to Algorithmic Resistance."

17 Rebecca Lewis, *Alternative Influence*, 25.

18 Xueling Zheng, Yiu Ming Lai, K.P. Chow, Lucas C.K. Hui and S.M. Yiu, "Sockpuppet Detection in Online Discussion Forums," proceedings for 2011 Seventh International Conference on Intelligent Information Hiding and Multimedia Signal Processing (2011).

19 Ben Schreckinger, "Chat Logs Show how 4chan Users Created #GamerGate Controversy," *Ars Technica*, 9 October 2015. https://arstechnica.com/gaming/2014/09/new-chat-logs-show-how-4chan-users-pushed-gamergate-into-the-national-spotlight/

20 Torill Elvira Mortensen, "Anger, Fear, and Games: The Long Event of #GamerGate," *Games and Culture*, 13:8 (2016), 793.

21 Leesha McKenny, "Joshua Ryne Goldberg Has Pleaded Guilty to Attempting to Enlist a Person to Bomb a September 11 Memorial Event," *SBS News*, 22 December 2017. https://www.sbs.com.au/news/us-troll-who-posed-as-an-australian-jihadist-facing-20-years-in-jail

22 Unknown, "Eine kleine Anleitung im Umgang mit Brandkonten auf YouTube." https://cdn.discordapp.com/attachments/337669621681356800/353709666204909569/Anleitung_Brandkonten.pdf [Accessed 14 September 2018].

23 Anonymous, "/cfg/ <MEME, PSYOP & SUBVERSION>," *4plebs*, 10 July 2016. https://archive.4plebs.org/pol/thread/80519343/

24 MYNUNUDONALDACCOUNT, 'Advanced Meme Warfare /cfg/', 6 July 2016. https://pastebin.com/hack9Z6G.

25 Katie Notopoulos, "How Trolls Locked My Twitter Account for 10 Days, and Welp," *BuzzFeed News*, 2 December 2017. https://www.buzzfeednews.com/article/katienotopoulos/how-trolls-locked-my-twitter-account-for-10-days-and-welp

26 Alice Marwick and Rebecca Lewis, *Media Manipulation and Disinformation Online* (New York: Data & Society Research Institute, 2017), 39.

27 Ben Schreckinger, "'Real News' Joins the White House Briefing Room," *Politico Magazine*, 15 February 2017. https://www.politico.com/magazine/story/2017/02/fa ke-news-gateway-pundit-white-house-trump-briefing-room-214781

28 Arturo Garcia, "Far Right Blogs, Conspiracy Theorists Attack Parkland Mass Shooting Survivor," *Snopes*, 20 February 2018. https://www.snopes.com/news/2018/02/20/ right-wing-media-david-hogg/

29 Cristina Laila, "SWEDENISTAN – McDonald's in Sweden Sends Out Mailers in Arabic to Accommodate Muslim Migrants," *Gateway Pundit*, 30 April 2017. https:// www.thegatewaypundit.com/2017/04/swedenistan-mcdonalds-sweden-sends-mailers-ar abic-accommodate-muslim-migrants/

30 Andrew Anglin, "Sweden: McDonald's Sends Out Ads in Arabic," *Daily Stormer*, 1 May 2017. https://dailystormer.name/sweden-mcdonalds-sends-out-ads-in-arabic/

31 Sputnik International, "Swedish McDonald's Learns to Speak Arabic Due to Popular Demand," 3 May 2017. https://sputniknews.com/art_living/201705031053224840-swe dish-mcdonalds-arabic/

PART III
Gender and sexuality

12

FROM ANGER TO IDEOLOGY

A history of the manosphere

It has long been the case that far-right movements have been dominated by men. Whether that be the hierarchies of the fascist dictatorships of the 20th century or the countless far-right movements of the postwar period, most have over-whelmingly been run by, and for, men. A belief in the unavoidable, natural or desirable hierarchical nature of gender relations, the idealisation of a virile hyper-masculinity and a belief in binary genders and fixed gender roles have resulted in a pronounced misogyny in most far-right groups. However, for the contemporary Alternative Right (both its racial nationalist alt-right wing and cultural nationalist alt-lite wing), anti-feminist and misogynist politics are not merely a result of their wider political outlook but rather a central pillar of the movement's ideology, riv-alling race and racism for *primus inter pares*. One major influence on the Alternative Right's understanding of gender politics is a parallel, and sometimes overlapping, collection of groups commonly known as the "manosphere."[1]

Broadly speaking, the manosphere refers to a loose collection of websites, forums, blogs, and vlogs concerned with men's issues and masculinity, oriented around an opposition to feminism. The prevailing interpretation within the manosphere is that feminism is about promoting misandry rather than gender equality. As Alice Marwick and Robyn Caplan explain, many within the mano-sphere view feminism as "[…] intrinsically prejudicial and threatening towards men."[2] This perception is central to understanding the manosphere, for whilst many of its interests and ideas are inherently sexist, anti-feminist, and misogynistic, others, such as concerns about male suicide, are not themselves expressions of these prejudices. Rather, they are viewed in the manosphere through a lens which places the blame for such issues at the feet of women, feminism, and progressive politics. Within the manosphere are numerous subdivisions, many of which interact with the Alternative Right due to their similar anti-feminist, mis-ogynist, and anti-progressive views.

Sections of the manosphere have entered the public eye in the past two decades, in particular the Pick-Up Artist community in the 2000s following the publication of Neil Strauss' 2005 bestseller *The Game: Penetrating the Secret Society of Pickup Artists*, the anti-feminist movement following the "Gamergate" harassment campaign in the mid-2010s, and the "Incel" community, following mass murders committed by self-described incels Elliot Rodger in 2014 and Alek Minassian in 2018. These factions and others slowly came together online throughout the late 2000s and by the mid-2010s were becoming both increasingly politicised and conspiratorial. What would result is a community that often places the blame for its members' injuries, real or perceived, not just at the feet of women and feminism, but moreover on progressive politics and sometimes the racial and religious targets of the broader far right.

The first wave: The manosphere wakes up

A key, early component of the manosphere was the online "Pick-Up Artist" (PUA) community which, as the Southern Poverty Law Center describes, focuses "on teaching men how to manipulate women into sex, all the while constantly disparaging women and the idea of consent."[3]

Prior to its online migration, the PUA "community" was more disparate, and within the United States centred around followers of the "speed seduction" ideas of Paul Ross (AKA Ross Jeffries), who published his book *How to Get the Women You Desire into Bed* in 1992. The online PUA community grew, especially, out of the alt.seduction.fast (ASF) USENET forum. The ASF forum was initially billed as a means to spread the ideas of Ross. As an early post on the group from 16 November 1994 describes:

> What is alt.seduction.fast? A discussion/ongoing exchange about the ideas, techniques and secrets of Speed Seduction. Speed Seduction is the creation of Ross Jeffries [...] Ross has developed methods that any man can use to attract the best looking women, quickly and easily, using [...] language/persuasion patterns specifically geared for seduction.[4]

The posts on ASF and similar forums, in turn, were collected and used for the first "guides" published online within the PUA community, with a "layguide" published online by Estonian PUA Tony Clink in January 1999 seen as a key documentation of these early forums' discussions. Crucially, however, the early PUA community was still largely non-politicised. As Daryush Valizadeh (AKA Roosh V), a key Alternative Right-linked manosphere blogger, argued in an episode of his "Kingmaker" podcast in January 2017, Clink's text and much of the early online PUA community was "void of cultural analysis of why [men] are doing this."[5] Nonetheless, Valizadeh and his interviewee "Samseau," argued that the underlying sentiments that would fuel the politicised manosphere were already present at the birth of the online PUA community. Noting a 1992 television appearance on NBC's Faith Daniels show, featuring Ross, "Men's Rights Activist" and founder of the National Center for Men, Mel Feit, and the feminist and ethicist Bruce Weinstein, they suggest that other than occasional media spots such as this, these topics "just had no coverage." In their view, what would drive the manosphere was "already there, it was just moving onto the internet and getting exposure 'cus it could not get any exposure through the TV."[6] This is evidenced by the wider online anti-feminist and misogynist activity that could be found on USENET groups such as alt.dads.rights and alt.feminazis.[7]

Most explicitly, it was manifesting too in the "Men's Rights" movement, of which Feit was noted as a member. Emerging in response to second-wave feminism, Men's Rights Activists (MRAs) initially supported feminism's aims but focused on how traditional masculinity also harmed men. In the 1980s and 1990s offshoots emerged who either reasserted traditional masculinity (the "mythopoetic" movement), or who judged – often implicitly white, cisgender, heterosexual – men to be undergoing systematic oppression at the hands of feminism and progressive movements more broadly. The MRA movement since then has predominantly carried on these offshoot traditions.[8]

Interaction between the PUA and MRA communities was marginal in these online groups in the early- to mid-1990s. This is evident by the scant mention of Jeffries in the alt.mens-rights group and likewise minimal discussion of, for example, Warren Farrell, an influential MRA writer at the time who is considered to have launched the modern MRA movement, amongst the seduction community. Other key strands within the modern manosphere were less established at this time, namely the radicalised element of the "involuntary celibate" or "incel" subculture (whose members blame their lack of sexual and romantic success on feminism and women), and the "Men Going Their Own Way" (or, "MGTOW") subculture (a gender separatist contingent, who reject or greatly minimise their interaction with women). For the former, this is potentially explained by the theory that this community developed as a response to disillusionment with the advice of PUAs, meaning it would develop later on after the PUA community itself first grew. The MGTOW movement, likewise, is generally understood to have developed in the early- to mid-2000s in response to fractures within the MRA community at the time, both with respect to MRA activists' differing willingness to cooperate with female MRAs and the wish by some not to function as a political collective.[9]

The second wave: incel radicalisation, MRA organising and the "Roissysphere"

The Pick-Up Artist (PUA) community began to move towards its more public image in the late 1990s and into the early 2000s, growing from forums to sites such as Eben Pagan's (AKA David DeAngelo's) doubleyourdating.com which heralded an increasingly commercialised environment of "seduction gurus" delivering seminars in person and offering programmes for a fee. This led to a backlash amongst some within the PUA community and the establishment of the

"PUAhate" forum on 22 September 2009. In addition to serving as a forum for criticising PUA "scams, deception, and misleading marketing techniques used [...] to deceive men and profit from them,"[10] the forum's "Shitty Advice" subforum was amongst those that nurtured the increasingly extreme, radicalised element of the incel community. Tim Squirrell, a researcher at Edinburgh University who has written extensively on incels, describes this change in the community as follows:

> Incel forums, which began as support groups in the late 1990s, now ubiqui-
> tously accept the concept of the "blackpill", which says that a man's life
> chances are fundamentally determined by his attractiveness, and nothing they
> can do will change their fate. The only options left to them, then, are living in
> misery or taking violent action against themselves and others. They feel
> wronged by the world and they blame women, whom they hold responsible
> for not giving them the affection they believe they are entitled to.[11]

As Squirrell notes, the incel community had pre-existed online since at least the late 1990s, initially with a broader interest in offering support, for example, with the term "involuntary celibate" first appearing in the alt.support.shyness USENET group on 21 April 1998 when a user proposed the creation of a group for those who were "involuntarily celibate."[12] However, the earlier online incel community exhibited less interest in anti-feminism and misogyny, as in the case of "Alana's Involuntary Celibacy Project" founded in 1997, which posted articles and featured a mailing list.[13] In an interview with the creator of the site in 2018, the BBC reported that it was created for people "struggling to form loving relationships" and that it welcomed both men and women.[14] The eponymous Alana noted that "There was probably a bit of anger [...] but in general it was a supportive place."[15]

However, even early on there were divisions. As Squirrell describes, from the mid-2000s there was antagonism between the misogynistic and "comparatively feminist" contingents within the community which saw the latter lose out, leading to:

> an ever-dwindling emphasis on support and rehabilitation, and an increasing
> pressure to take the blackpill (that is, to accept that the world is fundamentally
> stacked against incels and that nothing will ever change for them). [...] Whilst
> misogyny and advocacy of really extreme positions (e.g. pro-rape, pro-paedo-
> philia) were always present, they weren't dominant in the same way that they
> are on contemporary sites.[16]

This shift appears true not only for incel-related sites that emerged from other parts of the manosphere, such as the aforementioned PUAhate.com, but also for sites which were part of the pre-existing incel community online. As David Futrelle, a journalist who has monitored the manosphere since 2010, remarked in the same year, the "love-shy.com" incel site (registered online in 2003) had "so much see-thing resentment among the regulars, not only of those women who have rejected them but [of] women in general."[17] PUAhate and the incel community more broadly gained greater attention after it was revealed that Elliot Rodger, who murdered six people and injured fourteen others in Isla Vista, California as "revenge on humanity" because women had rejected him, before taking his own life on 23 May 2014, had been a regular poster on the forum. Following the attack the forum was closed by its administrators, before reappearing as the "Sluthate" forum on 26 May 2014. At the time of writing, this community continues to exist in the margins of manosphere amongst a few dedicated forums, including the "Lookism" forum, created on 27 June 2015, which grew out of the Sluthate forum.[18] Whilst some in the incel community have disavowed incel-motivated attacks, including one of the few public-facing, self-identified incels (though he has since renounced the label), Jack Peterson,[19] there remains widespread praise. Peterson himself reported that he received a backlash to this condemnation, telling *The Guardian* that the incel community's response was "'You're misrepresenting us: we really do hate women. We're not joking.'"[20] Moreover, as Jesselyn Cook noted in the *Huffington Post* in July 2018, at least three men who had likewise expressed support for Rodger's murders online had themselves gone on to commit mass-murders.[21]

The late 2000s also saw the creation of what would become the central online vehicle for the Men's Rights Activist (MRA) contingent of the manosphere, Paul Elam's "A Voice for Men" (AVFM) site, created on 22 July 2009. In 2015 he launched the linked podcast, "An Ear for Men." Elam (who is a friend of influential MRA Warren Farrell) and AVFM have run a number of extreme campaigns, including calling for October to be "Bash a Violent Bitch Month."[22] That Elam is seen as a central figure in the MRA movement today, and AVFM a central organising space, is an indication of the extremes which this contingent of the manosphere have for the most part moved towards. Another key MRA organisation to emerge in this period was the Justice for Men and Boys (J4MB) party in the UK, registered with the UK Electoral Commission on 21 February 2013.[23] J4MB was founded by Mike Buchanan, a former consultant to the Conservative party who quit in 2009 after the party's then leader, David Cameron, supported all-women parliamentary candidate shortlists.[24]

Whilst the MRA community had been politically-focused since its origins, the mid- to late-2000s saw the increased politicisation of the PUA community, in part because of the blogger James C. Weidmann (AKA Roissy in DC). Weidmann is widely credited within the manosphere and in the broader Alternative Right with introducing more of the "cultural analysis" that Valizadeh noted was not as central to the PUA community early on. Weidmann himself was a commenter on Valizadeh's earlier blog, "DC Bachelor" (itself following his first blog, Roosh.com, which began in 2001), and was encouraged by Valizadeh to start blogging himself. Weidmann created his initial blog, roissy.wordpress.com, in April 2007 and would go on to move onto the "Citizen Renegade" blog, and eventually the "Chateau Heartiste" blog on 7 May 2008 where he would establish himself as a central voice in the manosphere.

Weidmann – along with other PUA bloggers including Valizadeh and the "Rational Male" blog run by "Rollo Tomassi" – marked a change in this particular subsection of the manosphere. Specifically, those who had been PUA adherents (as well as many who had become disillusioned with it) began to increasingly interpret the initial motivation for PUA – i.e. men needing help to seduce women – as a symptom of a deeper social ill. These bloggers would offer their readers theories as to why their difficulties in seducing women were the result of the influence of feminism and wider progressive movements on society, supporting their explanations with pseudo-academic theories encompassing ideas from history, evolutionary psychology, and much else. In this way, Weidmann and others who took a similar approach to discussions of the themes of PUA had an impact inside and outside the PUA community. Internally, this rearticulated the grievances of the readers of PUA sites, as many now believed that the wool had been pulled from their eyes and they could see that what appeared to be simply something they struggled with – seducing women – was the result of a deeper societal effort resulting from progressive movements working against their interests.

Externally, this likely also drew many from the interests of PUA to the traditional topics of the MRA community, such as fathers' rights, which now many in the manosphere would interpret as under fire from the same progressive movements. This mindset was further crystallised by the manosphere's adoption of the "red pill" meme – "a metaphorical term used to describe the epiphany of the unpleasant truth of reality in a wide range of contexts" – that had already existed online since at least 2004.[25] This manifested itself most explicitly in the manosphere with the creation of the "r/theredpill" subforum of the popular forum site, Reddit.com, in 2012. The "red pill" subforum, which was revealed by *The Daily Beast* in 2017 to have been founded by then-Republican congressman for the New Hampshire House of Representatives, Robert Fisher, would go on to become a central online space within the manosphere.[26]

Moreover, however, this shift to addressing progressive politics beyond feminism – as was the focal concern of the MRA community – highlighted the slowly increasing overlap of parts of the manosphere with the wider far right. This is evident from a round-up of its key sites by the Southern Poverty Law Center in 2012.[27] Whilst the majority of sites listed maintained a focus primarily on men's issues, anti-feminism, and misogyny, the In Mala Fide blog, started by Matt Forney (AKA Ferdinand Bardamu) in 2009, is noted to have a wider set of interests alongside its underlying belief that "Feminism is a hate movement designed to disenfranchise and dehumanize men."[28] They note that Forney describes the blog as:

> [a]n online magazine dedicated to publishing heretical and unpopular ideas. Ideas that polite society considers "racist," "misogynistic," "homophobic," "bigoted" or other slurs used to shut down critical thinking and maintain the web of delusions that keep our world broken and dying.[29]

That Forney already had a broader political focus including race and notions of civilisational decline is insightful with regard to understanding how the wider manosphere was coming to see itself, since at this point it was only beginning to coalesce into a network which its constituent factions (PUA, MRA, MGTOW, etc.) recognised as knitted together. As the manosphere blogger "Dalrock" wrote in a May 2013 post entitled "What is the manosphere?":

> the concept of the manosphere only goes back a few years [...] Just a year or two back I would have offered a very simple definition [...] If you were somewhat regularly included in Ferdinand Bardamu's weekly link roundup, I would argue that this made you a de facto member of the manosphere. [...] I don't think it is an exaggeration to state that his link roundups played a central role in knitting together extremely different groups into a common conversation.[30]

Already as early as 2009, Forney's blog demonstrated this interaction from within the manosphere to the wider far right and early alt-right ideological tributaries. An archive of his "Friends of In Mala Fide" blogroll lists, amongst various manosphere sites, the future alt-right vlogger "RamZPaul," a blog focusing on a popular, racist pseudoscientific theory of the alt-right – "Human Biodiversity" – and the "2blowhards" blog, which gave rise to the blogger Curtis Yarvin (AKA Mencius Moldbug), influential within the alt-right tributary movement, "Neoreaction."[31]

During this period in the development of the manosphere, Forney was by no means an exception in this respect. In July 2008 Weidmann, for example, had already uploaded a long post praising "Sexual Utopia in Power,"[32] an influential essay within the alt-right and the manosphere by Frances Roger Devlin. Published in the white nationalist journal, *The Occidental Quarterly*, in 2006 it declares "Western woman has become the new 'white man's burden,' and the signs are that he is beginning to throw it off."[33] Likewise, Weidmann declared on his blog on 13 November 2008 that "Diversity is a wonderful thing to observe, if not necessarily to live amongst," a sentiment that would snowball into his now oft-repeated phrase, "diversity + proximity = war."[34]

Nonetheless, others in the manosphere did not share this support of the extreme racial politics of the emerging alt-right, including Paul Elam.[35] Likewise, whilst some in the alt-right were supportive of the manosphere, even inviting its key figures to conferences,[36] others were more reticent. Writing on the website of his white nationalist publishing organisation, Counter-Currents Publishing, in February 2015, central US alt-right figure Greg Johnson admitted his interest and praise of some writers in the manosphere, stating that, "For several years now, the website I read more than any other has been Chateau Heartiste, formerly known as Chateau Roissy. I also read Roosh V. from time to time." Despite this, in Johnson's view, whilst:

> The manosphere provides the New Right with all the theoretical premises necessary for a patriarchal sexual counter-revolution that reinstitutes traditional and – it turns out – biologically sound norms and institutions to govern sexuality, thereby promoting the individual happiness of men and women and the common good of society and the race in general. [...] in practical terms,

the manosphere does not promote such a restoration, but instead urges an ethic of "riding the tiger" (or perhaps the cougar), i.e., to personally wallow in – and thus to amplify and advance – the decadence that we are supposed to combat.[37]

The perception was shared amongst others at the time, with a comment on Johnson's post (which Johnson appeared to affirm), observing that:

> [The] Manosphere is becoming more overtly racial. And the more successful writers are being forced to pick sides. Heartiste has made outright overtures to the meme seeders from our Pro White camp (with both tweets and supporting post [sic] on his blog).[...] I would guess as things become more and more racial. [sic] Certain elements of Manosphere may clean up their acts and heed some of your advice. And I would bet other elements become more and more degenerate. The battle lines are drawn.[38]

Johnson's observation regarding the nihilism of elements of the manosphere was likely picking up on the "PUAhate" reaction to the PUA community and the growing incel subculture. Of course, this was also true of the wider manosphere as despite the galvanising effect of Weidmann, Forney, and others, more connectivity and a more conscious shared rejection of feminism could not resolve the fundamental divergences in how these various subcultures chose to respond to their shared enemy. Indeed, Johnson picked up on another disagreement in regard to this, when he judged that "the manosphere simply takes emancipated female sexuality as a given." This aligns with the view amongst some in the PUA community that MRA was inherently flawed because it attempted to advocate men's rights within a political arena which PUAs saw as weighted to progressive and feminist interests. For the most ardently sexist and misogynist PUAs (and others in other subcultures of the manosphere), they would argue that the very idea of equality between men and women is mistaken, since they view the latter as inferior to men and therefore not entitled to equal rights.

Yet, it is also clear that Johnson wasn't perhaps quite as au fait with the manosphere's internal politics as he may have suggested, since key figures within the manosphere had publicly rejected one another over many of these issues three years prior. After an attempted rapprochement beginning in 2009, in 2012 Valizadeh declared that "The Men's Right's Movement is Dead"[39] and was joined by others, including Jack Donovan, the advocate of "male tribalism" (described by Matthew N. Lyons as "a social and political order based on small, close-knit 'gangs' of male warriors"[40]), in rejecting the MRA movement.[41] In response to Valizadeh, Elam likewise rejected PUAs, a prominent blogger associated with MGTOW ("zed") and the contingent of the manosphere that was beginning to embracing the broader far right. Elam wrote:

> things in the sphere have changed a lot in recent times. Ferdinand Bardamu, after letting In Mala Fide devolve from a rigorously thoughtful source of counter-theory into a cesspool of white supremacy and anti-Semitism, mercifully checked out for good.[42]

Elam too recognised, however, that these divergences had existed throughout the attempts of the various subcultures of the manosphere to coalesce, adding that:

> The very expression, man-o-sphere, implicitly paints an image of connectivity; of shared purpose and identity. Aside from distaste for feminism, which anyone capable of critical thought will share, there is no real or abiding connection; no universality or even commonality, and that lacking manifests in how we tear ourselves, and each other, down, and always have.[43]

The third wave: the manosphere as ideology

Whatever disunity persisted, by the mid-2010s the manosphere was taking on a life of its own outside of its origins, in part because its central sentiment of "taking the red pill" and rejecting a plank of progressive politics – namely, feminism – continued to find resonance with the broader Alternative Right's rejection of various prevailing liberal-left principles. As such, it mattered less if the old guard of the Men's Rights Activists (MRAs), Pick-Up Artists (PUA), and other manosphere groups saw few points of agreement beyond anti-feminism, since those outside of these communities who shared grievances about feminism could nonetheless pick and choose from them as part of their broader commitment to the even bigger tent of the Alternative Right.[44]

The best demonstration of this was the "Gamergate" phenomenon. Ostensibly an effort to protect the male "safe space" of gaming from the perceived encroachment of feminist values, it unfolded from August 2014 onwards after a spurned boyfriend posted online alleging that his ex-girlfriend – a female game developer – had been unfaithful. This resulted in an organised harassment campaign against female and feminist game developers and critics, which resonated with the anti-feminist sentiment that united the manosphere and, as such, led to much support from within it. Gamergate would prove advantageous to both those in the manosphere who rejected the Alternative Right and those who had maintained a connection. For the former, it was a clear means of drawing in new recruits to the anti-feminist cause and for the latter, it was a canary in the coalmine for their future radicalising efforts online, indicating to those already within its ranks the extent of support – and online activism – they might be able to further muster amongst a contingent of angry, white, young men online. For many within this group involved in Gamergate, in fact, it served as the initial "red pill" (i.e. "progressives are controlling the gaming industry") on the path of more and more extreme conspiracy theories.[45]

At the same time, the role of conspiracy theories in further radicalising followers of the manosphere reflects back in an important way onto those of its constituents who claimed to reject the Alternative Right. What they reject primarily is the extreme positions on race espoused by the white nationalist alt-right, yet the Alternative Right also encompasses the "alt-lite," who maintain xenophobic, Western chauvinist, and nativist views but who do not wish to create white ethnostates. Such views sit comfortably with many in the manosphere who reject the alt-right's white nationalism, including Elam who, in a pre-recorded speech played at the 2018 International Conference on Men's Issues in London, voiced his support for the nationalist and populist surge in the US and Europe in recent years, before declaring that "the war against feminism is a war against the left."[46] This recourse to a further enemy is, moreover, integral to manosphere thought. As Christa Hoddap has highlighted, MRA's incoherent depiction of feminists as all-controlling yet irrational and unintelligent requires conceiving of them as "dupes" who are themselves "puppets of the powers that be."[47] She draws attention to the following quote from Elam:

> Feminism is not for feminists. Feminists are idiots, but they are useful idiots in the description previously reserved [for] the Soviet sycophants in Cold War America. Feminism, in reality, is for governments and corporations. And it is the most effective tool for control of the masses since the riot baton and water cannons. Feminists are not a bunch of nut cases that have taken over the world. They're just a bunch of nut cases that have assisted some really smart and devious people in erasing any impediments they might have ever had at putting a leash on all of us.[48]

Hoddap notes that Elam does not elaborate exactly on who these "devious people" are beyond being those found in "governments and corporations," though it is clear how this could open up ideological space for conspiratorial, far-right theories to enter the manosphere community, including antisemitic conspiracies. Indeed, Elam, who rejects antisemitism, noted in 2017 that AVFM had attracted anti-semites "for years."[49]

In contrast to those in the manosphere who more readily rejected far-right tendencies following the growth of outside interest in the manosphere, Valizadeh and others welcomed the spread as a means of promoting traditional masculinity (or as he and some others in the Alternative Right have termed it, "neomasculinity").[50] In the aforementioned podcast discussion on his Return of Kings website from January 2017, Valizadeh noted this, suggesting that the manosphere began to become more of a countercultural movement from 2011 onwards and was creating an altogether new ideology and had provided a "masculine justification"[51] that, he argued, played a key role in electing Donald Trump to the US presidency in 2016.[52] Even read charitably, this claim overlooks the more fundamental socio-economic drivers that undergird ostensibly gender-based support for Trump (or any other nationalist and populist leader). Nonetheless, the narrative Valizadeh is utilising is convincing for many of the "red-pilled" adherents of the Alternative Right, more broadly. As his interviewee summarised the manosphere in the aforementioned podcast:

> When the internet came out and men could discuss their problems anonymously now you could be honest without fear [...] What started with trying

to figure out how to get laid because you're living in a destroyed dating market [...] moved on to politics [...] and then when you have [...] guys like Trump saying, "we need to focus on ourselves, we can't just be focusing on the rest of the world, we can't just keep taking care of everyone who shows up on our doorstep, we need to have families again" [...] this is obviously going to resonate with this huge segment of men who've discovered over the internet that their culture has been destroyed, that their old culture is gone and that if they want to have a future for themselves in their civilization they have to act real fast.[53]

The above quote is especially concerned with the politicisation of the PUA community, yet its discussion of anonymous collectives of aggrieved men coalescing online describes a trajectory true of all the subsections of the manosphere. From MRAs to incels and even the anti-collectivist Men Going Their Own Way (MGTOW) movement, to an extent, the early web allowed a cohort of men harbouring implicit and explicit anti-feminist and misogynist views to come together. Throughout the 2000s and into the early 2010s the various factions of the manosphere began to see one another, as well as many in the Alternative Right, as part of a broader movement whose common enemy was the progressive world. Despite this, the manosphere remains a conglomeration with deep-running internecine disputes, given that they are based on political cleavages that have been in place since its origins. Furthermore, the extreme racial and religious politics of the Alternative Right does not enjoy uniform support across the manosphere. Given these fractures, the longevity of the already loosely tied network of the manosphere and its degree of overlap with the Alternative Right is questionable. However, as the most recent phase of the manosphere's development indicates, its lasting influence may be the embittered worldview that has been fostered online.

Prospects for the manosphere

The main subcultures of the manosphere by and large undermine their own political growth. The PUA community may act as a route into more politically-focused sub-cultures, but they themselves are primarily interested in altering individual lifestyles, as are MGTOW who, moreover, actively reject collective action. More complex are the prospects of MRAs and incels. The latter largely discourage political action, including collective action, and promote a deeply pessimistic worldview. However, some incels have and may continue to pose a violent threat, a response borne from the same pessimism. Moreover, as Ross Haenfler has highlighted, the pessimism for change, mutual discouragement and lack of traditional organisation found in incel communities does not mean they do not play a role in catalysing seemingly lone actor violence.[54]

The prospects for the MRA community are comparatively stronger, in part because they emphasise collective action and because they employ a framework of human rights activism. Yet, in both respects, their ideology also contains the contradictions which undermine their growth, and in a way that is instructive about problems for the longevity of manosphere ideology as a whole, despite its recent influence beyond its original web community.

Regarding collective action, despite banding together, MRAs often refuse to engage beyond their community, regularly rejecting mainstream institutions and political movements on the assumption that these are "gynocentric" (i.e. focused on a female or feminist point of view) and thus run contrary to their interests. Moreover, though a minority of MRAs engage in protests, marches, leafleting, and so on, central to the community since its online coalescence and following campaigns such as Gamergate, has been a focus on disrupting what they see as a society that is fundamentally hostile to men's wellbeing, and the promotion of the "truth" of feminist oppression of men's rights. In Elam's words, "Our one and only job is to fuck their shit up; to make them suffer the pain of truth, and to keep doing it till they have no place to hide."[55] This combative, silencing approach to engaging with others outside of their community undermines, of course, their capacity to grow, though MRAs believe that their efforts to reveal the "truth" about feminism will win them supporters who are rejecting feminism or who simply do not identify as feminists.

A recent example of this is MRA efforts to mobilise this supposed "non-feminist" segment of the population. MRAs follow a trend present in the broader contemporary far right of presenting themselves as martyrs for free speech; censored for merely trying to speak the "truth" about "dangerous" progressive ideas or religions, typically Islam in the present context. Such an approach to feminism is clear in the "Non-Feminist Declaration" published online by British MRAs in 2018, which stated, "Recognizing the growth of feminist aggression, we assert our right to exist and thrive without paying any respect to feminists or their ideology. We shall not permit feminists to dictate what we say, how we say it or how we interact with the world."[56] By promoting the idea that feminism is an authoritative, controlling ideology MRAs may indeed initially capitalise on a contingent who can be swayed from being non-feminists to anti-feminists, creating room for sexism and misogyny to be legitimised through the undermining of feminist reform.

However, whatever initial gains MRAs may make by attempting a less hostile interaction with the mainstream, a deeper internal contradiction of MRA beliefs found in their "human rights" framework, places a limit on their growth in the long run and that of the manosphere ideology moreover. Despite their claims to be working from a basis of human rights, the MRA analysis of the harms men face is better understood as the opposite: a decidedly non-universal political programme which implicitly relegates other groups' rights in the interests of maintaining a subsection of men's rights (and not to the latter's benefit either). As Christa Hoddap explains, at its core, this movement "[...] seeks a broad negative right of noninterference concerning the maintenance of hegemonic masculinity," where the agent of interference is identified as feminism and said interference is articulated as a system of oppression which drives the harms men face (typical MRA topics include male suicide, exposure to dangerous work, and prison sentencing).[57] By seeking to uphold a right (more accurately understood as an *existing* privilege for some) to maintain hegemonic masculinity in the name of "human" rights, MRAs advocate a conception of what it means to achieve genuine equality in society which in fact simply maintains the status quo and the current inequalities faced by other groups therein. This allows for the perpetuation of women's oppression through not addressing the features of hegemonic masculinity which systematically harm them, but the problems extend to other groups as well. As Hoddap notes, "There is no clear denial in most instances on the part of the [Men's Rights Movement] that certain men experience other oppressions such as racism, classism, homophobia, but the point is that these forms of oppression are often secondary to the overwhelming gender oppression men are claimed to experience."[58] It was noted above that antisemitic conspiracy theories can find a route into the manosphere through the explanatory gaps it allows in its analysis of supposed feminist power. Similarly, a relegation of other identity experiences leaves the MRA analysis of inequality inadequate in explaining harms experienced by different kinds of men, whilst a disinterest or outright rejection of intersectionality allows room for wider far-right prejudices to be fostered.

Not only does the MRA "human rights" framework in fact uphold inequalities, it also fails to adequately explain why men face the harms they do. The maintenance of hegemonic masculinity means the maintenance of many of these harms, but not for women or feminism's gain. For example, it can be argued that societal expectations on men to carry out dangerous work and engage in risk-taking behaviour for the sake of fulfilling their "protector" roles, is of benefit to military interests, which in turn are arguably of interest to others' imperial and economic interests. A multifaceted analysis such as this sidesteps the needless antagonism towards potential allies in groups also harmed by these exploitative interests, and gives men a path to counteracting the harms they face which doesn't also harm these allies. Crucially, it also, as Hoddap notes, does so without suggesting that the harms men face add up to a system of oppression which is uniquely aimed at men; many groups, after all, are subject to these kinds of exploitation. Hoddap draws attention to this distinction when quoting Marilyn Frye, who highlighted that "Human beings can be miserable without being oppressed, and it is certainly perfectly consistent to deny that a person or a group is oppressed without denying that they have feelings or suffer."[59] Overlooking the distinction between harm and oppression is arguably the fundamental mistake of MRA beliefs, and the manosphere ideology moreover. Indeed, in rejecting feminism and progressive politics more broadly, and so maintaining masculinity as it is, the manosphere can only offer men more of the same, which in the long run will only lead to disillusionment and attrition. As Hoddap notes, despite its claims to revealing the "truth" to men, MRA and the manosphere moreover, is ultimately a movement with "no momentum for change."[60]

Notes

1 For discussion of the wider understanding of gender and sexuality in the Alternative Right, see Chapter 14 "Sexuality and the Alternative Right" in this book.
2 Alice E. Marwick & Robyn Caplan "Drinking Male Tears: Language, the Manosphere, and Networked Harassment," *Feminist Media Studies*, 18:4 (2018), 543–559.
3 "Male Supremacy," *Southern Poverty Law Centre*. https://www.splcenter.org/fighting-ha te/extremist-files/ideology/male-supremacy. Alice Marwick and Rebecca Lewis note

that, "While dating advice broadly understood can help shy, awkward, or frustrated young men gain confidence in social interactions, the PUA community distorts this by dehumanizing women and granting all sexual agency to men." Alice Marwick and Rebecca Lewis, *Media Manipulation & Disinformation Online* (New York: Data & Society Research Institute, 2017), 15.

4 Alan L. Bostick, post on "alt.seduction.fast FAQ," 16 November 1994. https://groups. google.com/forum/#!original/alt.seduction.fast/yxBws4R0lSs/9baQQPbejR8J [Accessed 3 September 2018].

5 Roosh V, 2017, *How the Manosphere Crushed Feminism* [Online Video]. Available at: http s://www.youtube.com/watch?v=-WgAn6GFU0E [Accessed 3 September 2018].

6 Ibid.

7 Marwick and Caplan have demonstrated how key tropes in the manosphere, including an anti-feminist interpretation of the concept of "misandry," emerged early on in such groups and served a role in building the sphere's sense of community. Alice E. Marwick and Robyn Caplan, "Drinking Male Tears: Language, the Manosphere, and Networked Harassment," *Feminist Media Studies*, 18:4 (2018), 543–559.

8 As Marwick and Caplan describe it, the men's rights movement today is "defined as much against feminism as it is for men's rights." Ibid., 546.

9 The exact origins are a matter of conflicting interpretation within the manosphere, however. See: "MGTOW History," *MGTOW History.* https://web.archive.org/web/ 20130219174037/http://www.mgtowhistory.com/ [Accessed 5 September 2018]; Fedrz, "The History of Men Going Their Own Way," *No Ma'am,* 2 January 2006. http s://archive.is/BBgcl; "The Protocols of the Elders of MGTOW: the original MGTOW manifesto revealed!" *Reddit.* https://www.reddit.com/r/MGTOW/comments/3ust22/ the_protocols_of_the_elders_of_mgtow_the_original/ [Accessed 5 September 2018]. Outside of its growth online, most within the manosphere recognise that MGTOW attitudes were found amongst MRAs prior to it being termed "MGTOW." Even within the online history of MRA, such sentiments were expressed early on. A post on alt.mens. rights in 1994 called for a boycott of women's businesses, for example: Greg Gonzalez, post on "Boycott Women's Business," 7 September 1994. https://groups.google.com/ forum/#!topic/alt.mens-rights/QXX_B1zVOTE [Accessed 5 September 2018].

10 Katie J.M. Baker, "The Angry Underground World of Failed Pick-Up Artists," *Jezebel,* 2 May 2012. https://jezebel.com/5906648/the-angry-underground-world-of-failed-pickup-artists

11 Tim Squirrell, "Nathan Larson, The Self-Described Incel Paedophile, is Running for Congress. This is How he Groomed Vulnerable Young Men," *The Independent,* 5 June 2018. https://www.independent.co.uk/voices/nathan-larson-incel-paedophile-dark-web-congress-virginia-a8384391.html

12 Dan, post on "Proposal: alt.support.celibacy," 21 April 1998. https://groups.google. com/forum/#!searchin/alt.support.shyness/involuntary$20celibate|sort:date/alt.support. shyness/ekeQ76Ow0gI/KQA5YG2OYWkJ [Accessed 10 September 2018].

13 "Home," *Alana's Involuntary Celibacy Project.* https://web.archive.org/web/20030212170914/ http://www.ncf.carleton.ca:80/~ad097/ic-home.html [Accessed 10 September 2018].

14 Jim Taylor, "The Woman who Founded the 'Incel' Movement'," *BBC,* 30 August 2018. https://www.bbc.co.uk/news/world-us-canada-45284455

15 Ibid.

16 Tim Squirrell, "A Definitive Guide to Incels Part Three: The History of Incel," *Tim Squirrell,* 4 June 2018. https://www.timsquirrell.com/blog/2018/6/4/a-definitive-gui de-to-incels-part-three-the-history-of-incel

17 David Futrelle, "Love-Shyness and The Perpetual Resentment Machine," *We Hunted the Mammoth,* 21 December 2010. http://www.wehuntedthemammoth.com/2010/12/21/ love-shyness-and-the-perpetual-resentment-machine/

18 "Lookism" refers to discrimination on the basis of someone's appearance. As Allie Conti wrote for *VICE* regarding the forum, its users "obsess over the idea of the 'perfect face' in hopes of figuring out how they might reconstruct their own, however recklessly, so as to attract mates. A popular section of the site contains rate-me threads, where Incels post

selfies so anonymous commenters can make recommendations on how they can 'looksmax' – or get more attractive. Tips range from seemingly sane advice on a new hairstyle to admonishments to get expensive and brutal surgeries [...]." Allie Conti, "Learn to Decode the Secret Language of the Incel Subculture," *VICE*, 26 June 2018. https://www.vice.com/en_us/article/7xmaze/learn-to-decode-the-secret-language-of-the-incel-subculture

19 Melissa Jeltsen, "The Unmasking of an Incel," *The Huffington Post*, 6 July 2018. https://www.huffingtonpost.co.uk/entry/unmaking-of-an-incel_us_5b11a9a ee4b0d5e89e1fb519

20 Justin Ling, "Not as Ironic as I Imagined: The Incels Spokesman on Why He is Renouncing Them," *The Guardian*, 19 June 2018. https://www.theguardian.com/world/2018/jun/19/incels-why-jack-peterson-left-elliot-rodger

21 Specifically, Chris Harper-Mercer in Oregon, USA in October 2015, Nikolas Cruz in Florida, USA in February 2018 and Alek Minassian in Toronto, Canada in April 2018. Rodger is generally credited with being the first high-profile attack explicitly linked to the extreme misogynist element of the incel community, though other similar attacks have been tied to the manosphere more broadly. These include George Sodini, who engaged in a mass-shooting of a women's aerobics class in Pittsburgh, USA in August 2009 and was later revealed to have been interested in the Pick-Up Artist community and to have expressed his misogynist intentions online. See: Edecio Martinez, "Gym Killer Was Devoted Follower of Dating Guru," *CBS News*, 10 August 2009. https://www.cbsnews.com/news/gym-killer-was-devoted-follower-of-dating-guru/; Sean D. Hamill, "Blog Details Shooter's Frustration," *The New York Times*, 5 August 2009. https://www.nytimes.com/2009/08/06/us/06shoot.html

22 Paul Elam, "If You See Jezebel in the Road, Run the Bitch Down," *A Voice for Men*. 22 October 2010. https://www.avoiceformen.com/mens-rights/domestic-violence-industry/if-you-see-jezebel-in-the-road-run-the-bitch-down/. AVFM has claimed the article was intended as "satire of the Juvenalian variety."

23 It is important to note that MRA groups – and the manosphere moreover – can be found across the globe, including, for example, the Indian MRA organisation, "Save India Family Foundation," who have attended events organised by J4MB and AVFM.

24 Helen Nianias, "'Feminists Hate Men': Meet Mike Buchanan, the Leader of Britain's new Justice for Men and Boys Party," *The Independent*, 14 January 2015. https://www.independent.co.uk/news/people/feminists-hate-men-meet-mike-buchanan-the-lea der-of-britains-new-justice-for-men-and-boys-party-9977357.html. J4MB are electorally as marginal as they come, and in practice function as a pressure group carrying out small demonstrations to little attention, and only occasionally are engaged with by the media. More effective has been the party's ability to act as the central organisers of UK anti-feminist activity, and as a liaison to anti-feminists abroad. J4MB co-organised the 2018 (London), 2017 (Gold Coast, Australia), and 2016 (London) International Conferences on Men's Issues (ICMI), the key international meetup for anti-feminist activists, alongside anti-feminist groups in the US, India, Australia, and elsewhere (the first was organised by A Voice For Men and held in Detroit in 2014).

25 "Red Pill," *Know Your Meme*. https://knowyourmeme.com/memes/red-pill

26 Bonnie Bacarisse, "The Republican Lawmaker Who Secretly Created Reddit's Women-Hating 'Red Pill'," *The Daily Beast*, 25 April 2017. https://www.thedailybeast.com/the-republican-lawmaker-who-secretly-created-reddits-women-hating-red-pill

27 "Misogyny: The Sites," *Intelligence Report*, 1 March 2012. https://www.splcenter.org/fighting-hate/intelligence-report/2012/misogyny-sites. It is worth noting too that Forney's then-moniker was a character from a 1932 novel written by the antisemitic French writer Louis-Ferdinand Céline and, as the Southern Poverty Law Centre's *Intelligence Report* notes, at the time of writing the blog advertised the racist 1920s text, *The Revolt Against Civilization* by Lothrop Stoddard.

28 "Misogyny: The Sites," *Intelligence Report*, 1 March 2012. https://www.splcenter.org/fighting-hate/intelligence-report/2012/misogyny-sites

29 Ibid.
30 Dalrock, "What is the Manosphere," *Dalrock*, 15 May 2013. https://dalrock.wordpress.com/2013/05/15/what-is-the-manosphere/
31 "Home," Ferdinand Bardamu. https://web.archive.org/web/20091125135522/http://fbardamu.wordpress.com:80/ [Accessed 13 September 2018]. An archive of the blog's "About" page the same year is emblematic of the slow radicalising occurring throughout these fringe, far-right blogs, with Forney describing himself as only, "Conservative in politics, anarchist in nature, libertine by necessity, [and] misanthropic by choice." "About," Ferdinand Bardamu. https://web.archive.org/web/20091125135522/http://fbardamu.wordpress.com:80/ [Accessed 13 September 2018].
32 Chateau Heartiste, "Decivilizing: Human Nature Unleashed," *Heartiste*. 23 July 2008. https://heartiste.wordpress.com/2008/07/23/decivilizing-human-nature-unleashed/
33 F. Roger Devlin, "Sexual Utopia in Power," *The Occidental Quarterly*, 6:2 (2006), 30. Valizadeh embraced the alt-right later, but firmly showed his willingness to do so following a praising 2015 review of the core antisemitic text for the alt-right, Kevin MacDonald's 1998 book *The Culture of Critique: An Evolutionary Analysis of Jewish Involvement in Twentieth-Century Intellectual and Political Movements*. Roosh Valizadeh, "The Damaging Effects of Jewish Intellectualism and Activism on Western Culture," *Return of Kings*, 4 May 2015. http://www.returnofkings.com/62716/the-damaging-effects-of-jewish-intellectualism-and-activism-on-western-culture
34 Chateau Heartiste, "How American Women are Seen by Kazakhs," *Heartiste*, 13 November 2008. https://heartiste.wordpress.com/2008/11/13/how-american-women-are-seen-by-kazakhs/.
35 Paul Elam, "Adios, c-ya, good-bye man-o-sphere," *A Voice for Men*, 5 September 2012. https://www.avoiceformen.com/men/adios-man-o-sphere/
36 Most notably, Valizadeh and Forney's attendance of the 2016 National Policy Institute conference. David Futrelle, "Roosh V Denounced as Degenerate 'Muzzie' by White Supremacists He's Trying to Woo," *We Hunted the Mammoth*, 2 November 2015. http://www.wehuntedthemammoth.com/2015/11/02/roosh-v-denounced-as-degenerate-muzzie-by-white-supremacists-hes-trying-to-woo/. Interestingly, Canadian vlogger Stefan Molyneux, who would become a key web-presence in the Alternative Right, appeared at the 2014 International Conference on Men's Issues, the major annual MRA gathering. Stefan Molyneux, 2014, *#ICMI-Stefan Molyneux* [Online video]. Available at: https://www.youtube.com/watch?v=ErwrBCyCpd4&list=PLHLREeMe4S0OmV_BYAfWNWi0qQzu2FWzK&index=16 [Accessed 15 September 2018].
37 Greg Johnson, "Does the Manosphere Morally Corrupt Men?" *Counter-Currents Publishing*, 25 February 2015. https://www.counter-currents.com/2015/02/does-the-manosphere-morally-corrupt-men/
38 Ibid.
39 Roosh V, "The Men's Rights Movement Is Dead," *Roosh V*, 27 August 2012. http://www.rooshv.com/the-mens-rights-movement-is-dead
40 Matthew N. Lyons, *Ctrl-Alt-Delete: An Antifascist Report on the Alternative Right* (Montreal: Kersplebedeb Publishing, 2017), 9.
41 Jack Donovan, "Long Live the Manosphere," *Jack Donovan*, 9 September 2012. https://web.archive.org/web/20170715140531/http://www.jack-donovan.com/axis/2012/09/long-live-the-manosphere/. The view was reiterated by the popular manosphere site, The Spearhead, in 2015 prior to its folding: W.F. Price, 'Why MRA Has Been and Will Continue to Be a Failure," *The Spearhead*, 30 January 2015. https://web.archive.org/web/20150324035714/http://www.the-spearhead.com/2015/01/30/why-mra-has-been-and-will-continue-to-be-a-failure/
42 Paul Elam, "Adios, c-ya, good-bye man-o-sphere," *A Voice for Men*, 5 September 2012. https://www.avoiceformen.com/men/adios-man-o-sphere/. This was prior to Forney's later return to blogging.
43 Ibid.

44 Moreover, many in the manosphere – albeit often in a hyperbolic and grandiose tone – predicted that the anti-feminist sentiment driving the manosphere would increasingly affect mainstream politics, irrespective of the manosphere's unity. A blog post published on 1 January 2010 that proved influential within the manosphere, entitled "The Misandry Bubble," declared that: "The Western World has quietly become a civilization that has tainted the interaction between men and women [...] where male nature is vilified but female nature is celebrated. This [...] is a recipe for a rapid civilizational decline and displacement, the costs of which will ultimately be borne by a subsequent generation of innocent women, rather than men, as soon as 2020." Imran Khan, "The Misandry Bubble," *Singularity 2050*, 1 January 2010. http://www.singularity2050.com/2010/01/the-misandry-bubble.html

45 Hatewatch Staff, "McInnes, Molyneux, and 4chan: Investigating Pathways to the Alt-Right," *Southern Poverty Law Center*, 19 April 2018. https://www.splcenter.org/20180419/mcinnes-molyneux-and-4chan-investigating-pathways-alt-right

46 Paul Elam, 2018, *20 July 2018: Paul Elam – "The Men's Movement: Personal and Political" (ICMI18)* [Online video]. Available at: https://www.youtube.com/watch?v= KWK0Lx9X7x4. In a likely allusion to the raft of Alternative Right vloggers who advocate a return to traditional gender roles for men, Elam also warned viewers during this talk of anti-feminists who are not also MRAs. Whilst MRAs tend to defend much of traditional masculinity, they believe women and feminists seek to maintain traditional male roles – such as being "breadwinners" or "protectors" – for their own gain.

47 Paul Elam, 2018, *20 July 2018: Paul Elam – "The Men's Movement: Personal and Political" (ICMI18)* [Online video]. Available at: https://www.youtube.com/watch?v= KWK0Lx9X7x4. In Christa Hodapp, *Men's Rights, Gender, and Social Media* (Lanham: Lexington Books, 2017), 6–7.

48 Paul Elam, "The X%: What Feminism Is Really about and Why Anyone who Values Freedom Should Fight against It," *A Voice for Men*, 19 November 2013. https://www.avoiceformen.com/feminism/the-x-what-feminism-is-really-about-and-why-anyone-who-values-freedom-should-fight-against-it/

49 Paul Elam, "Beware the Jooze!" *A Voice for Men*, 15 May 2017. https://www.avoiceformen.com/a-voice-for-men/beware-the-jooze/.

50 Quintus Curtius, "The Origins of Neomasculinity," *Return of Kings*, 9 March 2015. http://www.returnofkings.com/58237/the-origins-of-neomasculinity. For example, Paul Joseph Watson, 2015, *Neomasculinity: The Male Backlash against Toxic Women* [Online video]. Available at: https://www.youtube.com/watch?v=3qHnIp-WzCI. Valizadeh also claimed to reject the "red pill" term because of the increasingly conspiratorial connotations it had garnered: Roosh V., "Neomasculinity," *Roosh V*, 4 March 2015. https://www.rooshv.com/neomasculinity

51 Roosh V, 2017, *How the Manosphere Crushed Feminism* [Online Video]. Available at: https://www.youtube.com/watch?v=-WgAn6GFU0E [Accessed 3 September 2018].

52 Ibid. Valizadeh's interviewee also notes that a thread started on Valizadeh's site's forum is the top search result on Google if you search for "Donald Trump thread." This is true at the time of writing.

53 Ibid.

54 The Fifth Estate, "Why incels are a 'real and present threat' for Canadians," *CBC News*, 27 January 2019. https://www.cbc.ca/news/canada/incel-threat-canadians-fifth-estate-1.4992184. In this regard, online incel radicalisation very much aligns with contemporary online far-right radicalisation as a whole. See: Joe Mulhall, "A Post-organisational Far Right?" *HOPE not Hate*. https://www.hopenothate.org.uk/research/state-of-hate-2018/online-radicalisation/post-organisational-far-right/

55 Paul Elam, "Fuck their shit up," *A Voice for Men*, https://www.avoiceformen.com/mens-rights/fuck-their-shit-up/

56 "The Non-Feminist Declaration," *Nonfeminist18*. https://nonfeminist18.wordpress.com/ [Accessed 29 March 2019].

57 Christa Hodapp, *Men's Rights, Gender, and Social Media* (Lanham: Lexington Books, 2017), 11.
58 Ibid., 10. Interestingly, perhaps as a hangover from its origins, Hoddap highlights that "This position is very similar to problematic assertions made by feminists in the second wave, carrying over in some degree to certain forms of current feminism. […] Such moves alienated many women from feminism, and it seems to have the same effect on the MRM [Men's Rights Movement], given its generally white, straight, middle class make-up. The old mistakes repeat themselves over and over – privileged positions become the 'human position.'" Christa Hodapp, *Men's Rights, Gender, and Social Media* (Lanham: Lexington Books, 2017), 10.
59 Marilyn Frye, "Oppression," 13, in: Bonnie Kime Scott, Susan E. Cayleff, Anne Donadey, and Irene Lara (Eds.), *Women in Culture: An Intersectional Anthology for Gender and Women's Studies* (Second Edition) (Chichester: Wiley Blackwell, 2017). In Christa Hodapp, *Men's Rights, Gender, and Social Media* (Lanham: Lexington Books, 2017), 101.
60 Christa Hodapp, *Men's Rights, Gender, and Social Media* (Lanham: Lexington Books, 2017), 60.

13

MASCULINITY AND MISOGYNY IN THE ALTERNATIVE RIGHT

The Alternative Right has conflicting viewpoints on numerous fronts, but broadly aims to establish identity and status for white men who feel aggrieved, is deeply antagonistic towards feminism, and holds that men and women – and the world more generally – should be ordered in strict hierarchies. A key influence on the development of this worldview is the manosphere, the online den for men "red pilled" (awoken) to their supposed emasculation by feminists.[1] A consensus has emerged across the manosphere and Alternative Right that white men have been persecuted by feminism and identity politics, leaving them downtrodden, feminised, and adrift in modern society.

In an attempt to capitalise on this resentment, the Alternative Right has indulged in highly idealised visions for the role of men and women in a world free from what Daniel Friberg, CEO of the central alt-right publisher Arktos Media, calls "the Leftist myth of the absolute equality and sameness of the sexes."[2] These visions are at their core confused and conflicted, and, crucially, unrealisable.

Masculinity and male-only enclaves

That there is a crisis of masculinity amongst the men of the Alternative Right could scarcely be more explicit. "Men are confused. They're bewildered. They have been lectured that the innate behaviours, feelings and characteristics that defined masculinity for generations, are sexist, malevolent, and need to be abandoned if men are to have any success with women," complains alt-lite YouTuber Paul Joseph Watson.[3] In an attempt to rectify this situation, the men of the Alternative Right have developed theories and practices aimed at, in Watson's words, "reasserting and reclaiming what it means to be a man."[4] Restoring masculine pride is a central project of the Alternative Right.

One important message emphasised across the Alternative Right is that despite the supposed attempts of feminists and "social justice warriors" (SJWs) to shame them, white men have a proud heritage, and can take credit for the civilisational achievements of previous generations of Western men. For example, alt-lite figurehead Milo Yiannopoulos has claimed that "What feminists allude to as the patriarchy is in fact, Western civilization,"[5] and Gavin McInnes' alt-lite Proud Boys fraternity, which proclaims to stand against the "pussified, weak, immoral culture of feminized failure,"[6] tells men that they should "no longer apologise for creating the modern world."[7] For the white nationalist alt-right, this message is explicitly racial; in propaganda for his National Policy Institute (NPI) think-tank, Richard Spencer seeks to connect his white viewers to "a culture, a history, a destiny, an identity that stretches back and flows forward for centuries," claiming that whites are "part of the people's history, spirit and civilization of Europe."[8] Raising the status of men in this way is, crucially, at the expense of other cultures/races. McInnes has stated that "I think the West is the best, I don't care what race you are, but I don't think other cultures are [just] different; I think they're worse,"[9] while Spencer has asserted that "Every ounce of civilization was given to [African countries] by Europeans."[10] Invoking historical achievements enables white men to feel entitled to their historical privileges, rendering the perceived attempts of "ungrateful" feminists/SJWs to degrade them all the more egregious. Such a narrative can be an effective mobiliser; as masculinities scholar Michael Kimmel writes, "white men's anger comes from the potent fusion of two sentiments – entitlement and a sense of victimization."[11]

Drawing on the manosphere, the alt-lite and alt-right have emphasised the importance of protecting male-only enclaves within which they can protect themselves from the supposedly feminising influence of women and affirm this sense of entitlement and victimisation to each other. As Angela Nagle points out in *Kill All Normies*, in doing so, the Alternative Right is following wider online trends; the 4chan culture from which the Alternative Right draws has long regarded the internet to be a male space to be defended against women.[12] The 2014 Gamergate scandal, when elements of the gaming community, manosphere, 4chan and 8chan forums, and burgeoning Alternative Right harassed female game developers, was essentially an effort to protect the male safe space of gaming. Yiannopoulos, one of the key Alternative Right exploiters of Gamergate, has continued to tap into this sentiment, writing "women are […] screwing up the internet for men by invading every space we have online and ruining it with attention-seeking and a needy, demanding, touchy-feely form of modern feminism."[13] In a telling article entitled "Reestablishing Masculinity: The Prequel," Andrew Anglin of the Daily Stormer designates his site "officially a boys club" and blocks women from contributing, admitting that he does so as "degradation" at the hands of women, rather than Jews or "other races," is a more commonly perceived grievance amongst "young men raised in a feminist society." Anglin, in his own words, recognises that the offer "we can free you from women and give you back your masculinity and your power, as well as your tribal male-bonding patterns" can resonate deeply with young men, and therefore banning women and focusing on male issues can help to drive traffic to his site.[14]

Whilst Anglin is unusually forthright, the message that establishing male-only spaces is vital to regaining masculinity is shared across the Alternative Right, and efforts have been made to establish such enclaves offline as well as on. Examples include the alt-lite Proud Boys (described by a prominent member as an "alpha male support group"[15]), and, on the extreme end, the manosphere's "male tribalist" Jack Donovan. A key early influence on the alt-right's conceptions of masculinity, Donovan advocates, in the words of scholar Matthew N. Lyons, "a social and political order based on small, close-knit 'gangs' of male warriors."[16] In Donovan's view, success amongst groups of men is vital for the achievement of manhood:

> A man is not merely a man but a man among men, in a world of men. Being good at being a man has more to do with a man's ability to succeed with men and within groups of men than it does with a man's relationship to any woman or any group of women.[17]

The alt-right sometimes refers to offline male-only groups as the "Männerbund," which are often attributed enormous importance. For example, the Männerbund is described by Joakim Andersen of the proto-alt-right think-tank Motpol as "the natural organizational form of the genuine Right,"[18] and by both Spencer[19] and Greg Johnson of Counter-Currents Publishing[20] as foundational to civilisation. Online or offline, such groups can be especially alluring to men who may be otherwise isolated.

However, within such male-only spaces, men are ranked in strict hierarchies that entail the persecution of other men regarded as less masculine.[21] Male competition for status is particularly acute in the Alternative Right, informed by the pre-occupation with "alpha males" and "beta males" it has inherited from the manosphere. Liberal and left-wing men, regarded as spineless for accepting their domination by women, are derided as effeminate "betas" and "soy boys" (referencing the theory that soy products, which these men are said to consume, boost oestrogen levels). Men who have rejected far-right views are ubiquitously derided as "cucks," a term that has, through pornography featuring the white wives of submissive husbands having sex with (usually) black men, become imbued with racial meaning and overtones of sexual humiliation.[22] Whilst there are several notable gay figures associated with the Alternative Right, homophobia is also commonplace, and anxiety around the innate homoerotic undertones of male-only spaces has led to periodic witch hunts in the alt-right aimed at outing gay men in the movement.[23]

In an attempt to distinguish themselves from these "lesser" men, the Alternative Right places a heavy focus on re-masculinising through "self-improvement."[24] Exercise, especially lifting weights, is key; Anglin has conceded that "a lot of our target demographic is going to be out of shape", and so encouraged his followers to "go to the gym together," continuing "We must have Chad Nationalism. That is what will make guys want to join us, that is what will make girls want to be our groupies" ("Chad" is manosphere slang for an alpha male).[25] Developing an aptitude for violence is also a prominent masculine trope;[26] McInnes has reportedly stated that members can achieve a higher rank in Proud Boys when they "get beat up, kick the crap out of an antifa."[27] The more extreme Donovan has written that violence is "the reserve that guarantees order."[28] For some, re-masculinising entails abstaining from masturbation as a means to exercise discipline, boost testosterone or, for alt-right bodybuilder-cum-lifestyle guru Marcus Follin (AKA "The Golden One"), so one can harness his "sexual energy" into endeavours such as mixed martial arts (MMA) training.[29] Masculine status can also be obtained by becoming an intellectually dominating "man of reason."[30] Despite a widespread penchant for conspiracy theories in the Alternative Right, figures such as Canadian YouTuber Stefan Molyneux fixate on their own self-proclaimed "logic" and "rationality" in the face of feminising "political correctness," an irrational mainstream media, and emotional, oversensitive, "triggered snowflakes." As Nagle states, the Alternative Right's elitism draws in part from a Nietzschean disdain for "feminized" mass culture.[31] By positioning themselves as radically aloof from mainstream culture, those on the intellectual end of the IQ-obsessed alt-right can then inhabit the role of intellectual "higher men."[32]

Opportunities for male bonding and the promise of regaining manhood provide a gateway into the Alternative Right, and subsequently the plethora of bigotry indulged across the loose movement. Anglin freely admits that he established his "boys club" in order to lure young men, who "have the option of living comfortably and playing video games," to engagement in a wider struggle against supposed Jewish control.[33] In addition, Kimmel has suggested in a study of violent rhetoric in pornographic chat rooms that "homosocial competition" between men can lead to the escalation of extreme and violent language.[34] Jostling for hierarchy in the Alternative Right's male-only spaces can contribute to a one-upmanship in "edginess" and aggression, meaning that these spaces can become echo chambers within which ever-more extreme rhetoric and ideas can take hold.

Women and the Alternative Right

Running parallel to re-masculinisation in male-only spaces, a core facet of restoring male pride is reasserting male dominance over women.[35] An argument common amongst the Alternative Right is that feminist inroads into the public sphere and the freedoms of the sexual revolution have led women to neglect their biological desire for children and their duties to family, and instead to seek self-aggrandisement through careers and cheap gratification through casual sex. This situation is deemed intolerable for men, as women's ability to choose sexual partners allegedly favours "alphas," leaving many men unable to find partners. The perceived result, as a post on Spencer's AltRight.com reads, is that "Both sexes are confused and set against one another like never before."[36] Therefore, as is typical for far-right groups, the Alternative Right generally emphasises a return to traditional family roles, in the words of Johnson, "men as protectors and providers, women as nurturers."[37]

The emphasis on "venerating the housewife," as the Proud Boys put it,[38] is common in far-right groups. This is in part because, as scholar Anne McLintock has written, women occupy a powerful role in nationalistic discourse as "symbolic bearers of the nation but are denied any direct relation to national agency,"[39] and because nations (whether geographical or racial) are frequently imagined using familial language and symbols.[40] As Iris Marion Young writes, traditional gender roles place men as the head and "protector" of the family, with women playing a reproductive and nurturing role, and by extension this logic frames men as "protectors" of the population, with their dominance over women often masked with notions of chivalry, natural duty, and love, rather than aggression.[41] Women defying their "natural" subordination by exercising their sexual and political enfranchisement can therefore be portrayed as not only leading to the breakdown of the family unit, but as a threat to the nation. For example, a video by alt-right YouTuber "Black Pigeon Speaks" states:

> If women's sexual preferences are liberated and go unchecked, they destroy civilisations. If women are allowed to choose, harems form. If women are allowed a voice in matters that pertain to the safety of a nation, then that nation will die, inevitably.[42]

By exerting dominance and subjugating women back into traditional familial roles, men are symbolically reclaiming the nation. Anglin writes: "The Alt-Right agenda is not simply about reclaiming our land, it is about reclaiming every aspect of our civilization, an important element of which is our women."[43] The alt-right therefore emphasises that women should focus on becoming "trad wives" (traditional spouses) and on boosting the white birth rate, a longstanding focus for racist groups, perceived as vital to reviving the strength of the nation. "Make sure you have at least three children and raise them well," Friberg writes to his female readers; "in this regard, the future of Europe rests squarely in your hands."[44]

The prominent female commentators in the Alternative Right similarly argue that women should focus on the domestic sphere and traditional family roles. The most well-known female figure in the alt-lite is former Rebel Media host Lauren Southern, who has argued for the "return of the traditional woman," claiming that "there is no purpose more noble than motherhood."[45] However, facing claims of hypocrisy, she has allowed for "exceptions to the rule," and stated that she will not get married purely to avoid being "called a degenerate on the internet."[46] The alt-right's most visible female figure, Lana Lokteff of Red Ice Creations, claims that women instinctively crave "beauty, family and home."[47] Vlogger Ayla Stewart (AKA "Wife With A Purpose"), a white nationalist mother of six, has challenged her viewers to "match or beat" her birth rate.[48] The alt-right's domestic ideals are sometimes celebrated online with Nazi propaganda images, featuring men at the head of Aryan families. As Sam Miller states in *Jacobin* magazine, the views of the likes of Lokteff on gender "essentially regurgitate the rhetoric of *Kinder, Küche, Kirche* (children, kitchen, church), from 1930s Germany."[49]

As Young highlights, for men to embody the masculine role of "protector" of women and the nation, an external threat is necessary, a "selfish aggressor who wishes to invade the lord's property and sexually conquer his women."[50] As scholar Kimberlé Crenshaw has highlighted, white masculinity is framed not just in relation to women but to ethnic Others, and the Alternative Right heavily invokes the spectre of the hypersexualised non-white/Muslim rapist, an enduring figure in far-right discourse.[51] Due to women's symbolic role in nationalist discourse, every sexual assault of a white woman by a non-white man is portrayed as an assault on the West as a whole; for example, Watson has described the 2015/2016 New Year's Eve sexual assault scandal in Cologne as the "Rape of Europe."[52] "Feminising" elites are held responsible, often powerful women who have rejected their "natural" role in the domestic sphere; for example, McInnes has written that "Childless hag Angela Merkel told the world there's no such thing as a rapefugee [...] She opened the floodgates to the rapists and they got to raping."[53] The alt-right commonly forwards the "white genocide" conspiracy theory, which alleges that elites (often Jews) are actively attempting to destroy white societies by degrading white masculinity, encouraging miscegenation, and opening borders to "animalistic" non-white sexual predators. In mounting a "defence" of white women, men hope to distinguish themselves against the effeminate "cucks" that have betrayed their women and homeland, and regain national pride.

Despite the heavy emphasis on men as warriors and protectors, the narrative of a looming sexual threat from non-whites has enabled some women to take a more active and public role beyond the confines of passive domesticity. For example, vlogger Brittany Pettibone has supported the 120 Decibels campaign, an attempt by female members of the European far-right youth movement Generation Identity (GI) to capitalise on the feminist #MeToo movement, but focussing solely on sexual assaults by Muslims and migrants.[54] Lokteff has claimed that, in the face of the current "emergency situation", whilst women are "too emotional for leading roles in politics, this is the time for female nationalists to be loud."[55] Public activism, however, rests uneasily with the simultaneous imperative to uphold traditional conceptions of femininity and docility. For example, Lokteff claims that "the women that I've met in this movement can be lionesses and shield maidens and Valkyries, but also [as] soft and sensual as silk."[56] Encapsulating this tension, a contributor to Red Ice known as "The Blonde Butter Maker," who primarily provides domestic tips, has modelled a "women's self defense corset holder" in which she can conceal her firearms whilst still appearing like a "seemingly defenceless white girl."[57] The adoption of an active position in the Alternative Right also commonly entails being targeted by some men in the movement, as we explore later in this chapter.

A vision unfulfilled

As Kimmel writes, in far-right circles women are often presented as a "prize" to which men will be entitled when they take up the cause, regain their manhood, and are able to offer women protection.[58] For example, Lokteff told the overwhelmingly male crowd at the 2017 Identitarian Ideas IX conference in Stockholm that "all the girls are starting to eye the bad boy who is the nationalist," continuing that:

European nationalists and the alt-right in America are a very attractive, very sexy bunch, which is also in our favour. Women are loving it, as they can have their pick of the best [...] I've been seeing matches made left and right, left and right, of the most beautiful, intelligent couples, so it's eugenic, it's a eugenic process.[59]

Despite Lokteff's words of encouragement, however, the reality often appears less ideal, as evidenced by the commonplace disillusionment and anger on display in the alt-right's interaction with online dating sites. Scottish vlogger Colin Robertson (AKA "Millennial Woes"), who functions as an alt-right agony uncle of sorts, has recommended that his lonely viewers use dating sites and be "shameless" about their desire for traditional relationships, as "certain female instincts are triggered" by such frank talk.[60]

However, complaints are commonplace that mainstream online dating sites are too progressive, are unfairly favouring women, or are encouraging miscegenation and the breakdown of the family. For example a post on the Return of Kings (RoK) website of pick-up artist (PUA)-turned-traditional relationship proponent Daryush Valizadeh (AKA "Roosh V"), a key manosphere influence on the Alternative Right, decries online dating as "a tool to fuel the female ego,"[61] and his site contains article with titles such as "Confused Beta Male Laments Realities of Online Dating."[62] A user of the Daily Stormer forums complains that the online dating service Match.com banned his profile, which read:

> Looking for that Aryan Princess. I know they are rare [...] Are you done being a degenerate whore? [...] Hopefully you don't have a history of sleeping with brown people, because that's disgusting. You must realize Jews are a fundamental problem in our society and must be dealt with.[63]

Whilst hard-line racist dating sites have existed for more than two decades,[64] the two most prominent openly racist dating sites currently active, WASP Love and WhiteDate, explicitly cater for the alt-right. However, the fundamental issue remains that users are overwhelmingly male. "Stonewall," the founder of WASP Love, told *VICE* that the service needed to "beef up the female members,"[65] and WhiteDate even had a section entitled "How to Invite Women to WhiteDate," complete with its own printable flyer.[66] This disproportionate gender balance extends to the alt-right as a whole. Spencer has reportedly claimed that women secretly desire alt-right boyfriends due to their "alpha sperm," despite the fact that – by his own estimates – women only constitute around one-fifth of the movement's followers.[67] Robertson has estimated that the male-female ratio of his followers is ten to one.[68] The very existence of the alt-right is possible due to the internet, which has enabled far-right activism beyond traditional, organisational structures, meaning that activists can be utterly isolated from likeminded individuals away from a computer screen. However, even online, the search for partners with the same views and desires appears seldom fruitful, with a sense of both loneliness and anger pervading alt-right discourse as a whole.

Targeting women

This anger is evident in the routine degradation of women as sexual objects by sections of the Alternative Right, which sits uneasily with the voiced desire for traditional marriage commonly expressed in the loose movement. Sexual success with women is a commonplace marker of masculine status, and as Lyons highlights, Valizadeh embodies the friction between the manosphere's simultaneous emphasis on traditional families and obsessive refining of seduction techniques;[69] indeed, RoK both bemoans the breakdown of marriage and posts articles such as "8 Essential Rules for Banging Married Chicks."[70] Nagle highlights that this hypocrisy is a symptom of male entitlement, of wanting "the benefits of tradition without its necessary restraints and duties."[71] It is fitting that a central rallying point of the Alternative Right was the campaign of Donald Trump against Hillary Clinton, a woman perceived as embodying the liberal "feminist" establishment. During his candidacy Trump claimed he was "for traditional marriage,"[72] but recordings also surfaced of him bragging about his ability to grab women "by the pussy" and his attempt to sleep with a married woman.[73]

Again undercutting any genuine concern for the wellbeing of women, the existence of white rapists is frequently downplayed or denied by the Alternative Right until politically expedient. For example, Southern has denied the existence of a rape culture in the West – granting its existence would damage notions of Western superiority.[74] Watson attempted to capitalise on the exposure of film mogul Harvey Weinstein as a serial sexual predator in October 2017, striking out at "left wing" Hollywood.[75] However, the opportunism of his attack is evident in the fact that he has elsewhere derided the #MeToo movement, of which the Weinstein revelations were a part, as a tool to attack men.[76] In accordance with Nils Christie's analysis, there is often a sharp demarcation made between "genuine" victims who are viciously attacked by deviant strangers, who are thus "worthy" of protection, and "blameworthy" victims who "invite" or "deserve" sexual violence.[77] For the alt-right, the assault of "naïve" liberal white women is sometimes almost celebrated as "learning experiences" for women portrayed as having "betrayed" their race, evident in the memes shared of battered white women with black partners.

Again undercutting pretences of "chivalry," the seething resentment of the Alternative Right regularly boils over into misogynistic harassment campaigns designed to force women back into the private sphere, often described as "thot patrols." A particularly divisive example was the so-called "Thotgate" scandal of late 2017. The affair was triggered after a photograph surfaced of a young Lauren Southern with her biracial then-boyfriend, which made her a "coal burner" (miscegenator) in the eyes of racial purists in the alt-right. The second key trigger was when alt-right YouTuber Tara McCarthy complained that "Women in the Alt Right are constantly harassed by low status anonymous trolls trying to put us in our place," continuing that "Men in the Alt Right are going to have to decide whether they will continue to passively/actively endorse this behaviour, or speak out against it."[78] The two events prompted a campaign of merciless harassment against prominent women in the Alternative Right, and sparked a debate about whether women should be ejected *en masse* from public roles. Robertson came to the defence of McCarthy and Southern in a now-deleted video, arguing that women have helped to change the alt-right on You-Tube from "a collection of despairing, frankly miserable men into what feels much more like a proper community today."[79] Anglin, revealing something of his own anxieties, labelled McCarthy and Southern "camwhores," writing that "They are stupid, they do not have ideas, they enter male spaces only to gain attention and destroy the concept of male spaces. Then they claim you're a wimp or a homosexual if you don't accept it."[80] The "faggot males" supporting McCarthy, who had the temerity to complain about her treatment, were also viewed by Anglin as legitimate targets for attack, as the act of defending her was viewed as non-masculine.[81]

At the extremes of the Alternative Right, a rhetoric is prevalent that advocates sexual abuse and other forms of violence against women. Valizadeh, for example, penned a notorious article advocating the legalisation of rape on private property (which he has subsequently dismissed as "a satirical thought experiment").[82] Manosphere racist Matt Forney has written an article entitled "How to Beat Your Girlfriend or Wife and Get Away with It," in which he recommends "spanking" women as "It's difficult for a girl to go down on you when she has a broken jaw," and as "All girls crave the firm hand of masculine authority on their behinds."[83] Andrew Auernheimer (AKA "weev"), who represents the most extreme elements of the alt-right, stated in a typically vile diatribe:

> I think at this point every woman in the Western world virtually needs rape [...] I definitely think that we need white men to do it but these skanks need proper rapings and beatings. I think it's just a reality is [sic] that women without the coercion of force will always fall, and we've had this for centuries; we've always treated women sort of with physical discipline, with public humiliation usually with some sort of instruments [sic]; if you don't beat and rape a bitch then she just turned to utter slime.[84]

Such violent rhetoric should not be shrugged off as mere fantasy; as Kimmel states, it is a longstanding masculine trope that, when suffering acute feelings of shame and emasculation, violence is viewed as a way to restore manhood.[85] *BuzzFeed* has reported that, in divorce filings, Spencer was accused of being "physically, emotionally, verbally and financially abusive" by his wife, who also alleged that he told her that the "only language women understand is violence"[86] (in court filings, Spencer said that he "denies each, every, and all allegations").[87] Matthew Heimbach, leader of the now-defunct alt-right-affiliated Traditionalist Workers Party (TWP), was arrested in March 2018 on domestic violence charges, and has subsequently pled guilty to beating the TWP co-founder Matt Parrott, Heimbach's father-in-law. The incident was reportedly sparked by Heimbach's affair with Parrott's wife.[88] Male jostling for hierarchy, violence, and a hypocritical disdain for marriage from a man proclaiming to venerate it, were all displayed in one extraordinary event.

The Alternative Right is a movement steeped in male feelings of political, social and sexual disempowerment and wounded pride. Free from restraint and accountability, the followers of the loose movement have assembled codes and hierarchies that rely on achieving a cartoonish maleness, and indulged fantasies which cloak their desire to dominate women with notions of "natural order." However, a chasm exists between such fantasies and the lived reality of most aspiring "alphas" hunched behind their keyboards. The subsequent angst and resentment cause men to subjugate each other and allow that contradictory male edict, to both protect and to exploit women, to be taken to extremes.

Notes

1 For more information on the manosphere, see Chapter 12 "From Anger to Ideology: A History of the Manosphere."
2 Daniel Friberg, *The Real Right Returns: A Handbook for the True Opposition* (United Kingdom: Arktos Media Ltd., 2015), 52.
3 Paul Joseph Watson, 2015, *Neomasculinity: The Male Backlash against Toxic Women* [Online video] Available at: https://www.youtube.com/watch?v=3qHnIp-WzCI&t=53s [Accessed 14 April 2017].
4 Ibid. In this quote Watson is specifically referring to "neomasculinity," a theory developed by manosphere writer Daryush Valizadeh (AKA Roosh V), who is discussed elsewhere in this chapter. See: "What Is Neomasculinity," *Roosh V*, 6 May 2015. https://www.rooshv.com/what-is-neomasculinity?doing_wp_cron=1554548745.4193220138549804687500
5 MILO, 2016, *MILO at Ohio University: What Is the Patriarchy?* [Online video]. Accessible at: https://www.youtube.com/watch?v=cAkuEyeoZ7c [Accessed 16 July 2017].
6 Derek Wray, "Radical Traditionalism – The New Western Conservatism," *Proud Boy Magazine*, 23 June 2017. http://officialproudboys.com/columns/radical-traditionalism-the-new-western-conservatism/
7 "'Proud Boys' Back in Canada Military after Crashing Indigenous Ceremony," *BBC News*, 31 August 2017. https://www.bbc.co.uk/news/world-us-canada-41116175
8 NPI / Radix, 2015, *Who Are We?* [Online video]. Available at: https://www.youtube.com/watch?v=3rnRPhEwELo [Accessed 15 July 2018].
9 PowerfulJRE, 2017, *Joe Rogan Experience #920 – Gavin McInnes* [Online video]. Accessible at: https://www.youtube.com/watch?v=qm9lfWTGmDY [Accessed 29 August 2018].
10 Richard Spencer (@RichardBSpencer), 11 January 2018, 8:51 pm. https://twitter.com/RichardBSpencer/status/951677997022699521
11 Michael Kimmel, *Angry White Men: American Masculinity at the End of an Era* (New York: Nation Books, 2017), x.
12 Angela Nagle, *Kill All Normies: Online Culture Wars from 4chan and Tumblr to Trump and the Alt-Right* (Croydon: Zero Books, 2017), 103.
13 Milo Yiannopoulos, "The Solution to Online 'Harassment' is Simple: Women should Log Off," *Breitbart News Network*, 5 June 2016. https://www.breitbart.com/social-justice/2016/07/05/solution-online-harassment-simple-women-log-off/
14 Andrew Anglin, "Reestablishing Masculinity: The Prequel," *Daily Stormer*, 30 March 2015. https://dailystormer.name/male-rehabilitation-saga-the-prequel/
15 SBS Dateline, 2018, *Defending Gender part 1 – Proud Boys* [Online video]. Accessible at: https://www.youtube.com/watch?v=i7f4b1o6BKM [Accessed 19 August 2018].
16 Matthew N. Lyons, "Ctrl-Alt-Delete: An Antifascist Report on the Alternative Right," *Political Research Associates*, 20 January 2017. https://www.politicalresearch.org/2017/01/20/ctrl-alt-delete-report-on-the-alternative-right/

17 Jack Donovan, *The Way of Men* (Milwaukie: Dissonant Hum, 2012), 1–2.
18 Joakim Andersen, *Rising from the Ruins: The Right of the 21st Century* (United Kingdom: Arktos Media Ltd., 2018), 169.
19 Richard Spencer (@RichardBSpencer), 6 October 2018, 12:10 pm. https://twitter.com/RichardBSpencer/status/1048651743565963265
20 Greg Johnson, "Homosexuality & White Nationalism," *Counter-Currents Publishing*, 4 October 2010. https://www.counter-currents.com/2010/10/homosexuality-and-white-nationalism/
21 R.W. Connell, *Masculinities* (2nd ed.) (Cambridge: Blackwell Publishers Ltd), 78.
22 Dana Schwartz, "Why Angry White Men Love Calling People 'Cucks'," *GQ*, 1 August 2016. https://www.gq.com/story/why-angry-white-men-love-calling-people-cucks
23 This is explored further in Chapter 14 "Sexuality and the Alternative Right." The phenomenon of "homohysteria" is outlined in Eric Anderson, "The Rise and Fall of Western Homohysteria," *Journal of Feminist Scholarship*, 1 (2011), 80–94.
24 Andersen, *Rising from the Ruins: The Right of the 21st Century*, 215.
25 Andrew Anglin, "PSA: When the Alt-Right Hits the Street, You Wanna be Ready," *Daily Stormer*, 19 August 2017. https://dailystormer.name/psa-when-the-internet-becomes-real-life-and-the-alt-right-hits-the-street-you-wanna-be-ready/
26 Connell, *Masculinities*, 83–84.
27 Gavin McInnes in: Christopher Mathias, "Pro-Trump Gang Seen in Footage Assaulting Anti-Fascist Protestors in Manhattan," *The Huffington Post*, 13 October 2018. https://www.huffingtonpost.co.uk/entry/proud-boys-new-york-assault-gavin-mcinnes_us_5bc20d60e4b0bd9ed55a96ee
28 Jack Donovan, "Violence is Golden," *Counter-Currents Publishing*, 8 December 2011. https://www.counter-currents.com/2011/12/violence-is-golden/
29 The Golden One, 2017, *The Golden One's 2017 Challenge of Willpower and Sexual Energy. 4 Steps 4 Months* [Online video]. Accessible at: https://www.youtube.com/watch?v=6ZbXaf5lD80&t=616s [Accessed 19 July 2017].
30 Connell, *Masculinities*, 164.
31 Nagle, *Kill All Normies*, 108.
32 For more on the fascist concept of "higher men", see: Matthew Feldman, Jorge Dagnino and Paul Stocker (ed.), *The "New Man" in Radical Right Ideology and Practice, 1919–45* (London: Bloomsbury Academic, 2018).
33 Anglin, "Reestablishing Masculinity: The Prequel."
34 Kimmel, *Angry White Men*, 115.
35 Connell, *Masculinities*, 77.
36 Hannibal Bateman, "The Sexual Revolution Has Left Broken Men and Women in its Wake,"   *AltRight.com*.https://altright.com/2017/10/03/the-sexual-revolution-has-left-broken-men-and-women-in-its-wake/
37 Greg Johnson, "The Woman Question in White Nationalism," *Counter-Currents Publishing*, 25 May 2011. https://www.counter-currents.com/2011/05/the-woman-question-in-white-nationalism/
38 Robert Culkin, "Proud Boys: Who Are They?" *Proud Boys Magazine*, 24 August 2017. http://officialproudboys.com/proud-boys/whoaretheproudboys/
39 Anne McClintock, "'No Longer in a Future Heaven': Gender, Race, and Nationalism," in Anne McClintock, Aamir Mufti and Ella Shohat (ed.), *Dangerous Liaisons: Gender, Nation, and Postcolonial Perspectives* (Minneapolis: University of Minnesota Press, 1997), 90.
40 Anne McClintock, "Family feuds: Gender, Nationalism and the Family," *Feminist Review*, 44 (1993), 61–80.
41 Iris Marion Young, "The Logic of Masculinist Protection: Reflections on the Current Security State," *Signs: Journal of Women in Culture and Society*, 29:1 (2003), 1–25.
42 Black Pigeon Speaks, 2016, *Why Women DESTROY NATIONS* / CIVILIZA-TIONS – and other UNCOMFORTABLE TRUTHS* [Online video]. Available at: https://www.youtube.com/watch?v=UxpVwBzFAkw&bpctr=1540315623 [Accessed 13 May 2018].

43 Andrew Anglin, "What Happens When You Liberate White Women?" *Daily Stormer*, 8 August 2017. https://dailystormer.name/what-happens-when-you-liberate-white-women/
44 Friberg, *The Real Right Returns*, 60.
45 Lauren Southern, 2017, *Return of the Traditional Woman – Cal Poly SLO* [Online video]. Available at: https://www.youtube.com/watch?v=HFW0z0Y5TR4 [Accessed 20 July 2017].
46 Lauren Southern, 2017, *Why I'm Not Married* [Online video]. Available at: https://www.youtube.com/watch?v=P-UKPpmQlys&t=34s [Accessed 11 May 2018].
47 Ice TV, 2017, *Lana Lokteff – How the Left is Betraying Women – Identitarian Ideas IX* [Online video]. Available at: https://www.youtube.com/watch?v=BjnH99slHmE [Accessed 18 July 2017].
48 Ayla Stewart in: Annie Kelly, "The Housewives of White Supremacy," *The New York Times*, 1 June 2018. https://www.nytimes.com/2018/06/01/opinion/sunday/tradwives-women-alt-right.html
49 Sam Miller, "Lipstick Fascism," *Jacobin*, 4 April 2017. https://www.jacobinmag.com/2017/04/alt-right-lana-lokteff-racism-misogyny-women-feminism/
50 Young, "The Logic of Masculinist Protection: Reflections on the Current Security State."
51 Kimberlé Crenshaw, "Whose Story is it, Anyway? Feminist and Antiracist Appropriations of Anita Hill," in Toni Morrison (ed.), *Race-ing Justice, En-Gendering Power. Essays on Anita Hill, Clarence Thomas, and the Construction of Social Reality* (New York: Pantheon Books, 1992), 402–440.
52 Paul Joseph Watson, 2016, *The Rape of Europe* [Online video]. Available at: https://www.youtube.com/watch?v=KUPuMs3E_k0&t=2s [Accessed 16 July 2017].
53 Gavin McInnes, "Politics as Fashion Is a Bad Look," *Taki's Magazine*, 29 January 2016. http://takimag.com/article/politics_as_fashion_is_a_bad_look_gavin_mcinnes/#axzz5Urd GKNz0
54 HOPE not hate online archive.
55 Lokteff, 2017, *Lana Lokteff – How the Left is Betraying Women – Identitarian Ideas IX* [Online video].
56 Ibid.
57 Red Ice TV, 2017, *Blonde Buttermaker: After Hours – Women's Self Defense Corset Holster* [Online video]. Available at: https://www.youtube.com/watch?v=UhfML-IgDvE [Accessed 2 May 2017].
58 Kimmel, *Angry White Men*, 272.
59 Lokteff, 2017, *Lana Lokteff – How the Left is Betraying Women – Identitarian Ideas IX* [Online video].
60 Millennial Woes, 2016, *Finding a Traditional Wife (Part 1) [O.S.]* [Online video]. Available at: https://www.youtube.com/watch?v=LchLM0zkhe0&t=1s [Accessed 3 April 2018].
61 Adrian Braxton, "The Ugly Reality of Online Dating," *Return of Kings*, 4 June 2017. http://www.returnofkings.com/122562/the-ugly-reality-of-online-dating
62 Winston Smith, "Confused Beta Male Laments Realities of Online Dating," *Return of Kings*, 29 July 2014. http://www.returnofkings.com/40716/confused-beta-male-laments-realities-of-online-dating
63 HOPE not hate online archive.
64 Les Back, "Aryans reading Adorno: Cyber-culture and Twenty-first-century Racism," *Ethnic and Racial Studies*, 25:4 (2002), 628–651.
65 Mack Lamoureux, "Inside the Sad World of Racist Online Dating," *VICE*, 19 December 2016. https://www.vice.com/en_uk/article/wndk85/inside-the-sad-world-of-racist-online-dating
66 "Mini Flyer – How to Invite Women to WhiteDate," *WhiteDate*. https://www.whitedate.net/miniflyer/
67 Richard Spencer in: Sarah Posner, "Meet the Alt-Right 'Spokesman' Who's Thrilled With Trump's Rise," *Rolling Stone*, 28 October 2016. https://www.rollingstone.com/politics/politics-features/meet-the-alt-right-spokesman-whos-thrilled-with-trumps-rise-129588/

68 Millennial Woes, 2018, *Milleniyule 2018: WhiteDate* [Online video]. Available at: http s://www.youtube.com/watch?v=7–iKVYAFyWc [Accessed 1 January 2019].

69 Lyons, "Ctrl-Alt-Delete: An Antifascist Report on the Alternative Right."

70 Donovan Sharpe, "8 Essential Rules for Banging Married Chicks," *Return of Kings*, 3 March 2015. http://www.returnofkings.com/57437/8-essential-rules-for-banging-ma rried-chicks

71 Nagle, *Kill All Normies*, 93.

72 Donald Trump in: Timothy Cama, "Trump: 'I'm for traditional marriage'," *The Hill*, 28 February 2015. https://thehill.com/blogs/ballot-box/presidential-races/246387-trump -im-for-traditional-marriage

73 Donald Trump in: Ben Jacobs, Sabrina Siddiqui and Scott Bixby: "'You can do anything': Trump brags on tape about using fame to get women," *The Guardian*, 8 October 2016. http s://www.theguardian.com/us-news/2016/oct/07/donald-trump-leaked-recording-women

74 Victoria Richards, "Woman holds sign at feminist rally saying 'there is no rape culture in the West'," *The Independent*, 10 June 2015. https://www.independent.co.uk/news/ world/americas/woman-holds-sign-at-feminist-rally-saying-there-is-no-rape-culture- in-the-west-10310370.html

75 Paul Joseph Watson, 2017, *The Truth about Hollywood* [Online video]. Available at: https:// www.youtube.com/watch?v=0Tr9LEgAwI4 [Accessed 15 October 2018].

76 Paul Joseph Watson (@PrisonPlanet), 16 January 2018, 2:41 am. https://twitter.com/ PrisonPlanet/status/953215573172936704

77 Nils Christie, "Ideal Victim," in: Ezzat A Fattah (eds.) *From Crime Policy to Victim Policy* (New York: St Martin's Press, 1986), 17–30.

78 Tara McCarthy in: Rachel Leah, "'Alt-right' women are upset that 'alt-right' men are treating them terribly," *Salon*, 4 December 2017. https://www.salon.com/2017/12/ 04/alt-right-women-are-upset-that-alt-right-men-are-treating-them-terribly/

79 HOPE not hate online archive.

80 Andrew Anglin, "Women Should Shut the Fuck Up," *Daily Stormer*, 8 December 2017. https://dailystormer.name/women-should-shut-the-fuck-up/

81 Ibid.

82 Daryush Valizadeh, "How to Stop Rape," *Roosh V*, 16 February 2015. https://www. rooshv.com/how-to-stop-rape

83 Matt Forney, "How to Beat Your Girlfriend or Wife and Get Away with It," *Matt Forney*, 23 June 2014. https://mattforney.com/beat-girlfriend-wife-get-away/

84 薄熙来, 2017, *Race Ghost Roast to Roast 3 – Eulogy for Ironmarch | Weev podcast* [Online video]. Available at: https://www.youtube.com/watch?v=uFkpkWagpBE&t=968s [Accessed 24 July 2018].

85 Kimm2el, *Angry White Men*, 92.

86 Talal Ansari, "White Nationalist Richard Spencer's Wife Says in Divorce Filings that He Physically and Emotionally Abused Her," *BuzzFeed News*, 23 October 2018. https://www. buzzfeednews.com/article/talalansari/richard-spencer-divorce-abuse-wife-allegations

87 Spencer also addressed the allegations on Twitter: (@RichardBSpencer), 24 October 2018, 4.36 pm. https://twitter.com/RichardBSpencer/status/1055241608742891520

88 Brett Barrouquere, "Days after Guilty Plea, Matthew Heimbach Re-emerges in New Alliance with National Socialist Movement," *Southern Poverty Law Centre*, 24 September 2018. https://www.splcenter.org/hatewatch/2018/09/24/days-after-guilty-plea-matthe w-heimbach-re-emerges-new-alliance-national-socialist-movement

14

SEXUALITY AND THE ALTERNATIVE RIGHT[1]

To some, it may seem incongruous that the term "alt-right," which has come to define a new generation of extreme bigotry and intolerance in the popular consciousness, was popularised by Milo Yiannopoulos, an openly gay man.[2] The broad Alternative Right, like other far-right movements, venerates traditional family structures, is fixated on perceived societal decline, and has a proclivity for scapegoating minorities. LGBT+ individuals have therefore historically been targeted by the far right, often portrayed as immoral, deviant, and subversive.

However, the Alternative Right is a loose collection of far-right ideologies and has competing and conflicting positions on numerous fronts, including a varied discourse around sexuality. Elements within both the Western chauvinist alt-lite and white nationalist alt-right have, to varying degrees, embraced or tolerated openly gay figures. This relationship is limited and deeply caveated, however, and the Alternative Right broadly ignores or actively rejects lesbians, transgender people, and people of other queer identities.

This chapter will provide an overview of attitudes towards sexuality held across the broad Alternative Right, from pro-Trump drag performances, to the pragmatic tolerance of some gay individuals, to calls for the purging of LGBT+ individuals from the alt-right movement and society as a whole.

The alt-lite: homonationalism and pinkwashing

The alt-lite has embraced some openly gay individuals as figureheads, and has engaged in a limited discourse with gay men, in part for strategic purposes. Positioning the *right* to be gay as a core Western value enables the alt-lite to attack Islamic and "Third World" cultures for their perceived intolerance, bolstering its argument that such cultures are incompatible with the West, and potentially making the movement appear more palatable to audiences with more liberal attitudes towards sexuality.

The concept of "homonationalism," developed by Rutgers University professor Jasbir K. Puar, is useful when considering the utilisation of queer identities and politics for nationalist causes.[3] As James Michael Nichols writes for the *Huffington Post*, homonationalism involves "conceptually realigning the ideas invested within the realm of LGBT activism to fit the goals and ideologies of neoliberalism and the far-right. This reframing is used primarily to justify and rationalize racist and xenophobic perspectives."[4] As pointed out by Robert Tobin for *The Gay and Lesbian Review*, such tactics are not unique to the alt-lite; there have long been openly gay, radical populist right and far-right leaders in Europe, for example Dutch politician Pim Fortuyn and the French Front National's former Vice President Florian Philippot.[5]

Drawing on the homonationalism of such European far-right leaders, the alt-lite has used gay rights to position LGBT+ individuals and liberal left-wingers against Muslims, who are presented as a monolith of hatred towards LGBT+ people. British vlogger Paul Joseph Watson has made this explicit, tweeting in 2017 "Liberals; Either you support Islam or gay rights. Pick one. You can't have both."[6] Former Rebel Media personalities Caolan Robertson and Lauren Southern distributed fliers in Luton, England bearing the words "Allah is a gay god,"[7] a stunt that was described as "a social experiment on Islamic attitudes to homosexuality and transgenderism" by Breitbart News Network.[8] Attempts by alt-lite figures to turn LGBT+ communities against Muslims intensified after Omar Mateen, a Muslim man, massacred 49 people at the gay nightclub Pulse in Orlando, Florida, in June 2016. Yiannopoulos penned a Breitbart article titled: "The Left Chose Islam over Gays. Now 100 People Are Dead Or Maimed In Orlando",[9] and Watson uploaded a video entitled "Dear Gays: The Left Betrayed You for Islam," in which he repeats that Islam has a "violent hatred towards gays."[10] In a typically provocative stunt, in the days following the massacre, Gavin McInnes, founder of the macho Proud Boys fraternity, gave a speech in Orlando during which he engaged Yiannopoulos in a kiss immediately after saying the words "fuck you Islam."[11]

The literal and figurative embrace of gay figures also serves to confound liberal and journalistic expectations of how far-right movements should appear. As Maureen O'Connor writes for *The Cut* magazine, Yiannopoulos' rise to significance was propelled by "the sheer cognitive dissonance between his flamboyant self-presentation and callous politics."[12] Yiannopoulos consciously uses his identity to deflect accusations of bigotry, admitting that he can "go on TV and say all manner of outrageous things about feminism only because [he's] a homosexual," as "it's very difficult to argue that a flamboyant homosexual who never shuts up about, you know, black boyfriends is in any way bigoted."[13]

As Donna Minkowitz writes in *Slate*, in entertaining such tactics the alt-lite is engaging in "pinkwashing"; appearing gay-friendly to moderate the image and broaden the appeal of far-right groups to millennials, who may be more supportive of gay rights than previous generations.[14] Whilst similar tactics have been used by European far-right figures, fitting into a wider trend of "modernisation," the alt-lite has taken the practice further than most. For example, Yiannopoulos named his college speaking tour "The Dangerous Faggot" and has his own drag persona, "Ivana Wall" (in reference to the Trump border wall). Similarly, Lucian Wintrich, the former White House correspondent for the website *The Gateway Pundit*, founded the "Twinks4Trump" project, which featured sexually suggestive photographs of young men in Make America Great Again (MAGA) hats, which was covered positively in Yiannopoulos' Breitbart article "How Donald Trump Made It Cool to Be Gay Again."[15] Association with gay figures adds a sheen of tolerance to heterosexual alt-lite figures, despite the fact they may hold a variety of far-right views; Yiannopoulos regards himself as "every straight white male's gay hall pass."[16]

The mask slips

Despite openly embracing some gay figures, the alt-lite draws a hard line between gay individuals and modern gay rights movements, which are often scornfully derided and associated with societal decline. This is in part because positioning the West against supposedly "barbaric" cultures entails the minimisation or denial of homophobia in Western societies, to which Western LGBT+ rights campaigns seek to draw attention. McInnes' Proud Boys claim to be "Pro-Gay," although in a video entitled "What's with Gay Pride?" he says that "look gays, your entire industry is based on homophobia and it's a myth. We don't care! Move on!"[17] Yiannopoulos, himself a Catholic, argues that significant homophobia "is coming from one religion. Just one," telling listeners to "Stop lying to people that, you know, there is some equivalence between, you know, the discomfort occasionally felt by Christians about gay marriage and Muslims murdering homosexuals."[18]

By delegitimising LGBT+ rights movements, the alt-lite can paint LGBT+ activists as overly sensitive, inherently selfish or actively malign. McInnes has called the notion of gay marriage "bullshit," and only desired by same sex couples to "bully Catholics."[19] Caolan Robertson, who is openly gay, encapsulated alt-lite attitudes with his coverage of the Pride in London 2017 parade for Rebel Media, which simultaneously focused on Islamic oppression of gay men and described attendees of the event as "degenerates" who "completely destroy[ed] the city [...] to protest nothing."[20] Yiannopoulos has also railed against modern gay rights movements, writing in 2015 that the "genteel, camp rightsists of the 1950s" have transformed into "brash, glitter-drenched Pride queens" who he implores to "get back in the closet."[21]

Yiannopoulos has elsewhere argued that gay people should actively maintain their marginalisation and uphold a Christian, conservative mainstream, as the existence of such a mainstream enables gay men to inhabit a transgressive identity. Yiannopoulos writes in his book *Dangerous*:

> When [alt-right neo-nazi website] *Daily Stormer* called me a "degenerate homosexual," they meant it as an insult. But I take it as a compliment: I became a homo precisely because it is transgressive. And I want homosexuality to continue being transgressive, and even degenerate.[22]

He later goes on to state that "Christianity is not your enemy; it is a secret friend. The Devil needs the Church to stay in business, and naturally mischievous gay men need a book of rules to break. We need to be told that we're wrong, we need to be told that we're degenerate."[23] However, much of Yiannopoulos' transgressive energy is aimed at offending or otherwise targeting other sexual and ethnic minorities. Nichols writes that "homonationalists are largely white gay people blinded by privilege and actively working against the well-being of the most vulnerable members of our community."[24] Yiannopoulos' desire to uphold a conservative mainstream appears to be, at least in part, fuelled by his enjoyment of abusing his privilege as an erudite, middle-class white male to ridicule lesbians, transgender individuals, and people of other queer identities.

The alt-lite as a whole generally ignores or actively denigrates lesbians; McInnes has accused lesbians of being "grumpy in ill-fitting denim pants" due to their alleged lack of sex,[25] and Watson has claimed that "militant lesbian feminists are usually very ugly and hate attractive women."[26] Yiannopoulos has accused lesbians of "penis envy,"[27] and has written that "It's time to stop lesbians from running the gay mafia and get them back where they belong: in porn."[28] He has elsewhere questioned the very legitimacy of lesbianism, stating "I don't entirely believe in lesbians," although acknowledging "a tiny proportion of, you know, the dungaree wearing types, you know, with the short haircuts, your, your gender studies professors who probably will never see a penis, more out of lack of options rather than preference."[29]

The alt-lite takes an even more aggressively hostile stance towards transgender people, who are subjected to astoundingly vicious abuse. Transgender people are presented variously as mentally ill (McInnes has written an article entitled "Transphobia is perfectly natural," in which he claims that transgender people "are mentally ill gays who need help, and that doesn't include being maimed by physicians"[30]), or as a danger to children (there are multiple Breitbart articles equating "transgender ideology" to child abuse).[31] Notions of gender fluidity and pro-transgender policies are held by the alt-lite to be the result of malign, corrupting "cultural Marxist" doctrines, and subject to constant ridicule. For example, in a stunt for Rebel Media, Lauren Southern even had her gender legally changed to male in order to mock Canadian gender identity policy.[32]

Whilst there are undoubtedly individuals active in the alt-lite who are motivated by a genuine concern around the attitudes in some Islamic communities towards LGBT+ individuals, much of the alt-lite's discourse on the issue boils down to little more than shallow, cynical realpolitik. The alt-lite retains strongly sexist beliefs, upholds rigid gender norms, and whilst it may claim to hold sexual freedom as a Western value, the alt-lite's conception of this freedom remains extremely narrow, largely restricted to a handful of gay men, used not to protect or celebrate diversity of sexuality or gender identity, but to attack other marginalised populations.

The alt-right: reluctant tolerance

Unsurprisingly, the more extreme and overtly fascistic alt-right forgoes any pretence about embracing gay rights as a Western value, with LGBT+ individuals relegated to the bottom of its cruel hierarchies. Whilst there have been a few openly gay men within the alt-right, gay men are considered at best repugnant nuisances, and at worst hostile parasites worthy of eradication.

Greg Johnson of Counter-Currents Publishing is unusual in arguing for a pragmatic tolerance towards homosexuality, warning against the damaging effects of "gay panics" in the alt-right. To Johnson, white nationalists should:

> uphold and defend heterosexuality as the norm but also recognize that not everyone fits that norm. But as long as homosexuals uphold healthy norms and have something positive to contribute, they can and do make our movement stronger, *if we stop worrying about it.*[33]

Johnson has sought to scapegoat Jews for fostering homophobia, alleging in a 2002 article, posted in 2010 to the Counter-Currents website, that "intolerance of homosexuality is Jewish," claiming that "Queer-bashers are in the grip of Jewry without even knowing it."[34] Johnson has also noted the virtues of pinkwashing, claiming that whilst he finds masculine gay men to be more tolerable, "even effeminate gay men can make a real contribution." He cites the "fruity persona" of Pim Fortuyn, which in Johnson's eyes meant that "The media found it difficult to paint a flamboyant old fop who fussed over floral arrangements and doted over his lapdogs as the next Hitler."[35]

Such a stance has enabled Counter-Currents' support of New Right intellectual James O'Meara, who, as Minkowitz writes, is one of two openly gay figures who have experienced a degree of acceptance from some factions of the alt-right, the other being Jack Donovan, who leads the "Cascadia" chapter of the pagan "tribe" Wolves of Vinland in the American Pacific northwest.[36] O'Meara authored the essay collection *The Homo and the Negro: Masculinist Meditations on Politics & Popular Culture*, which is advertised on Counter-Currents as bringing "a 'queer eye' to the overwhelmingly 'homophobic' Far Right." The Counter-Currents website states that whilst O'Meara considers the gay rights movement to be "largely subversive, he argues that homosexuals have traditionally played prominent roles in creating and conserving Western civilization."[37] O'Meara shares Johnson's basic aim of raising the status of gay white men at the expense of other traditionally marginalised groups.

Jack Donovan, on the other hand, has found his niche with his extreme veneration of masculinity and violence. Donovan is an advocate of "male tribalism," calling for, in the words of scholar Matthew N. Lyons, "a social and political order based on small, close-knit 'gangs' of male warriors."[38] Donovan has, alongside Swedish vlogger Marcus Follin (AKA "The Golden One"), become popular in part for uploading homoerotic pictures of their muscular bodies on social media. Donovan defines himself as an "androphile," which he applies to men who are attracted to other men but who reject "The highly vocal and visible queer fringe [that] publicly celebrates extreme promiscuity, sadomasochism, transvestitism, transsexuality and flamboyant effeminacy"[39] (it should be noted that the term "androphile" is used in other contexts quite separate to the alt-right or the manosphere). As O'Connor notes, Donovan is unusual for a figure associated with the alt-right in that he does regard the successes of previous generations of gay activists to decriminalise gay sex and organise during the AIDS crisis as positive.[40] However, he has also written that "Same-sex marriage [...] spells death for civilizations, and that society has a rational interest in promoting big, patriarchal families above all other arrangements."[41] For gay men, association with the alt-right requires accepting inferiority in the eyes of the movement as a whole, and both O'Meara and Donovan's limited acceptance in the alt-right has required a strict conformity to masculine and heterosexual norms.

Homophobia and homohysteria

Donovan and O'Meara are notable exceptions in the alt-right, which remains overwhelmingly male, obsessed with increasing white birth rates and establishing strict masculine hierarchies, enabling an intense and deep-rooted anxiety around homosexuality and fostering a deeply "homohysteric" culture. Homohysteria, a term coined by Eric Anderson, refers to "men's fear of being homosexualized, through association with feminized behavior,"[42] and is "characterized by the witch-hunt to expose who they [homosexuals] are."[43] The concept has been illuminatingly applied by George J. Severs to analyse anti-gay sentiment in the 1980s and 1990s period of the British National Party (BNP).[44]

Richard Spencer, the de facto figurehead of the alt-right, at one time appeared to take a more liberal attitude than some of his peers towards homosexuality. For example, Spencer tweeted in 2014 that "Homosexuality has been a part of European societies and culture for millennia. It's not going away, not something to get worked up about,"[45] and hosted Donovan as a speaker at his National Policy Institute (NPI) conferences. However, more recently his public line has shifted. In his ongoing row with Greg Johnson, he described the article in which Johnson propounds his theory that homophobia is the product of Jews as "Very creepy stuff," using Johnson's relative tolerance of homosexuality as evidence of his untrustworthiness.[46] Spencer has also written that "In the Alt-Right, effectively all infighting derives from gays, scorned women, incel nerds, and gay nerds."[47] Exploiting the homohysteric atmosphere of the alt-right, he has sought to undermine Yiannopoulos' support by claiming that individuals within the alt-right who do not hate him are "themselves homosexuals."[48] Spencer's change of line may simply be due to him feeling more able to express his own homophobia, or he may have yielded to pressure within the alt-right, which has included the questioning of his own sexuality.

The alt-right's emphasis on establishing male-only spaces has led to a keen angst around the homoeroticism prevalent in these spaces. For example, the alt-right nazi Gabriel Sohier Chaput (AKA "Zeiger") complained in an article for The Right Stuff (TRS) that a "culture of tolerance for homosexual behavior" has made all-male gatherings, or even an embrace between two male friends, vulnerable to being interpreted as "suspect." In Chaput's view:

In order to counter this general tolerance for homosexuality (which triggers this acute paranoia about being perceived "effeminate"), we have to create a strong taboo against all forms of effeminacy and degeneracy in the alt-right. Mocking and ridicule must be accompanied by a total shunning of anyone homosexual, advocating homosexuality or even tolerance for homosexuality.[49]

Chaput makes explicit that he advocates extreme prejudice against gay people due to a homohysteric fear of being considered gay, simply for engaging in acts of male bonding.

Following in extreme right traditions, sections of the alt-right have framed LGBT+ movements and notions of gender fluidity as existential threats towards the white race, sometimes as a tool of a Jewish conspiracy. Racist manosphere writer Francis Roger Devlin has written that "The homosexual bathhouse view of sex as merely a means to personal pleasure attacks our race from within and at its source."[50] Andrew Joyce, in a virulently homophobic three part series "The Alt-Right and the Homosexual Question" for AltRight.com, described tolerance of homosexuality as part of a culture "cultivated" for "demographic assassination,"[51] and indulges the far-right trope that gay people are conspiring against whites, akin to Jews and other alleged "subversives" within society.[52]

Framing gay people as threatening the white race from within enables some within the alt-right to entertain violent fantasies towards the LGBT+ community. Rather than opportunistically exploiting Muslim violence against homosexuals as a means to radicalise liberals, the Daily Stormer has celebrated the internment of gay men in Chechen concentration camps.[53] Some alt-right voices, such as "Butch Leghorn" of TRS, viewed the Orlando shooting as a cynical opportunity to "Make it cool to be anti-Muslim."[54] However, the likes of manosphere racist Matt Forney, whilst claiming that he has "no love for Muslims," had sympathy for the murderer:

> No functioning, healthy society would allow Pulse – or the kinds of men who frequented it – to exist. No healthy society would mourn their passing. Indeed, depending on your perspective, Mateen was just taking out the trash, eliminating societal parasites via natural selection.[55]

Forney asks, in light of the progress of gay rights struggles, "Why *should* Muslims want to become part of this disgusting culture? Why *shouldn't* they want to destroy it?"[56]

Forney goes on to attack the more "tolerant" figures within the alt-right, stating that "the traitors and infiltrators in the right-wing ranks must be outed and removed," including "open sodomites like Grindr Greg Johnson."[57] Johnson in particular has long faced speculation and subsequent attacks over his sexuality, especially as his feud with Spencer and Arktos Media CEO Daniel Friberg has intensified. In 2019, a recording surfaced of Johnson conversing with the blogger Francis Nally (AKA "Pilleater"), which was interpreted by Spencer as evidence of a "secret homosexual cabal within the Alt-Right that [Johnson is] a part of."[58] Evan McLaren, the former Executive Director of the NPI, has claimed that Johnson "networks and coordinates activity through a secret group of white-nationalist-minded homosexuals."[59] Johnson has disputed such allegations. Along the alt-right dictum, "don't punch right," whilst the more "moderate" or practical elements of the alt-right are often reticent to censor extreme homophobes associated with their movement, the extreme fringes often delight in attacking the more moderate elements.

Regardless of how the broad Alternative Right wishes to portray itself, a far-right movement it remains. Whilst there is a spectrum of attitudes towards LGBT+ rights across the loose, often unstable Alternative Right, at best this tolerance remains narrow, almost solely focused on men, reflecting the wider gender politics of the movement. Whilst some in the alt-lite may hold a sincere concern for gay people, others have as little genuine compassion towards LGBT+ individuals as they do the Muslims they target. This is certainly evident on the alt-right. Whilst sections may tolerate gay men willing to adopt heterosexual norms, the movement generally forgoes any pretence of compassion and embraces an open, ugly prejudice that, at its worst, cheerleads for violence.

Notes

1 Several points made in this chapter were originally published on the HOPE not hate website in an article entitled "Gay Men and the Alternative Right: An Overview" on 8 April 2018, written by Clay Bodnar. These points are repeated here with his permission.
2 Allum Bokhari & Milo Yiannopoulos, "An Establishment Conservative's Guide to the Alt-Right," *Breitbart News Network*, 29 March 2016. https://www.breitbart.com/tech/2016/03/29/an-establishment-conservatives-guide-to-the-alt-right/
3 Jasbir K. Puar, *Terrorist Assemblages: Homonationalism in Queer Times* (Durham and London: Duke University Press, 2007).
4 James Michael Nichols, "Understanding Homonationalism: Why Are There Gay People Supporting Trump?" *The Huffington Post*, 5 October 2016. https://www.huffingtonpost.co.uk/entry/gay-people-supporting-trump homonationalism_us_57f3e545e4b01b16aaff4bff
5 Robert Tobin, "Gays for Trump? Homonationalism Has Deep Roots," *The Gay & Lesbian Review*, 26 April 2017. http://glreview.org/article/gays-for-trump-homonationalism-has-deep-roots/
6 Paul Joseph Watson (@PrisonPlanet). 13 July 2017, 5:19 pm. https://twitter.com/prisonplanet/status/885654972242812932?lang=en
7 "Why 3 anti-Islam activists were refused entry to the UK," *BBC News*, 14 March 2018. https://www.bbc.co.uk/news/blogs-trending-43393035
8 Jack Montgomery, "22-year-old conservative Lauren Southern claims 'lifetime ban' from UK for 'Allah is gay' social experiment," *Breitbart News Network*, 27 March 2018. https://www.breitbart.com/europe/2018/03/27/lauren-southern-given-lifetime-ban-uk-allah-gay-social-experiment/
9 Sophie Wilkinson, 'Is It Okay to Be Gay (and in the Far-Right)?', *VICE*, 12 March 2018. https://www.vice.com/en_uk/article/ywqd55/is-it-okay-to-be-gay-and-in-the-far-right
10 Paul Joseph Watson, 2016, *Dear Gays: The Left Betrayed You for Islam* [Online video]. Available at: https://www.youtube.com/watch?v=PlqXgXwzkPg [Accessed 14 September 2018].
11 Rebel Media, 2016, *Gavin McInnes and Milo Yiannopoulos Lock Lips in Orlando!* [Online video]. Available at: https://www.youtube.com/watch?v=q_2WkJSPOOs [Accessed at 12 September 2018].
12 Maureen O'Connor, "The Philosophical Fascists of the Gay Alt-Right," *The Cut*, 20 April 2017. https://www.thecut.com/2017/04/jack-donovan-philosophical-fascists-of-the-gay-alt-right.html

13 The Rubin Report, 2015, *Milo Yiannopoulos and Dave Rubin Discuss Gay Rights and Cultural Libertarians* [Online video]. Available at: https://www.youtube.com/watch?v= M0505RbdG5k [Accessed at 17 September 2018].

14 Donna Minkowitz, "How the Alt-Right Is Using Sex and Camp to Attract Gay Men to Fascism," *Slate*, 5 June 2017. http://www.slate.com/blogs/outward/2017/06/05/how_a lt_right_leaders_jack_donovan_and_james_o_meara_attract_gay_men_to.html

15 Milo Yiannopoulos, "How Donald Trump Made It Cool to Be Gay Again," *Breitbart News Network*, 11 August 2016. https://www.breitbart.com/social-justice/2016/08/11/ trump-brought-subversion-decadence-back-gay-culture/

16 Milo Yiannopoulos, *Dangerous* (USA: Dangerous Books, 2017), 152.

17 Rebel Media, 2017, *Gavin McInnes: What's with Gay Pride?* [Online video]. Available at: https://www.youtube.com/watch?v=verl_8US1c0 [Accessed at 20 September 2018].

18 PowerfulJRE, 2016, *Joe Rogan Experience #820 – Milo Yiannopoulos* [Online video]. Available at: https://www.youtube.com/watch?v=LnH67G7vAu4 [Accessed at 20 September 2018].

19 Rebel Media, 2017, *Gavin McInnes: What's with Gay Pride?* [Online video]. Available at: https://www.youtube.com/watch?v=verl_8US1c0 [Accessed 17 September 2018].

20 Rebel Media, 2017, *The Rebel in London for Gay Pride* [Online video]. Available at: http s://www.youtube.com/watch?v=UTJmJTEJVN0 [Accessed 18 September 2018].

21 Milo Yiannopoulos, "Gay Rights Have Made Us Dumber, It's Time to Get Back in the Closet," *Breitbart News Network*, 17 June 2015. https://www.breitbart.com/politics/ 2015/06/17/gay-rights-have-made-us-dumber-its-time-to-get-back-in-the-closet/

22 Yiannopoulos, *Dangerous*, 143.

23 Ibid., 151.

24 Nichols, "Understanding Homonationalism."

25 RWW Blog, 2018, *RWW News: Gavin McInnes and Alex Jones Complain about "Sexless, Depressed, Old, Chubby Dikes"* [Online video]. Available at: https://www.youtube.com/ watch?v=iLy7qkMic0E [Accessed 23 September 2018].

26 Paul Joseph Watson (@PrisonPlanet). 25 August 2015, 4.28 am. https://twitter.com/ PrisonPlanet/status/636137948245835776

27 Milo Yiannopoulos, "Attack of the Killer Dykes!" *Breitbart News Network*, 7 May 2015. https://www.breitbart.com/europe/2015/05/07/attack-of-the-killer-dykes/

28 Yiannopoulos, *Dangerous*, 152.

29 MILO, 2016, *Milo Yiannopoulos Tells Lesbian She Doesn't Exist* [Online video]. Available at: https://www.youtube.com/watch?v=eSt62K70o0E [Accessed 28 September 2018].

30 "Proud Boys," *Southern Poverty Law Centre*. https://www.splcenter.org/fighting-hate/ extremist-files/group/proud-boys

31 For example: Neil Munro, "Transgender Ideology Abuses Kids, Say Doctors," *Breitbart News Network*, 12 October 2017. https://www.breitbart.com/politics/2017/10/12/tra nsgender-ideology-abuses-kids-say-doctors/ and Dr. Susan Berry, "Camille Paglia: 'Transgender Propagandists' Committing 'Child Abuse'," *Breitbart News Network*, 7 September 2017. https://www.breitbart.com/politics/2017/09/07/camille-paglia-tra nsgender-propagandists-committing-child-abuse/

32 Rebel Media, *Lauren Southern Becomes a Man* [Online video]. Available at: https://www. youtube.com/watch?v=gGpZSefYvwM [Accessed 20 September 2018].

33 Greg Johnson, "Gay Panic on the Alt Right," *Counter-Currents Publishing*, 18 March 2016. https://www.counter-currents.com/2016/03/gay-panic-on-the-alt-right/

34 Greg Johnson, "Homosexuality & White Nationalism," *Counter-Currents Publishing*, 4 October 2010. https://www.counter-currents.com/2010/10/homosexuality-and-white-nationalism/

35 Ibid.

36 Minkowitz, "How the Alt-Right Is Using Sex and Camp to Attract Gay Men to Fascism."

37 "The Homo & the Negro: Masculinist Meditations on Politics & Popular Culture," *Counter-Currents Publishing*, 25 October 2017. https://www.counter-currents.com/product/ the-homo-the-negro-masculinist-meditations-on-politics-popular-culture/

38 Matthew N. Lyons, "Ctrl-Alt-Delete: An Antifascist Report on the Alternative Right," *Political Research Associates*, 20 January 2017. https://www.politicalresearch.org/2017/01/20/ctrl-alt-delete-report-on-the-alternative-right/

39 Jack Donovan, *Androphilia: Rejecting the Gay Identity, Reclaiming Masculinity* (Third edition - electronic) (Milwaukie: Dissonant Hum, 2012), 206.

40 O'Connor, "The Philosophical Fascists of the Gay Alt-Right."

41 Jack Donovan, *The Way of Men* (Milwaukie: Dissonant Hum, 2012), 235.

42 Eric Anderson, "The Rise and Fall of Western Homohysteria," *Journal of Feminist Scholarship*, 1 (2011), 80–94.

43 Eric Anderson, *Inclusive Masculinity: The Changing Nature of Masculinities* (London: Routledge, 2012), 86.

44 George J. Severs, "The 'Obnoxious Mobilised Minority': Homophobia and Homohysteria in the British National Party, 1982–1999," in *Gender and Education*, 29:2 (2017), 165–181.

45 Richard Spencer (@RichardBSpencer), 31 October 2014, 8:59 pm. https://twitter.com/richardbspencer/status/528395974666764288?lang=en

46 Richard Spencer (@RichardBSpencer), 19 June 2017, 4:43 pm. https://twitter.com/RichardBSpencer/status/876586206389305344

47 Richard Spencer (@RichardBSpencer), 6 October 2018, 12:10 pm. https://twitter.com/RichardBSpencer/status/1048651743565963265

48 Richard Spencer, 2017, *Why Milo Will Fail* [Online video]. Available at: https://archive.org/details/youtube-gQUBjN4fpa0 [Accessed 4 February 2019].

49 Gabriel Sohier Chaput (AKA Zeiger), "Homosexuality and the Alt-Right," *The Right Stuff*, 12 July 2016. https://blog.therightstuff.biz/2016/07/12/homosexuality-and-the-alt-right/

50 F. Roger Devlin, "Sexual Liberation & Racial Suicide," *Counter-Currents Publishing*, 3 July 2015. https://www.counter-currents.com/2010/11/sexual-liberation-racial-suicide/

51 Andrew Joyce, "The Alt-Right and the Homosexual Question – Part 3," *AltRight.com*. https://altright.com/2017/09/27/the-alt-right-and-the-homosexual-question-part-3/

52 Severs, "The 'obnoxious mobilised minority'."

53 Jez Turner, "Chechnya Rounding Up Homos and Locking Them in Concentration Camps," *Daily Stormer*, 11 April 2017. https://dailystormer.name/chechnya-rounding-up-homos-and-locking-them-in-concentration-camps/

54 Minkowitz, "How the Alt-Right Is Using Sex and Camp to Attract Gay Men to Fascism."

55 Matt Forney, "The Orlando Nightclub Shooting and the Moral Sickness of Whites," *Matt Forney*, 12 June 2017. https://mattforney.com/orlando-nightclub-shooting/

56 Ibid.

57 Ibid.

58 Richard Spencer (@RichardBSpencer). 25 February 2019, 8.15 am. https://twitter.com/RichardBSpencer/status/1100066752057077760

59 Evan McLaren (@EvanMcLaren). 25 February 2019, 2:53 am. https://twitter.com/EvanMcLaren/status/1099985838258163713

PART IV
International

15

JAPAN AND THE ALTERNATIVE RIGHT

Whilst excavating the ideological roots of the Alternative Right leads to Europe, unearthing its online origins leads to East Asia. Specifically, to a Japanese nationalist movement that predates the Alternative Right and has numerous striking parallels; the *Netto Uyoku* ("the online right"). Both the Alternative Right in the US and Europe and the *Netto Uyoku* emerged from similar wellsprings. The Western Alternative Right, which developed in the late 2000s and grew during the early- to mid-2010s, comprises broadly privileged contingents (by some tentative estimates[1]) of the population, reacting to perceived Western decline inflicted by "Cultural Marxists," liberal "globalists" and, predominantly Muslim, non-Western, and non-white migrants. The *Netto Uyoku* emerged prior to this in the early- to mid-2000s, in the wake of events such as the 2002 FIFA World Cup (hosted in Japan and South Korea) which gave rise to greater anti-Korean sentiment, and the anti-Chinese, revisionist backlash against the publication of a historical comic concerning the Nanjing Massacre.[2] The *Netto Uyoku* is also believed to be largely privileged,[3] and – like the Alternative Right – their political attitudes and actions have been, in a fundamental way, shaped by the internet. Moreover, both movements depart from the establishment right, and decry the "politically correct" mainstream media's positive coverage of minorities and migrants.

Yet, the relationship between the Alternative Right and Japan runs deeper than merely the former's parallels with the *Netto Uyoku*. Japanese culture has influenced and inspired the Alternative Right, perhaps to a greater degree than any other non-Western nation. Certain Japanese websites are literal precursors to online sub-cultures that have been vital in the formation of the Alternative Right, and certain tropes regarding Japan – from elements of the country's pop culture exports, to its ethnic homogeneity, and its perceived conservatism – have been deeply fetishised by elements of the Alternative Right. Whilst there are significant differences too, the links nonetheless make for a unique relationship, and have even led to some collaboration between the Alternative Right and its Japanese sympathisers.

Channels of hate: the Alternative Right and the *Netto Uyoku*

A highly formative component of the Alternative Right was "Online Antagonistic Communities."[4] These are reactionary online communities built around various interests, but which all engage in exclusionary, antagonistic behaviour (be it through trolling, creating and spreading offensive symbolism or just espousing hatred and contempt). In particular, the forum 4chan.org, founded in October 2003, and its notorious "politically incorrect" subforum 4chan.org/pol/, founded in October 2011, have been hugely influential on the development of the Alternative Right's hateful rhetoric, imagery, juvenile humour, and online organisational tactics, such as coordinated harassment campaigns and media manipulation.

The creator of 4chan, Christopher Poole, consciously imitated a Japanese forum referred to as the "Futaba Channel," launched in 2001 and itself a spin-off of an earlier forum, '2channel' (which became 5ch.net in October 2017). 2channel was created on 30 May 1999 by Hiroyuki Nishimura, then a student at the University of Arkansas. As *WIRED* magazine's Lisa Katamaya described in a 2008 interview with Nishimura, what made the site innovative was its "openness" – it is anonymous and inactive posts are briefly archived before deletion – and its timing; Nishimura "read the air and realized that what Japan needed was an outlet for unfettered expression."[5] 2channel courted controversy by this design, with the lack of restraints appearing to lend itself to expressions of the extreme.[6] By copying its design, Poole created a popular online environment which did much the same, and through the antagonistic community it helped nurture which would eventually overlap with the far right, helped radicalise many to the far right. Indeed, this design gave rise to the same phenomenon on 2channel, with the emergence of the *Netto Uyoku*, whom the journalist Furuya Tsunehira described in 2016 as:

> a new breed of neo-nationalists who interact almost entirely within their own cyber community, shut off from the rest of society. Their most conspicuous characteristic may be their harshly anti-Korean views, but they also share a fierce animosity toward China, the mainstream media [...], and the so-called "Tokyo Trial view of history," with its acknowledgment of wrongs committed by Japan before and during the war.[7]

Despite obvious differences in the subjects of hate, and the Japanese far right's greater focus on historical revisionism, the image painted by Tsunehira chimes with the reactionary outlook of the Alternative Right.

Netto Uyoku have since engaged in online campaigns such as *enjō*, which Rumi Sakamoto of the University of Auckland describes as a "rush of critical or accusatory comments [...] to a specific blog or [social networking site]" which targets "left/liberal opinions and sites".[8] In addition, more technologically sophisticated campaign techniques, including the use of bots, have been documented as being employed by the *Netto Uyoku*.[9]

A related parallel in the origins of these two movements is their supporter base's social detachment and its seeming contribution to their radicalisation. In an article examining the history of 4chan, writer Dale Beran, who had monitored it since prior to its rightward turn, highlighted how many of its users maintained "a culture of hopelessness," a worldview reflected in the self-perception of many within these online communities.[10] This includes a deep sense of social as well economic failure or despair, exemplified by a popular self-identity of these users being "NEET," a term originating from a 1999 UK government report classifying those aged 16–24 who were "Not in Education, Employment or Training."[11] Similarly, as *Global Voices* reported in 2017, some self-confessed former members of the *Netto Uyoku* put their extreme social isolation – a phenomenon, especially amongst the young, referred to in Japan as *hikikomori* – down as a contributor to their process of radicalisation.[12] As one woman explained:

> When I was *hikikomori* [...] I was reading only those websites that collected foreigners' admiration towards Japan [...] At that time, I thought of myself as a total dropout from society in every aspect. The only thing that remained was that I was "Japanese". So, when I saw people expressing their love for Japan I felt like they loved me as well... As I continued my habit of visiting those websites, their links and references often brought me to other websites where I found a lot of racist comments directed at China and Korea. By then I had become an avid believer of "Japan is great!" so I was easily convinced that all those negative comments towards the two countries were true.[13]

Others also mentioned the role of a conspiratorial mindset in contributing towards their radicalisation, something that has been core to Alternative Right radicalisation:

> I was lonely and had nothing to do at that time. So I spent a lot of time on the Internet. This was just as "*matome*" meme aggregator websites were just becoming popular in Japan. After reading websites that focused on discrimination, I felt great because I thought I had gained knowledge that they did not teach in school nor you could not get by watching TV. [...] The topics we were discussing were often about how to set the world right. So, I felt I was someone important.[14]

To the streets

The Alternative Right first gathered steam online and their coordinated online hate campaigns have been a hallmark of the movement. A catalysing moment for the Alternative Right was the 2014 "Gamergate" scandal, a vitriolic harassment campaign triggered by the perceived encroachment of feminist values into gaming culture. Gamergate quickly evolved into a broader fightback against "political correctness" and the left, laying the foundations for an online, far-right reactionary culture fired-up to lash out at a perceived left-liberal hegemony. Despite its effective weaponisation of the internet, however, the Alternative Right has proved unable to organise professionally offline, especially in the wake of the death of anti-racist activist Heather Heyer in August 2017 at the Alternative Right "Unite the Right" rally in Charlottesville, Virginia.

The *Netto Uyoku* has likewise mainly been active online, with less of a regular and well-organised offline presence, though with one particularly prominent exception: the "Association of Citizens against the Special Privileges of the Zainichi," or the *Zaitokukai* (the Zainichi are Japanese residents who emigrated from, or are descendants of, colonial Koreans during Japanese rule). Established by Makoto Takata (AKA Makoto Sakurai), the *Zaitokukai* has expanded its initial anti-Zainichi attitudes to encompass a broader anti-immigrant outlook (although the contemporary Japanese far right uses less overtly racialised rhetoric and so in many ways reflects the more culturally-concerned "alt-lite" wing of the Alternative Right, in contrast to the explicitly white nationalist alt-right). The group grew rapidly between 2007 and 2010 and, in contrast to the broader *Netto Uyoku*, regularly used street demonstrations. Whilst Takata's focus since August 2016 has been his far-right *Nihon Daiittō* (Japan First) party, the *Zaitokukai* remains active and is distinctively similar to organised Alternative Right activism in a number of ways. Professor Naoto Higuchi of Tokushima University notes that, compared to the traditional Japanese far right, recent movements such as the *Zaitokukai* have less dependence on "existing social groups such as religious organisations and associations of war veterans" and instead have "succeeded in mobilizing citizens unaffiliated with existing groups," especially online.[15]

This mirrors the Alternative Right's capitalisation on the recent wave of populism and anti-elite attitudes more broadly, which has seen them reject mainstream political groups, religious institutions, and the media, appealing instead to disparate individuals communing online. For the *Zaitokukai*, Higuchi even claims that they have relied "solely on the Internet to recruit core activists as well as rank-and-file members."[16] Mirroring the Alternative Right's symbiotic relationship with 4chan.org/pol/, he argues the likes of 2channel allowed "nativist discourse" to be "used in abandon" in Japan's online world in the early 2000s and that this "virtual free space" resulted in the creation of groups such as the *Zaitokukai*.

Contextualising the *Netto Uyoku* and *Zaitokukai*

Despite the overlaps between the Alternative Right and the *Netto Uyoku*, it is important to place the latter more in the context of the changing Japanese far right so as to draw attention to the divergences between these movements. Higuchi divides the Japanese radical right into three waves: that descended from prewar, fascist, imperialist organisations characterised by anti-communism and which maintained links to organised crime; the imperialist, historical revisionist, traditionalist religious right and that associated with the war veteran community; and the more recent, prominently nativist, web-mobilised contemporary radical right associated with the *Netto Uyoku* and *Zaitokukai*.[17] Whilst the first section has receded somewhat to the extent that anti-communism has receded as a driving issue for the Japanese right,[18] both it and the second remain and have fed somewhat into the third and most recent element.[19]

Whilst overlaps exist with the prior waves, Higuchi argues that the distinctive ideological overlap of the contemporary European and American far right with that of Japan is the degree to which nativism is a prominent part of their platforms. The postwar establishment right in Japan pursued nativist policies and social movements in the country have held "extremely nativist" positions, but nativism has not been "a core aspect," Higuchi argues, viewing "the ideology of the post-war Japanese right wing as authoritarian traditionalism, symbolized by [reverence for] the Emperor System and anti-communism."[20] In this regard, the *Netto Uyoku* and *Zaitokukai* are a novel development as they have brought forth an organised "social movement publicly touting nativism as its stance" in Japan for the first time.[21] (Such a stance within the Western far right is not novel, of course, but it remains central to their platform also.)

Despite this, Higuchi claims there is a divergence on this with regard to the motivations for nativism:

> Japanese nativism reflects relations with Japan's nearest neighbors rather than an influx of migrants, and it is based on colonial settlement and the Cold War. The nativist movement primarily hates Koreans because they remind the Japanese of a disgraceful period in their history, which requires redress of rights lost in the process of decolonization. As the European radical right has been taking advantage of wars in the Middle East and the influx of refugees from there, Japan's nativism uses tensions with neighboring countries for its own ends.[22]

Higuchi is correct to draw out the differing historical and geopolitical contextual drivers for nativism becoming a core feature of both the contemporary European/American and Japanese far right. In particular, in noting the focus on anti-Korean positions over the targeting of other ethnic minorities in Japan who are more ethnically dissimilar to the Japanese, including Brazilians and Filipinos, he brings out the deeper motivation for this nativism, in comparison with the straightforward racial supremacism of the alt-right. Despite this, Higuchi seems to overlook the way in which the Japanese nativists' historical revisionist backlash to the decolonising redress of rights parallels the anti-social justice narrative of the Alternative Right. Whilst imperialism is not typically glorified by this movement, they view efforts at recognising and remedying its continued harms today to various groups in society as an attack, and in response glorify a mythologised white, Western past. The alt-lite Proud Boys organisation describes its membership as "Western chauvinists who refuse to apologize for creating the modern world."[23] This ties into a broader denunciation of progressive policy, including that of welcoming migrants and of promoting multiculturalism, which they interpret as a sign of Western nations "selling-out" their country out of a sense of guilt.

Fetishising Japan

A common theme in the Alternative Right is the deep fetishisation of Japanese culture, frequently invoking an idealised vision of Japanese society, with many in the alt-right especially seeing the nation as a model for their desired white ethno-states in Europe and the US. A post from a writer using the pen name "Makoto Fujiwara" on the misogynist manosphere blog, Return of Kings, from August 2017 details "3 Ways Japan is Naturally Alt-Right." The article lists its low refugee intake, its low crime-rates (which the author notes the Alternative Right put down to Japanese cultural and ethnic homogeneity), and its brand of nationalism, which involves Japanese politicians "maintaining a public face of supporting globalist regimes, while inwardly pushing forward national agendas."[24] Such tropes, common in the Alternative Right, are devoid of nuance. Japan's low-crime rates, for example, are due to a complex set of factors including a greater focus on rehabilitation in prison[25] and archaic sexual violence laws,[26] rather than necessarily because they have fewer migrants and ethnic minorities, as those belonging to the Alternative Right are prone to claim.

Teen Sheng's analysis in Plan A magazine also explains how the Alternative Right's attraction towards Japan goes deeper than merely using it to justify ethno-states. Sheng notes that the Alternative Right wishes "to harvest [...] as [alt-right figurehead Richard] Spencer put it, the 'rich conception' of Japanese identity that they believe imbues Japanese life with the kind of ethnic meaning and social connection that is denied [...] especially [to] modern white Americans."[27]

An affinity for Japan in the Alternative Right is especially evident in the broader fetishisation of Asian women by many in the movement. In part, this is reflected in the use online of imagery from Japanese anime cartoons, especially that which involves highly-sexualised female characters.[28] Yet, this fetishisation extends offline too. Writing for the The New York Times in January 2018, Audrea Lim listed the many high-profile Alternative Right figures who, despite their Western chauvinism or racial nationalism, had had partners who were Asian or of Asian descent.[29] Indeed, the same contributor to Right of Kings aforementioned, Makoto Fujiwara, also detailed in February 2018, "3 Things American Girls Can Learn from Japanese Women," and denigrated American women for falling short of the conservative gender standards which they believe Japanese women exemplify.[30]

Prospects for collaboration

Sheng puts the Alternative Right's "strange embrace" of Asia, and Japan in particular, down to the movement's perception that "with its deep traditions preserved by a social and political conservatism, [Japan] should serve as the template for an ideal American state."[31] But how reciprocal is this embrace and what are its prospects?

Aside from the above nods to Japanese culture, there is not extensive evidence of concrete interaction between the Alternative Right and the contemporary Japanese far right. In part, this is due to the language barrier between the two, but also given their differing interests guided by their historical and geopolitical contexts (note, for example, that Japan's far right is not in a position to capitalise on rising levels of immigration). Indeed, Jared Taylor of the key alt-right organisation American Renaissance, who was born in Japan and resided there until he was sixteen, argued in his 1983 book *Shadows of the Rising Sun: A Critical View of the Japanese Miracle* that Japan was not an appropriate model for America to emulate because of the nations' vastly different histories[32] (although, speaking to *Splinter News* in January 2018, Taylor still praised the "good culture[s]" of east Asia).[33]

However, a degree of ideological affinity has led to some attempts to establish links. Lana Lokteff of the leading alt-right media platform Red Ice Creations interviewed Japanese right-wing vlogger Yoko Mada in July 2017, agreeing that "nationalists across the globe" have "to work together" to stop their common "globalist" enemy. Acting as a potential bridge in the alt-right media is the Canadian-born vlogger "Black Pigeon Speaks," who now resides in Japan and who through a joint video discussion in February 2018 exposed Mada as well as the Japanese vlogger, "Nobita," to the audiences of his and fellow US-born and Japan-based YouTuber, "Renegade of Funk."[34]

December 2017 saw the first Japanese Conservative Political Action Conference (J-CPAC) in Tokyo, a spin-off event of the largest US conservative activist conference, "CPAC." The event featured Steve Bannon, former head of central alt-light platform Breitbart News Network and former Chief Strategist to Trump, as a speaker. In his speech, Bannon praised the ultra-nationalist Japanese Prime Minister, Shinzō Abe, and declared that "Japan has every opportunity to seize its destiny, to re-establish its national identity (and) in true partnership with the United States, reverse what the elites have allowed to happen."[35] Whilst in Japan, Bannon was pictured with Yoko Mada and a former candidate for *Kibō no Tō* (Party of Hope), Hidetoshi Ishii.[36]

In 2018, Makoto Takata increased his Japan First party's efforts to interact with the US far right, including figures associated with the Alternative Right. From 28 January to 2 February Takata visited Washington DC, during which time he met William Johnson of the American Freedom Party, white nationalist Jared Taylor, and Virgil Goode, a former State Senator for Virginia.[37] Later, from 15–17 June, Takata and Nakamura Kazuhiro, also of Japan First, spoke at the Nationalist Solutions conference in Tennessee, co-organised by the American Freedom Party and the Council of Conservative Citizens. Notably, this featured figures from both the US and Europe.[38] A post on Takata's blog from 14 June 2018 indicated that those gathered would be planning how to work in alliance internationally.[39] In addition to anti-Chinese and anti-Korean sentiments during his speech in Tennessee, Takata – who was being translated by Kazuhiro – attacked the "Simon Centre" in what appeared to be reference to the Simon Wiesenthal Center's (SWC) criticisms of the Japanese pop group Kishidan in 2011, after the group wore outfits with a clear resemblance to SS uniforms.[40] He also told the crowd that in 2014 the SWC criticised Takata's anti-Korean protests, to which he told them that if they didn't stop their criticisms then his group (he does not specify whether this was in reference to Japan First or the *Zaitokukai*) would "go to the center of Tokyo [...] to start to protest all the Jews."[41] Takata told the crowd that "after that letter the Simon Centre stopped disturbing our group" before adding that he thinks this was "the first time in [Japan's] history that there's a guy who really complained and [fought] with the Jew in Japan."[42]

In Europe, the clearest indication of interaction comes from evidence that Takata was invited to speak at the London Forum – a key platform for far-right and alt-right speakers within the UK, prior to it becoming dormant in 2017 – and at a meeting of the far-right Traditional Britain Group (TBG), in October 2017.[43] The TBG is run by Gregory Lauder-Frost, head of the UK branch of the alt-right publishers, Arktos Media. In September 2017, however, Takata indicated on his personal blog that the visit had been cancelled due to security concerns.[44]

Despite these developments, the future of the relationship between the *Netto Uyoku*, or the broader Japanese far right, and the Alternative Right is hard to predict. Given their differing surface-level interests they ostensibly would have little to gain by increased cooperation, especially offline. Yet, if not materially, the reciprocity of their relationship could come down to a joint trading of visions; Japan continuing to be an idealised ethno-state that motivates the Alternative Right, and the latter providing a supremacist ideology for the former's dissident right to shape their anti-migrant and minority messages around. Even though the *Netto Uyoku* and the Alternative Right emerged quite independently on forums over a decade ago, perhaps now they will begin – just as the latter did when it bridged the Atlantic – to coalesce across the Pacific.

Notes

1 Brian Resnick, "Psychologists surveyed hundreds of alt-right supporters. The results are unsettling," *Vox*, 12 August 2018. https://www.vox.com/science-and-health/2017/8/15/16144070/psychology-alt-right-unite-the-right
2 Rumi Sakamoto, "Koreans, Go Home! Internet Nationalism in Contemporary Japan as a Digitally Mediated Subculture," *The Asia-Pacific Journal*, 9:10 (2011), 4.
3 Furuya Tsunehira, "The Roots and Realities of Japan's Cyber-Nationalism," *Nippon.com*, 21 January 2016. https://www.nippon.com/en/currents/d00208/
4 For further discussion of these, see Chapter 9 "The Role of the Troll: Online Antagonistic Communities and the Alternative Right" in this book.
5 Lisa Katayama, "Meet Hiroyuki Nishimura, the Bad Boy of the Japanese Internet," *WIRED*, 19 May 2008. https://www.wired.com/2008/05/mf-hiroyuki/?currentPage=all. Coming full circle, Nishimura bought 4chan from Poole in September 2015, with multiple statements from Nishimura appearing to some of its users to be dog-whistles to the Alternative Right. In reply to a question on 4chan asking "What do you think Western Civilization will be like in 25 years?", he said "maybe we'll not use the word. more Spanish speaking people in US, more Muslim will stay in EU. there will be no 'Western'." "AN HIRO Q&A DISCUSSION THREAD (Part 4)," 4chan. https://archive.4plebs.org/pol/thread/52311067/#52318012 [Accessed 4 September 2018]. Likewise, after reports that the forum site Reddit was censoring the Alternative Right, 4chan's Twitter account tweeted that there would be "'No censorship on 4chan.' 4chan regards Freedom of speech as important." 4chan (@4chan) 25 November 2016, https://twitter.com/4chan/status/802257259338207232. 5ch.net has similarly fallen into related

forum hands, after it was acquired by US-born and Philippines-based Jim Watkins in 2014 (who had previously hosted the site on his servers and is also the owner of the extreme far-right forum, "8chan") in disputed circumstances from Nishimura. Akky Akimoto, "Who Holds the Deeds to Gossip Bulletin Board 2channel?" *Japan Times*, 20 March 2014. https://www.japantimes.co.jp/life/2014/03/20/digital/who-holds-the-deeds-to-gossip-bulletin-board-2channel/#.W9NjlY7Yq3A. The site came under the ownership of Loki Technology Inc. in 2017.

6 As *WIRED* reported at the time: "2channel is becoming increasingly controversial. There have been stalking incidents and suicide pacts supposedly planned through the site." Lisa Katayama, "Meet Hiroyuki Nishimura, the Bad Boy of the Japanese Internet," *WIRED*, 19 May 2008. https://www.wired.com/2008/05/mf-hiroyuki/?currentPage=all

7 Furuya Tsunehira, "The Roots and Realities of Japan's Cyber-Nationalism," *Nippon. com*, 21 January 2016. https://www.nippon.com/en/currents/d00208/

8 Rumi Sakamoto, "Koreans, Go Home! Internet Nationalism in Contemporary Japan as a Digitally Mediated Subculture," *The Asia-Pacific Journal*, 9:10 (2011), 4.

9 Fabian Schäfer, Stefan Evert, and Philipp Heinrich, "Japan's 2014 General Election: Political Bots, Right-Wing Internet Activism, and Prime Minister Shinzo Abe's Hidden Nationalist Agenda," *Big Data*, 5:4 (2017).

10 Dale Beran, "4chan: The Skeleton Key to the Rise of Trump," *Medium*, 14 February 2017. https://medium.com/@DaleBeran/4chan-the-skeleton-key-to-the-rise-of-trump -624e7cb798cb

11 The Social Exclusion Unit, *Bridging the Gap: New Opportunities for 16–18 Year Olds Not in Education, Employment or Training, Presented to Parliament by the Prime Minister by Command of Her Majesty* (London: Stationery Office, 1999).

12 Izumi Mihashi, "Confessions of Former Japanese 'Netto-Uyoku' Internet Racists," *Global Voices*, 23 March 2015. https://globalvoices.org/2015/03/23/confessions-of-form er-japanese-netto-uyo-internet-racists/. A 2016 estimate by the Cabinet Office of Japan suggested there were over half a million *hikikomori*. Nicolas Tajan, Hamasaki Yukiko and Nancy Pionnié-Dax, "Hikikomori: The Japanese Cabinet Office's 2016 Survey of Acute Social Withdrawal," *The Asia-Pacific Journal*, 15:5 (2017), 1. A 2015 study by Yukiko Uchida and Vinai Norasakkunkit highlighted psychological commonalities between the NEET and *hikikomori* phenomena. Yukiko Uchida and Vinai Norasakkunkit, "The NEET and Hikikomori Spectrum: Assessing the Risks and Consequences of Becoming Culturally Marginalized," *Frontiers in Psychology*, 6:11 (2015), 2.

13 Izumi Mihashi, "Confessions of Former Japanese 'Netto-Uyoku' Internet Racists," *Global Voices*, 23 March 2015. https://globalvoices.org/2015/03/23/confessions-of-form er-japanese-netto-uyo-internet-racists/

14 Ibid.

15 Naoto Higuchi, "The Radical Right in Japan," in: Jens Rydgren, (ed.), *The Oxford Handbook of the Radical Right* (Oxford: Oxford University Press, 2018), 685.

16 Ibid.

17 Ibid., 682–684.

18 Ibid., 695.

19 Higuchi, *Japan's Ultra-Right* (Melbourne: Trans Pacific Press, 2016), 8–9.

20 Ibid., 7.

21 Ibid., 7.

22 Higuchi, "The Radical Right in Japan," 695.

23 'Home', *Proud Boys USA*. http://proudboysusa.com/. [Accessed 30 March 2019].

24 Makoto Fujiwara, "3 Ways Japan is Naturally Alt Right," *Return of Kings*, 11 August 2017. http://www.returnofkings.com/127855/3-ways-japan-is-naturally-alt-right. A notable example of the Alternative Right's admiration for Japanese nationalism, in particular, is reverence for Yukio Mishima, a writer and founder of the *Tatenokai* militia which attempted a coup in 1970. Mishima is a recurring figure of interest for the Alternative Right. US alt-right figure Jack Donovan, for example, previously maintained a blog, "Headlessgod.com," dedicated to Mishima. Moreover, Mishima remains of

interest for the broader far right, including parts of the European New Right which influenced the Alternative Right. See: James Kirchick, "A Thing for Men in Uniforms," *The New York Review of Books*, 14 May 2018. https://www.nybooks.com/daily/2018/05/14/a-thing-for-men-in-uniforms/

25 "Forced to Confess," *The Economist*, 5 December 2015. https://www.economist.com/leaders/2015/12/05/forced-to-confess

26 Masami Ito, "Shifting Attitudes Toward Sexual Violence in Japan," *Japan Times*, 6 January 2018. https://www.japantimes.co.jp/news/2018/01/06/national/social-issues/shifting-attitudes-toward-sexual-violence-japan/#.W9Dfx47Yq3A

27 Teen Sheng, "No Conflicts: The Alt-Right's Embrace of Asian Women," *Plan A*, 8 January 2018. https://planamag.com/no-conflicts-the-alt-rights-embrace-of-asian-women-92eb5c16eef0

28 A similar trope popular within the Alternative Right is the idea of a "waifu," referring to "one's favorite female [...] anime character." "Waifu," *Know Your Meme*. https://knowyourmeme.com/memes/waifu [Accessed 6 September 2018]. The alt-right social media personality Tim Gionet (AKA "Baked Alaska") describes a story of him "marrying" a cushion with his waifu printed on it in his 2018 book *Meme Magic Secrets Revealed* (Anchorage: Infinite Manifest Press, 2017), 79–85.

29 Audrea Lim, "The Alt-Right's Asian Fetish," *The New York Times*, 6 January 2018. https://www.nytimes.com/2018/01/06/opinion/sunday/alt-right-asian-fetish.html

30 Makoto Fujiwara, "3 Ways Japan is Naturally Alt Right," *Return of Kings*, 11 August 2017. http://www.returnofkings.com/127855/3-ways-japan-is-naturally-alt-right

31 Teen Sheng, "No Conflicts: The Alt-Right's Embrace of Asian Women," *Plan A*, 8 January 2018. https://planamag.com/no-conflicts-the-alt-rights-embrace-of-asian-women-92eb5c16eef0

32 Jared Taylor, *Shadows of the Rising Sun: A Critical View of the "Japanese Miracle"* (New York City: William Morrow & Co, 1983), 21.

33 Clio Chang, "The Alt-Right's 'Asian Exception' Is Cribbed Directly from the White Mainstream," *Splinter*, 25 January 2018. https://splinternews.com/the-alt-rights-asian-exception-is-cribbed-directly-from-1822421189

34 The Renegade of Funk, 2018, *Japan Political Discussion: Black Pigeon Speaks, RandomYoko, Nobita, The Renegade of Funk* [Online video] Available at: https://www.youtube.com/watch?v=QeGMfqSY5V8&t=11s [Accessed 6 September 2018].

35 Tomohiro Osaki, "Former Trump Strategist Steve Bannon Praises Abe's Nationalist Agenda," *Japan Times*, 17 December 2017. https://www.japantimes.co.jp/news/2017/12/17/national/politics-diplomacy/former-trump-strategist-bannon-praises-abes-nationalist-agenda/

36 Michael Yon, Facebook Status Update, 15 November 2017, available at: https://www.facebook.com/MichaelYonFanPage/photos/pcb.10155097838665665/10155097825590665/?type=3&theater [Accessed 6 September 2018]. *Kibō no Tō* was formed by Yuriko Koike, the Governor of Tokyo at the time of writing, who has previously been an executive member of the nationalist and revisionist *Nippon Kaigi* organisation. Jake Adelstein, "The Pride and (Anti-Korean) Prejudice of Tokyo Governor Yuriko Koike Is A Big Problem," *Forbes*, 19 October 2017. https://www.forbes.com/sites/adelsteinjake/2017/10/19/the-pride-and-anti-korean-prejudice-of-tokyo-governor-yuriko-koike-is-a-big-problem/#6d839baf774f

37 Makoto Sakurai, 'ワシントンD.C.からの帰国報告', *Doronpaの独り言*, 2 February 2018. https://ameblo.jp/doronpa01/entry-12349650206.html

38 "About," Nationalist Solutions. http://nationalistsolutions.com/about/ [Accessed 6 September 2018]. Speaking alongside Takata were Tomislav Sunic, James Edwards, Kevin MacDonald, David Duke, Bill Johnson, Adrian Krieg, Virginia Abernethy, Michael Hill, Earl Holt, Dominic Lüthard, and Rachel Pendergraft.

39 Sakurai, '訪米のお知らせ', *Doronpaの独り言*, 14 June 2018. https://ameblo.jp/doronpa01/entry-12383205056.html

40 Justin McCurry, "Japanese Pop Group Kishidan's 'Nazi' Outfits Force Sony to Apologise," *The Guardian*, 2 March 2011. https://www.theguardian.com/world/2011/mar/02/kishidan-nazi-uniforms-japan-aplogy

41 yoyevrah, 2018, *Japan First* [Online video] Available at: https://vimeo.com/280826187 [Accessed 3 October 2018].

42 Ibid.

43 Sakurai, '英国保守系団体からの訪英要請について', *Doronpa*の独り言, 30 July 2018. https://ameblo.jp/doronpa01/day-20170730.html

44 Sakurai, '英国遠征についての報告', *Doronpa*の独り言, 13 September 2017. https://ameblo.jp/doronpa01/entry-12310380583.html

16

RUSSIA AND THE ALTERNATIVE RIGHT

The broad Alternative Right rallied around Donald Trump and was, at least until his election, strongly supportive of him. However, if there is one political leader that has competed for the movement's affections, it is Vladimir Putin. Key figures in the movement see Putin, his government, leadership style, and Russia more generally as an ideal that the United States, and Europe, should emulate. Putin has pushed Russia in an increasingly illiberal direction and promoted policies that the Alternative Right has generally supported. Sections of the far-right movement have similarly expressed support for other illiberal rulers, including Syrian President Bashar al-Assad, Rodrigo Duterte of the Philippines and more recently Jair Bolsonaro in Brazil. However, the connections between far-right individuals and groups in Russia, Europe, and the US are more complex than superficial admiration for an illiberal leader.

Ahead of the 2016 US Presidential election, the conglomerate movement that is the Alternative Right consolidated around a pro-Trump, anti-establishment, and nativist message. Just weeks before the election it was revealed that the Kremlin was involved in the leak of emails from the Democratic National Committee, to the benefit of the Trump campaign.[1] Characteristically, the Alternative Right was bolstered by this series of events, which aligned well with its cause. While the mainstream media warned of the failure of the electoral system, Alternative Right activists generally made it a matter of principle to take the opposing position. Key activists generally discarded any accusation of Russian state support for Trump's campaign, with alt-lite conspiracy theorist Stefan Molyneux calling it a "witch-hunt."[2] Others ridiculed the widespread idea that "bots" were behind Trump's success. Although there was significant evidence for a social media driven interference campaign, sometimes exaggerated and in some cases unfounded assertions that Trump-supporting accounts on Twitter were bots (accounts automated by computer software) controlled by Russian actors was effective material to assert that the mainstream media was spreading "fake news" to discredit Trump and his supporters.

In the online spaces of the race nationalist alt-right, such as the 4chan forum's /pol/ board and Twitter clone Gab, pro-Russian sentiments were and remain common. On /pol/, Russia and the potential election interference were discussed extensively, but the responses were not those of alarm or anger. Instead, replies to posts on the topic, broadly speaking, garnered two types of responses that radically differed from the alarm espoused by mainstream political commentators, scholars, and media. Users often denied possible interference, or more dishearteningly, supported it. One user posted on Gab: "I am 64 and have grown up with #Russia always seen as the enemy. I can't believe I trust #Putin more then #Obama right now but I do."[3]

Election interference

Several months after the conclusion of the election, the investigation into the interference operation revealed more details of the state-sponsored influence campaign orchestrated by Russia, primarily on Twitter and Facebook. It was run through the Kremlin-connected Internet Research Agency (IRA) which used social media accounts, often impersonating Americans or US-based political groups. It also set up websites which published fake news content and bolstered legitimacy of the bogus accounts.[4] Data released by Twitter in November 2017, with further additions in October 2018, revealed that the content posted from the IRA associated accounts perpetuated a variety of narratives aiming to sow division ahead of the election. The strategy involved accounts championing far-right and racist narratives as well as progressive causes, such as Black Lives Matter and anti-Trump views.[5]

However, much of the content was pro-Trump, and made use of far-right and often conspiratorial rhetoric and ideas that often aligned well with those of the Alternative Right. Some of these accounts were also remarkably successful, and many posts were shared widely. One of the larger IRA controlled accounts was @TEN_GOP, an account posing as an independent Tennessee Republican.[6] It regularly shared the content of Western chauvinist alt-lite profiles such as Alex Jones of the conspiracy site InfoWars and his associate, British YouTuber Paul Joseph Watson, as well as conspiracy theorist Mike Cernovich, and its posts were regularly retweeted thousands of times per day. Across all the IRA-associated accounts released by Twitter, Watson was retweeted over 3,000 times.[7] In return, the Alternative Right shared their content. Both American alt-lite "citizen journalist" Jack Posobiec and Cernovich shared the @TEN_GOP account's posts.[8]

While it is clear that the narrative advanced by the IRA accounts sometimes aligned well with, or even mimicked that of the Alternative Right, the similarity in rhetoric in the interference operation does not itself imply an ideological agreement or direct cooperation between the Kremlin and the Alternative Right (the single most shared tweet by the IRA campaign was anti-Trump and not pro, for example). If anything, it highlights the efficacy of sowing division using these narratives on (US) social media platforms. The motives should not be interpreted as outright support, but the IRA's activity nonetheless helped give both activists as well as outside observers the impression that the Alternative Right had gained a powerful ally abroad, while also raising interest in Russia among Alternative Right supporters more generally.

Overlapping ideals

The relationship between Russia and the extreme right in Europe and the US has not been consistent over time. For much of the postwar period, Soviet communism was seen as the enemy of the West and, by many sections of the extreme right, Jewish interest as being behind the Bolshevik Revolution. For example, the founder of the American Nazi Party, George Lincoln Rockwell, argued that the Soviet Union was a vehicle of a Jewish conspiracy that sought to destroy the White race,[9] writing that "the 'Russian' revolution was not Russian at all, but the CAPTURE of Russia, by a gang of criminal JEWS!"[10] There were of course pro-Soviet exceptions, such as Francis Parker Yockey, who in his work *Imperium* imagined a reborn Western civilisation including large parts of what now is Russia.[11] The European New Right (ENR) was also largely pro-Soviet in the 1980s and saw American individualism as a greater threat than communism.[12] However, especially since the end of the Cold War, Russia has taken the place that the US formerly occupied as the closest manifestation of an ideal society for a section of the contemporary far right. Russia has also come to be seen as a counterweight to supposed Jewish power, which is now also seen as being exerted through global capitalism instead of, or in addition to, communism.[13]

Therefore, the Alternative Right's infatuation with Russia should not merely be reduced to their perceived common support for Donald Trump's presidency and opposition to Hillary Clinton and the Democratic Party, nor should it be seen as an entirely new phenomenon. The relationship between the Alternative Right and Russia needs to be seen in the context of the far-right movement's rejection of liberalism, globalism, and egalitarian and progressive ideals. The most prominent theorist of the ENR, Alain de Benoist, an ideological inspiration for sections of the Alternative Right, exemplifies this. The ENR idealises Europe and its cultures and traditions but puts this in direct conflict with the idea of "the West," its Anglo-Saxon dominance, liberal ideals, materialism, and individualism which are argued to be inherently destructive and the cause of Europe's perceived cultural decline, increasing immigration, and social degeneracy.[14] These are ideas which have also become central to the rhetoric of the Alternative Right.

For many, Russia has come to be perceived as the cultural and political antipole of the United States and is viewed by sections of the far right, including much of the alt-right, as a last bastion of traditionalist values. Writing about Russia for one of the movement's founding blogs (as well as one of its more clearly pro-Russian outlets), alternative-right.blogspot.com, now renamed affirmativeright.blogspot. com, a pseudonymous author explains why supporters of the alt-right are a better fit in Russian than American society:

In many ways, Russians remind me of how Americans used to be. It is only recently, with cultural elites enforcing the will of social engineers and colluding with soulless politicians, that social liberalism has seeped into American culture and destroyed our will to fight for the right values, tradition, and protecting our culture. [...] No one [in Russia] speaks about how they hate Westerners, only that they hate the sexual liberalism and cultural liberalism that America seems eager to push around the world.[15]

Prominent ENR figure and Archeofuturism theorist, Guillaume Faye, also summarised this idea in an interview with Sputnik News in connection with a conference in Moscow in 2012:

Without Russia Europe does not exist. And even if all European peoples have been sickened by the Americanization of culture, the replacement of a population by immigration, and the phenomenon of decadence, nevertheless Russia is the country that, in spite of all, has still preserved and kept its sanity.[16]

Whilst initially viewed as a liberal leader in the early 2000s, Putin has taken large strides in the direction of conservatism and authoritarianism, a process that accelerated after the start of his second term in 2012. Some of the most publicised developments in this broader trend are the anti-LGBT+ law passed in June 2013, as well as Russia's intervention in Syria in support of Assad. An indication of the Kremlin's increasing conservatism is also the rising influence of the country's Orthodox Christian church after the collapse of the Soviet Union.[17] Furthermore, Putin's anti-Western rhetoric, including his opposition to NATO, has been interpreted as a move against interventionism, features of globalisation, and, among the antisemitic alt-right, a stand against alleged Jewish influence.[18]

Putin's regime has, alongside embracing several traditionalist ideas, also turned increasingly authoritarian, and to a degree, made use of rhetoric that could be called ethno-nationalist.[19] Such rhetoric intensified during the invasion of Ukraine in 2014, during which Russia annexed the Crimean Peninsula. Putin justified the annexation in ethnic terms by referring to Crimeans as ethnic Russians.[20] However, even earlier, after the two "colour revolutions" in Ukraine and Georgia in the early 2000s, the Russian regime turned to nationalistic, anti-Western, and anti-American rhetoric as a means to stave off similar developments at home. Consequently, Putin moved from being seen as a pro-West, largely liberal leader to positioning himself and Russia as the West's antithesis, a move that may in part explain increasing authoritarian changes.[21] These developments have raised the interest of the Alternative Right in Russia and in Putin himself, whose actions have been glorified by a large contingent of the movement.

Related to the shared attitude of anti-globalism is Russia's and the Alternative Right's common stance against international military interventions. The previously mentioned support for Russia's military intervention in Syria can be explained by it being initiated after a request by the Syrian government for aid against rebel groups, which made it legitimate in the eyes of most of the alt-right. Trump's decision to intervene in Syria however brought criticism from a wide section of the Alternative Right, even among those who had generally supported him. Cernovich, for example, wrote on Twitter: "This is unbelievable. This is not what we voted for. This is definitely not what we voted for."[22] Several alt-right activists also clearly expressed admiration for Assad. Richard Spencer, one of the key figures in the racial nationalist wing of the Alternative Right, described him as "one of the most civilized leader[s] in the Middle East."[23] There is also an antisemitic driver for some of the Alternative Right's support for Assad, with some lauding him for being vociferously anti-Israel. A contingent of the alt-right has also been supportive of Russia's intervention in Syria on the side of Assad for its potential to undermine US control in the Middle East. Colin Liddell, co-founder of affirmativeright.blogspot. com, argues this control "is built on a fragile foundation of corrupt oil sheikdoms" and an alliance with Israel.[24]

Building a network

Unsurprisingly, expressions of support for Russia by figures associated with the Alternative Right, especially the alt-right, as well as the wider far right are common. Spencer has publicly criticized NATO[25] and stated that Russia is the "sole white power in the world."[26] Moreover, at the now infamous Charlottesville rally in August 2017, attendees could be heard shouting "Russia is our friend!"[27] David Duke, the former Grand Wizard of the Ku Klux Klan who has since associated himself with the alt-right, previously owned a flat in Moscow, where he lived for five years.[28] He has also released one book in Russian which, according to him, "was a bestseller and sold in the Duma book store."[29] Furthermore, Duke was one of the speakers at a conference held in Moscow titled "The White World's Future" in 2006, organised by Russian far-right journal *Athenaeum*.[30] The primary idea behind the conference was the idea of "Euro-Russia," which is described in a study by Richard Arnold and Ekaterina Romanova as the "notion [of] [...] turning Siberia into a living space for the peoples of the white world, an area abundant with natural resources that will be able to stand independently of the rest of the world."[31] The attendees were from Russia, Europe, and the US.

One of the most fervent supporters of Russia among the alt-right is Matthew Heimbach and his now defunct Traditionalist Worker Party (TWP). Heimbach regularly calls Russia an ally. In September 2015 Matt Parrott, co-founder of the group, wrote on TWP's official blog that "Russia is currently at the center of the nascent development of a Traditionalist dipole against the forces of Modernity based in the West and Israel."[32] Heimbach and the mother organisation of TWP, the Traditionalist Youth Network (TYN), were also invited to another far-right conference in Russia, held in St Petersburg in 2015. The conference coordinated the launch of the World National-Conservative Movement and was organised by the nationalist party Rodina and the far-right Russian Imperial Movement (RIM). RIM is infamous for organising paramilitary training camps with attendees from the

Russian and European far right, including members of the Nordic Resistance Movement (NMR), who were also invited to the conference.[33] The invitation letter sent out ahead of the conference opened by stating that "in the majority of countries, the predominating governing ideology is one of liberalism, multi-culturalism and tolerance, all of which are realised in the process of globalization"; it then went on to say that the EU and NATO were part of a "global cabal."[34]

The conference represented another attempt to increase the cooperation between the international far right. It spread the net wide and invited radical right parties such as France's Rassemblement National as well as organisations like the TWP, the NMR, the neo-Confederate League of the South and Jim Dowson, founder of the far-right British street movement Britain First. Heimbach failed to attend but he continued to support RIM and met with a representative of the organisation, Stanislav Shevchuk, in Washington DC the following spring.[35] They posted several pictures together posing with the Russian Imperial flag (the flag officially used until 1883 in pre-revolutionary Russia but now mainly used by far-right groups and sympathisers) alongside the Confederate flag in front of the White House and Confederate monuments.

Important to note, however, is that following the Russian invasion of Ukraine in 2014 there has been a split within the alt-right as well as the wider far right, with some groups and individuals siding with Russia and others taking a pro-Ukrainian position and finding the annexation in conflict with the movement's principle of non-intervention and self-determination. Greg Johnson argued in an article on the website of Counter-Currents Publishing that the invasion was illegitimate and it was up to Ukrainian nationals themselves to peacefully divide the state into ethnically homogenous communities.[36] Affirmativeright.blogspot.com and Liddell generally supports Putin but in the case of Ukraine published several critical articles. In one article titled "Putin Vs. The Nationalists," Russian activist Dimitry Savvin argued that "[b]oth the Crimean annexation and the attempt to prevent the revolution, which successfully began in Maidan, is an attempt to prevent Ukraine finally overcoming its Soviet legacy and Neo-Bolshevism."[37] Kevin Alfred Strom, founder of the nazi National Vanguard, on the other hand argued that "[i]n order to weaken Russia, and eventually install a pro-Jewish government there, the Jewish/US axis has engineered a coup d'etat in Ukraine" which he suggests justifies the intervention.[38]

Alexander Dugin

Based on the understanding that the Alternative Right sees the West to be in a cultural decline, it is perhaps not surprising that the far right has looked eastward for ideological inspiration and that certain ideas from Russia have attracted a significant following in the West. Russian far-right activist and theorist Alexander Dugin has, since the early 1990s, made a name for himself in far-right circles, and has become a frequently quoted ideologue by the alt-right and, to a degree, also the alt-lite. He bases much of his work on European far-right thought, has close ties to the ENR, and has praised Alain de Benoist, who he has called the "the greatest European thinker of our time."[39] Much of Dugin's work has been that of an aggregator, adapting far-right thought and ideology to a Russian context, then combining it with pre-existing ideological streams of thought in Russia. Julius Evola is another European far-right figure favoured by Dugin, who did the first Russian translation of Evola's *Pagan Imperialism* in 1981.[40]

Since the 1990s, Dugin has successfully attracted a considerable following outside of Russia and built a wide network of far-right activists in Europe and North America, some of which are now part of the alt-right. It has been his criticism of liberalism and, perhaps counterintuitively, his strong anti-Western rhetoric that has made him appreciated by the Alternative Right and broader far right in the West. His dramatic language, often painting a picture of a world on the brink of global war or the total collapse of Western society because of materialism, individualism, and the pervasiveness of liberal values has also helped win him many fans. In his book *The Fourth Political Theory*, he summarises his views and gives a clear indication of the overlaps with European far-right theorists:

> I share the vision of René Guénon and Julius Evola, who considered modernity and its ideological basis [...] to be the cause of the future catastrophe of humanity, and the global domination of the Western lifestyle as the reason for the final degradation of the Earth.[41]

The Fourth Political Theory (FPT), also often dubbed "Neo-Eurasianism," is an ideology that Dugin has promoted since the 1990s and has developed in articles and in his 1997 textbook, *The Foundations of Geopolitics*.[42] The FPT is a critique of the three central 20th century ideologies, fascism, communism, and most importantly, liberalism. It is superficially based on the doctrine of Eurasianism that emerged in the 1920s and 1930s from Soviet émigrés in Europe, a nationalist stream of thought positioning Russia, and the Eurasian continent, as a unique geopolitical sphere that is neither Asian, nor European. It is an isolationist stream of thought that asserts Eurasia's difference from the West in that it is non-liberal, undemocratic, and anti-individualistic.[43] Dugin's version of Eurasianism shares relatively little with the original. Shekhovtsov and Umland, two academics who have studied the Russian far right and its international connections extensively, argued that he adopted the term because it "has allowed Dugin to disguise his more important non-Russian [...] ideological roots," including those from European far-right thinkers such as Julius Evola and de Benoist.[44] Dugin does not develop and adapt the original Eurasianism to the post-Soviet era so much as compile European far-right ideas while retaining parts of classic Eurasianist terminology. Even his anti-Western ideas are mainly adaptations of the European far-right's critiques of the liberal West as indicated by his acknowledgement of his shared vision with René Guénon and Julius Evola.

However, like classic Eurasianism, Dugin continue to divide up the world into tellurocracies (land powers) and thalassocracies (maritime powers) and this remains central to his ideology. A state's geopolitical position is, according to Dugin, determinant of its cultural traits. Not afraid to generalise, Dugin asserts that maritime states are liberal and individualistic whereas tellurocracies are collectivist and traditionalist. Dugin's concern is however concerned with land powers in a more general sense than the classic Eurasianists. Whereas classic Eurasianism more narrowly defined Eurasia as roughly the region of the Soviet empire stretching from Eastern Europe to North East Asia, Dugin's Neo-Eurasianism focus is much wider as well as more ambiguous. For him, tellurocracies include any land powers across the world and he envisions these joining together against the USA and Atlanticism. This ambiguity has likely helped Dugin's thoughts find adherents outside of Russia. José Pedro Zúquete has argued that the broadening of the ideology "has the potential to attract all those movements that challenge the status quo of liberalism, atlanticism, and the global oligarchy associated with them."[45]

Dugin shares Evola's idea that a new world will be remade from the ruins of the current one, and the regenerative power of destruction is a familiar idea to much of the alt-right. According to Marlene Laruelle, in her biographical chapter on Dugin in *Key Thinkers of the Radical Right*, "he cultivates the cult of war as a unique regenerative tool to destroy the old world and create a new one."[46] In contrast to classic Eurasianism's isolationist view, Dugin's dichotomous division of the world believes in an inevitable clash between the land and sea powers. The sea powers necessarily need to expand in order to satisfy consumerism's ever-growing need for resources and Russia, being inherently imperial, will have to counter the expanse of the maritime powers in order to survive, but also in order to live up to its purpose as the centre of a "Eurasian empire" which he argues is closely tied to its national identity.[47]

Dugin, however, argues that he opposes biological racism and the white supremacist ideas of fascism. His Neo-Eurasianism focuses on nations, states, and "civilisations," concepts which he uses interchangeably but does not define in biological terms. This view is part of his critique against fascism.[48] Inspired by de Benoist's ethnopluralism, he denies a hierarchy between groups of people while continuing to fervently argue that ethnic groups are inherently different. Neither is he outright Islamophobic; Muslim countries are included in his Eurasian empire.[49] However, his denial of biological racism hides an equally disturbing worldview. Dugin has made statements resembling the metaphysical or spiritual racism espoused, for example, by Evola, who suggested that races are not defined so much by their biology as by a "metaphysical mission" which the physical body is a representation of, thereby endowing them with different qualities.[50]

Although international commentators have sometimes claimed that Dugin has meaningful influence in the Kremlin, and has even been described as an influence on Putin himself, this is an overstatement.[51] Dugin's success is, perhaps paradoxically, greater abroad than at home. In Russia his influence has been fluctuating over time and despite having had periods of success, he never reached the inner circles of the Kremlin.[52] One of his greatest successes in Russia remains the publication of his textbook *The Foundations of Geopolitics* in 1997. The textbook was commissioned by the Minister of Defence at the time, Igor Rodionov, and its publication gave Dugin a large readership in military circles. The book also helped him secure a position to teach at the Military Academy of the General Staff of the Armed Forces and attain an advisor position to Duma speaker Gennadiy Seleznyov in 1998.[53]

Dugin made (failed) attempts to reach direct political influence with his Eurasian Party, founded in 2002 on a platform based on his own teachings, emphasising geopolitics-based foreign policy and anti-Americanism. In 2003, Dugin founded the International Eurasianist Movement (IEM) in another attempt to promote neo-Eurasianism and disbanding the unsuccessful party structure. The aim was to spread the ideas also outside of Russia and branches were established in most of the former Soviet states and several European countries.[54] IEM at first received support from a meaningful number of individuals in powerful positions.[55] However, after a promising start it eventually failed to attract enough members. While it aimed to distance itself from the white supremacist far-right groups this also failed when marches organised by IEM attracted more demonstrators from the extreme right than from IEM itself, including nazi skinheads and members of the virulently antisemitic organisation Pamyat.[56]

In 2008, Dugin made another entry into an established institution when he got the opportunity to create the *Center for Conservative Research* within the Sociology Department at Moscow State University (MSU) (the university already had a reputation of being a conservative institution). However, this recognition was relatively short lived. Between 2012 and 2014 the Kremlin was more welcoming to conservative ideas as the new Putin-led government attempted to oust liberal voices, meaning Dugin was again allowed to participate in public forums and the mainstream media but during the Russian annexation of Crimea in 2014 Dugin's dramatic and often critical rhetoric backfired on him.[57] Dugin supported the invasion but criticised its execution for not being hardline enough towards Ukrainian nationalists. In an interview with an Abkhazian news agency he called on Russia to "kill, kill, kill" Ukrainian nationalists. This likely contributed to his marginalisation from mainstream platforms and he also lost his position at MSU after a petition focusing on his statement to the Abkhazian news agency was signed by over 10,000 people.[58]

Internationally, however, Dugin has fared better and built a network with far-right groups and individuals across Europe and the United States including the aforementioned European New Right but also with key activists from the alt-right. Although arguing that he opposes white supremacist ideas, he chose to appear at the inauguration of Matthew Heimbach's TWP via Skype in 2015. In the speech he warned that people with European heritage in the US are endangered.[59] Dugin was prevented from entering the US as he was included on a sanctions list following his fervent support for the invasion of Crimea a year earlier.[60] He has also regularly contributed to Richard Spencer's ventures, AltRight.com and the *Radix Journal*.[61] Spencer has returned the favour and written for Dugin's website.[62] Several of his books are also published by Daniel Friberg's Arktos Media, one of the largest far-right book publishers in the world and until August 2018 part of Spencer's transatlantic AltRight Corporation, alongside the National Policy

Institute and white supremacist online radio and TV outlet, Red Ice Creations.[63] He has also frequently appeared on US conspiracy theorist Alex Jones' InfoWars show and been pictured alongside David Duke.[64] Spencer's estranged wife Nina Kouprianova was born in Russia and is the translator of Dugin's works into English.[65] He has also had links to sections of the alt-lite. In 2018 he was interviewed by the North American vloggers Lauren Southern and Brittany Pettibone,[66] and Posobiec has tweeted saying that he's read Dugin's books.[67]

Dugin has become an influential figure for the international far right and at the same time has attempted to bring European far-right ideas into Russia, adapting them and incorporating them into his Russian works. Additionally, his, admittedly fluctuating, access to mainstream media exemplifies how extreme ideas themselves are not necessarily a hindrance to accessing these platforms, as long you are a supporter of the Russian nationalist project and its regime.

The Kremlin's support

Evidence of direct support for the far right abroad by the Russian state is a more complicated issue than expressions of support for Russia by the far right in the West. There is considerable evidence of support for radical right parties in Europe. Anton Shekhovtsov has, in his monograph *Russia and the Western Far Right: Tango Noir*, detailed how connections have been tied with far-right groups and activists in Europe, especially in Italy, France, and Austria.[68] That Marine Le Pen's Rassemblement National (previously Front National) has been given loans by Russian banks with Kremlin connections is also well documented.[69] The Russian regime's overall motive should, however, be seen as aiming to secure Russian allies and influence rather than direct support for these organisations' causes. Indeed, it has shown itself to be tactical in choosing whom to support. In the case of France, state funded media outlets including RT and Sputnik News switched from supporting Le Pen and Rassemblement National between 2013 and 2015 to François Fillon in the run up to the 2017 presidential election, and then back again to Le Pen as she overtook Fillon in support.[70] As James Sherr puts it in his book *Hard Diplomacy and Soft Coercion: Russia's Influence Abroad*, Russia's overarching aim is "the creation of an international environment conducive to the maintenance of its system of governance at home."[71]

Despite these efforts, Russia has faced increased foreign critique by Western politicians and international organisations as a consequence of the decline of human rights and its introduction of illiberal policies. These include the much publicised anti-LGBT+ law passed in June 2013, as well as Russia's intervention in Syria, and the 2008 war in Georgia. In response, the Russian regime has sought new allies in the West as a way to retain some level of support in the international community. As support from mainstream politicians and parties was generally out of reach the Kremlin sought to establish connections with the radical far right who had already shown them support. European radical right parties and organisations have also served to legitimise pro-Russian separatist movements in former Soviet republics and similarly appeared as election observers in these regions, as well as in Russia.[72] Russia, for example, invited both Rassemblement National and the Austrian Freedom Party as observers in the 2014 referendum in Crimea.[73]

Radical right parties and anti-establishment actors often see a partial ideological convergence with the Russian interest and, in some cases, also see an opportunity to gain legitimacy through association with a global power.[74] Additionally, business and funding opportunities have motivated engagement from both sides. The Kremlin has preferred to support radical right parties, rather than far-right activist groups, as the former are closer to the mainstream and have more legitimacy than the latter. One should therefore not expect to see clear evidence of direct support for far-right groups by Russia. In many cases, activist groups are also in competition with the more mainstream actors. To collaborate with these more extreme groups risks compromising the relations with more influential radical right actors.[75]

It is also with this interest in mind that we should understand the Kremlin-owned international TV channel RT (formerly "Russia Today"), which has played a central role in both whitewashing actions by the Russian regime and disseminating ideas that bolster the far right internationally. The channel is broadcast in six languages and often gives a platform to not only radical right party leaders, but conspiracy theorists and far-right activists.[76] Alt-lite figurehead Milo Yiannopoulos, for example, did an extensive interview with the channel in May 2018.[77] Richard Spencer has commented on US-Russian relations and the war in Libya on the channel.[78] Ingrid Carlqvist, a Swedish Holocaust relativist and, at the time, editor of the anti-Muslim online publication *Dispatch International*, was also invited to comment on riots in the suburbs of Stockholm in 2013.[79]

The far right in Russia

Identifying an intentional counterpart to the Alternative Right in Russia is difficult. Groups with characteristics similar to the European and American movement on the popular Russian social media site VK, as well as on Russian-language groups on Facebook and the Russian messaging app Telegram, are relatively small in size. Russians also engage relatively little on online messaging boards popular with the Alternative Right such as 4chan's /pol/ board.[80]

There are also instances of groups inspired by identitarianism, an ideology developed by the ENR, including an offshoot group of the Generation Identity youth movement that remains active in Russia both online and with occasional street actions.[81] However, it is difficult to discuss the state of the far right in Russia without putting it into the context of the colour revolutions in Ukraine and Georgia that helped motivate the Kremlin's increase its anti-Western and illiberal rhetoric and policy changes. This resulted in both the clamp down on the anti-Kremlin far right as well as the de-marginalisation of the pro-Kremlin contingent of that scene, including ultraconservative, imperialistic, and far-right ideologues.[82] The fear of an equivalent to the uprisings in Ukraine and Georgia warranted repression of anti-Kremlin groups. Therefore, the perception that the Kremlin directly and straightforwardly supports Russian far-right groups and causes, similarly to how it has been documented to aid radical right actors in Europe, is an oversimplification.

Like other sections of the Kremlin's opposition, the oppositional far right is now quite harshly suppressed, which has affected its ability to organise effectively. During the first decade of the 2000s there was a resurgence of extreme-right groups in Russia, with an increase in organisations as well as violent attacks. Since 2004 at least 4,000 people have been killed or injured by far-right groups according to Russian far-right watchdog SOVA.[83] The organisation stresses that these figures are likely under-estimates, since they are manually collected and often the crimes go unreported. Many of the murders are attributed to racist skinhead groups, a subculture that has long comprised the majority of Russia's racist street movement scene.[84] There has, how-ever, been a marked decline from the peak in the number of attacks in 2008.

Perhaps the clearest case of active suppression is the increase in arrests of far-right activists.[85] An example of the impact of state repression is the actions taken to hinder what is known as the Russian March, a yearly march on the state holiday, National Unity Day, on 4 November. For several years it attracted thousands of far-right activists in Moscow and other cities. The Russian March was first encouraged by the authorities as it was one of the few events to take place on the newly created National Unity Day, a replacement for the disbanded holiday commemorating the October Revolution of 1917. However, over time its organisers turned more out-spokenly anti-Kremlin, accelerated by the invasion of Ukraine in 2014, which split and weakened Russian far-right street movements. In 2014 there were two marches with the same name in Moscow, one side supporting what had transpired in Crimea and the other not. The Russian March now has more or less been decimated, with several of the organisers incarcerated. In 2017 it was dispersed by police and many participants were arrested.[86] In their place have come groups that do not challenge the current regime. This includes those connected to, mostly, pro-Kremlin ideologues like Dugin and some of his numerous activist organisations. One such group is the Eurasian Youth Union, the youth wing of the previously mentioned Eurasian Party which Shekhovtsov argues was founded with the explicit aim of proactively defending against a similar uprising by engaging young people in a pro-regime movement. The organisation remains active and mobilises around, among other of Dugin's core ideas, strong anti-Americanism.[87]

Another movement that has avoided suppression is the Orthodox fundamentalists. Russian Orthodox Christian fundamentalists commonly reject concepts of democracy and human rights, oppose Western influence, and demand restrictions on non-Orthodox confessions.[88] In October 2017 the film *Matilda*, which depicts the life of Tsar Nicholas II and his relationship to the ballet dancer Matilda Kshesinskaya, caused outrage among Russian Christian Orthodox fundamentalists and led to a violent off-line campaign, involving threats to theatres and Molotov cocktails thrown into the studio of the director.[89] The event was also followed by online protests and targeted harassment towards the director and cinemas showing the film, indicating that these groups are increasing their capacity to engage in online activism.

Conclusion

Primarily the alt-right, but also parts of the alt-lite, have found ideological and strategic reasons to make connections with Russian far-right groups and to support Russia in the context of international politics. The core of this convergence is the central critique of liberalism, globalism, and egalitarian movements which are argued to be undermining "Western civilisation" by the Alternative Right and several far-right movements that came before it. Russia has come to be seen as one of the few significant powers that could hold back the supposed deepening influence of what the Alternative Right considers to be destructive. The perception and reality of increasing authoritarianism and opposition to progressive values in Russia has also helped Russian state actors form connections with the far right in Europe and North America. The point of view has been expressed by current figureheads of the movement such as Richard Spencer, but also parts of the older generation now associated with the alt-right, such as David Duke.

Suggestions of direct support from the Kremlin to activists of the Alternative Right should, however, be taken with a pinch of salt. Generally, the Alternative Right's idea of Russia, and especially its President, is an idealised and heavily simplified one. The support that some activists believe they have from the Kremlin, due to its apparent favouring of Trump over Clinton and the usage of narratives that the Alternative Right also espouses, is not a sign of direct support, nor genuine ideological agreement with the movement. Rather, it shows that the Kremlin has found far-right rhetoric to be one of several effective tools to obstruct the democratic process in democratic Western states.

The strategic nature of this rhetoric as well as support for far-right candidates in Europe and elsewhere makes it no less worrying, however. Whether the choice of a narrative relying on nativism and populism was a strategic choice or a result of trial-and-error, as suggested by the many progressive messages also originating in the Russian influence campaign in the 2016 US Presidential election, it appeared at least partially successful and they will, therefore, be unlikely to stop employing it. While it is important not to externalise and reduce the issue of a growing far right to just foreign interference, Russia's interests as well as the possibility of them amplifying far-right ideas should not be underestimated, especially on online platforms. Except for hidden operations on social media, completely open channels continue to amplify far-right actors to promote narratives useful to the Kremlin. RT and its live video subdivision, Ruptly, have made it their forte to broadcast live on YouTube from far-right rallies, affording the events attention and legitimacy. Alongside the well-documented support for radical right parties in Europe, this shows that the Kremlin's interests, at least for the moment, overlap well with those of the wider far right and that it is willing to invest resources in order to strengthen its influence through this route.

Notes

1 US Department of Homeland Security, "Joint Statement from the Department Of Homeland Security and Office of the Director of National Intelligence on Election Security," 2016. https://www.dhs.gov/news/2016/10/07/joint-statement-department-homeland-security-and-office-director-national

2 Stefan Molyneux, 2018, *Civil War MAGA: President Donald Trump vs. Steve Bannon* [Online video]. Available at: https://www.youtube.com/watch?v=apB2J_rhV7g [Accessed 10 October 2018].

3 Insane Orange (@InsaneOrange). 30 December 2016, 3:53 pm, https://gab.com/Insa neOrange/posts/3438438

4 Donie O'Sullivan, "The biggest Black Lives Matter page on Facebook is fake," *CNN*, 9 April 2018. https://money.cnn.com/2018/04/09/technology/fake-black-lives-matter-fa cebook-page/index.html

5 Leo G. Stewart, Ahmer Arif, and Kate Starbird, "Examining Trolls and Polarization with a Retweet Network," *MIS2*, 2018, 3.

6 Aaron Kessler, "Who Is @TEN_GOP from the Russia Indictment? Here's What We Found Reading 2,000 of its Tweets," *CNN*, 17 February 2018. https://edition.cnn. com/2018/02/16/politics/who-is-ten-gop/index.html

7 Luke O'Brien, "Twitter Ignored This Russia-Controlled Account during the Election. Team Trump Did Not," *The Huffington Post*, 11 November 2017. https://edition.cnn. com/2018/02/16/politics/who-is-ten-gop/index.html

8 Sean Gallagher, "How Russia's 'Influence Operations' Targeted the Midterms (and How They Still Do)," *Ars Technica*, 23 October 2018. https://arstechnica.com/tech-p olicy/2018/10/how-russias-influence-operations-targeted-the-midterms-a nd-how-they-still-do/

9 George Michael, "Useful Idiots or Fellow Travelers? The Relationship between the American Far Right and Russia," *Terrorism and Political Violence*, 31:1 (2019), 65.

10 George Lincoln Rockwell, *White Power* (Arlington, VA: American Nazi Party, 1967).

11 Kevin Coogan, *Dreamer of the Day: Francis Parker Yockey and the Postwar Fascist International* (New York: Autonomedia, 1999), 113–29. George Michael, "Useful Idiots or Fellow Travelers?" 66. See also: Joe Mulhall, "The Unbroken Thread: British Fascism, Its Ideologues and Ideologies, 1939–1960," Ph.D. dissertation, Royal Holloway, University of London, 2016, 160–164.

12 Roger Eatwell, *Fascism: A History* (London: Pimlico, 2003), 314.

13 George Michael, "Useful Idiots or Fellow Travelers?" 68.

14 José Pedro Zúquete, *The Identitarians: The Movement against Globalism and Islam in Europe* (Notre Dame: University of Notre Dame Press, 2018), 230–231.

15 Cainus Maxus, "'Russia's Orthodox Jihad' and the Reflections of an American Living in Russia," *Affirmative Right*, 12 February 2015. https://affirmativeright.blogspot.com/ 2015/02/russias-orthodox-jihad-and-reflections.html

16 Sputnik France, "La Russie sauvera l'Europe!" 16 November 2012. https://fr.sputni knews.com/analyse/201211061022497470-la-russie-sauvera-l-europe/

17 Richard Arnold and Andreas Umland, "The Radical Right in Post-Soviet Russia," in Jens Rydgren (ed.), *The Oxford Handbook of the Radical Right* (New York, NY: Oxford University Press, 2018), 582.

18 Greg Johnson, "Ukraine, Russia, & the Jewish Factor," *Counter-Currents Publishing*, 5 September 2014. https://www.counter-currents.com/2014/09/ukraine-russia-and-the-jewish-factor/

19 Richard Arnold and Andreas Umland, "The Radical Right in Post-Soviet Russia," 589–590.

20 Ibid.

21 Anton Shekhovtsov, *Russia and the Western Far Right: Tango Noir* (New York: Routledge, 2018), 92–93.

22 David Smith, "Doves and Hawks: How Opinion Was Divided about Airstrikes in Syria," *The Guardian*, 8 April 2017. https://www.theguardian.com/us-news/2017/apr/ 08/doves-and-hawks-how-opinion-was-divided-about-airstrikes-in-syria

23 Richard Spencer (@RichardBSpencer). 8 April 2018, 6:28 pm, https://twitter.com/ RichardBSpencer/status/983018873950793732

24 Colin Liddell, "Putin reading Alt-Right?" *Affirmative Right*, 16 September 2015. http s://affirmativeright.blogspot.com/2015/09/putin-reading-alt-right.html

25 Richard Spencer (@RichardBSpencer). 22 March 2016, 7:14 pm, https://twitter.com/ richardbspencer/status/712341728980705280

26 David Weigel, "Trump Moves Praise for Putin Closer to the Mainstream of the GOP," *The Washington Post*, 9 September 2016. https://www.washingtonpost.com/politics/ trump-moves-praise-for-putin-closer-to-the-mainstream-of-the-gop/2016/09/09/ ccf2853c-7693-11e6-8149-b8d05321db62_story.html

27 Oliver Laughland, "White Nationalist Richard Spencer at Rally over Confederate Statue's Removal," *The Guardian Post*, 14 May 2017. https://www.theguardian.com/ world/2017/may/14/richard-spencer-white-nationalist-virginia-confederate-statue

28 David Duke (@DrDavidDuke). 17 February 2017, 12:09 am, https://twitter.com/drda vidduke/status/832366195819044870.

29 Ibid.

30 Richard Arnold and Ekaterina Romanova, "The 'White World's Future?' An Analysis of the Russian Far Right," *Journal for the Study of Radicalism*, 7:1 (2013), 81–82.

31 Ibid., 85.

32 Matt Parrott, "Techno-Traditionalism against Modernity," Traditionalist Worker party, 26 September 2015. https://web.archive.org/web/20180116221955/https://www.tra dworker.org/?p=51359

33 Nordfront.se, "Ny gränsöverskridande nationalkonservativ rörelse har bildats," 29 December 2015. https://www.nordfront.se/ny-gransoverskridande-nationalkonservativ- rorelse-har-bildats.smr. Also: Expo, "Nordiska motståndsrörelsen (NMR)," 7 March 2019. https://expo.se/fakta/wiki/nordiska-motst%C3%A5ndsr%C3%B6relsen-nmr

34 Anton Shekhovtsov, "Russian Politicians Building an International Extreme Right Alliance," *Anton Shekhovtsov's blog*, 15 September 2015. http://anton-shekhovtsov.blogsp ot.com/2015/09/russian-politicians-building.html

35 Casey Michael, "Russian, American White Nationalists Raise their Flags in Washington," *Think Progress*, 22 September 2017. https://thinkprogress.org/russian-american-na tionalists-washington-5bd15fd18eaf/

36 Greg Johnson, "The Ukraine Crisis," *Counter-Currents Publishing*, 3 March 2014. https:// www.counter-currents.com/2014/03/the-ukraine-crisis/

37 Colin Liddell, "Putin Vs. The Nationalists," *Affirmative Right*, 30 January 2017. https://a ffirmativeright.blogspot.com/2017/01/putin-vs-nationalists.htm

38 Kevin Alfred Strom, "Jewish Aggression, Part 2," *Kevin Alfred Strom*, 16 August 2014. http://www.kevinalfredstrom.com/2014/08/jewish-aggression-part-2/

39 José Pedro Zúquete, *The Identitarians: The Movement against Globalism and Islam in Europe* (Notre Dame: University of Notre Dame Press, 2018), 232.

40 Marlene Laruelle, *Aleksandr Dugin: A Russian Version of the European Radical Right?* (Washington, DC: Kennan Institute Occasional Papers, 2006), 10.

41 Alexander Dugin, *The Fourth Political Theory* (London: Arktos, 2012), 193.

42 Alexander Dugin, *Osnovy geopolitiki: geopolitičeskoe budušćee Rossii* (Moscow: Arktogeja, 1997).

43 V. A. Shnirel'man, "The Idea of Eurasianism and the Theory of Culture," *Anthropology & Archeology of Eurasia*, 36:4 (1998).

44 Anton Shekhovtsov and Andreas Umland, "Is Aleksandr Dugin a Traditionalist? 'Neo-Eurasianism' and Perennial Philosophy," *The Russian Review*, 68:4 (2009), 675.

45 José Pedro Zúquete, *The Identitarians: The Movement against Globalism and Islam in Europe* (Notre Dame: University of Notre Dame Press, 2018), 232.

46 Marlene Laruelle, "Alexander Dugin and Eurasianism," in Mark Sedgwick (ed.), *Key Thinkers of the Radical Right: Behind the New Threat to Liberal Democracy* (Oxford: Oxford University Press, 2019), 161.

47 Ibid., 160.

48 Alexander Dugin in: Lauren Southern, 2018, *Aleksandr Dugin on Millennials, Modernity and Religion* [Online Video]. Available at: https://www.youtube.com/watch?v= sl2-OHvxK4 [Accessed 22 October 2018].

49 Laruelle, "Alexander Dugin and Eurasianism," 162.

50 Andreas Umland, "Pathological Tendencies in Russian 'Neo-Eurasianism': The Significance of the Rise of Aleksandr Dugin for the Interpretation of Public Life in Contemporary Russia," *Russian Politics & Law*, 47:1 (2009), 78.
51 See: Anton Barbashin and Hannah Thoburn, "Putin's Brain," *Foreign Affairs Group*, 31 March 2014. https://www.foreignaffairs.com/articles/russia-fsu/2014-03-31/putins-brain
52 Laruelle, "Alexander Dugin and Eurasianism," 158.
53 Umland, "Pathological Tendencies in Russian 'Neo-Eurasianism': The Significance of the Rise of Aleksandr Dugin for the Interpretation of Public Life in Contemporary Russia," 76.
54 Alexander Dugin, *Eurasian Mission: An Introduction to Neo-Eurasianism* (United Kingdom: Arktos Media Ltd, 2014), 28.
55 Umland, "Pathological Tendencies in Russian 'Neo-Eurasianism': The Significance of the Rise of Aleksandr Dugin for the Interpretation of Public Life in Contemporary Russia," 80.
56 Wayne Allensworth, "Dugin and the Eurasian controversy: Is Eurasianism 'patriotic'?" in Marlène Laruelle (ed.), *Russian Nationalism and the National Reassertion of Russia* (New York: Routledge, 2009), 104.
57 Laruelle, "Alexander Dugin and Eurasianism," 158.
58 Change.org, Требуем увёльнения прёфессёра факультета сёциёлёгии МГУ А. Г. Дугина!. https://www.change.org/p/ректёру-мгу-им-лёмёнёсёва-академику-в-а-садёвничему-требуем-увёльнения-прёфессёра-факультета-сёциёлёгии-мгу-а-г-дугина [Accessed 4 January 2019].
59 George Michael, "Useful Idiots or Fellow Travelers? The Relationship between the American Far Right and Russia," *Terrorism and Political Violence*, 31:1 (2019), 77.
60 Kathrin Hille, "Blacklist Putin loyalists, says Navalny," *Financial Times*, 11 March 2015. https://www.ft.com/content/0e21a4b4-c80a-11e4-8210-00144feab7de
61 Alexander Dugin, "MAKE DASEIN GREAT AGAIN," *Radix Journal*, 18 March 2016. https://radixjournal.com/2016/03/2016-3-18-9g6g8wrlcugqzwq7aiwju912smr0in/
62 Richard Spencer, "Will Trump Really Make America Great Again?" *Katheon*, 25 January 2017. http://katehon.com/article/will-trump-really-make-america-great-again
63 Arktos Media Ltd., "Departure from the AltRight Corporation," *Arktos*, 3 August 2018. https://arktos.com/2018/08/03/departure-from-the-altright-corporation/
64 David Duke, "Jewish Attacks on Russian Parliamentarians Reveal Their Own Hypocrisies," *DavidDuke.com*, 26 January 2005. http://web.archive.org/web/20050308111116/http://www.davidduke.com:80/index.php?p=224
65 Casey Michel, "Meet the Moscow Mouthpiece Married to a Racist Alt-Right Boss," *The Daily Beast*, 20 December 2016. https://www.thedailybeast.com/meet-the-moscow-mouthpiece-married-to-a-racist-alt-right-boss
66 Alexander Dugin in: Lauren Southern, 2018, *Aleksandr Dugin on Millennials, Modernity and Religion* [Online Video]. Available at: https://www.youtube.com/watch?v=sl2-OHvxK4 [Accessed 22 October 2018].
67 Tweet by Jack Posobiec, 13 June 2017, HOPE not hate Online Archive.
68 Shekhovtsov, *Russia and the Western Far Right: Tango Noir*.
69 Gabriel Gatehouse, "Marine Le Pen: Who's Funding France's Far Right?" *BBC Panorama*, 3 April 2017. https://www.bbc.com/news/world-europe-39478066
70 Shekhovtsov, *Russia and the Western Far Right: Tango Noir*, 253.
71 James Sherr, *Hard Diplomacy and Soft Coercion: Russia's Influence Abroad* (London: Chatham House, 2013), 96. Italics from original removed.
72 Antonis Klapsis, *An Unholy Alliance: The European Far Right and Putin's Russia* (Brussels: Wilfried Martens Centre for European Studies, 2017), 44.
73 Halya Coynash, "The Crimean Referendum's Neo-Nazi Observers," *Kharkiv Human Rights Group*, 16 March 2014. http://khpg.org/index.php?id=1394946269
74 Shekhovtsov, *Russia and the Western Far Right: Tango Noir*, xxvii.
75 Ibid., 252.
76 "About RT," RT, Accessed 20 October 2018. https://www.rt.com/about-us/

77 RT UK, 2013, *EXCLUSIVE: RT Speaks to Milo Yiannopoulos ahead of Day for Freedom Rally* [Online Video]. Available at: https://www.youtube.com/watch?v=WurmJ-ki5IM [Accessed 25 October 2018].
78 RTQuestionMore, 2013, *Richard Spencer RT TV Exclusive Interview* [Online Video]. Available at: https://www.youtube.com/watch?v=dTKw7CD9v6Q [Accessed 25 October 2018].
79 RTQuestionMore, 2013, *Stockholm Riots: Immigrant Anger* [Online Video]. Available at: https://www.youtube.com/watch?v=nTz3GrXQAk8 [Accessed 25 October 2018].
80 Gabriel Emile Hine et al., "Kek, Cucks, and God Emperor Trump: A Measurement Study of 4chan's Politically Incorrect Forum and Its Effects on the Web," *Presented at the 11th International AAAI Conference on Web and Social Media (ICWSM'17)* (2017), 4.
81 "Идентаристы Рёссии," VK group page. https://vk.com/generation_identity [Accessed 14 October 2018].
82 Shekhovtsov, *Russia and the Western Far Right: Tango Noir*, 92.
83 SOVA Center, "Database," https://www.sova-center.ru/database/ [Accessed 20 October 2018].
84 Alexander Verkhovsky, "Future Prospects of Contemporary Russian Nationalism," in Marlène Laruelle (ed.), *Russian Nationalism and the National Reassertion of Russia* (New York: Routledge, 2009), 92.
85 Richard Arnold and Andreas Umland, "The Radical Right in Post-Soviet Russia," 590.
86 Mariya Petkova, "The Death of the Russian Far Right," *Al Jazeera*, 16 December 2017. https://www.aljazeera.com/indepth/features/2017/11/death-russian-171123102640298.html
87 Shekhovtsov, *Russia and the Western Far Right: Tango Noir*, 76–77.
88 Aleksandr Verkhovsky, "The Role of the Russian Orthodox Church in Nationalist, Xenophobic and Antiwestern Tendencies in Russia Today: Not Nationalism, but Fundamentalism," *Religion, State and Society*, 30:4 (2002), 334.
89 Mansur Mirovalev, "The Rise of Russia's 'Violence-prone Alt-right'," *Al Jazeera*, 27 October 2017. https://www.aljazeera.com/news/2017/10/rise-russia-violence-prone-alt-171025103935875.html

17

MYTH, MYSTICISM, INDIA, AND THE ALT-RIGHT

A glance at the comments section of any alt-right website will confront the viewer with crude racism towards people of non-white ethnicities, not least people of Indian origin, who are variously degraded as "Pajeets," "street-shitters," or stereotyped as sexual harassers. Of course, this is unsurprising for a movement rooted in white supremacy. However, upon delving deeper into many of these same websites one may also encounter allusions to the "Indo-European" heritage of Aryan peoples, passages from Hindu texts, images of Eastern deities, and references to notions of cyclical time and the "Kali Yuga."

Some important figures and institutions of the alt-right – which attracts cranks from a variety of far-right philosophies – have, in search of mystical/spiritual underpinnings, drawn from the teachings of a number of esoteric movements and fascist gurus of the 20th century. These thinkers and movements have subsequently gained a renewed reach through alt-right publishing houses and websites. This chapter builds on the work of historian Blake Smith[1] and journalists Carol Schaeffer,[2] Joshua Green,[3] and Maria Margaronis[4] to explore how in drawing from such arcane figures and movements, factions of the broad alt-right have come to appropriate elements of Hindu philosophy, and have some interesting (although limited) links to Hindu nationalism (Hindutva) today.

Alt-right ideologue Greg Johnson, editor-in-chief of Counter-Currents Publishing – one of the two major publishing houses of the alt-right – wrote in a review of author Farnham O'Reilly's "racial nationalist fantasy" novel *Hyperborean Home* (2011) that "facts are not enough" to inspire a white nationalist movement:

> What we need is a myth, meaning a concrete vision, a story of who we are and who we wish to become. Since myths are stories, they can be understood and appreciated by virtually anyone. And myths, unlike science and policy studies, resonate deeply in the soul and reach the wellsprings of action. Myths can inspire collective action to change the world.[5]

In order to elevate the gutter racism of the movement, elements of the alt-right have sought to invoke, sometimes semi-ironically, sweeping mythologies that stretch from the semi-divine origins of "Aryans" to the end and rebirth of the world itself.

The Aryan homeland

The opening paragraph of Richard Spencer's "meta-political manifesto for the Alt-Right movement" – released by his AltRight Corporation the day before the disastrous "Unite the Right" Charlottesville event – reads:

> Race is real. Race matters. Race is the foundation of identity. "White" is shorthand for a worldwide constellation of peoples, each of which is derived from the Indo-European race, often called Aryan. "European" refers to a core stock – Celtic, Germanic, Hellenic, Latin, Nordic, and Slavic – from which related cultures and a shared civilisation sprang.[6]

The central motivating issue for the alt-right is the preservation of a white "Aryan" race, often held to share common ancestry with ancient northern Indians. "The Western Identity is entirely Indo-European," an article on Spencer's *Radix Journal* alleges.[7]

According to Nicholas Goodrick-Clarke's *Black Sun: Aryan Cults, Esoteric Nazism and the Politics of Identity*, the Aryan mythology that has been adopted by factions of the far right originated in the Enlightenment. Drawing on apparent similarities between Nordic and Indian languages and traditions, Friedrich Schlegel (1772–1829) posited that an ancient superior race originating in northern India – whom he dubbed Aryans – had swept across the West, founding the world's great civilisations.[8] As the narrative provided a non-Biblical (and therefore non-"Semitic") origin story for Europeans, antisemites such as Christian Lassen (1800–1876) held the heroic Indo-European Aryans in a dualism with their supposed lowly counter-image, the Jews.[9]

As Goodrick-Clarke writes, myths around a prehistoric Aryan homeland were developed by Bal Gangadhar Tilak (1856–1920), known as the "father of Indian unrest" for his militant Indian nationalism.[10] Tilak believed the Hindu holy texts, the Vedas, were authored by the descendants of ancient Aryans, and that his studies of the texts suggested that some 10,000 years ago the Aryans had existed in a spiritually superior civilisation in the Arctic, which was lost in an exodus to the south with the onset of the last Ice Age.[11] For Tilak, the "vitality and superiority" of the Aryans was evident in "their conquest, by extermination or assimilation, of the non-Aryan races with whom they came into contact," and could only be explained by the "high degree of civilisation in their original Arctic home."[12]

The Arctic Aryan homeland theory was adopted by Western far-right thinkers, including the Italian Julius Evola (1898–1974), a key figure in the school of Traditionalism. In his most famous work, *Revolt against the Modern World*, Evola posited that the "Hyperborean" people dwelled in the Arctic before being compelled to migrate south due to a cataclysm.[13] Evola believed that "The memory of this Arctic seat is in the patrimony of the traditions of many people,"[14] holding that allusions to a polar land exist in the ancient texts of numerous civilisations.[15] According to Thomas Hakl and Joscelyn Godwin, there is evidence that Evola was in contact with the SS *Ahnenerbe* (Research Community for Ancestral Heritage), the Nazi institute that sought to prove the polar origins of the Aryans.[16]

Also important to mention is the European New Right (ENR), an important ideological foundation of the alt-right.[17] ENR thinker Alain de Benoist's embrace of paganism is in part due to his belief that it represents a more authentic Indo-European spirituality than Christianity. De Benoist penned an overview of Indo-European scholarship early in his career, an expanded English translation of which was released by alt-right publishing house Arktos Media in 2016, entitled *The Indo-Europeans: In Search of the Homeland*. Other significant ENR figures include the German Pierre Krebs, who founded the Thule-Seminar as a research group into Indo-European culture.[18] "Thule" refers to a mythical northern island alleged to be the homeland of the Aryan peoples, another expression of the Arctic homeland myth.

Both Evola and the ENR are key influences on the Russian thinker Alexander Dugin, who has been credited as an influential ideologue within the Kremlin[19] (albeit in an undoubtedly exaggerated fashion[20]). As Marlene Laruelle notes, Dugin's notions of Hyperborea draw from Hermann Wirth, co-founder of the SS *Ahnenerbe*. In Dugin's view, "Thousands of years ago, our land welcomed the descendants of the Arctic, the founders of the Hindu and Iranian civilizations. We (especially as Orthodox Christians) are the most direct heirs of the Arctic, of its ancient traditions."[21] Dugin has elsewhere written that "there was something divine in the barbarian invasions" of the Hyperboreans, which "wrought destruction, ruin and death, but also injected new life, new blood, and fresh energy" to the inferior "effeminized" civilisations of the South.[22]

Dugin has multiple links to the alt-right, billed as a speaker at Spencer's National Policy Institute (NPI) conference in Budapest, Hungary in 2014 (although he was barred from entering the country), and his work appears on Spencer's AltRight. com. The first English language translation of Dugin's work was published in 2012 by Arktos Media, the premier English-language publisher of the ENR and alt-right. Arktos was founded in 2009 by Swede Daniel Friberg and American John Morgan, and was based in Goa, India, for the first years of its existence. Since its founding Arktos has mostly published works by Western far-right figures such as Dugin, Evola, de Benoist, and Krebs. However, other works in the Arktos catalogue include *The Saga of the Aryan Race* by Mumbai-based writer Porus Homi Havewala, the first volume of which outlines "the Great Migration of the ancient Aryans from their homeland at the North Pole,"[23] and Tilak's *The Arctic Home in the Vedas*, which is described as making "a compelling case which is not easily refuted."[24] Carol Schaeffer, in her thorough article on Arktos and the alt-right's links to India and Hinduism for *The Caravan* magazine, quotes Morgan as stating that the publisher was so-named in order to invoke a "European tradition and 'northernness.'"[25] An excerpt of Evola's work entitled "The Mystery of the Pre-historical Arctic – Thule" has been published through Arktos' online journal.[26]

Whilst discussions around polar Aryan homelands remain niche within the alt-right, and some figures in the movement have mocked the indulgence of such obscure fables,[27] others have suggested the Hyperborean myth holds an innate value even if historically inaccurate. The alt-right's go-to expert on all matters Indo-European is Tom Rowsell. A former journalist who has written for Breitbart News Network, Rowsell runs the YouTube channel "Survive the Jive," which contains instructional videos such as "How to pray like an Indo-European pagan"[28] and documents his journeys to India, which he regards to be the sole country to have preserved "Indo-European pagan traditions."[29] In a video entitled "Real Hyperboreans – Ancient North Eurasians", Rowsell admits that Tilak's theories seem absurd "from a literal perspective," but tentatively suggests such myths may arise from "some kind of ancestral memory of a migration from the north into the Pontic-Caspian steppe" by the Ancient North Eurasian peoples. However, even if such myths are factually false, he claims "the polar origin myth is not without merit, because there is still the esoteric aspect to consider."[30] Joakim Andersen, who co-founded the proto-alt-right Swedish think-tank Motpol with Friberg, writes, "The myth of Hyperborea, like similar myths about Thule and Atland/Atlantis, is interesting, whether interpreted literally or not. They illustrate how several Indo-European peoples meant that the real enlightenment came from the north."[31] The flirtation of elements of the alt-right with such myths helps to enrich the lore of the movement, similar to previous racist movements.

By indulging in myths that recast whiteness as a remnant of superior or semi-divine origins, followers of the alt-right can vicariously credit themselves, through their alleged ancestors, to be the architects of the world's great civilisations, from ancient India to Egypt, Rome, and Persia. Claiming Indo-European Aryan heritage excuses the appropriation of Eastern cultures by Western racists as a revival of their own tradition. For example, a post on Spencer's *Radix Journal* states that "even today there is a higher amount of Caucasian blood in the Brahman caste. Ergo, Yoga as an ancient practice of the Brahmans was a White invention. This is not appropriation; it is a rediscovery of our Indo-European heritage."[32] The myth of a utopian lost civilisation also provides a core fascist trope; that of a glorious, racially pure past that has been lost, but the essence of which the alt-right wishes to recapture. The aims of Counter-Currents are open: to "lay the intellectual groundwork for a white ethnostate in North America."[33]

The Kali Yuga

John Morgan left Arktos in 2016 to join Counter-Currents, an organisation that views itself as a North American equivalent to the European New Right.[34] The "guiding principles" of Counter-Currents are taken directly from French philosopher René Guénon (1886–1951). "History is cyclical," the Counter-Currents website states:

We live in a Dark Age, in which decadence reigns and all natural and healthy values are inverted. Even in the depths of the Dark Age, there are hidden Golden Age counter-currents: survivals of the past Golden Age that sustain the world and serve as seeds of the Golden Age to come [...] Counter-Currents also aims to promote the survival of essential ideas and texts into Golden Age [sic] to come.[35]

Guénon is best known as the father of Traditionalism, a school of thought holding that behind reality lies a metaphysical truth (Tradition), which is enshrined in the material world through various primordial spiritual creeds, such as Hindu Vedanta (a school of Hinduism). This truth is also manifested in authentic religions such as Islam and medieval Catholicism (Guénon himself was a convert to Sufi Islam).[36] Guénon adopted the Vedic concept of the yugas, four cyclical epochs of time, holding that the current cycle, which began in the Hyperborean land of Tula (Thule), was nearing its end.[37] According to Guénon, humanity is passing through the Kali Yuga (or Dark Age), a time of spiritual estrangement from Tradition, during which the world will be destroyed and reborn into a new age.[38]

Guénon was highly influential on Evola, who developed an unwaveringly hierarchical form of Traditionalism, holding that humanity had been in decline ever since the Hyperborean Aryans were forced to migrate from their Arctic homeland.[39] Evola viewed Hinduism as rooted in untarnished Aryan traditions, its legitimacy evident in its caste system, which represents "the embodiment of the metaphysical ideas of stability and justice."[40] In Evola's view the West, however, has become disconnected from "traditional and Aryan doctrine," mired in a "spiritually tortuous and chaotic situation" in which the caste system has crumbled and races are mixed.[41] Whilst he believed that true tradition could only be reinstated following the end of the modern world,[42] Evola also held that it was possible to transcend the spiritual deterioration of the Kali Yuga, and emphasised action as a value of kshatriya, or the warrior caste, with which he considered himself to be aligned.[43] Evola's ideas would go on to inspire far-right terrorism in Italy.[44]

As Blake Smith writes for the Los Angeles Review of Books, "the importance of Evola's ideas to the emergence of the alt-right is difficult to overstate."[45] Johnson has written that the Traditionalism of Guénon and Evola "has deeply influenced my own outlook and the metapolitical mission and editorial agenda of Counter-Currents Publishing."[46] Morgan, in a 2015 speech, claimed that the outlook of Arktos is best understood by Evola's term "true right."[47] Spreading the works of Evola and other Traditionalists remains a major focus for both outlets.

A vital perspective that the alt-right's intellectuals have inherited from the Traditionalist conception of cyclical time is the interpretation of the onset of modernity and progressive liberalism as a signifier of cosmic decline.[48] Johnson has written:

There is no question that technology, science, and medicine are making remarkable advances. But from a White Nationalist point of view, everything is getting worse politically, culturally, and racially. This is why so many White

Nationalists are attracted to Traditionalism, which explains contemporary events in terms of the myth that history moves in cycles – beginning with a Golden Age then declining through Silver, Bronze, and Iron (or Dark) Ages, until a new Golden Age dawns.[49]

This outlook enables the alt-right to present its fascist ideals and actions as heroic efforts to transcend the decay, or, as per Counter-Currents, "laying the ground-work" for the coming Golden Age. For example, an article for The Occidental Observer by alt-right intellectual Andrew Joyce begins with a quote from Savitri Devi (discussed below), continuing:

> There are many glaring ways in which degeneracy is embraced in this slow unfolding of the Kali Yuga. The ancient Hindus, closely related to us by blood, believed that prior to an age of rebirth, the last stage in the cyclical existence of the world would be a time of great strife and hardship for the righteous. The Kali Yuga (Age of the Demon) would be typified by lying governments, the mass migration of peoples to the wealthier portions of the globe, increased addiction to drugs and alcohol, and rampant sexual permissiveness.[50]

The article then proceeds to argue favourably for eugenics. Even the Daily Stormer has promoted audio narrations of excerpts of Guénon's The Crisis of the Modern World[51] and long passages from Hare Krishna leaders outlining the symptoms of the Kali Yuga.[52] The narrative of cyclical time allows the alt-right to pretend its efforts to bring back segregation and establish ethnostates are of epochal importance, rather than base race hate.

The influence of the Traditionalists stretches beyond the intellectual core of the white nationalist alt-right, however. Historian Mark Sedgwick describes Dugin as "the centrally important" Russian Traditionalist,[53] although unlike Guénon and Evola he primarily focuses on Eastern Orthodox Christianity rather than Hinduism or Sufi Islam.[54] Dugin wrote in his book The Fourth Political Theory (an English translation of which is available via Arktos) that:

> I share the vision of René Guénon and Julius Evola, who considered modernity and its ideological basis (individualism, liberal democracy, capitalism, consumerism, and so on) to be the cause of the future catastrophe of humanity, and the global domination of the Western lifestyle as the reason for the final degradation of the Earth.[55]

According to Laruelle, Dugin, drawing in part from Evola, "cultivates the cult of war as a unique regenerative tool to destroy the old world and create a new one," and, alongside his indulgence of Hyperborean myths, believes that "an ancient caste of warriors [will] reemerge and take the lead of the new world."[56] Dugin has also impressed the need of organising in the face of decline, stating in a 2012 interview with Arktos that "we must create strategic alliances to overthrow the present order of things, of which the core could be described as human rights, anti-hierarchy, and political correctness – everything that is the face of the Beast, the anti-Christ or, in other terms, Kali Yuga."[57]

Guénon and Evola have also both been referenced by Steve Bannon, the former head of central alt-lite outlet Breitbart News Network and former Chief Strategist to US President Donald Trump. In his 2017 work *Devil's Bargain*, Joshua Green reveals that as a young man Bannon discovered Guénon through his interest in Eastern metaphysics, considering his 1925 book *Man and his Becoming According to the Vedanta* to be "a life-changing discovery."[58] Bannon, reportedly enchanted with the notion of the Kali Yuga, perceived globalism and immigration to be destroying the remaining remnants of the traditional. In a 2014 speech at the Vatican, Bannon claimed that the present would one day be considered "a new dark age."[59]

It is unclear to what extent Bannon, a Catholic, has ever sincerely held a belief in cyclical ages and the Kali Yuga. It is also important to note other influences on Bannon's understanding of societal decay and rebirth; for example, he has expressed admiration for William Strauss and Neil Howe's "Fourth Turning" theory – the notion that history develops in 80-year cycles, divided into four seasonal "turnings" of "growth, maturation, entropy and destruction," as *The New York Times* puts it.[60] Whatever the case, as Green points out, it is certainly true that Breitbart is obsessed with the decline of the West at the hands of liberals, immigrants, and Muslims.[61] To Morgan, the very fact that he would reference Guénon "indicates that on some level there is a very deep similarity between Bannon's worldview and ours."[62] Similarly, Spencer told *The New York Times* that Bannon's awareness of Evola and the Traditionalist school "means a tremendous amount," going on to say that:

> Even if he hasn't fully imbibed them and been changed by them, he is at least open to them. He at least recognizes that they are there. That is a stark difference to the American conservative movement that was ignorant of them or attempted to suppress them.[63]

At the February 2017 "Rising from the Ruins" conference, organised by Friberg and Andersen's Motpol think-tank (and named in apparent reference to Evola's 1953 book), Jason Reza Jorjani, then Arktos' editor, announced the launch of AltRight Corporation. The stated aim of the venture, headed by Spencer, was to become a "Breitbart for the age to come, not the one that has passed."[64] Later that year, HOPE not hate caught Jorjani on camera bragging that he was the alt-right's "link man" with the Trump administration via Bannon.[65] Far from its own lofty ambitions, AltRight Corporation has collapsed, and the Iranian-American Jorjani has left both Arktos and AltRight Corporation to form the Iranian United Front, which aims to rid Iran of the Islamic Republic and usher in an "Indo-European World Order."[66] Bannon himself has endured a remarkable fall from grace, being ousted from the White House in August 2017 and then from Breitbart after a public spat with Trump.

However, Bannon's place in the history of the alt-right is assured. Whilst Breit-bart under his leadership avoided direct endorsements of white nationalism, it also arguably did more to provide the elements of the alt-right cover, and therefore extend the movement's reach, than any other organ. Bannon continues to preach a message of Western decline, and remains active in global far-right politics, attempt-ing (albeit with a number of setbacks) to launch a foundation that would unify European right-wing populist and far-right parties against the liberal consensus. Whilst Dugin's influence may have been exaggerated, it is sobering to note Green's observation that, even if it was not to last, through Dugin and Bannon Traditionalist ideas gained "a proximity to power not seen since the 1930s and '40s."[67]

Esoteric Hitlerism

Joakim Andersen writes in the opening pages of his book *Rising from the Ruins: The Right of the 21st Century*, published by Arktos in 2018:

> In many Indo-European myths the gods' avatars – in the shape of Kalki or Saoshyant – step in to punish the godless just when everything looks pitch-black. A new order and a new Golden Age follow, and the process goes full circle and starts to repeat itself again. The possibility for regeneration does exist and it is up to us to identify the possible sources for such a possibility.[68]

Andersen's reference to Kalki, the avatar of Vishnu set to battle the demons of the Kali Yuga and usher in the new age, serves as a nod towards the flirtation of ele-ments within the alt-right with "Esoteric Hitlerism," a quasi-religion blending Hitler-worship with Hindu traditions, developed by Savitri Devi (1905–1982) and Miguel Serrano (1917–2009).

Born Maximiani Portas in France, Devi moved to India in the early 1930s. According to Goodrick-Clarke, Tilak's Arctic homeland theory "strongly influ-enced [Devi's] view of India, its culture and its people,"[69] and she became obsessed with preserving the Aryan bloodline of the Brahmins (members of the highest, priestly caste).[70] Devi considered Hinduism to be "the custodian of the Aryan and Vedic heritage down through the centuries, the very essence of India,"[71] and viewed Hitler's Third Reich as the rebirth of Aryan paganism in the Western world. Devi developed a belief system that alleged that Hitler was a "Man against Time," the penultimate avatar of Vishnu, sent to battle the demonic materialistic forces of the Kali Yuga (which Devi called the "reign of the Jew"[72]). The untold misery caused by Hitler to Europe's Jewish population was in fact clearing the ground for Vishnu's final incarnation, Kalki the Avenger, a narrative that, as Smith points out, handily reframes Hitler's miserable failure as a spiritual triumph.[73]

Further developing Devi's ideas was Serrano, a Chilean diplomat who served as ambassador in India, during which time, according to Goodrick-Clarke, he culti-vated links to Prime Minister Nehru, Indira Gandhi, and the Dalai Lama.[74] As a young antisemite Serrano joined a Chilean esoteric order allegedly allied to a secretive group of Brahmins based in the Himalayas who regarded Hitler as the saviour of Indo-European Aryan peoples.[75] Also drawing from Tilak, Serrano's belief in the polar origins of the Hyperboreans (Aryans) led him to blend Hindu and Nordic traditions, holding Hitler to be an avatar of the gods Vishnu, Shiva or Wotan.[76] In Goodrick-Clarke's words, Serrano viewed Hitler's war against the supposedly Jewish-controlled Soviet Union and the United States to be "an all-out avataric battle against the demonic hosts of the Kali Yuga in order to turn the cycle from the dark age into a new golden age."[77]

Whilst Devi has been an influence on occult nazism in the USA for decades,[78] no Western figure has done more to spread the works of Devi in the 21st century than Greg Johnson, described by the BBC's Maria Margaronis as probably "the greatest living expert on Savitri's work."[79] Johnson has claimed that he found common ground with Devi due to his sympathies to "National Socialism, Indo-European paganism, and the Traditional cyclical conception of history,"[80] and has established the online Savitri Devi Archive under the alias "R.G. Fowler," as well as republishing Devi's books via Counter-Currents. The tagline of Counter-Currents, "Books against Time," is a reference to Devi's notion that Hitler was a "Man against Time," i.e. against the decline of the Kali Yuga and for "Golden Age ideals."[81] Devi was also something of a stepping-stone for Morgan; as Schaeffer notes, whilst Morgan considers Devi "an interesting, if problematic figure," it was through Goodrick-Clarke's biography, *Hitler's Priestess: Savitri Devi, the Hindu-Aryan Myth and Neo-Nazism*, that he developed his fixation with Evola and Guénon.[82]

Devi's works are analysed on some alt-right blogs; for example, a post on the Occidental Dissent ponders whether parallels between the myths of Kalki and Christ could be "a sign of some sort of super-mind or racial soul among our people."[83] Serrano's writing also appears on Counter-Currents, and his books have been translated and published by Alex Kurtagic, an early co-editor at Spencer's AlternativeRight.com, and a contributor to many of the alt-right's central outlets. Kurtagic considers Serrano "a highly accomplished literary artist and a man of vast erudition, able to produce sublime prose, rich with lyrical beauty and spiritual and cultural profundity."[84] The Daily Stormer has promoted the podcast series "Aryan Esoterica," in which pseudonymous host Sven Longshanks discusses Serrano's book *Adolf Hitler: The Ultimate Avatar*, and notorious nazi hacker Andrew Auernheimer (AKA "weev") of the Daily Stormer has claimed that he can quote "huge bodies" of Serrano (among other prominent nazis) from memory.[85]

Whilst the likes of Johnson and Kurtagic may have a genuine intellectual interest in Esoteric Hitlerism, a serious pursuit of such ideas remains fringe within the alt-right. Figures hoping to provide a rational sheen to white supremacy, such as Jared Taylor of American Renaissance, have steered well clear of the notion, as with other esoteric ideas discussed here. However, part of the alt-right's novelty is its sense of mischievousness and penchant for developing detailed, semi-ironic lore. Devi and Serrano's eccentricity, extremeness, and esotericism has seen them, to some extent, incorporated into 4chan-style meme culture, which blurs the boundary between irony and genuine belief. For example, The Right Stuff writer Lawrence Murray has reimagined Devi's ideas as "Esoteric Kekism" (about which, he claims, he is "only half-joking").[86] Murray imagines that the alt-right's mascot Pepe the Frog, by way of Kek (an ancient Egyptian deity, of which Pepe is said to be a modern incarnation), "may well represent Kalki the Destroyer, bringer of the end of the Dark Age."[87] Richard Spencer has jokingly deified Trump as an incarnation of Kalki,[88] and the Daily Stormer has posted Serrano quotes and memes, including describing itself as "The World's #1 site for Serrano Esoteric Hitlerism."[89] Such references are patently not serious – Anglin has elsewhere strongly advised his readers against creating "a religious cult as a vehicle for your political ideology"[90] – but, as with the cult of Kek, the alt-right can signal in-group status by becoming fluent in the jargon and memes around this mythos.[91] Nods towards Esoteric Hitlerism, as with Hyperborea and the Kali Yuga, have helped to provide the alt-right with a "spiritual aura," as Smith puts it, which can be alluring to those with an interest in arcane and taboo beliefs.[92] As Smith has also pointed out, the alt-right's tongue-in-cheek references to Devi and her beliefs ultimately constitute a slow drip of de-stigmatisation around extreme antisemitism and Hitler-worship.[93]

Hindutva

In June 2016, alt-right nazi Gabriel Sohier Chaput (AKA "Zeiger") shared on the Daily Stormer a *Reuters* report on the celebration of Trump's 70th birthday by a group of far-right Hindu nationalists. Chaput wrote:

> While India is now a brown mess, Aryans used to control the region thousands of years ago. They formulated a grand religion, which in a modified form is still practiced today by the inhabitants of the peninsula. Considering this, it's only natural that Hindus today would come to worship Donald Trump as Kalki, the savior of humanity [...] Indians have had to deal with these Moslems for hundreds of years now. They understand better than anyone why you'd want these people out of your country. Interesting though that even other brown people hate Moslems though.[94]

Putting Chaput's hateful commentary aside, there have been news reports from legitimate outlets on support for Trump among some Hindu nationalist groups both in the US and in India.[95] The ascent of Narendra Modi's populist Bharatiya Janata Party (BJP), which exploited antipathy towards Muslims to gain victory in India in 2014, has been viewed by some journalists as a precursor to Trump's 2016 success.[96] Whilst it is important not to draw ill-fitting comparisons between modern Hindutva and the alt-right, there are some interesting links between the two.

Devi's nephew, the left-wing journalist Sumanta Banerjee, told BBC Radio 4 that "members of the present Modi-led BJP government have imbibed Savitri Devi's ideology," meaning the desire for a Hindu rashtra (Hindu nation).[97] During the 1930s, Devi worked for the Hindu nationalist group Hindu Mission, and in 1939 released the book *A Warning to the Hindus*, still popular with Hindu nationalists today,[98] in which she encourages the cultivation of a *"predominant Hindu nationalism* in each individual Hindu."[99] Through Hindu nationalist circles Devi became acquainted with the founder of Hindutva ideology, V.D. Savarkar (who in 1938 infamously advocated treating Muslims as Hitler did Jews[100]), was an important influence on the formation of her "Hindu-Aryan" ideology.[101] Savarkar's ideas would also serve as an inspiration for the Hindutva paramilitary Rashtriya Swayamsevak Sangh (RSS), from which the democratic BJP split in 1980.

Tilak is viewed as a forefather of Hindu nationalism in part due to promotion of resolute resistance against the Raj, but also, as Margaronis states, because his theory that Aryans had authored the Vedas has enabled Hinduism to be interpreted as a racially Aryan religion.[102] The belief that India is an inherently Hindu nation, and should remain so, is the official position of Modi's BJP,[103] although the notion that the Aryans invaded India from an external northern homeland is vigorously rejected by Hindu nationalists, who hold that the Aryans were indigenous to India.[104]

Modi's reactionary, anti-Muslim politics have won him support from far-right actors in the West, including Bannon, who has described the BJP's victory as part of a "global revolt,"[105] and reportedly once intended to establish a Breitbart office in India to support the party.[106] Whilst the racist alt-right has largely paid little attention to the BJP, some important figures have viewed the ascent of the party as signalling the beginning of a new epoch. Joakim Andersen writes that the BJP:

> provides an interesting example of an ancient civilization trying to find political paths most fitting to its own identity [...] it is also a sign of a new world emerging, when a party of the so called "extreme Right" now rules one of the most populous countries in the world.[107]

Friberg has described the BJP's ascent to power, alongside Trump, as part of a "historic paradigm shift."[108] This is interesting in light of Schaeffer's reports that Arktos' management met with members of the BJP and RSS on at least two occasions, and that "Friberg claims to have conducted over a hundred meetings with influential figures in India, including politicians, religious leaders and publishers."[109] Whilst it took place prior to the BJP's election in 2014, attendees at one meeting included Ram Madhav and Ravi Shankar Prasad, who now occupy lofty positions in India's ruling government.[110] Friberg has confirmed the meetings, but dismissed them as networking opportunities for "publishing reasons" rather than a "shady conspiracy."[111] Nonetheless, it is worth noting that a December 2013 post on Arktos' Facebook page claims that at one meeting with BJP officials:

> We discussed possibilities for cooperation between traditionalist and conservative movements in Europe and Asia, as well as potential strategies to counter liberal globalist hegemony, and, of course, future book projects. [...] Arktos intends to become the Indian Right's gateway to the Western world, which will be fruitful both for our friends in India as well as for those interested in contemporary India elsewhere, and the lessons it can offer us worldwide[112]

Regardless of the true extent of the links between Arktos and the alt-right and Hindu nationalism, appropriating and distorting Hindu and Indian traditions has helped the alt-right provide itself a certain sensationalism and illusion of depth. Tomislav Sunic, an ENR thinker active in alt-right circles, wrote in an article on Evola's racial theories that "The best cultural weapons for our White 'super-race' are our common Indo-Aryan myths, our sagas, our will to power – and our inexorable sense of the tragic."[113] Indeed, the ugly online invective of the alt-right, often aimed at ethnic Indians, is indicative of the fact that the movement is comprised of angry white men seeking a sense of identity and purpose. It can therefore be powerful for such feckless followers to entertain a mix of Indo-Aryan mythology that connects white men to a "superior" bloodline, with a heroic past and an equally glorious future. Such myths, however, ultimately provide a justification for an old bigotry, and a new form of tyranny.

Notes

1 Blake Smith, "The Alt-Right Apocalypse: Hindu Eschatology and the Reactionary Mind," *Marginalia: Los Angeles Review of Books*, 17 August 2017 https://marginalia.lareviewofbooks. org/alt-right-apocalypse/ and Blake Smith, "Writings of French Hindu who Worshipped Hitler as an Avatar of Vishnu Are Inspiring the US Alt-right," *Scroll*, 17 December 2016.
   https://scroll.in/article/823142/writings-of-french-hindu-who-worshipped-hitler-as-an -avatar-of-vishnu-are-inspiring-the-us-alt-right

2 Carol Schaeffer, "Alt-Reich: The Unholy Alliance between India and the New Global Wave of White Supremacy," *The Caravan*, 1 January 2018. https://caravanma gazine.in/reportage/unholy-alliance-india-white-supremacy

3 Joshua Green, *Devil's Bargain: Steve Bannon, Donald Trump, and the Storming of the Presidency* (New York: Penguin Press, 2017).

4 Maria Margaronis, *Savitri Devi: From the Aryans to the Alt-right*, BBC Radio 4, Broadcast 3 November 2017, https://www.bbc.co.uk/programmes/p05lxqgl and Maria Margaronis, "Savitri Devi: The Mystical Fascist Being Resurrected by the Alt-right," *BBC News Magazine*, 29 October 2017. https://www.bbc.co.uk/news/magazine-41757047

5 Greg Johnson, "Hyperborean Home," *Counter-Currents Publishing*, 8 July 2011. http s://www.counter-currents.com/2011/07/hyperborean-home/

6 Richard Spencer, "What It Means to Be Alt-Right: A Metapolitical Manifesto for the Alt-Right Movement. THE CHARLOTTESVILLE STATEMENT," *AltRight.com*, 11 August 2017. https://altright.com/2017/08/11/what-it-means-to-be-alt-right/

7 No listed author. "The Occidental Identity: An Oriental Perspective," *Radix Journal*, 8 October 2014. https://radixjournal.com/2014/10/2014-10-8-the-occidental-identity/

8 Nicholas Goodrick-Clarke, *Black Sun: Aryan Cults, Esoteric Nazism and the Politics of Identity* (New York and London: New York University Press, 2002), 89.

9 Ibid., 90.

10 Ibid., 91.

11 Ibid., 91.

12 Bal Ghangadhar Tilak quoted in: Goodrick-Clarke, *Black Sun*, 91.

13 Ibid., 59.

14 Julius Evola quoted in: Joscelyn Godwin, *Arktos: The Polar Myth in Science, Symbolism, and Nazi Survival* (Kempton, Illinois: Adventures Unlimited Press, 1996), 58.

15 Ibid., 58.

16 H. Thomas Hakl and Joscelyn Godwin, "Julius Evola and Tradition," in Mark Sedgwick (ed.), *Key Thinkers of the Radical Right: Behind the New Threat to Liberal Democracy* (Oxford: Oxford University Press, 2019), 63.

17 The influence of the European New Right on the alt-right is explored in Chapter 1 "The European Roots of Alt-Right Ideology."

18 "Homepage," *The Thule-Seminar*. http://www.thule-seminar.org/ [Accessed 6 July 2018].

19 Anton Barbashin and Hannah Thoburn, "Putin's Brain: Alexander Dugin and the Philosophy Behind Putin's Invasion of Crimea," *Foreign Affairs*, 31 March 2014. http s://www.foreignaffairs.com/articles/russia-fsu/2014-03-31/putins-brain

20 Marlene Laruelle, "Alexander Dugin and Eurasianism," in Mark Sedgwick (ed.), *Key Thinkers of the Radical Right: Behind the New Threat to Liberal Democracy* (Oxford: Oxford University Press, 2019), 163.

21 Alexander Dugin quoted in: Marlene Laruelle, "Aleksandr Dugin: A Russian Version of the European Radical Right?" *Woodrow Wilson International Center for Scholars; Kennan Institute Occasional Papers Series #294* (2006), 14–15.

22 Alexander Dugin, "Hyperborea and Eurasia (Beyond the Polar Mountains)," *The Fourth Political Theory*.http://www.4pt.su/en/content/hyperborea-and-eurasia

23 "The Sage of the Aryan Race (vol. 1–2)," *Arktos Media*. https://arktos.com/product/the-saga-of-the-aryan-race-vol-1-2/

24 "The Arctic Home in the Vedas," *Arktos Media*. https://arktos.com/product/the-arctic-home-in-the-vedas/

25 Schaeffer, 'Alt-Reich'.

26 Julius Evola, "The Mystery of the Prehistorical Arctic – Thule," *Arktos Media*, 5 December 2018. https://arktos.com/2018/12/05/the-mystery-of-the-prehistorical-arctic-thule/

27 Brad Griffin (AKA "Hunter Wallace"), "Why Vanguardists Never Win," *Occidental Dissent*, 28 December 2010. http://www.occidentaldissent.com/2010/12/28/why-vanguardists-never-win/

28 Survive the Jive, 2018, *Indo-European Prayer and Ritual* [Online video]. Available at: https://www.youtube.com/watch?v=Wzjx4yneCZs [Accessed 6 July 2018].

29 Survive the Jive, 2018, *A Passage to India: From Aryans to Empire* [Online video]. Available at: https://www.youtube.com/watch?v=6WxtDribi7I [Accessed 6 July 2018].

30 Survive the Jive, 2017, *Real Hyperboreans – Ancient North Eurasians* [Online video]. Available at: https://www.youtube.com/watch?v=Imj0_UhfMLs [Accessed 6 July 2018].

31 Translated from the original Swedish. Joakim Andersen, "Alexander och Hyperborea," *Motpol*, 31 January 2011. https://motpol.nu/oskorei/2011/01/31/alexander-och-hyperborea/

32 "Downward Dog: Yoga and Cultural Appropriation," *Radix Journal*, 15 February 2015. https://radixjournal.com/2015/02/2015-2-14-downward-dog/

33 Greg Johnson, "Theory & Practice," *Counter-Currents Publishing*, 30 September 2010. https://www.counter-currents.com/2010/09/theory-practice/

34 Johnson, "Theory & Practice."

35 Greg Johnson, "About Counter-Currents Publishing & North American New Right," *Counter-Currents Publishing*.https://www.counter-currents.com/about/

36 Goodrick-Clarke, *Black Sun*, 56–57.

37 Godwin, *Arktos*, 21.

38 Goodrick-Clarke, *Black Sun*, 56–57.

39 Julius Evola, *Revolt against the Modern World* (Rochester, Vermont: Inner Traditions International, 1995), 189.

40 Evola, *Revolt against the Modern World*, 89.

41 Julius Evola, "The Aryan Ethos: Loyalty to One's Own Nature," *Counter-Currents Publishing*, 15 June 2018 [original source listed as: *La Vita Italiana*, March 1943]. http s://www.counter-currents.com/2018/06/the-aryan-ethos/

42 Hakl and Godwin, "Julius Evola and Tradition," 61.

43 Mark Sedgwick, *Against the Modern World: Traditionalism and the Secret Intellectual History of the Twentieth Century* (New York: Oxford University Press, 2004), 100.

44 Ibid., 181.

45 Smith, "The Alt-Right Apocalypse."
46 Greg Johnson, "Remembering René Guénon: November 15, 1886 to January 7, 1951," *Counter Currents Publishing*, 15 November 2015. https://www.counter-currents.com/2017/11/remembering-rene-guenon-7/
47 Schaeffer, "Alt-Reich."
48 Smith, "The Alt-Right Apocalypse."
49 Greg Johnson, "Metapolitics & Occult Warfare, Part 1," *Counter-Currents Publishing*, 10 December 2012. https://www.counter-currents.com/2012/12/metapolitics-and-occult-warfare-part-1/
50 Andrew Joyce, "Eugenics and the Age of the Demon," *The Occidental Observer*, 27 June 2015. https://www.theoccidentalobserver.net/2015/06/27/eugenics-and-the-age-of-the-demon/
51 "Radio Stormer Narrations: The Social Chaos," *Daily Stormer*, 4 May 2015. https://dailystormer.name/radio-stormer-narrations-the-social-chaos/
52 "Symptoms of the Kali Yuga (Age of Hypocrisy)," *Daily Stormer*, 1 May 2014. https://dailystormer.name/symptoms-of-the-kali-yuga-age-of-hypocrisy/
53 Sedgwick, *Against the Modern World*, 222.
54 Ibid., 225.
55 Alexander Dugin, quoted in: James Heiser, "A Review of Dugin's 'The Fourth Political Theory'," *The New American*, 31 October 2014. https://www.thenewamerican.com/reviews/books/item/19427-a-review-of-dugin-s-the-fourth-political-theory
56 Laruelle, "Alexander Dugin and Eurasianism," 161.
57 Alexander Dugin, "If You are in Favor of Global Liberal Hegemony, You are the Enemy: Interview with Alexander Dugin in New Delhi, India, 19 February 2012," *Eurasian Mission: An Introduction to Neo-Eurasianism* (United Kingdom: Arktos Media Ltd., 2014), 175.
58 Green, *Devil's Bargain*, 206.
59 Ibid., 207.
60 Jeremy W. Peters, "Bannon's Worldview: Dissecting the Message of 'The Fourth Turning'," *The New York Times*, 8 April 2017. https://www.nytimes.com/2017/04/08/us/politics/bannon-fourth-turning.html
61 Andrew Prokop, "Inside Steve Bannon's Apocalyptic Ideology: 'Like [Karl] Rove on an Acid Trip'," *Vox*, 21 July 2017. https://www.vox.com/policy-and-politics/2017/7/21/16000914/steve-bannon-devils-bargain-josh-green
62 John Morgan. "#3: Devil's Bargain." *Counter-Currents Radio Podcast No.184* [Podcast audio]. Available at: https://www.counter-currents.com/2017/07/counter-currents-radio-weekly-3-devils-bargain/ [Accessed 6 March 2018].
63 Jason Horowitz, "Steve Bannon Cited Italian Thinker who Inspired Fascists," *The New York Times*, 10 February 2017. https://www.nytimes.com/2017/02/10/world/europe/bannon-vatican-julius-evola-fascism.html
64 Richard Spencer, "Our Vision for AltRight.com," *AltRight.com*, 12 June 2017 [page archived]. https://archive.is/2aOtJ
65 Patrik Hermansson, "My Year inside the International Alt-Right," *HOPE not hate*, 19 September 2017. https://alternativeright.hopenothate.com/my-year-inside-the-international-alt-right
66 Jason Reza Jorjani, "My Resignation from the Alt-Right," *Jason Reza Jorjani Blog*, 15 August 2017 [page archived]. https://web.archive.org/web/20170825001718/https://jasonrezajorjani.com/blog
67 Joshua Green, "Inside the Secret, Strange Origins of Steve Bannon's Nationalist Fantasia," *Vanity Fair*, 17 July 2017. https://www.vanityfair.com/news/2017/07/the-strange-origins-of-steve-bannons-nationalist-fantasia
68 Joakim Andersen, *Rising from the Ruins: The Right of the 21st Century* (United Kingdom: Arktos Media Ltd., 2018), 6.
69 Goodrick-Clarke, *Black Sun*, 91.
70 Ibid., 91–92.

71 Ibid., 92.
72 Savitri Devi, "The Jews & the Dark Age," *Counter-Currents Publishing*, 2 October 2014. [The article contains the following Editor's Note: "The following is an excerpt from chapter 16 of Savitri Devi's *The Lightning and the Sun*. The title is editorial."]. https://www.counter-currents.com/2015/06/the-jews-and-the-dark-age-2/
73 Smith, "Writings of French Hindu who Worshipped Hitler as an Avatar of Vishnu Are Inspiring the US Alt-right."
74 Goodrick-Clarke, *Black Sun*, 176–177.
75 Ibid., 176.
76 Ibid., 180–181.
77 Ibid., 188.
78 Mattias Gardell, *Gods of the Blood: The Pagan Revival and White Separatism* (USA: Duke University Press, 2003), 183.
79 Margaronis, *Savitri Devi.*
80 Greg Johnson (AKA R.G. Fowler), "Savitri Devi: The Woman Against Time – Looking back with R.G. Fowler," *Mourning the Ancient*. http://www.mourningtheancient.com/savitri.htm
81 Savitri Devi, *The Lightning and the Sun* (USA: Samisdat Publishers Ltd, no date provided), 34.
82 Schaeffer, "Alt-Reich."
83 Marcus Cicero, "The Return of Kalki the Destroyer: Green Lights Flash across Mexico City during Massive Earthquake," *Occidental Dissent*, 8 September 2017. http://www.occidentaldissent.com/2017/09/08/the-return-of-kalki-the-destroyer-green-lights-flash-across-mexico-city-during-massive-earthquake/
84 Alex Kurtagic, "Miguel Serrano's *The Golden Thread*," *Counter-Currents Publishing*, 28 June 2010. https://www.counter-currents.com/2010/06/the-golden-thread/
85 Andrew Aurenheimer (AKA weev), post on KiwiFarms.net, 7 October 2017. https://kiwifarms.net/threads/i-am-weev-ama.35025/page-4
86 Lawrence Murray, "Esoteric Kekism, or Kek as a Bodhisattva of Racial Enlightenment," *The Right Stuff*, 14 August 2016. https://blog.therightstuff.biz/2016/08/14/esoteric-kekism-or-kek-as-a-bodhisattva-of-racial-enlightenment/
87 Murray, "Esoteric Kekism, or Kek as a Bodhisattva of Racial Enlightenment."
88 Richard Spencer (@RichardBSpencer), 19 October 2016, 6:02 pm
     https://twitter.com/RichardBSpencer/status/788908195527987200
89 Colonel Gunter Brumm and Ragnar Talks, "Memetic Monday: A Word from Colonel Gunter Brumm," *Daily Stormer*, 18 July 2016. https://dailystormer.name/memetic-monday-a-word-from-colonel-gunter-brumm/
90 Andrew Anglin, "PSA: When the Alt-Right Hits the Street, You Wanna be Ready," *Daily Stormer*, 19 August 2017. https://dailystormer.name/psa-when-the-internet-becomes-real-life-and-the-alt-right-hits-the-street-you-wanna-be-ready/
91 David Neiwert, "What the Kek: Explaining the Alt-Right 'Deity' behind Their 'Meme Magic'," *Southern Poverty Law Centre*, 8 May 2017. https://www.splcenter.org/hatewatch/2017/05/08/what-kek-explaining-alt-right-deity-behind-their-meme-magic
92 Smith, "The Alt-Right Apocalypse."
93 Smith, "Writings of French Hindu who Worshipped Hitler as an Avatar of Vishnu Are Inspiring the US Alt-right."
94 Gabriel Sohier Chaput (AKA Zeiger), "Hindus Celebrate Trump's Birthday, Hailing Him as King of the World," *Daily Stormer*, 14 June 2016. https://dailystormer.name/hindus-celebrate-trumps-birthday-hailing-him-as-king-of-the-world-2/
95 Aadita Chaudhury, "Why White Supremacists and Hindu Nationalists Are so Alike," *Al Jazeera*, 13 December 2018. https://www.aljazeera.com/indepth/opinion/white-supremacists-hindu-nationalists-alike-181212144618283.html
96 Pankahj Mishra, "The Incendiary Appeal of Demagoguery in Our Time," *The New York Times*, 13 November 2016. https://www.nytimes.com/2016/11/14/opinion/the-incen

diary-appeal-of-demagoguery-in-our-time.html?mtrref=undefined&gwh=3788FE2A42
0F3B4E1499DF1594C83C61&gwt=pay&assetType=opinion
97   Margaronis, *Savitri Devi*.
98   Chaudhury, "Why White Supremacists and Hindu Nationalists Are so Alike," *Al Jazeera*.
99   Emphasis in original. Savitri Devi, *A Warning to the Hindus* (Calcutta: Brahmacharis Bijoy Krishna, 1939), 100.
100 Roger Griffin, *Terrorist's Creed: Fanatical Violence and the Human Need for Meaning* (Great Britain: Palgrave Macmillan, 2012), 120.
101 Nicholas Goodrick-Clarke, *Hitler's Priestess: Savitri Devi, the Hindu-Aryan Myth, and Neo-Nazism* (New York and London: New York University Press, 1998), 45.
102 Margaronis, *Savitri Devi*, BBC Radio 4.
103 Ibid.
104 Sitaram Yechury, "Govt Is Rewriting History, Taking India to the Brink," *Hindustan Times*, 22 September 2015. https://www.hindustantimes.com/columns/govt-is-re writing-history-taking-india-to-the-brink/story-HFgsvcV7oM395DweDEQmtJ.html
105 Steve Bannon quoted in J. Lester Feder, "This Is How Steve Bannon Sees the Entire World," *BuzzFeed News*, 16 November 2016. https://www.financialexpress.com/ world-news/steve-bannon-once-described-narendra-modis-victory-as-part-of-globa l-revolt/447518/
106 Asawin Suebsaeng, "Inside Steve Bannon's Failed Breitbart India Scheme," *Daily Beast*, 3 February 2017. https://www.thedailybeast.com/inside-steve-bannons-failed-breitbart-india-scheme
107 Andersen, *Rising from the Ruins*, 157.
108 Right On, 2016, *Daniel Friberg: Europe rising – Freedom Congress (Wismar, Germany, 2016)* [Online video]. Available at: https://www.youtube.com/watch?v=QyAgW2VgBcs [Accessed 17 June 2018].
109 Ibid.
110 Schaeffer, "Alt-Reich."
111 Arktos, 2018, *The Evolution of a Metapolitical Warrior* [Online video]. Available at: http s://www.youtube.com/watch?v=MybaxeU5b2g [Accessed 19 June 2018].
112 Arktos Media, post on Facebook, 31 December 2013. https://www.facebook.com/ Arktos/photos/a.296492987045025/766331276727858/?type=1&theater [Accessed 17 June 2018].
113 Tomislav Sunic, "Julius Evola on Race," *The Occidental Observer*, 1 May 2010. https:// www.theoccidentalobserver.net/2010/05/01/sunic-evola-on-race/

CONCLUSION

The Unite the Right rally in Charlottesville, Virginia, August 12, 2017, was a defining moment for the alt-right, but not in the way the movement had hoped. Announced in the context of escalating violence at alt-right events, Unite the Right was intended to be the moment that the primarily online-based movement demonstrated that its various factions and figures could stand in solidarity for white nationalism, wielding power on the streets against all opposition.

As events transpired, Unite the Right was defined by ferocious violence that resulted in dozens of injuries, culminating in the death of anti-fascist activist Heather Heyer after James Fields, a self-described neo-nazi, drove a car into a crowd of counter-protestors. In 2019, at a US District Court in Charlottesville, Fields plead guilty to 28 federal counts of hate crime acts causing bodily injury and involving an attempt to kill, and one count of a hate crime act that resulted in death.[1] Whilst the alt-right has long attempted to portray itself as a fresh alternative to stale, thuggish, traditional American white supremacism, in the wake of Charlottesville media outlets across the globe were adorned with images of leading alt-right figures alongside nazi flags, Klansmen and shield- and helmet-clad activists with makeshift weapons.[2] The scope of negative coverage was magnified by US President Donald Trump's failure to adequately condemn the white supremacists.

Charlottesville was a hubristic attempt to capitalise on the momentum of Trump's election, but instead gave the alt-right its most infamous moment. Whilst some alt-right figures attempted to claim the abortive event was a victory, Charlottesville significantly intensified negative attention on the alt-right, which in the aftermath has found itself operating in an even more hostile environment and facing a number of considerable challenges. The alt-right will forever be associated with the events of that day, and while the demonstration brought them worldwide attention, it also marked the moment that the movement went into sharp decline. The years that have followed have been marred by infighting and splits, paradoxically meaning that "Unite the Right" was the catalyst for the disintegration of many of the already tenuous links that held this "movement" together. While Charlottesville does not represent the wholesale collapse of the alt-right in America, it has resulted in significant tactical shifts and altered the nature of the movement.

Emblematic of the effect of Charlottesville was when, a year later, organiser Jason Kessler unwisely sought to hold "Unite the Right 2" and faced pre-emptive condemnation across the alt-right for attempting to hold a sequel march to the first abortive rally. Kessler was able to muster a dismal turnout of just 20 activists in Washington DC, down from as many as 1,500 at the previous rally, vastly outnumbered by counter-protestors.[3]

While the alt-right has undoubtedly endured a long and bruising few years since Charlottesville, the miserable attendance at Unite the Right 2 did not represent the death of the movement, but rather a change in tack. The alt-right has continued to host private conferences, bringing together the biggest American and European names in the alt-right and providing networking opportunities and fostering a sense of community. Speeches can subsequently be uploaded to YouTube and other sites, greatly expanding their potential audience. The Daily Stormer and The Right Stuff have also advocated the organisation of smaller-scale private meetups, referred to as "Book Clubs" and "Pool Parties" respectively, aimed at extreme-right community-building.[4] As such, the post-Charlottesville online deplatformings, lawsuits, and infighting endured by the alt-right in the wake of Charlottesville have forced white nationalists to pause, readapt, and reconsider strategy both online and offline.

Hostile environment

The alt-right has, since its earliest days, primarily operated online. Whilst many thousands of internet users may identify with the alt-right, only a fraction of these will have engaged in offline activism. As explored in Part II of this book, Culture and Activism, the alt-right uses the internet to recruit, to target its perceived enemies, and to engage in "metapolitics" – the dissemination of ideas and cultural values, laying the foundation for long-term political change. While Unite the Right was an attempt by alt-right figureheads to venture into street politics, getting boots on the ground still depended on the use of online tools, for example advertising the event, allowing event organisers to communicate, and crowdfunding travel costs. The subsequent catastrophe led many on the alt-right to abandon the endorsement of planned public events, in favour of retreating online and continuing to engage in the culture war through digital means. Online activists can be anonymous, avoiding the doxing and lawsuits that Charlottesville brought on them. "We had successfully been lured out of our element, out of the place we were winning by engaging the culture, into a place where we could not win," wrote Andrew Anglin of the Daily Stormer in March 2018.[5]

However, post-Charlottesville the alt-right has found that the internet is no longer quite the safe haven it once enjoyed. Alongside actions by anti-fascist hackers – for example, Red Ice Creations, the alt-right's premier media network, claimed to have had its social media hacked and its membership database stolen on the day of the rally[6] – public outcry has prompted a renewed digital crackdown aimed at alt-right-associated accounts on social media platforms, payment providers, and advertising platforms. This has, as explored in Chapter 10 "Alt-Tech: Co-opting and Creating Digital Spaces," forced some on the alt-right to seek solace in alternative online platforms, sometimes created by the alt-right or its sympathisers. These are marketed for their "free speech" policies and, in the case of payments, can provide greater anonymity. These alternative platforms have had varying degrees of success, however, and engagement in mainstream platforms remains a major area of focus for the alt-right, which has in some areas continued to grow online post-Charlottesville.

Anglin's Daily Stormer has been victim to particularly severe responses post-Charlottesville, partly due to the outlet branding Heyer a "fat, childless, 32-year-old slut"[7] and site administrator Andrew Auernheimer (AKA "weev") claiming that he was seeking to "get people on the ground" at her funeral.[8] Shortly after Unite the Right, the Daily Stormer's domain name was seized by Google and its hosting provider, GoDaddy, kicked the site off its servers. The Daily Stormer has subsequently moved between hosting providers and has had over a dozen domain names seized, enabling Anglin to call his site the "most censored publication in history."[9] "In less than a year between the election and that fateful day in August, we went from the highest high to the lowest low," Anglin wrote in March 2018.[10] Despite all this, Anglin claimed in June 2018 that "Daily Stormer traffic is better than ever," and the site remains the most significant nazi website in the world.[11] Elsewhere the website of Greg Johnson's Counter-Currents Publishing, which suffered online DDOS attacks after Charlottesville, reported a spike in visitors in August 2017, although it returned to approximately 150,000 visitors per month by June 2018, a small increase from spring 2017.[12]

The alt-right has also been hurt financially by online payment providers Stripe and PayPal, both of which have cancelled contracts with high profile alt-right websites and activists. This began with the pre-Charlottesville cancellation of the accounts of alt-lite personality Kyle Chapman (AKA "Based Stickman"), alt-right blog Occidental Dissent and WeSearchr, the crowdfunding site that offered a bounty for the antifascist who punched alt-right figurehead Richard Spencer in January 2017. The crackdown accelerated after Unite the Right, with the accounts of Spencer's National Policy Institute (NPI), the now-defunct Identity Evropa (replaced by the American Identity Movement in 2019) and Counter-Currents all facing sanctions. Bans by payment providers have been piecemeal, however, and Stripe remains as the processor of several sites connected to the alt-right. As a result the alt-right has sought to establish replacement funding platforms, but with limited success. The Patreon alternative Hatreon, for example, collapsed in early 2018. This has increased the already existing interest in cryptocurrencies, such as Bitcoin and Monero. As decentralised systems they are virtually impossible to censor and allow for a degree of anonymity that is impossible with, for example, a credit card. The rapid rise in the price of Bitcoin during the fall of 2017 helped drive the use of the currency and most public alt-right activists now have cryptocurrency wallets.

However, dependence on effort-intensive payment methods such as crypto-currencies and cheques has, for some, caused difficulties. Greg Johnson of Counter-Currents announced in August 2018 that his organisation had received just $8,497.94 so far that year, well short of its $70,000 target for the year and significantly less than previous years.[13] Johnson has, however, done well from cryptocurrencies; his wallet was worth over $100,000 in December 2017, thanks to the high price of the currency at the time.[14] Others have fared even better; Auernheimer had received a staggering $1,676,039 to his bitcoin wallet as of August 2018.[15] These numbers highlight the tech-savvy nature of the alt-right, a movement looking to stay a step ahead.

Post-Charlottesville many social media platforms also made a renewed effort to ban accounts associated with the alt-right. Twitter has banned numerous high profile activists, especially after policy changes in December 2017. Gab has quickly gained traction in the alt-right as a Twitter alternative and some of those blocked on Twitter, such as Anglin, have established themselves as among Gab's most prominent users. Gab has, however, largely failed to establish a loyal user base. Many users contribute little to the site, simply maintaining accounts as backups in case of Twitter bans, resulting in comparatively low levels of discussion and interaction between users compared to other social media platforms. This highlights the fact that the alt-right is reluctant to move to alternative platforms unless forced. Platforms such as Gab, Reddit alternative Voat and Facebook alternative VK risk alt-right ghettoisation, which limits the potential to reach new audiences and pull off attention-grabbing media stunts afforded by mainstream platforms. Bans on alt-right accounts can meaningfully limit the alt-right's reach, but such bans have been inconsistent across platforms while some influential users have simply returned to Twitter under different user names.

Despite facing huge challenges post-Charlottesville, alt-right content producers have continued to see growth on YouTube, which is both central in disseminating their message and, whilst it has banned a small number of extreme accounts, is relatively lenient towards the alt-right. YouTube also allows alt-right accounts, such as Colin Robertson (AKA 'Millennial Woes'), to monetise their live streams with "Super Chats," which allow viewers to "tip" the creator of the video, now a common way for alt-right YouTubers to monetise their channels, supplanting platforms like Patreon where users may have been blocked.

One corner of the internet has remained relatively untouched, however, and as such continues to be a haven for online alt-right activity. Impervious to content bans are image messageboards such as 4chan and 8chan, which tolerate almost any kind of content, no matter how extreme. The /pol/ board of 4chan has been essential to the movement's growth, and both 4chan and 8chan remain central hubs for the development of alt-right propaganda and online strategies, such as deliberate misinformation and ad hoc hate campaigns, through which the alt-right's culture war is fought. However, in the wake of the murder of 51 people in New Zealand by a far-right terrorist in March 2019, multiple internet service providers in Australia took the decision to block access to websites that spread video footage of the attack and this included both 8chan and 4chan, meaning that not even these might be safe spaces for the alt-right in the near future.[16]

Splits and division in the alt-right post-Charlottesville

Unite the Right has, ironically, left the movement more fragmented than ever before, with many activists attempting to shift blame for the mess, and some dissociating from the movement altogether. "There's disarray, there's discord and there's infighting – endless fucking infighting, vendettas" said Colin Robertson in March 2018, summarising simply: "we are fucked."[17]

Since Charlottesville there has been intense backlash against figures continuing to engage in street politics and planned public events. Following Charlottesville Richard Spencer continued on his tour of American colleges, protected by his black-clad nazi bodyguards of the Traditionalist Workers Party (TWP). The expensive tour culminated at Michigan State University in March 2018, when 25 people were arrested after TWP activists violently clashed with anti-fascists, all so that Spencer could address a near-empty auditorium.[18] TWP dissolved just weeks later after leader Matthew Heimbach was arrested on domestic violence charges, eventually pleading guilty to beating the TWP co-founder Matt Parrott, Heimbach's father-in-law. The incident was reportedly sparked by Heimbach's affair with Parrott's wife.[19] The whole debacle was deeply humiliating for the alt-right.

The predictable violence at planned street protests such as Charlottesville has also enabled lawsuits against big name alt-right figures, including a suit brought on behalf of ten counter-protestors injured at Charlottesville and against event organisers.[20] "I am under attack and I need your help," Spencer said in an April 2018 video. "Some of the biggest and baddest law firms in the United States are suing me."[21] Coupled with deplatformings from funding sites, such lawsuits have been devastating for some figures; Spencer was reportedly so broke in May 2018 that his credit card was declined for a $4.75 drink.[22] Spencer's AltRight.com was taken down by its hosting provider after being targeted by a civil rights group in May; it is now back online but dormant. "It will take the movement years to recover from the bad decisions of 2017," wrote Greg Johnson, "I doubt that Richard Spencer and his various operations like the National Policy Institute will recover at all."[23]

The start of 2019 saw an existing schism in the alt-right widen significantly when two central figures, long antagonists, reopened their war. The feud that has been rumbling on at the very heart of the white nationalist alt-right between Greg Johnson and Daniel Friberg – the respective heads of the central publishers of the alt-right, US-based Counter-Currents Publishing and Hungary-based Arktos Media – has again erupted, with accusations of grooming, doxing, alcoholism, and criminality being levelled. Whilst some leading figures have tried their best to remain impartial, Johnson has attempted to force figures to take sides, claiming that:

> I will not deal with people who deal with Friberg and Forney. I will not do business with people who do business with Friberg and Forney. I cannot, in good conscience, have anything to do with them. They are just cancer, they are just poison, and they are so dishonest. And all their little fanboys, and their enablers, I'm declaring war on you too.[24]

Splits are nothing new to far-right movements but after two years of post-Charlottesville division this major rupture at the heart of the movement has only served to further divide an already fragmented scene.

In the face of such opposition and internal strife and division one is forced to ask, does the alt-right even exist anymore? Media commentators, many of whom were late to notice its existence, were quick to pronounce its death over the past few years. Even within the movement many have dropped the moniker of "alt-right" – Greg Johnson has gone back to talking of the "white nationalist movement" – and some, such as Anatoly Karlin in the Unz Review simply declared, "The Alt Right Is Dead."[25] However, the alt-right was never, as some believed, a simple, formal, structured, and homogenous far-right movement with an identifiable formation and end date. In our introduction, we defined the International "Alternative Right" as:

> An international set of groups and individuals, operating primarily online though with offline outlets, whose core belief is that "white identity" is under attack from pro-multicultural and liberal elites and so-called "social justice warriors" (SJW) who allegedly use "political correctness" to undermine Western civilisation and the rights of white males. Put simply, the "Alternative Right" is a far right, anti-globalist grouping that offers a radical "alternative" to traditional/establishment conservatism. The eclectic and disparate nature of its constituent parts make for large areas of disagreement yet, together, they are united around a core set of beliefs.

While there have been periods of unity and cooperation – the Trump election causing the greatest period of formal coordination – and periods of division, and variable amounts of offline organisation, the amorphous movement as we define it still exists. The alt-right trolls still plague social media, the alt-right content producers still pump out endless hours of videos and podcasts, alt-right writers still publish reams of articles and alt-right organisers still hold conferences around the world with well-known figures travelling to speak at them. Just because the alt-right does not collectively identify or seek to demonstrate together as they did in Charlottesville, does not mean that the alt-right does not exist. The movement was always a decentralised, distributed network, and it is merely more decentralised again.

Notes

1 Gary Robertson, "Killer of Heather Heyer Pleads Guilty to Hate Crimes Tied to Virginia Riot," *Reuters*, 27 March 2019. https://www.reuters.com/article/us-virginia-protests/kill er-of-heather-heyer-pleads-guilty-to-hate-crimes-tied-to-virginia-riot-idUSKCN1R81V8
2 Ainara Tiefenthäler and Natalie Reneau, "Swastikas, Shields and Flags: Branding Hate in Charlottesville," *New York Times*, 15 August 2017 [Online video]. https://www.google. com/search?q=charlottesville+swastika+flag&oq=charlottesville+swastika+flag&aqs= chrome..69i57.5046j0j7&sourceid=chrome&ie=UTF-8

3 "Unite the Right: White Nationalists Outnumbered at Washington Rally," *BBC*, 13 August 2018. https://www.bbc.co.uk/news/world-us-canada-45165656
4 "Alt Right Moving from Online to Real-World Activity," *Anti-Defamation League*, 13 February 2017. https://www.adl.org/blog/alt-right-moving-from-online-to-real-world-activity
5 Andrew Anglin, "Decision Time for the Alt-Right: Which Way, White Man?" *Daily Stormer*, 22 March 2018. https://archive.is/J5lp2
6 Red Ice TV, 2017, "Red Ice Websites Hacked – Someone Really Hates Us" [Online Video]. Available at: https://www.youtube.com/watch?v=uWF5i0qvf3Q [Accessed 31 March 2019].
7 Andrew Anglin, "Heather Heyer: Woman Killed in Road Rage Incident was a Fat, Childless 32-Year-Old Slut," *Daily Stormer*, 13 August 2017. https://dailystormer.name/heather-heyer-woman-killed-in-road-rage-incident-was-a-fat-childless-32-year-old-slut/
8 Andrew Auernheimer (AKA weev) quoted in: Will Worley, "Neo-Nazi Website Asks Readers to Target Funeral of Heather Heyer who Died in Charlottesville Violence," *The Independent*, 16 August 2017. https://www.independent.co.uk/news/world/americas/america-top-neo-nazi-website-daily-stormer-orders-followers-harass-funeral-heather-heyer-victim-a7895496.html
9 "The most censored publication in history" is the Daily Stormer's website subheader.
10 Anglin, "Decision Time for the Alt-Right: Which Way, White Man?"
11 Andrew Anglin, "Daily Stormer Traffic Is Better than Ever," *Daily Stormer*, 20 June 2018. https://dailystormer.name/daily-stormer-traffic-is-better-than-ever/
12 Greg Johnson, "Happy Birthday to Us!" *Counter-Currents Publishing*, 11 June 2018. https://www.counter-currents.com/2018/06/happy-birthday-to-us-8/
13 Greg Johnson, "New Directions at Counter-Currents," *Counter-Currents Publishing*, 10 August 2018. https://www.counter-currents.com/tag/countercurrentstv/
14 Joe Mulhall, "Huge Bitcoin Windfalls for the Alt-Right," *HOPE not hate*, 29 January 2019. https://www.hopenothate.org.uk/2018/01/29/huge-bitcoin-windfalls-alt-right/
15 Ibid.
16 Alexandra Ma, "4chan, 8chan, and LiveLeak Blocked by Australian Internet Providers for Hosting the Livestream of New Zealand Mosque Shootings," *Business Insider*, 20 March 2019. https://www.businessinsider.com/new-zealand-shootings-isps-block-4chan-8chan-liveleak-over-stream-2019-3?r=US&IR=T
17 Millennial Woes, 2018, "Welcome to 2018" [Online Video]. Available at https://www.youtube.com/watch?v=BCdjoOQkQVc [Accessed 31 March 2019].
18 Simon D. Schuster and Susan Svrluga, "'Nazis Go Home!' Fights Break out at Michigan State as Protesters, White Supremacists Converge for Richard Spencer Speech," *The Washington Post*, 5 March 2018. https://www.washingtonpost.com/news/grade-point/wp/2018/03/05/michigan-state-braces-for-white-nationalist-speech-as-protesters-converge/?noredirect=on&utm_term=.606ec28cf8e7
19 Brett Barrouquere, "Days after Guilty Plea, Matthew Heimbach Re-emerges in New Alliance with National Socialist Movement," *Southern Poverty Law Centre*, 24 September 2018. https://www.splcenter.org/hatewatch/2018/09/24/days-after-guilty-plea-matthew-heimbach-re-emerges-new-alliance-national-socialist-movement
20 Aaron Katersky, "Charlottesville Rally Lawsuit to Proceed despite Nathan Damigo's Bankruptcy Filing," *ABC News*, 19 February 2019. https://abcnews.go.com/US/charlottesville-rally-lawsuit-proceed-nathan-damigos-bankruptcy-filing/story?id=61149383
21 Kelly Weill, "Richard Spencer Was Supposed to Lead the Alt-Right to Victory. Now He's Begging for Money," *Daily Beast*, 2 May 2018. https://www.thedailybeast.com/richard-spencer-was-supposed-to-lead-the-alt-right-to-victory-now-hes-begging-for-money
22 Kate Bernot, "White Supremacist Richard Spencer's Card Was Declined for a $4.75 Bar Tab," *The Takeout*, 9 May 2018. https://thetakeout.com/white-supremacist-richard-spencers-card-was-declined-fo-1825899667
23 Greg Johnson, "Interview on Unite the Right 1 & 2," *Counter Currents*, 9 August 2018. https://www.counter-currents.com/2018/08/interview-on-unite-the-right-i-and-ii/

24 Greg Johnson, quoted in: David Lawrence, "Arktos Vs Counter Currents Feud Splits Alt-Right," *HOPE not hate*, 5 March 2019. https://www.hopenothate.org.uk/2019/03/05/arktos-vs-counter-currents-feud-splitting-alt-right/

25 Anatoly Karlin, "The Alt-Right Is Dead," *The Unz Review*, 25 March 2018. http://www.unz.com/akarlin/the-alt-right-is-dead/

INDEX

0–9

#MacronLeaks 127
#MeToo movement 186, 188
120 Decibels campaign 186
1980s nostalgia 111, 114
2blowhards 87,
2channel 135, 208, 210, 215
4chan 4, 48–49, 108, 110, 113, 115–116,
   123–131, 134, 135n3–4, 136n9–n19,
   137n40, 138n49, 140, 154, 156–157,
   182, 208–210, 214n5, 219, 228, 243, 254;
   /pol/48, 123, 125–126, 128–129, 132,
   156–157, 208, 210, 219, 228, 254
5ch 208, 214
8chan 59, 115, 136, 182, 215, 254

A

Abe, Shinzo 213
accelerationism 82, 83, 86, 96
Adam Smith Institute 96
Adult Swim 113
al-Assad, Bashar 218
Alinsky, Saul 68
alpha/beta males 118, 183–184, 187
Alt.seduction.fast (internet forum) 164
AlternativeRight.com 28, 125, 243
AltRight Corporation 11–12, 16, 20,
   65–66, 184, 200, 226, 236, 241, 255
AltRight.com see AltRight Corporation
Alt-tech 140–143, 145–147, 149, 253
American Civil Liberties Union (ACLU)
   56–57

American Freedom Party 213
American Identity Movement 68, 109, 253
   see also Identity Evropa
American Society for the Defense of
   Tradition, Family and Property 96
Amerimutt/Le 56% Face (meme) 108
Andersen, Joakim 15, 20, 39, 56, 108, 183,
   238, 242, 245
androphilia 198
Anglin, Andrew 6, 49, 108–111, 117–118,
   127, 130, 145, 182–185, 189, 244,
   252–254
Angry Goy 115
Anissimov, Michael 84, 87–88, 92
Anonymous (activist group) 124
anti-Americanism 16–18, 27–28, 73–74,
   221, 226, 229
Anti-Defamation League (ADL) 66, 116–117
anti-feminism: and the alt-right 3, 5, 163,
   182–190; and incels 130, 166, and
   Gamergate 164, 171, 182; and the early
   internet 165; and misandry 165n7;
   international networks of 167n24 see also
   manosphere
antisemitism 18, 35, 38, 45–53, 54, 78n36,
   90, 108, 112–114, 172, 244
American Renaissance (AmRen) 15, 17, 28,
   37–38, 66, 108, 146, 213, 243
Archeofuturism 3, 11, 13, 18, 82,
   111, 221
Arktos Media Ltd 11, 15–16, 31, 67, 69, 72,
   77n16, 107, 181, 200, 214, 226,
   237–242, 245–246

Aryan Nation Liberty Net 141
Aryans 236–237, 239, 243–245
Aryan Polar origin myth 236–239, 242–243
Athenaeum 222
Atkins, Brian 93
Atalante Québec 71
Auernheimer, Andrew 110, 131, 139, 149,
    189, 243, 253, 254
Austria 19, 30, 41, 61, 67, 75, 77n15,
    79n43, 82, 102n100, 227, 228
Austrian Freedom Party 228
automated social media accounts *see* bot
A Voice for Men 167

B

Bannon, Steve 12, 19, 95, 213, 241–242, 245
Banerjee, Sumanta 244
Beam, Louis 141
Beale, Theodore 115
Bell, Michael 116,
Benjamin, Carl 127
Bennett, Hadley 89
Benoist, Alain de 3, 13–20, 27, 31–32, 38,
    66, 220, 224, 225, 237
Bharatiya Janata Party (BJP)
    244–245
BitChute 144–146, 149
Bitcoin 149, 253–254
Black Panther (film) 114
Black Pigeon Speaks 185, 213
Blackpill 166
Bloc Identitaire 27, 41, 66
Blonde Butter Maker, The 186
bloodsports 133
Bolsonaro, Jair 218
bots 127, 208, 218
Bougas, Nick 5
Bowden, Jonathan 12
Bowman, Sam 96
Brahmin caste 242–243
Breitbart News Network 12, 67, 95, 126–127,
    139, 195, 196, 197, 213, 238, 241–242, 245
Brimelow, Peter 15, 37, 79n40, 93
British National Party (BNP) 96, 199
Buchanan, Mike 167, 177n24
Buchanan, Pat 25, 37
Budapest, Hungary 16, 237

C

Cantwell, Christopher 55, 59–60
Carlyle, Thomas 82, 87, 99n55
Carlqvist, Ingrid 228
Cathedral, The 81, 84, 98n25

Center for Applied Rationality (CFAR) 94
Cernovich, Michael 143, 146, 219, 222
Champetier, Charles 14, 27, 66
Chapman, Kyle 132, 145, 253
Chaput, Gabriel Sohier 110, 199–200, 244
Charles Martel Society 47
Charlottesville 1, 7, 11, 15, 20, 56, 59, 69,
    117, 139, 140, 143, 153, 158, 210, 222,
    236, 251–256
Chateau Heartiste *see* Weidmann, James C.
classical art 68, 99n55, 109–111, 119n18,
Clink, Tony 164
Clinton, Hillary 109, 131, 138n49, 156,
    188, 220, 230
Cloudflare 147
Colour Revolutions 221, 228
Committee for Open Debate on the
    Holocaust 50
communism 17, 59, 220, 224
    and anti-communism 56, 210–211
Conservative Political Action Conference
    (CPAC) 69, 213
conspiracy theories 4, 46–47, 143, 157–158,
    171, 175, 184, 186, 218–220, 227–228, 245
Council of Conservative Citizens 213
Counter-Currents Publishing 11, 15; Arktos
    split and 255; Charlottesville and 253;
    classic art and 110; culture and art 118;
    Dark Enlightenment and 90; and funding
    254; gaming and 116; Globalism and 26;
    homosexuality and 198; identitarianism
    and 66, 72, 80n56; Traditionalism and
    238–240; manosphere and 169, 183;
    New Right and 15–16; parody music and
    112; race and white nationalism and 39,
    235, 238; Savitri Devi and 243; social
    media bans and 140; technological
    utopianism and 100n62; trolling and 134;
    Ukraine and 223
Counter.Fund 141
Counter-Jihad movement 6
Crimea 221, 223, 226, 228–229
Cryptocurrency 148, 253–254
cuck/cuckservative 76n8, 112, 135n5,
    183, 186
Cultural Libertarianism 55, 97n13
Cultural Marxism 46–47, 115, 116
CYBERNΔZI 111, 115

D

Daily Shoah, The 49, 52, 112
Daily Stormer: 4chan and 126, 130, 131;
    Aantisemitism and 50, 52, 127;
    community building and 252;

cryptocurrency and 149; Defend Europe and 67; deplatforming and 139–140, 145, 147, 253; fashwave 110–11; gaming 115; Holocaust denial 50; homosexuality 196, 200; Kali Yuga and 240; Kek and 108; misogyny and 182, 187; Serrano and 243–244; style guide 49
Dalrock 169
Damigo, Nathan 68–70, 77n14, 117
Dampier, Henry 89
Damore, James 141
Danelaw, Natt 115
dating sites 144, 165, 187
decentralisation 148–149
deep state 56
Defend Europa 145, 147
Deist, Jeff 61
Deleuze, Gilles 82–83
Democratic National Committee 218
demographic 'replacement' (conspiracy theory) 27n13, 42, 66, 70, 73–75, 200, 221 see also Great Replacement; white genocide
Derbyshire, John 89, 93
Devi, Savitri 240, 242–245
Devlin, Francis Roger 37, 169, 200
Dickinson, Pax 91, 140–141
Discord (messaging application) 115, 139, 155
Dispatch International 228
distributed denial-of-service attack (DDOS) 147, 253
Donovan, Jack 31, 37, 66, 89, 183–184, 198–199, 215n24
Dowson, Jim 223
Dugin, Alexander 3, 11, 13, 20, 223–227, 229, 232–233, 237, 240, 242, 247–248
Duke, David 67, 113, 117, 216n38, 222, 227, 230
Duke University 13
Dunstan, Jesse 112
Duterte, Rodrigo 218

E

Echoes (meme) 51–52
Egypt 108, 238, 244
Elam, Paul 167, 169, 170–172, 174
Elizabeth I 84
Enoch, Mike see Peinovich, Mike
Esoteric Hitlerism 242–244
ethnocultural identity 33n13, 41–42, 71–72
ethnopluralism 14, 20, 27, 41, 42, 65–66, 72, 85–86, 225
eugenics 39, 240
Eurasianism 3, 13, 224–226

Eurasian Youth Union 229
European New Right (ENR) see New Right
Evola, Julius 12–13, 19, 82, 99n55, 224–225, 236–241, 243, 246
EXPO Magazine 11

F

Facebook 78n30, 91–92, 134, 139–140, 142–143, 146, 148, 219, 228, 245, 254
family 184–187, 194
Farnsbarns, Charlie 107
Farrell, Warren 165, 167
Fash the Nation 112
fashion 107, 116–118
fashwave 110–111, 114, 118, 119n18
fashy haircut 117
Faye, Guillaume 3, 13, 17–19, 27–29, 37, 67–68, 82, 107, 111, 221
Fédération des Québécois de souche 71
femininity 184–186
feminism 127, 181–182, 195; Gamergate and 115, 126, 156, 171, 182, 209; men's rights movement and 165, rejection of 2, 163, 165n8, 168, 170–171; and the left 172; and conspiracy theory 46, 163, 172; and non-feminists 174; and hegemonic masculinity 174–175; and lesbianism 197
Feit, Mel 165; see also anti-feminism
Fields, James 251
film 51, 107, 112–114, 116, 118, 188, 229
Fisher, Robert 168
Follin, Marcus 115–116, 184, 198
Forney, Matt 55, 115, 168–170, 178n31, 189, 200, 255
Fortuyn, Pim 195, 198
Foucault, Michel 20
Fourth Political Theory (FPT) see Dugin, Alexander
Fowler, R.G. see Johnson, Greg
France 3, 13, 17, 19, 27, 41, 65, 79n43, 223, 227, 242
Francis, Sam 20
François, Stéphane 17
Frankfurt School 46
Franklin, Warg 89
Fred Perry 117
Free Speech Tech Alliance 141, 147
Freedomain Radio 40, 58
Freezoxee 147
French New Right see Nouvelle Droite
Freud, Sigmund 112
Friberg, Daniel 11, 15–16, 18, 20, 107, 181, 185, 200, 226, 237–238, 241, 245, 255

Friedman, Milton 92
Friedman, Patri 92
Fuerza Nacional-Identitaria 75
Furie, Matt 108
Future Primaeval, The (Blog) 89
Futurism 111

G

Gab 141–143, 145–147, 150, 219, 254
Galef, Julia 94
Gamergate 115, 126–127, 136n19, 156,
     164, 171, 174, 182, 209
gaming culture 113–116, 209
Gateway Pundit, The 157–158, 196
gay marriage 196
Generation Identity: antisemitism and
     70n36; activism and 65, 67–68, 68n15,
     72; Austria and 13, 19, 30, 41, 75; France
     and 27, 41, 66; UK and Ireland and 67;
     Italy and 67; imagery and 68–69; Canada
     and 70–72, 71n38; Slovenia and 71; race
     and 42, 73; Russia and 228; the USA and
     68–70, 68n18, 69n23; female members of
     186; Patriot Peer and 69
Gillespie, Austin Mitchell 59
Gionet, Tim 55, 145, 216n28
Goa, India 237
Goad, Jim 55
GoDaddy 139, 253
GoFundMe 145
Golden One, The see Follin, Marcus
Goode, Virgil 213
Google 52, 139, 141, 147–148,
     179n52, 253
Gottfried, Paul 55, 61, 62, 93
Gould, Stephen Jay 36
GoyFundMe 145
Gramsci, Antonio 14–15, 29, 128
Great Replacement, The 66 see also white
     genocide; demographic 'replacement'
     (conspiracy theory)
GRECE see New Right
Greene, Donovan 90
Griffin, Brad 31, 70, 107
Griffin, Nick 96,
*Groupement de recherche et d'études pour la
     civilisation européenne see* New Right
Guattari, Félix 83
Guénon, René 224, 238–241, 243

H

Habitable Worlds (blog) 88
Happy Merchant (meme) 51, 52, 108

Hare Krishna 240
Hatreon 145, 253
Havewala, Porus Homi 237
HBD chick 39–40
HBD-o-sphere see Human Biodiversity
Heidegger, Martin 13
Heimbach, Matthew 189, 222, 223, 226, 255
Herrnstein, Richard 36, 62
Hestia Society for Social Studies 86, 88–90, 96
Heyer, Heather 69, 139, 210, 251, 253
Hinduism 237, 239, 240, 242, 245
Hindu Mission 244–245
Hindu nationalism/Hindutva 235, 244–246
Hikikomori 209, 215n12
Holocaust 1, 18, 45–47, 49–52, 228
homohysteria 199–201
homophobia 2, 175, 183, 194, 196,
     198–201, 227
homonationalism 194–195
HOPE not hate 7, 11, 77n23, 123, 241
Hopkins, Katie 67
Hoppe, Hans-Hermann 61–62, 82, 84, 93
Howe, Jared 58–59, 62
Howe, Neil 20, 23n65, 241
Human Biodiversity (HBD) 36, 38–42, 169
Hyperboreans 235–239, 243
Hyde, Sam 113, 115

I

identitarianism: anti-Americanism and 73–
     74; activism and 72; antisemitism and 73;
     Arktos Media and 69; Austria and 19;
     Christianity and 74n48; defining
     41–42, 65; Chile and 75; demographic
     change and 70; Defend Europe and 67;
     Canada and 70–72; Donald Trump and
     70; European New Right and 3, 13, 21;
     France and 19, 66; hipsters and 117;
     geopolitics and 75; Germany and 33n13,
     156–157; globalisation and 31; the
     internet and 71n37; Italy and 33n13, 67;
     Latin America and 74–76; and LGBT+
     19–20; metapolitics and 29, 70;
     nationalism and 31; Operation Homeland
     and 69; regionalism and 72n44; Russia
     and 75n56; transnationalism and 31, 67,
     69, 71n40; 72–75; trolling and 131; race
     and 17, 31, 41–42, 70, 72–75; the
     Nouvelle Droite and 11, 65; UK and
     Ireland and 67; *see also* Generation
     Identity; Identity Evropa; ethnopluralism;
     ethnocultural identity
Identitäre Bewegung Österreich 19
Identitarian Ideas IX conference 11, 186, 241

Identity Acadia 72n44
Identity Evropa (IE) 65–66, 68–70, 75,
    77n13, 77n20, 78n34, 79n44, 109, 117,
    147, 253
Identity Vanguard 65
Imanuelsen, Peter 158
India 6, 177n23–24, 235–246
    Indian caste system 239, 242
Indo-Europeans 235–238, 241–243
InfoWars 46, 127, 143, 145, 219, 227
Instagram 146
International Conference on Men's Issues
    (ICMI) 172, 178n36, 177n24
International Eurasianist Movement (IEM) 226
Internet Research Agency (IRA) 219
In Mala Fide see Forney, Matt
involuntary celibate community (incels) 130,
    136n13, 164–167, 166, 170, 173, 176n18,
    177n21, 179n54, 199; forums 166–167
Iranian United Front 241
Iron March 110
Irony 82, 108, 111–113, 118, 130–132,
    134, 243
Irving, David 47
Ishii, Hidetoshi see Mada, Yoko
Islam 30, anti-Islam 18, 28, 32, 132, 194;
    Eurasianism and 225; identitarianism
    and 5, 66, 74–75; Iran and 241;
    'Islamification' 66, 73–75; 'Islamisation'
    73–74,; LGBT+ and 195–197; Mens
    Rights Activists and 174; Terrorism 68;
    Sufi 239–240

J

Jazzhands McFeels 112
Jewish Question 47
Johnson, Charles C. 67, 139, 141, 146
Johnson, Greg 6, 18, 256; antisemitism and
    26 Counter-Currents publishing and
    15, 253–255; film and 112–114; gender
    and sexuality and 169–170, 183–184,
    198–201; identitarianism and 66, 68,
    80n56; mysticism and 235, 239, 243;
    neoreaction and 90; race and 17, 39;
    Russia and Ukraine and 80n56, 223;
    trolling and 134–135
Jones, Alex 4, 143, 145, 219, 227
Jordan, Colin 6
Jorjani, Jason Reza 1, 11, 241
Joyce, Andrew 200, 240
JQ see Jewish Question
Justice for Men and Boys (J4MB) 167,
    177n24

K

Kaldenberg, Wyatt 51
Kali Yuga 235, 238–244, 246
Kalki 242–244
Karlin, Anatoly 256
Katehon 12
Kazuhiro, Nakamura see Nihon Daiitto
Kek (meme) 108, 132, 244
Kekistan see Kek
Kessler, Jason 252
Kickstarter 145
Klansman see Ku Klux Klan
Kollerstrom, Nick 49
Kouprianova, Nina 227
Krebs, Pierre 237
Kremlin 218, 219, 221, 225–230, 237
Ku Klux Klan (KKK) 3, 5, 67, 112–113,
    116, 141, 222, 251
Kurtagic, Alex 28, 38, 89, 243

L

Land, Nick 82, 84–89, 96, 99n41, 102n99,
    103n114
Lassen, Christian 236
Lauder-Frost, Gregory 214
Leave.EU 67
Le Bon, Gustave 20
League of the South 223
Leghorn, Butch 200
lesbianism 194–195, 197 see also LGBT+
Leuchter, Fred 50
LessWrong 87, 94–95, 102n97, 103n98
LGBT+ the alt-lite and 2, 194–197; the
    alt-right and 2, 197–201; identitarianism
    and 19–20; gender fluidity 197, 200;
    non-binary gender identity 131;
    binary gender identity 163; and
    multiculturalism and 71; see also queer,
    homonationalism, lesbianism,
    transgenderism, Twinks4Trump
Lichtmesz, Martin see Semlitsch, Martin
Liddell, Colin 55, 222–223
Lind, William 46
Lipstadt, Deborah 47
Lokteff, Lana 185–187, 213
London Forum 15, 47, 214
Longshanks, Sven 243
Lord of the Rings 114, 118
Louis XIV 84
Ludwig von Mises Institute 61
lulz 50, 130, 136n9
Lynch, Trevor see Johnson, Greg

M

MacDonald, Kevin 18, 46–48, 79n40, 131, 178n33, 216n38
Machine Intelligence Research Institute (MIRI) 92–94
Mada, Yoko 213
Madhav, Ram 245
MakerSupport 145
male-only spaces 181–184, 199
male tribalism 170, 198
manosphere: alpha and beta males 183; androphilia and 197, 199; antisemitism and 172, 175; conferences 7; defining the 163; Donald Trump and 172n52, 172–173; homosexuality and 200; incels and 130, 166, 167n21, 173, 175; India and 167n23; Japan and 212; mainstreaming of 164–165, 171n44; Men Going Their Own Way (MGTOW) and 28, 165n9; Men's Rights Activism (MRA) and 167, 174; the mythopoetic movement and 165; gamergate 115, 171, 182; gynocentrism and; Pick-Up Artists (PUA) and the 164, 167; race and 168–170; 'red pill' and the 168; violence against women and 189 *see also* neomasculinity; anti-feminism; feminism
Männerbund 183
Marx, Karl 17
Marxism 15, 86 *see also* Marx, Karl; Gramsci, Antonio; Cultural Marxism
Mateen, Omar 195, 200
Matrix, The (film) 114
McCarthy, Tara 188–189
McInnes, Gavin 2, 37, 55, 117, 182–183, 186, 195–197
McLaren, Evan 200
meme aesthetics 108–109
Men Going Their Own Way (MGTOW) 165, 168, 170, 173, 176n9
Men's Rights Activism (MRA) 165, 167–168, 170–175, 176n9, 177n23, 178n36; and second-wave feminism 175n58
Merkel, Angela 186
metapolitics 14–16, 29, 68, 70, 107, 118–119, 128, 252
Metzger, Tom 51
Mencken Club 41, 90, 96
Michigan State University 117, 255
Millennial Woes *see* Robertson, Colin
Million Dollar Extreme (MDE) 113
Milo *see* Yiannopoulos, Milo
Mises, Ludwig von 61, 82, 84
Mishima, Yukio 215

mixed martial arts (MMA) 184
Modi, Narendra 244
Moldbug, Mencius *see* Yarvin, Curtis
Molyneux, Stefan 40, 46, 55, 58, 143, 155, 178n36, 184, 218
Moon Man (meme) 113, 115
MoreRight (blog) 87–88
Morgan, John 11, 16, 72, 237–239, 241, 243
Motpol 15, 39, 56, 108, 183, 238, 241
Murdoch Murdoch 113
Murray, Charles 36, 62
Murray, Lawrence 243–244

N

Nally, Francis 200
National Action 77n14, 110, 148, 150
National Alliance 113
national anarchism 4
National Center for Men 165
National Policy Institute (NPI) 7, 11, 16, 19, 47, 66, 109, 131–132, 139, 178n36, 182, 199–200, 237, 253, 255
National Vanguard 223
National Socialist Movement 5
Nationalist Solutions Conference 213, 213n38
NATO 221, 223
Nazi Party 13, 109
NEET 130, 209, 215n12
Nehlen, Paul 147
neocameralism 84–85, 86, 92
neoliberalism 195
neomasculinity 172 *see also* manosphere
Neoreactionary 20, 30, 58, 81, 84, 86–88, 90–91, 92n74, 94, 99n43; and the reactosphere 81, 86–87, 89, 99n44
Netto Uyoku 207, 208–211, 215n12
New Balance 117
New Right: American New Right 15, 17 see also Counter Currents Publishing and Greg Johnson; European New Right (ENR) 3, 11, 13–20, 25, 27, 29, 31, 37–38, 66, 68, 74, 107, 117, 119, 128, 220, 221, 224, 228, 237, 246; French New Right 14; *Nouvelle Droite* 11, 14–15, 17–19, 25, 65, 128; Research and Study Group for European Civilisation (*Groupement de recherche et d'études pour la civilisation européenne*) (GRECE) 3, 13–18
New York Forum 15
New Zealand 67, 74, 81, 254
Nietzsche, Friedrich 12–13, 184
Nihon Daiitto see Takata, Makoto

Nishimura, Hiroyuki *see also* 2channel 208, 214–215n5
Nordic Resistance Movement (NMR) 223
North American New Right *see* New Right
North West Forum 15, 47
Nouvelle Droite see New Right

Property and Freedom Society (PFS) 62, 93, 101n88
Protocols of Zion 46
Proud Boys 117, 182–184, 184, 195–196, 211
Pulse nightclub shooting, Florida 195, 200
Putin, Vladimir 218–219, 221, 223, 225–226

O

Occidental Dissent 31, 70, 107, 243, 253
Occidental Observer, The (TOO) 47, 240
Occidental Quarterly, The (TOQ) 47, 169
O'Meara, James 66, 198–199
O'Reilly, Farnham 235
Online Antagonistic Communities 3, 6, 123, 128, 154
Orlando shooting *see* Pulse nightclub shooting, Florida
Orthodox Christianity 237, 240
Outside In (blog) 87–88
Overcoming Bias (blog) 87

Q

Queer 194–195, 197–198 *see also* LGBT+, homonationalism, lesbianism, transgenderism, Twinks4Trump

R

Radish Magazine 87, 89, 99n55
Radix Journal 30, 132, 139, 147, 226, 236, 238
Ramsey, Paul 55, 169
RamZPaul *see* Ramsey, Paul
Rand, Ayn 54, 55, 61
Rashtriya Swayamsevak Sangh (RSS) 245
Rationalist Sphere (blogging community) 87
Raymond, Benjamin 110
Reaction Times 86
Rebel Media 127, 185, 195–197
red pill (meme) 92, 114, 168, 171, 179n50
Reddit 30, 48, 101n74, 125–126, 136n14, 141–142, 168, 214n5; r/theredpill (Internet forum) 168
Red Ice Creations 11, 144, 185, 186, 213, 227, 252
Regnery, William H. II 47
Renouf, Michèle 50
Research and Study Group for European Civilisation *see* New Right
Rassemblement National 223, 227, 228
Return of Kings (RoK) (website) 172, 187–188, 212,
Right Stuff, The (TRS) 49, 52, 131, 199, 243, 252
Right Wing Death Squad (RWDS), (music) 111–112
Rockwell, George Lincoln 220
Rockwell, Llewellyn, Jr. 60–61
Robertson, Caolan 195–196
Robertson, Colin 89, 100n59, 140, 144, 146, 155, 187, 189, 254–255
Rodger, Elliot 164, 167, 177n21
Rodina (political party) 222
Rodionov, Igor 225
Roissy in DC *see* Weidmann, James C.
Rollo Tomassi 167
Rome 238
Ron, Paul 55, 58–61

P

paganism 198, 237–238, 242–243
Palantir 91
paleolibertarianism 60–62
Palmgren, Henrik 11
parody music 111–112
Parrott, Matt 90, 189, 222, 255
Patreon 145, 253, 254
PayPal 91, 139, 141, 147, 253
Peinovich, Mike 49, 51, 112, 131
Pepe the Frog 51–52, 108–109, 131–132, 138n49, 143, 244
Persia 238
Peterson, Jack 167
Pettibone, Brittany 67–70, 145, 186, 227
Philippot, Florian 195
Pick-Up Artistry (PUA) 164–168, 170–171, 173, 177n21, 187
Pierce, William Luther 113
Pilleater *see* Nally, Francis
pinkwashing 194–196
PJ Media 36
Pokémon Go 115
political correctness 2, 4, 46, 51, 126, 141, 184, 209, 241, 256
Poole, Christopher 135n3, 136n13, 208, 214n5
Popovic, Srdja 68
Posobiec, Jack 127, 219, 227
Post-Anathema (blog) 89, 88n55
Prasad, Ravi Shankar 245

Roosh V *see* Valizadeh, Daryush
Roosh.com *see* Valizadeh, Daryush
Ross, Paul 164–165
Rothbard, Murray 55, 60–62, 84
Rowsell, Tom 238
RT (TV network) 227–228,
Rudolf, Germar 50
Rubin, Dave 93
Rubin Report 93
Russia 5–6, 12; far right in 223–226,
   228–229; foregin influence 218–220,
   227–228, 230; media outlets 158, 221,
   227–228, 230; National Unity Day 229;
   Russian Imperial Movement (RIM) 222;
   Russian March 229; western far right and
   220–226, 230

S

Sailer, Steve 39, 41, 55, 89
Sakurai, Makoto *see* Takata, Makoto
Sargon of Akkad *see* Benjamin, Carl
Sartre, Jean-Paul 45, 50
Savarkar, V.D. 245
Saved by the Bell (TV show) 114
Scandza Forum 134
Sceptic community 132
Scharlach 88
Schlegel, Friedrich 236
Schmitt, Carl 12–13, 28
sci-fi tropes 110–111
Scott, Alexander 87, 102n97
Seattle 15, 26
Seasteading Institute 92, 94
Seleznyov, Gennadiy 226
Sellner, Martin 41–42, 67, 70, 72, 74
Semlitsch, Martin 66
Serrano, Miguel 242–244
Seventh Son *see* Dunstan, Jesse
Sheeeit (meme) 108
Shevchuk, Stanislav 223
shitposting 108, 130, 132, 134
Silensky, Anton 89
Silicon Valley 81, 82, 91–92, 94–96, 97n13,
   102n99, 141, 143, 147
Simmons, Harvey 18
Simon Wiesenthal Center 213
skinhead 117, 226, 229
Slate Star Codex (Blog) 87
Sloterdijk, Peter 20
sockpuppet 156–157
socialism 3, 14, 56, 61
social justice warrior (SJW) 2, 115, 131, 133,
   182, 256
Social Matter (website) 88–90, 96

Southern, Lauren 67, 127, 145, 155, 185,
   188–189, 195, 197, 227
Southern Poverty Law Center 35, 69, 109,
   164, 168, 175
Southern Nationalists of Identity Dixie 65
SOVA Center for Information and
   Analysis 229
Soviet Union 16, 220–221, 243
Spencer, Richard: Alt-right and 15, 37, 61,
   125; Alt-Right Corp and 11; American
   and 6, 17; Assad and 222; Charlottesville
   and 255; classical motifs 109;
   cryptocurrency 149; deplatforming of
   140, 142, 145, 147, 253; fashion and 118;
   gaming and 116; homosexuality 199;
   identitarianism and 65–67; 69, 73; Japan
   and 212; libertarianism and 55, 62l; music
   and 111; National Policy Institute (NPI)
   11, 47, 139, 182; neoreaction 89, 93;
   New Right and 16, 18; race and 2, 38,
   236; Russia and 226, 228, 230; Schmitt
   and 13; Taki's Magazine 26–27;
   traditionalism and 12; trolling
   and 131
Spengler, Oswald 12–13, 20
Sputnik News 158, 221, 227
SS Ahnenerbe 237
Strauss-Howe 20, 23n65
Strauss, William 20, 241
Steam (gaming platform) 115
Stewart, Ayla 185
Steves, Nick B. 88, 96
Stockholm, Sweden 7, 11, 186, 228
Stoekel, Sabine 93
Storey, Rik 59–60,
Stormfront 125–126, 136n13, 141
Stripe 253
Strom, Kevin Alfred 223
Students for Western Civilization 71
Sunić, Tomislav 16, 37, 62, 79n40, 93,
   216n38, 246
Survive the Jive *see* Rowsell, Tom
Swift, Taylor 111, 118
Sydney Traditionalist Forum 96

T

Tair, Amelia, 129
Tait, Joshua 58, 83–85, 98n25, 102n100,
Takata, Makoto *see also Zaitokukai* and
   Nihon Daiitto, 210, 213, 214, 216n38
Taki's Magazine 26, 39, 55
Taylor, Jared 2, 6, 15, 17, 37–39, 42, 55, 62,
   67, 79n40, 89, 93, 111, 117–118, 146,
   213, 243

Telegram (messaging application) 228
television 107, 112–114, 116, 118, 164
They Live (film) 114
Thiel, Peter 81, 91–97, 100n73,
Thomas Carlyle Club for Young
    Reactionaries 87
"Thotgate" harassment campaign
    188–189
Thule 237–239
Thule-Seminar 237
Tilak, Bal Gangadhar 236–238, 242–243, 245
Tlon 92
Traditionalism 12, 211, 238–242
Traditional Britain Group 96, 214
Traditionalist Workers Party (TWP) 5, 90,
    117, 189, 222–223, 226, 255
Traditionalist Youth Network 222
transgenderism 194, 195, 197
Trump, Donald: Andrew Anglin and 117;
    globalisation and 25; anti-government
    militias and 5; Steve Bannon and 12, 19,
    95, 213, 241; the Democratic National
    Committee leaks and 218; drag and 194;
    identitarianism and 70; intervention in
    Syria and 222; Esoteric Hitlerism and
    244; Hindu nationalism and 244–245;
    Charlottesville and 1, 251; Kyle
    Chapman (AKA Based Stick Man) and
    132; LGBT+ and Trump support 196;
    masculinity and 172n52, 172–173; Pepe
    the Frog and 109; Peter Thiel and 81, 95;
    race science and 35; Richard Spencer and
    132; Russia and 218–220, 222, 230;
    women and 188
Trump Jr., Donald 47
Turner, Hal 124
Twinks4Trump 196
Twitter 35, 87, 124, 127, 139, 140,
    142–143, 146, 155, 157, 218–219,
    222, 254

U

Uber 139
Ukraine 221, 223, 228–229
Uncuck the Right 112
Unite the Right Rally *see* also
    Charlottesville 11, 15, 55–56, 59, 69,
    77–79n28, 139, 153, 158, 210, 236,
    251–253, 255
Unite the Right 2 *see* also Charlottesville 252
University of Warwick 82
Unqualified Reservations (Blog) 82, 87
Unz Review 39, 256
Urbit 92, 94

V

Valizadeh, Daryush 164, 167, 169, 170, 172,
    178n33, 179n50, 179n52, 187, 188–189,
    190n4
Vardon, Philippe 19
Vedas 236–237, 239, 242, 245
VDARE 15, 37, 39, 47
Vishnu 242–243
VK 228, 254
Voat 141, 142, 146, 254
Vox Day *see* Beale, Theodore

W

waifu 216n28
Wallace, Hunter *see* Griffin, Brad
Warski, Andy 155
Warwick, Tarl 60
Washington DC 11, 37, 61, 69, 213, 223, 252
WASP Love 144, 187
Watkins, Jim 214–215n5
Watson, Paul Joseph 6, 32, 46, 143, 181,
    186, 188, 195, 197, 219
weev *see* Auernheimer, Andrew
Weidmann, James C. 167–170
Weinstein, Eric 94
Weinstein, Harvey 188
WeSearchr 67, 141, 145, 253
Wirth, Hermann 237
White Aryan Resistance (WAR) 51
WhiteDate 144, 187
white genocide 47, 186
White World's Future, The (conference) 222
Wife With A Purpose *see* Stewart, Ayla
Willinger, Markus 19, 30, 75
Wintrich, Lucian 196
Wolves of Vinland 198
World National-Conservative Movement 222
World Union of National Socialists 6
WrongThink 146

X

Xbox Live 114
Xurious 111

Y

Yarvin, Curtis 20, 58, 81–87, 89, 92–96,
    98n25, 102n97, 102–103n108, 169
Yiannopoulos, Milo 32, 55, 67, 95–96,
    102n100, 115, 126, 139, 146, 182,
    194–197, 199; Dangerous Faggot Tour,
    The 196, 228

Yockey, Francis Parker 220
Youcis, Emily 113
YouTube 38, 50, 58, 60, 93, 112–113, 132, 133, 139, 143–146, 155–157, 181, 184–185, 188, 213, 219, 230, 238, 252, 254
Yudkowsky, Eliezer 87, 93–94, 95

Z

Zaitokukai see also Takata, Makoto 210–211, 214
Zeiger *see* Chaput, Gabriel Sohier
Zündel, Ernst 49

For Product Safety Concerns and Information please contact our EU
representative GPSR@taylorandfrancis.com
Taylor & Francis Verlag GmbH, Kaufingerstraße 24, 80331 München, Germany

www.ingramcontent.com/pod-product-compliance
Lightning Source LLC
Chambersburg PA
CBHW051956270326
41929CB00015B/2680